The Meaning Makers

PEFC/16-33-111
CATG-PEFC-052
www.pefc.org

NEW PERSPECTIVES ON LANGUAGE AND EDUCATION
Series Editor: Professor Viv Edwards, *University of Reading, Reading, Great Britain*
Series Advisor: Professor Allan Luke, *Queensland University of Technology, Brisbane, Australia*

Two decades of research and development in language and literacy education have yielded a broad, multidisciplinary focus. Yet education systems face constant economic and technological change, with attendant issues of identity and power, community and culture. This series will feature critical and interpretive, disciplinary and multidisciplinary perspectives on teaching and learning, language and literacy in new times.

Full details of all the books in this series and of all our other publications can be found on http://www.multilingual-matters.com, or by writing to Multilingual Matters, St Nicholas House, 31–34 High Street, Bristol BS1 2AW, UK.

NEW PERSPECTIVES ON LANGUAGE AND EDUCATION
Series Editor: Professor Viv Edwards

The Meaning Makers
Learning to Talk and Talking to Learn
2nd edition

Gordon Wells

MULTILINGUAL MATTERS
Bristol • Buffalo • Toronto

Library of Congress Cataloging in Publication Data
A catalog record for this book is available from the Library of Congress.
Wells, C. Gordon.
The Meaning Makers: Learning to Talk and Talking to Learn/Gordon Wells.-2nd ed.
Includes bibliographical references.
1. Children—Language. 2. Language acquisition. 3. Literacy. 4. Language arts.
I. Title.
LB1139.L3W443 2009
372.6—dc22 2009026142

British Library Cataloguing in Publication Data
A catalogue entry for this book is available from the British Library.

ISBN-13: 978-1-84769-199-6 (hbk)
ISBN-13: 978-1-84769-198-9 (pbk)

Multilingual Matters
UK: St Nicholas House, 31–34 High Street, Bristol BS1 2AW, UK.
USA: UTP, 2250 Military Road, Tonawanda, NY 14150, USA.
Canada: UTP, 5201 Dufferin Street, North York, Ontario M3H 5T8, Canada.

The policy of Multilingual Matters/Channel View Publications is to use papers
that are natural, renewable and recyclable products, made from wood grown in
sustainable forests. In the manufacturing process of our books, and to further
support our policy, preference is given to printers that have FSC and PEFC Chain
of Custody certification. The FSC and/or PEFC logos will appear on those books
where full certification has been granted to the printer concerned.

Typeset by Techset Composition Ltd., Salisbury, UK.
Printed and bound in Great Britain by the MPG Books Group.

Contents

Acknowledgements

Behind this book lie 15 years of longitudinal research, to which many people contributed. First, the research team, whose work in making, transcribing and coding the recordings, observing and testing the children, interviewing the parents and teachers and then analysing all these different types of data provided the foundation on which this work of interpretation is built. Although they are too numerous to mention individually, I should like to take this opportunity of thanking them for their unflagging commitment to the project and for their enthusiasm and support.

Second, I should like to acknowledge the support received from the various institutions that have funded the research: The Social Science Research Council of Great Britain (now the Economic and Social Research Council), the Nuffield Foundation, the Boots Charitable Trust, the Spencer Foundation (USA) and the Department of Education and Science. I should also like to thank the University of Bristol for providing a home for the project and the many other facilities without which the research could not have been carried out; also the County of Avon Education Authority for allowing us to observe the children in their classrooms.

My greatest debt of gratitude, however, is to the children themselves and to their parents and teachers. Their cooperation over the successive phases of the investigation has been more complete and freely given than I could ever have dared to hope. If any of them recognize themselves, despite the use of pseudonyms, in the pages that follow, I hope they will not be offended by the way in which their words have been presented. To all of them I wish to express my thanks for their patience and generosity.

In illustrating my discussion of different ways of working with children at school, I have made use of quotations from the work of other researchers. These are acknowledged in the notes. However, I should particularly like to thank Harold Rosen for allowing me to quote extensively from *The Language of Primary School Children* and Moira McKenzie, Warden of the Inner London Education Authority's Centre for Language in Primary

Education, for letting me use the video recordings that were made under her direction for the *Extending Literacy* ETV series.

In writing this book, I have received help from many people. Discussions with teachers (many of whom are also parents) taking courses with me both in Bristol and Toronto have forced me to clarify my ideas about the broad issues with which it is concerned. In particular, I gained enormously from my collaboration in Toronto with Ann Maher and the members of the *Developing Inquiring Communities in Education* collaborative research group. I have also benefited from the comments of colleagues who have seen drafts of individual chapters. Three people deserve a special mention: Margaret Spencer, who read the whole of the first draft and helped me to see in what ways it needed revising; and Marion Lowden and Natalie Bernasconi, who acted as critical readers of the additional chapters in the second edition. I am grateful to both of them for their very positive and constructive suggestions. But my most unfailing source of help and encouragement was Jan Wells, herself a parent and teacher. It was she who originally persuaded me to write the book and, in numerous ways, made it possible for me to bring it to completion. To all these people I wish to express my sincere thanks.

Prologue to the Second Edition

As more than a quarter of a century has passed since the start of the Bristol Study, I need to start by explaining why I believe that a second edition is appropriate. First and foremost, although the context in which children learn to talk may be somewhat different today from what it was 25 years ago, the ways in which children's learning proceeds have not changed, as has been confirmed by more recent studies. And because the Bristol Study remains the largest and most representative longitudinal investigation of this process, *The Meaning Makers* can still provide food for thought concerning both the early stages and the transition from home to school. At the same time, there have also been significant changes in the intervening years, and some of these call for a reevaluation of the findings of the study. These I address in the final chapters.

From the perspective of these changes, it is interesting to consider how I might redesign the study if I were about to embark on it today. From a research point of view, one of the most significant developments has been in the field of information technology. When we began the study, the wireless microphone had just been invented and needed considerable modification for a one-year-old to wear it. Handheld video cameras and user-friendly computers were still a dream for the future. Now, almost every researcher has several video cameras and a laptop computer with a wide variety of software programmes for data analysis. With these tools researchers have been able to carry out both experimental and naturalistic studies of children learning a significant proportion of the world's languages, enabling them to formulate and test a variety of hypotheses about what is universal and what is context-dependent about children's language development (see Chapter 11). Nevertheless, I still would not use a video camera to record in children's homes, as the presence of a camera operator would certainly compromise the authentic naturalism that was a prime aim of our approach. On the other hand, a similar study today would certainly benefit from the ability to computerize the tasks of transcription, coding and quantitative analysis.

But it is not only the possibilities for research that have been transformed by technology. Recent inventions have also changed the contexts in which talk occurs. Today, many people seem to spend more time talking on their cell phones than in face-to-face conversation; young children play with walkie-talkies, and their older siblings listen to iPods, communicate on My Space, and spend much time playing computer games of increasing complexity and addictiveness. These changes in the part played by electronic communication and entertainment devices in people's lives has certainly affected what children talk about and how they spend their leisure time. Whether it has changed how they initially learn to talk is more debatable.

However, one significant social change that has almost certainly made a difference to the opportunities for language learning is that far more mothers now have full-time jobs, which means that, from a much earlier age, many children spend less time interacting with their mothers and other family members and much more in child care settings, which have a very different adult to child ratio than at home. If I were starting again, I would certainly want to include children whose parents are employed outside the home; a comparison between the interactions that a child experiences at home and those experienced in the various care settings would be particularly informative.

Schools, too, have changed. Many more schools today include children from a wider range of ethnic background as a result of the significant increase in emigration by families from countries racked by war or endemic poverty. For the children, the adjustment to a new culture and a new language is challenging, and extremely so for those who arrive in later childhood or adolescence; it is also a challenge for their teachers, who have to find ways to meet their emotional and social needs as well as ensuring their academic progress while they struggle to master the language of instruction. It would be particularly interesting to learn more about the effect of age of arrival or of starting preschool on the ease with which such children learn a second language outside the home.

The political and economic changes that have resulted from increasing globalization have also had a considerable impact on pedagogy and curriculum, as international competition has led to greater emphasis being placed on accountability at school and district levels. This, in turn, has led to a greater centralization of curriculum planning and an increased emphasis on testing, leading inevitably – in a high proportion of schools – to a focus on what will be tested rather than on encouraging students to develop their individual talents and interests. While making observations in school would still be very similar, the task of assessing achievement would be very much easier. In the 1970s we had to develop our own forms of assessment; today, this would certainly not be necessary!

But, equally important, I, too, have changed in the intervening years. First, I have been strongly influenced by the work of Vygotsky and his colleagues. Although Vygotsky died before I was born, his ideas only became known in the English-speaking world in the 1980s, following the publication of *Mind in Society*, an edited translation of some of his most important writings. Since then, the more I have read and thought about Vygotsky's theory of learning and development, the more it has seemed to provide the sort of encompassing theoretical framework that I needed to integrate my understanding of children's learning of their first language (and subsequent ones) with the goals and means of education. For this reason, in recent years cultural historical activity theory (CHAT) – as the current embodiment of Vygotsky's ideas is referred to – has formed the basis for my teaching and writing as well as my research.

The second major personal change has been in my stance as a researcher. In carrying out the Bristol Study, I adopted the traditional role of a social scientist: I selected a stratified random sample and proceeded to make regular observations of them. To the extent possible, I and my colleagues made every effort to avoid 'contaminating the data' by not engaging in discussion of the observations with the parents and teachers concerned and by not sharing our underlying hypotheses with the 'subjects' of the research. This, I still believe, was the appropriate stance to adopt, given the aim of the project – to describe the naturally occurring opportunities for language learning by a representative sample of children.

However, in 1984, at the conclusion of the Bristol Study, I moved to Toronto to join the Department of Curriculum, Teaching and Learning at the Ontario Institute for Studies in Education.[1] Henceforth, although I would also be contributing to the doctoral programme, I saw my major responsibilities as continuing to carry out research in classrooms and to teach practicing teachers who were studying part-time to gain a Master's degree in Education. Indeed, I hoped to find ways of integrating these two activities. However, knowing little about schools in Canada, I felt ill prepared to undertake my new responsibilities. Furthermore, despite having formed some strong convictions about the relationship between learning and teaching, and the central role of language in both, I had not previously thought about how to present them to practicing teachers, nor was I sure how they would be received in the Canadian context. Clearly, I needed to spend time in classrooms, getting to know them from the teachers' and students' perspectives.

This was a new situation for me. Up until then I had visited classrooms as a researcher, attempting to be the unobserved observer, recording my observations, evaluating them, and telling the 'truth' about what I had seen when invited to speak or write about my research. Given this traditional 'objective' stance, I had not shared my observations with the teachers, nor had I asked them about their intentions for the lessons I observed or for their own evaluations about what had been more or less successful. If I were to work *with* teachers, I realized, this stance would not be appropriate. I would have to become a participant before I could presume to offer my researcher's opinions and I would have to treat them as co-investigators with me rather than as providers of data for my personal research.

The need to change was very forcibly brought home to me during the new longitudinal research project that I started in Toronto. In planning this project, which was designed to investigate the school experiences and progress of children from different language backgrounds: Portuguese, Greek, Cantonese and English, I had planned to share the observations that my research team was making with the teachers, in the hope that they could form the basis for collaborative explorations of ways of better supporting English language learners. However, this did not prove easy, as many of the teachers – perhaps having already been 'subjects' for other researchers – were reluctant to become involved in the way I had hoped. This became very apparent as we prepared for the second year.

At the end of the first year the children we were observing moved up a grade and so we had to secure the cooperation of the new group of teachers into whose classes these children would be entering. Fortunately, despite not having been consulted in the initial planning stage, in all but one case, these new teachers were willing to have us make observations in their classrooms. But one grade three teacher absolutely refused.

Immediately I learned of her refusal, I went to talk with her and she gave the following explanation. Two years earlier she had attended a conference in Toronto at which I had been a guest speaker. During my presentation, I had played short extracts from some of the Bristol classroom recordings and offered my comments on the opportunities for learning that each provided. About one particular teacher-whole class discussion I had been rather critical, pointing out how the teacher had engaged her grade one children in an extended episode of 'guess what's in teacher's mind' instead of listening to what they had found interesting about the visit they had just made to a nearby castle.

'You're not going to do that to me,' she declared. And as I listened to her, I knew she was right. The stance I had taken in the past was both unethical and unproductive. In effect, I had been exploiting my 'subjects', not only giving little in return for their participation but also sometimes criticizing them in public (even though, of course, anonymously) when they had no chance to put their own points of view. But even from the point of view of a collector of data, my approach had also been misguided, if my aim was to understand the reality of learning and teaching as it happens in a particular place and time. Classrooms are communities in which, over time, the participants develop particular ways of acting and interacting; these cannot be understood by an outsider who pays occasional visits to collect and take away for analysis limited stretches of observational data, extracted from their organic historical context.

Fortunately, this teacher did eventually agree to participate – and she also taught me an important lesson in the process. Equally fortunate, in the second year, several teachers took up the offer to become co-investigators with me and I discovered how much more could be achieved by approaching research as a collaborative activity, in which the teacher and I would work together to make sense of the events in which we and the children were all involved and, on that basis, to consider changes that might be made. Ever since then I have carried out all my research as a collaborative action researcher.

In the light of all these developments, I was very pleased to be invited to prepare a second edition of *The Meaning Makers*. Not only is this an opportunity to re-present some of the key findings of the Bristol Study that challenge the current emphasis on accountability as the mechanism that is supposed to improve the quality of education for all children – as in the 'No Child Left Behind' legislation in the United States; but it also provides an opportunity to revisit the Bristol Study and to consider how its findings can contribute to ongoing efforts to improve the quality of public education. In many important ways, I believe, the questions raised in 1986 are still of supreme importance today: What are we educating children for? How can schools give equal emphasis to fostering initiative and innovation, on the one hand, while maintaining continuity with the achievements of the past, on the other? And how should we prepare the teachers of today so that, through them, we can positively influence the values and dispositions that the citizens of tomorrow form in the classrooms in which they learn today?

In thinking about how to rework the original edition, I wondered about the best way to bring it up to date. In the end, I decided to leave the original chapters more or less as they were, since the data and findings have not changed; but I have included references to more recent research where appropriate. On the other hand, I have added three new chapters and extended the final chapter in order to give an overview of the ways in which understanding about early language development and the role of language in learning and teaching has developed since the first edition was published.

The first of these new chapters (Chapter 11) reviews the research on children's language development from a contemporary, 'functional' perspective. What is new about this perspective is the serious attention it gives to the relationship between the development of language by the human species and the language development of contemporary individuals. As the result of empirical research in a wide range of disciplines, from neurolinguistics to archaeology, and from studies of higher primates to longitudinal studies of human infants, a consensus is developing which rejects the assumption that language development requires a species-specific 'language organ' – an 'innate language acquisition device' – as proposed by Chomsky and others. Instead, from this functional perspective, the emergence of language in the human species is seen to be the outcome of *cultural evolution* which, co-occurring and interacting with *biological evolution* of the brain and vocal tract, exploited humans' increased oral capabilities to serve the needs of inter-generational learning and teaching which, itself, was made possible by the prior biological evolution of human infants' predisposition to see other humans as intentional agents like themselves and to learn from them. Further support for this explanation comes from the parallelism between the two time scales – phylogenetic (species) and ontogenetic (individual) – with respect to the sequence of development. On both these time scales, speech is seen to emerge from earlier forms of interaction and communication in which action and gesture are the earliest forms of sharing intentions and making meaning.

The recordings of the children in the Bristol Study cannot throw any light on the very earliest forms of communication since they registered only sound. However, from the beginning, as we listened to the tapes, two features of the children's communication were very apparent. First was its functional orientation. As Halliday (1975) found in his longitudinal study of Nigel, it was nearly always possible to interpret the children's communicative intentions (e.g. indicating, requesting), even when the specific entity or event being referred to was unclear from the utterance itself. And second was the systematic use of intonation to distinguish between possible intentions. Taken together, these two features convinced us that what was driving the children's language development was the desire to share intentions. The adults with whom the children communicated also seemed, for the most part, to understand this, as was evidenced by their frequent checking to make sure they had understood the child's intention before replying, and by their evident concern – on most occasions – to help the children to explore their intentions further. Looking back, I think I can claim with considerable confidence that our interpretation of the data we had collected was an early contribution to the functional theory of language development that has since been developed and which I describe in Chapter 11.

In Chapter 12, I take stock of what has been learned from research over the last 50 years about the importance of language for children's social, emotional and intellectual development and about how adults – both parents and teachers – can support and enrich their development through the activities and interactions in which they engage with them. In schools, in particular, much of this research has been influenced by the ideas of Vygotsky and Bakhtin, leading to an increasing emphasis on dialogue in both whole-class and small group activities and on collaborative knowledge building rather than on teacher transmission and on competition between students as individuals. In this chapter, I report on many important initiatives that hold promise for the future. Unfortunately, though, the pervasive governmental emphasis on accountability by means of high-stakes testing has meant that there has, as yet, been little change in practice in the majority of classrooms.

The final additional chapter (Chapter 13) extends the work in Bristol by describing my most recent research, which has involved collaborative investigations with teachers to explore ways of improving opportunities for learning in schools. As explained earlier, as a result of observing the Bristol children in school, I had come to realize that the ways in which language was used in the classroom were, for the most part, very different from its use for the sort of collaborative meaning making that children experienced at home. It was not that the teachers I observed were not interested in the children in their charge or not keen to help them develop their command of language in its spoken and written forms. Rather, the problem seemed to be that many did not recognize that this development most readily occurs through using language to explore new ideas and solve authentic problems that are of importance to everyone involved. In most of the classrooms I had observed, it was the teacher who, following the curriculum guide, decided what would be talked or written about, who asked the questions, and who decided what were acceptable answers. As a result, children quickly learned that their own ideas were of little significance; their task was to answer the teacher's questions, not to ask their own. In effect, by being constrained in the ways they used language, they were also becoming constrained as thinkers; rather than being encouraged to pose their own problems and explore ideas that interested them, they were being made dependent on the teacher's judgment about what was worth doing or knowing.

From observations in a small number of excellent classrooms, both in England and in Canada, by 1990 I thought I knew how classrooms might be organized differently. But rather than trying to test my ideas through an intervention project, I believed it would be more effective to work in collaboration with practising teachers to explore a variety of possible approaches. In Chapter 13, I describe an eight-year collaborative action research project, undertaken in Toronto, in which, together, school and university educators attempted to create communities of inquiry in our respective classrooms and how this led to significant changes in the use of language. In every case, curriculum units became more inquiry oriented and both whole class and small group discussion became more dialogic.

As I write this prologue in December 2008, the world is engulfed in an economic crisis that has been brought on, at least in part, by an ethos of unbridled individualism and a lack of concern for the disenfranchised and for the well-being of society as a whole. The need for change has rarely been so apparent. And for this to occur, there must be change in the way we educate the young people who will take over the responsibility for solving the problems that, as a society, we have colluded in bringing about.

As Dewey presciently wrote nearly a century ago,

> In directing the activities of the young, society determines its own future ... Since the young at a given time will at some later date compose the society of that period, the latter's nature will largely turn upon the direction children's activities were given at an earlier period. (Dewey, 1916)

It is my hope that what has been learned through the research reported here will contribute to the achievement of the necessary changes.

Note

1. Now incorporated within the University of Toronto. Several times I suggested that, in the name of the department, the order of the terms should be reversed; an understanding of the nature of learning is a prerequisite for the development of a theory of effective teaching, and only then is it appropriate to design curriculum.

Introduction to First Edition

I still remember the excitement I felt when I first read Chomsky's claim that 'language is a window on the mind'. By studying the underlying regularities of the sentences that a speaker of a language can produce or understand, he suggested, we can discover the nature of the knowledge that he or she must possess, and from that we can draw conclusions about the workings of the mind itself. Heady stuff for someone concerned with the education of young children!

Reading further, I found that these were not merely philosophical speculations. Chomsky believed that his claims were empirically verifiable and that the study of children's language development was one way of carrying out such a test. Fortunately, my younger daughter was of a suitable age and I immediately embarked on an observational study.

According to my understanding of the theory, learning a language was very much a matter of arriving at appropriate rules of various kinds. I say 'arriving at' since Chomsky argued that these rules were not taught; neither could they be deduced in any simple way from the sentences that the child might hear. The only possible explanation, therefore, was that they were in some way latent in the structure of the mind. The rules that I decided to investigate were those involved in the formation of questions to which the answer is either 'yes' or 'no'. In abstract, these rules state that a yes/no interrogative sentence can be formed from its associated declarative sentence by taking the first auxiliary element of the verb group in the main clause and permuting it with the subject noun phrase of the same main clause or, in the absence of an auxiliary verb, by adding the auxiliary 'do' to the verb group and then permuting as before. This is apparently what every young child who can ask a question knows!

At this stage, Deborah had no auxiliary verbs in her repertoire and her yes/no questions all relied on rising intonation to achieve their effect. For example, when she wanted me to admire her bright new sweater, she said, 'Like my new sweater?' Even when asked to repeat my 'model' question, she still failed to imitate it correctly, saying instead, 'Uh like my new sweater?' Every 10 days I recorded her spontaneous speech, waiting for the first well-formed interrogative to appear. But, just in case she knew the rules but wasn't using them, I also tried to elicit interrogatives by such strategies as asking her to go and ask her mother if she wanted a cup of coffee. For several weeks, all her questions continued to be asked with intonation only: 'Want a cup of coffee, Mummy?' she asked, as she obligingly relayed my question.

Then one day, in carrying out the same procedure, I heard her say, 'DO you want a cup of coffee, Mummy?' and then she came straight back to where I was sitting and asked, 'Can I have my little book a moment?' Within five or 10 minutes, she had produced several more well-formed interrogative sentences, with 'will' and 'have' as auxiliaries. And then, after I had switched off the tape recorder, I heard her say to her elder sister, as they were playing on the stairs, 'We can climb up the stairs, can't we?' – her first 'tag-question', the description of which involved even more complicated rules.

In what sense she could be said to 'know the rules' I was not sure, but there was no doubt that, apparently in one step, she had discovered and was making use of a principle of very wide generality. I was hooked. I wanted to know more. Fortunately for me, the opportunity arose a few years later to engage in a larger and more systematic piece of research and, at one level, this book is the story of that investigation.

At the start, the Bristol Study was planned as an investigation of language development in the years before entry to school. The aim was to chart the course of development of a group of British children learning English as their first language and, on the basis of what was discovered, to try to answer the more difficult questions about the causes of development.

As my own informal research had shown, by the age of two the process is well under way. By that age, the majority of children have begun to put words together to form rudimentary sentences, and they can clearly understand a considerable amount of what is said to them. But how do they initially crack the language code and, indeed, how do they discover that there is a code to be cracked?

Parents are delighted when they find that they are able to communicate with their children through words. Together they can now begin to explore the world through talk as well as through action. They also find that they can discover more precisely the needs of their children rather than having to rely on the interpretation of cries, smiles, and other nonverbal gestures. Equally important, parents are no longer dependent on physical means to exert control over their children when this is necessary. As a result, during the next few years children in almost every home engage in a great deal of talk, much of it with their parents or other caregivers. How important is this for their language development? Should parents deliberately set out to teach language, or will their children learn to talk whatever their parents do or do not do?

We were also interested in possible differences between children. In appearance and in rate of physical development, children vary considerably. Is the same true of their linguistic development? Do they all follow the same route, or are there important individual differences? We should probably expect some children to develop more rapidly than others, but how wide is the gap between the fastest and the slowest? What are the causes of this variation, and what are the consequences for progress at school?

Questions concerning consequences cannot be answered from a study of the preschool years alone and, having already carried out the first stage of a longitudinal study, it became clear that we should try to extend it at least into the first stage of schooling. There was a further, and more political, reason for doing so. In the late 1960s and early 1970s, both in Britain and in North America, considerable sums of public money were being spent on trying to improve the educational achievement of children from families of lower socioeconomic status (SES). Various explanations were offered for the underachievement of many low-SES children, but most of them attributed at least part of the problem to some form of mismatch between the language of the home and the language of the school. At that time, however, there was little systematic relevant evidence based on observations of the same children at home and at school.

By following some of the children that we had first recorded at the age of 15 months into school, we hoped to be able to provide some much-needed information. If the language of the school is different from that of the home, what is the nature of these differences and do they affect all children equally? It has often been suggested that children from low-SES families are at a particular disadvantage in this respect and that this is a major cause of the relatively lower educational achievement of many of these children. Is there a causal connection between socioeconomic status, language experience in the preschool years, and educational achievement? If so, what are the specific linguistic skills, important for success in school, that are associated with membership of one social group rather than another, and what can be done to give children from all types of family background a more equal opportunity to succeed at school?

Children's language development before they come to school takes place very largely through talk – through the conversation that they have with the members of their immediate family circle. As soon as they enter school, however, they are expected to learn to read and write and, by the time they are seven or eight years old, a substantial part of their learning is dependent on their ability to cope with written language. Some children have little difficulty in mastering these skills and, from the beginning, are keen to explore the possibilities that literacy opens up to them. There are others, however, for whom written language seems to have little meaning.[1] Despite much time and effort they are unable to reach the stage of 'independence' in communicating through reading and writing and, as a result, their progress in other areas of the curriculum is jeopardized. All too often they come to be seen – and to see themselves – as failures. What is it that is required, then, for children to be able to extend their command of language to include the written mode? Are there preschool experiences that prepare some children more effectively than others to take the learning of writing in their stride? If so, what sort of experiences at school can best help children to make up for what they have missed at home?

In order to try to provide answers to these questions – insofar as this is possible on the basis of a single study carried out in one particular cultural environment – we followed 32 of the original representative sample of 128 children through to the final year of their elementary education. Using tests, assessments by the teachers, interviews with the parents, the teachers and the children themselves, as well as direct observations, we tried to identify the major linguistic influences on the children's educational achievement. The information that we obtained provides the basis of the story of language development that this book attempts to tell.

Some readers may be surprised at my use of the word 'story'. But I have chosen it quite deliberately. Stories are a way of making sense – of giving meaning to observable events by making connections between them. However, for any set of events there is almost always more than one possible interpretation – as a day in any courtroom would amply demonstrate. Carrying out research is, in this respect, like any other form of inquiry based on evidence. Only a certain number of events can be observed and although, like good detectives, researchers have hunches to guide them in choosing what events to observe and what clues to look for, in the last resort they have to go beyond the evidence in order to present a coherent account. The available evidence is given meaning by being embedded in a story in which it makes sense.

Stories, like other language forms, are created in the telling. They are influenced, of course, by other stories – in this case, the work of others who have thought and written about language development and its relation to education. They also have a history in the accumulated experience of the storyteller. But, most important, a story is the expression of the present attempt by the teller to find meaning in those experiences. My purpose in writing this book, therefore, is to make sense of the evidence that was collected during the research project and of the ideas that I have obtained through reading and discussion, and to tell the meaning that I have made to others who share my concerns.

Seen from this perspective, there can be no true stories. The evidence is never so complete or so unambiguous as to rule out alternative interpretations. The important criteria in judging the worth of a story are: does it fit the facts as I have observed them and does it provide a helpful basis for future action? It is my hope that many who are concerned with the care and education of young children – parents, teachers and educational policy-makers – will feel that, on these criteria, the story was worth the telling.

Notes on Transcriptions of Dialogue Extracts

In order to convey something of the pace and tone of the conversational extracts, I have used the following conventions:

Emphasis. Where a word or syllable is spoken with extra emphasis it is presented in boldface type.

Simultaneous speech. Where two people speak at once, the overlapping portions of their utterances are underlined.

Incompleteness. Where an utterance is interrupted or otherwise left incomplete, this is indicated by a hyphen. This often occurs within a speaking turn when the speaker stops and makes a fresh start at what he or she wants to say.

Pausing. Both between and within utterances, there are sometimes noticeable pauses. These are indicated by one or a series of dots. Each dot represents approximately one second of silence. Where the pause lasts for 5 seconds or longer, this information is stated in brackets.

Unintelligibility. Where an utterance is unintelligible, the number of asterisks corresponds to the number of words judged to have been spoken.

Note: Transcriptions of the recordings of a representative sample of the children in the Bristol Study can be accessed at the *Child Language Data Exchange System* (http://childes.psy.cmu.edu/).

Chapter 1

The Children and Their Families

'It's half past nine. Where's Rosie?'
'She got a knife in her hands, Dad'
'Oh, my God!'

This was our first meeting with Rosie. Up to that point unnoticed, as she sat quietly under the table playing with a knife, she became briefly the focus of attention. Then, the knife removed, she was left once again to her own devices.

Rosie

It was shortly after breakfast on 27 July 1973, and we were making our first observation of Rosie. But an observation with a difference. The only evidence of our interest in Rosie was a slight bulge under her dress at the front and a rather larger hump between her shoulders at the back. This was the bugging device – a pair of miniature microphones and a battery-operated radio transmitter – left in her home on the previous afternoon. Her elder brother and sisters were naturally intrigued. A little later, when Rosie had fallen asleep on the sofa, Kelvin (age eight) and his friend Mike took a closer look.[1]

Mike:	What's it connected to? her ears or her mouth?
Mother:	Eh? No, she just got it on . she got a square thing over her shoulders and round to the back
Kelvin:	Mike, look at this . there it is . look
Mother:	The round thing there is the microphone
Mike:	How does the noise come out, then, if it ain't in her mouth?
Mother:	I don't know . you see there's a wire going over there and a wire going over that side
Mike:	Is there a wire in her mouth?

Mother:	No . there's another microphone there . when she speaks it goes on that recorder in there [pointing to a box in the corner of the room]
Mike:	Can you hear her speak?
Mother:	No . they're coming tonight to play it back … and if there's anything comes out what we wants rubbed off, they'll rub it off

Like most of the children, at 15 months Rosie wasn't saying much that we could interpret with confidence. She also slept for quite a lot of the day. But this first recording gave the family an opportunity to get used to having the recorder in their home (there were very few references to the equipment on subsequent recordings). It also gave us our first glimpse of them and of their relationships with each other.

Rosie and her family lived in the inner city in a small terrace house built in the year of Queen Victoria's Jubilee. Father, a labourer, was not regularly employed and spent most of his time around the house. So, with two adults and five children – ranging from Kelvin, age eight, to Donna, only a year older than Rosie – as well as a large dog, there was not much space in the house when all of them were at home. With little money, providing for the children was a fairly constant preoccupation and so, although they were clearly fond of Rosie and concerned for her welfare, her parents did not find time to give her a great deal of individual attention. As she grew older, however, her brother and elder sisters included her in their activities, and by the time she went to school, she and Donna were almost inseparable.

Abigail

Abigail, whom we first met a few weeks later, was another child with several older siblings. She, however, lived on the other side of the city centre in a spacious four-floor house in a Regency terrace with a large garden. Like Rosie, though, she tended to get overlooked when all the family was at home – at least until she had learned to take part in the conversation. On one occasion, her mother found her in one of her sisters' bedrooms, playing alone with materials for tie-and-dye.

Abigail:	[asking about the bottles of dye] What's those?
Mother:	Did you take anything out?
Abigail:	Yeh
Mother:	[under her breath] Oh, my God … oh, Christ . [then, to Abigail] open your mouth

Fortunately, it was a false alarm. Abigail had not tried to drink the dye.

What both these narrow escapes illustrate (though more dramatically than usual) is just how much of parental speech to the one- to two-year-old is likely to be concerned with the child's safety and welfare, particularly when, with older and more verbal children competing for their attention, parents only notice what the youngest is up to when the damage is done. In fact, for many of the children at this age, controlling utterances, together with exclamations and endearments, provided the majority of the speech addressed to them. While Mother is talking to Rosanna, Abigail has gone into the garden with no shoes on and stepped in a puddle.

Abigail: [shouts with glee]
Mother: [looking out of the door] Oh, Abby! for goodness
sake! . you've come out in your tights after I've just dressed
you . taken ages to get you ready
[She picks Abigail up, takes her inside, and returns to her conversation with Rosanna.]

Notice, though, that such controlling utterances can also provide quite a lot of information about the way things are – or, perhaps, about the way they should or should not be. As we eavesdropped on these families, we came to realize very clearly that learning to talk is just one facet (albeit probably the most important one) of learning to be a member of a particular culture, with all the taken-for-granted assumptions of what is important, what is approved or disapproved of, and what that entails. Here is another example.

Abigail, now 21 months old, has been to the supermarket with her mother. On the way home, Abigail has been exploring the box of groceries and has found a packet of stock cubes. She is now sucking one of them.

Abigail: *
Mother: Oh, yucky! . oh, where's the packet gone, darling?
[No response, as Abigail continues to suck the cube.]
Mother: It's for cooking, sweetheart . look, it's for putting in a
cooking pot to make a stew

Abigail's parents, both professional people, were involved in a Franco-British society and, on several of the occasions when we observed her, there were young French people staying in the house. This led to many interesting conversations about places and customs that the visitors had remarked on or that were drawn to their attention. Thanks to her microphone, we were able to eavesdrop on these conversations, just as Abigail was. What she made of them we cannot tell, but there is no doubt that, compared with many other children, the range of language to which she was exposed as a listener was extremely wide and varied.

By 24 months, Abigail had acquired sufficient linguistic resources to begin to join in the conversation, provided the other person gave her his or her full attention. In the following extract, she was talking with her father about the jigsaw puzzle that they were doing together.

Abigail: [referring to a figure in the puzzle] Mummy
Father: [confirming] That's Mummy . and who's that?
Abigail: Man
Father: Very good .. and who's that?
Abigail: Bike
Father: Bicycle
Abigail: Bicycle
Father: And that?
Abigail: And car
Father: And a car .. oh, look!
Abigail: Man
Father: Lots of men

Three months later, she was well on her way to mastering the adult language. In the following extract, we find her alone with her mother, engaged in drawing and colouring.

Abigail: There Teddy . there 'tis
Mother: Is that your teddy?
Abigail: Yes it is
Mother: Do you want to draw a teddy?
Abigail: [referring to a crayon] I have that one
Mother: Can I colour him in with that one?
Abigail: Yeh
Mother: Oh no, it won't colour . can I have another colour to colour him in?
Abigail: Yeh . have that one [handing her a crayon]
Mother: A brown teddy . oh, that one's nearly gone too [nearly worn out]
Abigail: Green one . can I have green one? [Whispers to self] We haven't done green .. greeny one . purple, green . [softly to self] we haven't got green one . [addressing mother again] those are too big!

Gary

Our first impression of Gary was of a child with a healthy appetite – perhaps because much of his parent's speech to him during the first two observations was about food. The following extract comes from the second, at 18 months.

Gary: [crying] Look
Father: What do you want?
Mother: Come here
Gary: [wanting to look in the cupboard] Look
[Father lifts him up to the cupboard at which he's pointing. Gary takes out the biscuit (cookie) tin.]
Father: [to Mother, amused] Hey, Joyce, look! [To Gary] That what you wants?
Gary: Uh [yes]
Father: What d'you want?
Gary: [taking a handful of biscuits] That
Father: He don't take one [only one]
Mother: He got to take two
Father: [to Mother]: Yes [To Gary] All right?
Gary: Uh [yes]
Father: Get down?
Gary: Uh
[Father puts him down, the biscuit still in reach. Mother and Father talk together for a minute.]
Gary: Hey, Dada! look! [Gary gives one biscuit each to Mother and Father and has two left in his hand.]
Father: Is that one for Sandra? [his sister]
Gary: Mm [Makes no attempt to give it to her.]
Father: How come you got two?
Gary: [running off] Ha!

Gary's sister was just under two years older than him and, like the other two children we have met, he was often overshadowed by her – at least to begin with – and there were many minor tiffs. But they also played happily together, as in the following extract, when Gary was 27 months. Gary and Sandra are pretending to go shopping.

Mother: Where is you going?
Gary: Going up the shops
Mother: All right

Sandra:	[to Mother] I won't be late [To Gary] Right, get in the car then
Gary:	All right
Sandra:	[with a sudden change of plan] We're going to be married now
Gary:	Here comes the bride
Sandra:	Here comes the bride [They continue, shouting together.]

Gary's father was a diesel engine mechanic and his working hours meant that he was quite often at home during the day. He would spend some of this time in his garage, working on his car or motor bike. Gary often went to 'help' him, playing with the tools and 'mending' his favourite toys, a tractor and a pedal car. But he also enjoyed helping his mother, as in the following extract, at 33 months, when Mother was doing the ironing.

Gary:	[referring to the nylon thread that he is using as his washing line] I break it, Mummy
Mother:	No, you won't be able to . it's nylon
Gary:	Why, Mum?
Mother:	No, you won't be able to break it, Gary . that's to hang your washing on
Gary:	Oh What- what have you got there? [asking about what Mother is ironing]
Mother:	Mm?
Gary:	Hang my washing out . that's my washing line, isn't it? I can put some clothes on there, can't I?
Mother:	All right
Gary:	I'm going to put some clothes on there [he hangs up some hankies] hang them up .. I shall hang them up

This was the longest conversation that Gary had had up to this point in our observations, and it is significant, I think, that it took place when he was 'helping' his mother with the ironing. Parents are busy, most of the day, with the routine business of running the household; only a minority in our study took time to play with their children, joining in the children's activities. From time to time, of course, they would ask about or comment on what the child was doing, or respond to requests for help. But such conversations were, on the whole, brief and undeveloped. When a mother or father had the time and patience to allow the child to become engaged in her or his adult activities, on the other hand, quite long and interesting conversations often occurred.

There are two reasons for this, I suspect. On the one hand, children have a natural desire to try out those adult activities that they understand (as we see in the sort of role play illustrated above in the shopping episode), and talking about them is one of the ways in which they come to understand them better. And, on the other hand, from the adult's point of view, the purposefulness of the task gives purpose to the conversation. Under these conditions, children's questions and observations are more easily understood and hence are more likely to receive more satisfying responses.

Penny

While Gary liked best to help his Dad (when he was allowed to), Penny was from an early age a regular little housewife. Here she is at 24 months. Father, a firefighter just returned from work, is having his dinner in the front room, and Penny is running to and fro from the kitchen to serve him.

Penny: I've got more dinner
Father: Get a piece of bread and butter, please
Penny: Want some bread and butter?
Father: Yes, to put over these
Penny: [running into kitchen] Me going to get bread
Mother: He's a nuisance . he ought to have done it himself . he's lazy
Penny: I take in Daddy's bread . Daddy wants some tea?
Mother: I expect so . here you are . go and give that to Daddy
[Penny runs into the front room and gives bread to her father]
Father: Thank you

Of all the children introduced so far, Penny was the most linguistically advanced when we first met her at 15 months. This was the very first interchange on the tape. Penny is playing with a clock.

Mother: Oh-oh-oh! what's that?
Penny: Tick-tock
Mother: It's a tick-tock

No child was so obviously into the 'naming game' as Penny, as both she and her mother asked and answered the question 'What's that!' about household objects and pictures in a mail-order catalogue. At 18 months, looking at a picture book of clocks and watches, her mother encouraged her to count, which she did, somewhat erratically:

Mother: One, two, ...
Penny: Three

Mother: Three, four, five ...
Penny: Six, seven, ten
Mother: [firmly] Seven, eight ...
Penny: Ten

At the same age, she pretended to read a picture book by herself, while her mother was busy in the kitchen. Surprisingly, though, we never heard anybody read a story to her. Penny, too, had older siblings: two brothers, five and six years older than her. However, her situation was very different from that of the other children we have so far considered, for the two boys spent much of their time playing with their friends and were much less frequently competing with Penny for their parents' attention. Indeed, although not spoiled, she was quite obviously the whole family's pride and joy, and they all enjoyed playing and talking with her. The following extract comes from the recording already quoted above, just after her father had finished his dinner. Penny is playing with her teddy, which is in her doll's pram (carriage).

Penny: Teddy isn't * * [two unintelligible words]
Father: Eh? Teddy isn't what?
Penny: Er ... [sighs]
Father: All right now?
Penny: Yeh
Father: Is he in the pram?
Penny: Yeh
Father: Good . put the blanket over him, then
[Penny covers Teddy with the blanket.]
Father: Not over his face . he won't be able to see
Penny: Come on, Teddy
Father: Want me to do it?
Penny: Yeh
Father: [whispers] All right
Penny: [shouts to Sam?, the dog] Stay there!
Father: Shh!
Penny: Shh!
Father: [referring to Teddy] He's going night-nights . say
               'Night-night, Teddy'
Penny: Night-night, Teddy
[Penny wheels the pram into the kitchen.]
Penny: He asleep, Mummy
Mother: Who?
Penny: Teddy . he's a bad

Mother:	Bad, is he? Oh, poor Teddy!
Penny:	He's got a bad leg
Mother:	Oh, poor Teddy!

The other striking characteristic of Penny's family life was the constant stream of visitors: relatives, friends, neighbours and their children. Not a single observation passed without at least one visitor calling for an hour or two. A friendly, vivacious child, Penny benefited enormously from this wide range of playmates and conversational partners. In other homes, however, the effect of visitors could be very different. Some mothers, of course, invited friends with children, in order to ensure that their own children had friends of the same age to play with, and the adults would keep a watchful eye on them while they drank a cup of tea or coffee, occasionally entering into the children's play. Others, though, were so relieved to have another adult to talk to that they resented any interruption from the child. Already short of adult conversation, Rosie, for example, would be almost completely ignored while a visitor was in the house.

Anthony

This sometimes seemed to be the case with Anthony, the only child of somewhat older parents. Mother had had a management position in a large company before Anthony was born and, although she was obviously very fond of him, she sometimes seemed to find the continuous company of a young child rather irksome.

[Anthony is playing with the stick used for stirring the bucket of soiled nappies (diapers).]

Mother:	Oh, Tony! don't put that in your mouth . Ugh!

[Anthony puts the stick down, goes to the socket where the fridge is plugged in, and tries to switch it on and off.]

Mother:	Now what are you up to? . you know what? . you and I are going to have a little chat-
Anthony:	* *
Mother:	-about plugs, for a start, and not-
Anthony:	* *
Mother:	-switching them on and off . right? especially the one that's plugging in the fridge
Anthony:	* [begins to hit his mother.]
Mother:	Who are you thumping?
Anthony:	*
Mother:	[crossly]: You sit down there

An only child – or one with much older brothers and sisters – can put a severe strain on a parent who is at home alone all day. With no other children to play with, such a child is dependent on the adult for company and stimulation as well as for physical care. When the latter proves difficult – for example, when the child is not cooperative – it is not surprising that some parents easily lose their patience.

Mother: [trying to dress Anthony in order to go out] Tony! It's very not funny . it's hard . it's difficult . and you're not making it any easier . stand up! don't be so stupid!

Anthony: That pom-pom [swinging it so that he hits his mother's face]

Mother: [crossly] Don't ever do that again, Tony! [struggling to get his gloves on] Tony! concentrate on what I'm trying to do, will you, there's a good boy

Anthony: Mm

Mother: There's nothing worse than trying to put gloves on somebody who's not concentrating

Not all Anthony's conversational experience was like this, of course. There were many more enjoyable exchanges. But there was no doubt that his mother found the toddler stage hard work and perhaps looked forward to the day when he would be able to engage in intellectually more stimulating conversation. Anthony was, in fact, rather slow in learning to talk and, although his mother tried to be patient, she obviously found his limited abilities frustrating on occasion. The following extract comes from the recording made when he was 30 months old. They were looking at a picture book together, and Mother had asked him to find a mouse in the picture.

Anthony: Where's it gone, Mummy?

Mother: It's sitting on a little boat

Anthony: Uh?

Mother: Here you are- sitting on a little boat

Anthony: All gone, Mummy

Mother: It's on that page right in front of you [Anthony still can't see the mouse] ever such a tiny little mouse

Anthony: Uh?

Mother: Can you see it? . [trying a new tactic] can you see the sheep? . see the baby sheep? . well, just in front of the baby sheep is a little tiny mouse

Anthony: All gone, Mummy

Mother: [under her breath] Oh, God! [to Anthony] what's that?

Anthony: Little, Mummy

Mother: Can you see the baby chicken?
Anthony: Huh?
Mother: Can you see a baby chicken?
Anthony: Er . all gone, Mummy
Mother: You look for the baby chicken
Anthony: [excitedly]There it is!
Mother: There it is . a daddy chicken and a mummy chicken and a
              baby chicken
[With a sigh of relief, she moves away, leaving Anthony with the book.]

Jonathan

Jonathan was also an only child with older-than-average parents. But in his case, family life seemed to a much greater extent to revolve around him. Not that he was spoiled. Rather, it appeared that, from an early age, parents and child enjoyed doing many things together. Jonathan was a great lover of books and stories. On the very first observation, when Jonathan had a cold and an ear infection, Mother produced a book as soon as he had finished breakfast and looked at it with him in order to cheer him up.

Jonathan: [moans]
Mother: Shall we look at your book? . come and look at your book?
Jonathan: [mumbles.]
Mother: Come on then
Jonathan: [showing interest] Doddy [doggy]
Mother: [checking] Who's that? [Jonathan coughs] dog
Jonathan: Dog
Mother: Dog
Jonathan: [coughs] Dog
Mother: [turning to next picture] Baloo [name of the bear in the
              book] . bear
Jonathan: Bear [coughs]
Father: [entering the room] If that cough gets any worse,
              take him to the doctor's
Mother: I shall, darling . honestly, I'm sure you think I neglect him
[Jonathan gives the book to Father.]
Father: Thank you
Mother: [to Jonathan] Say 'my Mum don't neglect me . she just
              weighs up which I'm likely to do worse by - sitting in the
              doctor's surgery [office] getting coughed and spit all over,
              or being cured at home!'

The significance of books and stories in Jonathan's life can be gauged from the following account of what happened during the day of our second observation, when Jonathan was 18 months old. The timing device on the tape recorder was programmed to switch on for 90 seconds at approximately 20-minute intervals between 9:00 a.m. and 6:00 p.m. From the 24 samples recorded in this way at each observation, 18 were selected for transcription. In Jonathan's case, nine included some activity involving a book.

9:19 a.m.	Mother is ironing. Jonathan points to a book, saying, 'There, there', asking to be read to. 'Let Mummy just iron the anorak', says Mother. She finishes and starts to read.
9:51 a.m.	Jonathan is eating an apple. Mother opens a picture book. 'Teddy there', says Jonathan. They continue to look at the book.
10:07 a.m.	Mother is putting on Jonathan's shoes. 'Find the shoes in the book', says Mother, looking at the Mothercare catalogue.
12:09 p.m.	Jonathan is just waking up from his morning nap. He is sitting on his mother's lap, looking at a picture book with her.
1:03 p.m.	After his lunch, Jonathan is looking at his picture book.
1:17 p.m.	Mother has joined him, and they look at the book together.
2:55 p.m.	Jonathan's nose is blocked and he has difficulty breathing. Mother reads a book to distract him from his discomfort.
3:57 p.m.	'Do you want to look at this new book?' asks Mother. Jonathan, who is sitting on her lap, is eager to do so.
5:59 p.m.	Mother sings nursery rhymes to Jonathan as she gets him ready for bed. He recognizes the figures on a poster by his bed as those he has seen in one of his books.

On these early occasions, the books are almost always picture books, and the 'reading' is essentially matching words and pictures. But these are soon replaced by picture storybooks, which, because they are much longer, are more widely spaced through the day. When Jonathan is 36 months old, his mother insists, as she finishes a story, 'I told you I'm only reading one book now'. On another occasion, she refuses to read him a story because he's just wet his pants instead of asking to go to the toilet.

Because of his work as a motor mechanic maintaining machines in a factory, Jonathan's father was rarely at home during the observations. When he was at home, though, he joined in the story-reading as well, as we found in our observation at 27 months. However, not all Jonathan's interests were so literary. Our observations show him engaging in many other joint activities with his mother, such as playing with toy bricks, helping with the baking and the cleaning and, of course, just talking.

Jonathan was, in fact, the most advanced of this group of children when we completed the last round of the home observations. At three and a half, he had already mastered the basic grammar of English and had an estimated vocabulary of several thousand words. With these resources, he was able to converse effectively on a wide range of topics, as the following extracts demonstrate. In the first, he is offering his mother some of the imaginary dinner he has just cooked with play dough.

Mother:	You're cutting my food up for me, are you? . can't I cut it myself?
Jonathan:	There's just a chance because I'm going to have a bit of it before and then a bit of the big one . and then you're going to have a bit of the little one, then a bit of the big one .. but you eat that bit of the little one
Mother:	Oh, that was delicious!
Jonathan:	That's my best meal
Mother:	You cooked it beautifully . how did you cook it?
Jonathan:	Let me show you . well ... I rolled it first, right?
Mother:	Yes
Jonathan:	Then, when it was too big, right-?
Mother:	Yes
Jonathan:	When it was dropping, right? . I folded it over again, right?
Mother:	Yes
Jonathan:	Then rolled it again
Mother:	And was that how it was so nice- because you kept rolling it?
Jonathan:	I rolled it like that, right? . and flattened it again . I rolled it bigger and bigger and bigger and bigger
Mother:	And you put one of those to crumble up, don't you? [indicating a pretend ox-bullion-cube] . because Mummy does
Jonathan:	[uncertainly] Well I don't crumble it up
Mother:	Crumble it up and make the gravy nice
Jonathan:	Well that is to make it so nice

Unfortunately, at this moment, the recorder switched off, so we shall never know what other delicacies Jonathan cooked that day. Not many of the conversations that we recorded in these early observations were sustained over so many turns. This in itself is an indication of Jonathan's relative linguistic maturity. But is interesting to note that the majority of extended conversations developed around topics like this, which arose from shared activities to which both participants were giving their full attention.

The last extract also involves play dough, from which Mother has been making a model figure. In its wry humor, this conversation captures another side of the quality of family life in Jonathan's home.

Jonathan: What are you making?
Mother: Wait and see what I'm making
Jonathan: [after waiting several seconds] What are you making?
Mother: A man with a cigarette in his mouth [laughs]
Jonathan: Make- make his feet . shall I give you some play dough to
           make his feet?
Mother: There's his feet . there
Jonathan: Where is his feet?
Mother: One, two
Jonathan: Why is he a little man?
Mother: Because he's only tiny . smoking's stunted his growth
Jonathan: He'll grow big, won't he?
Mother: If he gives up smoking, yes
Jonathan: He's giving up smoking
[Father coughs loudly in the background.]
Mother: You'd better take the cigarette out of his mouth then,
           hadn't you?
Jonathan: I know . coo! he's growing and coughing
Mother: Growing and coughing
Jonathan: Because he shouldn't have a cigarette in his mouth,
           should he?
Mother: No
Jonathan: He's a silly man, isn't he?
Father: [kisses Jonathan] See you later [Father is going
           to work]
Jonathan: See you later . he's a silly man, too [referring to his father]

Choosing the Children

Rosie, Abigail, Gary, Penny, Anthony and Jonathan are just six of the 32 children that we studied from shortly after their first birthdays until the last year of their primary (elementary) schooling. However, the 32 children were themselves selected from a larger sample of 128, picked from a random sample of more than 1000 names of preschool children resident in the city of Bristol, England, drawn from Health Department records.[2] Each family was interviewed and, on the basis of the information obtained, the 128 children were picked from those families who agreed to participate (more than 87% of those interviewed). In selecting the children, an equal number of boys and girls at each age were chosen, and season of birth and the full range of family background were equally represented.[3] Half the children were three-and-a-half years old when we first observed them. These children were observed until they were just over five years old. (We shall be meeting some of them in later chapters.) The others were 15 months old, and it was exactly half of this group who were selected for the full longitudinal investigation.

Each child was recorded every three months over a period of 42 months. The recordings were made by means of a radio-microphone worn by the child. This was left at the child's home on the day before the observation and collected on the day following. During the actual observation, there was no observer present, as we did not want in any way to interfere with the spontaneity of the family's normal activities. In order to obtain information about the contexts in which the short samples of speech were recorded, the person who was to transcribe the tape called at the child's home in the evening, after the observation was finished, and asked questions about each of the recorded samples to find out who had been present, where they had been, and what they had been doing. Questions were also asked about any utterances that were unclear or in other ways difficult to understand, and any other information was noted that would make it easier to understand the conversation. In this way, by the end of this phase of the study, we had made more than 1200 recordings and collected a corpus of nearly a quarter of a million child utterances, all of which were transcribed and coded.

At about the same time as each recording, in a playroom at the university, we tested the children's comprehension and their ability to imitate the sentences in a simple story and, when each child was three-and-a-half years old, we interviewed the parents in order to gain further information about the home environment and about the parents' views on bringing up their children. Then, over the next five years, we carried out a variety of analyses of this material in order to try to answer questions about the sequence of language development and about the influences of the home environment on that development. These answers and the conclusions that I believe we can draw from them will be the subject of the following chapters.

However, the material we collected has more to tell us than can be revealed by this sort of quantitative analysis. Learning to talk is more than acquiring a set of linguistic resources; it is also discovering how to use them in conversation with a variety of people and for a variety of purposes. To understand children's language development, therefore, we need to study it in its context of interaction: people talking to each other as they go about their normal business. And it is this embeddedness of conversation in the texture of everyday life that is the strongest impression one gets from listening to the recordings that we made and from reading the resulting transcripts. In the following chapters, I shall quote from them at some length in order to try to convey something of this texture as well as to illustrate the conclusions we arrived at.

Some examples have already been given in the first part of this chapter. From them one gains a strong sense of the individuality of each child's experience and of the enormous variety that is to be found in any representative sample of children. Every child is unique, and so is every family. However, reading through the transcripts also convinces one of the very great degree of similarity that exists between children and families, if not in detail then at least in broad outline. And in trying to explain the universal accomplishment that language learning represents, these similarities are perhaps even more important than the differences.

One of the most striking features that is common to all families is the repetitiveness of the everyday life of a young child. Meals, dressing and undressing, and the performance of bodily functions provide the content of talk in sample after sample. (A whole book could be written on the different approaches to toilet training and on the varied vocabulary involved!) As a result, the same sorts of conversation occurred over and over again, different in small details from family to family but in function essentially the same. In all families, too, there was a concern with safety – both the child's and that of the property of other members of the family: 'Don't touch! That's Daddy's.' It is not surprising, therefore, that there is great similarity between children in the sorts of utterances that they first produce. For example, the 's marker of possession appears quite early in the speech of almost all the children.

Another striking characteristic is the brevity – not to say the disjointedness – of a large proportion of the conversations. The examples quoted earlier in this chapter are nearly all longer and more coherent than average. In fact, the average length of a conversation was 3.3 exchanges (that is to say, a total of about six speaking turns by all participants) at 18 months and still only 4.0 exchanges (or about eight turns) at 42 months. There are several reasons for this. Perhaps the most obvious is that young children are very limited in what they are able to say (though probably not so limited in the meanings they try to express), and quite a lot of their utterances are uninterpretable, even by their parents, who know them well. Sometimes the adult just doesn't have the time or the patience to discover what the child is trying to say, so the conversation comes to an abortive end. On other occasions the adult may understand all too well but decide that feigning incomprehension or not hearing is easier than having to refuse a request and cope with the consequences. 'We'll see' or 'When you've done——'are strategies that we observed many parents using to avoid confrontation.

A further reason for the brevity and for much of the apparent incoherence is the close relation between what is said and the activity in which the speech is embedded. What to an eavesdropper is incoherent may make perfect sense to the participants, who can see what the speaker is looking at and who have a very good idea what he or she wants them to do or think about it. The following conversation took place between Penny and her mother when Penny was two-and-a-half years old.

1	**Penny:**	I wants that one
2	**Mother:**	Mm
3	**Penny:**	A ball . I get it back
4	**Mother:**	Yes
5	**Penny:**	Our ball out there
6	**Mother:**	Which one do you want?
7	**Penny:**	That one
8		Get them all there . in there now
9		Is that yours, Ma?
10	**Mother:**	Yes
11	**Penny:**	Yes? . mine is hot, Ma

At first sight, this appears almost incomprehensible. In fact, it is two different conversations that are interwoven: the first about the dinner that Mother is serving and the second about the ball that Penny notices in the garden as she looks through the window. Lines 1, 2, 6 and 7 concern Penny's choice of plate; in lines 9–11 she checks that the other plate is her mother's; in line 12 she comments on the heat of her own plate. It is this conversation – and the activity of serving the dinner to which it is related – that is at the focus of the mother's attention. The second conversation, lines 3–5 and 8, are on a topic of Penny's choosing, to which the mother gives only the minimum of attention, in the form of an acknowledgment. Nevertheless, both conversations succeed in achieving their purposes: Mother serves the dinner in a way that meets with Penny's approval (a very important matter – as we discovered from listening to many episodes in which children objected because they hadn't been given the right spoon or because the ketchup was obscuring the picture on the plate, etc.), and Penny shares with her mother her interest in the ball she has noticed. She also appears to recognize – with no words spoken at all – that her intention, 'I get it back', will have to be deferred until later. Most conversations involving young children, then, like this one, are rooted in the here and now of perception, intention and action and so can be inexplicit and even fragmentary, yet still be successful for the purpose at hand.

When more extended conversations did occur, they were likely to be of a more discursive or exploratory nature: recalling past events, discussing what could be seen from the window, explaining how things work or considering what might happen – to the speakers themselves or to characters in stories or on television. For such conversations to take place, it seems, attention needs to be freed from the demands of ongoing action so that it can be devoted to the attempt to achieve mutual understanding. Young children not only have restricted powers of expression, they also have an understanding of the world that is both limited and naive. If adult and child are to succeed in elaborating a shared meaning over a number of turns, the adult has to make the effort to understand the child's intended meaning and to extend it in terms that the child can understand. This requires a willingness to listen sympathetically and an intuitive ability to pitch what one says at the right level – both intellectually and linguistically. Most parents are able to talk with children in this way, we discovered, but the pressure of other concerns meant that some of them rarely found the time to do so.

These pressures, in some cases, were considerable: family breakdown, shortage of money, ill health and overcrowded housing, to mention only the most obvious. But in no family did we observe a child for whom the parents did not show love and affection and a concern for his or her well-being – even though the manner in which this was expressed varied considerably and was not always consistent. We were also struck by the amount of humour: parents joking with the children and teasing them in a friendly fashion, and parents joking with each other about their children's annoying characteristics as well as the more obviously endearing ones.

These, then, were the homes in which the children were growing up – enormously varied, yet sharing many common characteristics in their patterns of everyday life and in the conversations that arose from them. This was the experience through which the children learned to talk and, through talk, also learned about the world in which they lived. How did they do it? The following chapters offer the beginnings of an answer.

Notes

1. Some of the extracts from the recordings contain words and grammatical structures that are features of the local dialect. Although these may be unfamiliar to

some readers, I have retained them in order to preserve the authenticity of the material.

2. A number of categories of children were excluded, including those with any known handicap, those in fulltime care, and those whose parents' first language was not English. In all, these categories amounted to less than 10% of the initial random sample.

3. In calculating the index of family background, equal weighting was given to each parent's occupational status (using the Registrar-General's classification) and to the extent of their fulltime education.

Chapter 2
Learning to Talk: The Pattern of Development

How do children learn to talk? This is a question to which many parents and teachers would like to know the answer, for then they would know better what sort of help they should give. But to ask the question in this way is to assume that all children – or at least the majority of them – are sufficiently similar for one single answer to be possible. From the point of view of the concerned parent or teacher, of course, it would be much easier if that proved to be the case; but it certainly should not be assumed without question.

On the face of it, there are quite strong reasons for expecting the opposite. The evidence of differences between children in rate of learning is overwhelming, as is the evidence for the wide divergences between families in the ways they use language and so in the model that they provide. These differences were clearly apparent just from listening to the recordings we made – as could be seen in the extracts quoted in the previous chapter. When we consider the much greater differences that exist between different cultural groups who happen to speak the same language, as, for example, in England, the United States and West Africa, and the still greater differences between communities that speak different languages, there are even stronger reasons for wanting evidence that the sequence of learning is essentially the same in all children before assuming that an answer to the question about how they learn can be given in a form that applies to all.

There are, in fact, two different questions involved: what children learn and how they learn it. Of course, these questions are not independent, since the context, both material and sociocultural, in which children are growing up will almost certainly affect what is *available* to be learned. Indeed, there already exist a number of studies that have been carried out in different parts of the world that clearly show very considerable differences in the context of language learning (e.g. Gaskins, 1999; Heath, 1983; Schieffelin & Ochs, 1986). However, these differences do not in themselves rule out the possibility of a universal answer to the question about how they learn. This latter question will be discussed in later chapters. For the moment, though, it is the first question that I want to consider.

One way of tackling the 'what' of learning is to compare the sequence of development across a large sample of children who are all learning the same language. To the extent that they all show essentially the same sequence, there will be a basis for continuing to seek a universal explanation of how learning takes place. On the other hand, strong evidence of dissimilarity would be a reason for doubting the feasibility of such an attempt. If similarity were found in one language, the next step would be to make the same sort of comparisons in a number of different languages, for only if there is a common sequence within every language can a universal explanation be considered.[1]

In very general terms, of course, the answer to the question concerning the sequence in which children learn to talk is already known. Children produce what appear to be random vocalizations and babbling before they begin to produce gestures and recognizable words; two-word utterances occur before two-clause utterances; direct imperative requests in all situations precede the appropriate matching of the various forms of indirect request to the particular status of the person addressed. But, within this general outline, there is room for considerable individual variation in the detail of the developmental sequence and, at this level, there is much less available information.

It was in order to provide this sort of detailed information about the sequence of development in English that we started to analyse the material we had collected.

The Sequence of Development

In order to understand what we discovered, a brief explanation of the method we used is probably necessary at this point. This can best be given by means of a particular example. Suppose we take what I shall call a *linguistic system*, such as the personal pronoun system: 'I', 'me', 'you', 'he', 'she', 'it', and so on. In the recordings of the speech of any particular child, these words are going to occur for the first time in a particular order. And if these first occurrences are widely separated in time, there will be reasonable grounds for thinking that the order in which they occur corresponds to the order in which they were learned. When we look at the recordings of another child, we shall again find that the pronouns first occur in a particular order. What will be interesting, though, is to compare the two children to find out if the order for the second child is the same as that found for the first or whether it is different. This procedure can then be extended until all the children have been included in the comparison and a large number of linguistic systems have been investigated in this way.[2]

The linguistic systems that we investigated can be divided into three groups: those concerned with the *functions* for which children use language (e.g. to make requests, ask questions, give explanations, etc.); those concerned with the *meanings* they express (the objects, states, events and relationships that they talk about); and those concerned with the *form* of their utterances (i.e. with their grammatical structure). Altogether, we investigated some 35 linguistic systems across these three groups.

The results of our analysis can be told very briefly. For each system and for all systems combined, the evidence strongly suggested a single common sequence of development. Despite their differing experiences, therefore, it seemed that all the children were learning in the same sort of way.

To illustrate this sequence, extracts will be presented from the speech of one particular child. Each extract will be followed by a discussion of the main characteristics appearing at that stage. It must be emphasized, of course, that referring to 'stages' is nothing more than a convenient way to describe the child's development. In fact, this development is more or less continuous, with no sharp boundaries between successive stages. Not surprisingly, therefore, the extracts that follow contain some examples of characteristics that are more typical of the following stage as well as occasional occurrences of immature forms that are characteristic of earlier stages. In this sense, almost any extract represents a period of transition.

Stage 1

Unfortunately, our observations did not begin until after the stage at which most children had begun to produce recognizable words, so we can say very little about the very early stages of language development.[3] However, some of the children in our sample were, at 15 months, still at the stage before the emergence of language in a recognisable form and the recordings of these children are probably representative of the earliest stage in all children. From about nine months or so, most children are beginning to communicate with a combination of gestures and idiosyncratic 'words'. For example, a child may point to an object while vocalizing 'oo', which might be a version of 'look'. Or she or he may produce a nasal vocalization 'nn' while reaching for a feeding bottle. These types of utterance can be described as *Operator + Referent*, where just one of the two terms is vocalized. (Of course there may be 'utterances' that consist only of gestures, but these don't show up in an audio recording!) At this stage, the child's utterances are probably only interpretable by the child's parents and other family members. Nevertheless, this stage signals the beginning of language development. (See Halliday, 1975 for a detailed study of this early stage.)

Mark, the child from whose recordings the following extracts are taken, was not one of the children in the main study. I started observing him the year before the study began in order to try out the recording techniques. For convenience, instead of taking many short samples, the recorder was switched on at a time unknown to his mother and allowed to run continuously for an hour or more. Most of the recordings took place during the course of the morning – the time, as we later discovered, when the greatest amount of conversation typically occurs. Mark was the elder of two children (his sister was nine months old at the time when the observations began) and, as it turned out, his development proceeded rather more rapidly than we later found to be the norm. He was also somewhat atypical of the children we observed in having a mother who spent quite long periods of time talking with him (though he was by no means unique in this respect). As a result, I was able to select particularly long stretches of conversation to illustrate the successive stages of development.

Stage 2

Mark is in the kitchen with his mother and his sister Helen. He is holding a mirror in which he sees reflected now himself and now his mother.

[Note: \ indicates falling intonation, / rising intonation, and V fall-rise intonation.]

1	**Mark:**	Mummy V . Mummy V
2	**Mother:**	What?
3	**Mark:**	There . there Mark\ *[sees himself in mirror]*
4	**Mother:**	Is that Mark?
5	**Mark:**	Mark\
6		Mummy/ *[pointing to reflection of Mother]*
7	**Mother:**	Mm
8	**Mark:**	Mummy/ *[pointing to reflection of Mother]*
9	**Mother:**	Yes, that's Mummy
10	**Mark:**	Mummy\
11		Mummy\

12		Mummy V
13	**Mother:**	Mm
14	**Mark:**	There /\ . Mummy/
15		Mummy, there- Mark there\ [seeing his own reflection]

[A minute later, looking out of the window at the birds in the garden]

16	**Mark:**	ëea\ (= look-at-that) . birds\, Mummy
17	**Mother:**	Mm
18	**Mark:**	Jubs\ (birds)
19	**Mother:**	What are they doing?
20	**Mark:**	Jubs bread\ (birds eating bread)
21	**Mother:**	Oh look! they're eating the berries, aren't they?
22	**Mark:**	Yeh\
23	**Mother:**	That's their food . they have berries for dinner
24	**Mark:**	Oh\

[Some minutes later]

25	**Mark:**	Er fwa/, Mummy (asking for water)
26	**Mother:**	What?
27	**Mark:**	Er fwa/
28	**Mother:**	No
29	**Mark:**	Fwa/
30	**Mother:**	No
31	**Mark:**	Fwa/
32	**Mother:**	No
33	**Mark:**	Fwa/
34	**Mother:**	No V
35	**Mark:**	No V (imitating)
36		Fwa/
37	**Mother:**	No, Mark *[with tone of finality]*

As in Stage 1, in the early part of Stage 2 there are still many utterances that make use of Operators, such as 'there', 'look', 'that', 'want', 'more', and 'all gone', either alone or in combination with the name of the object referred to. Essentially, what such utterances communicate is what is being referred to (the meaning) and what is to be done about it (the function). Mark provides several examples of this sort of utterance: for example, 'There Mark' (line 3) and 'Er fwa' (line 25). Although the objects may be very varied, depending on what is of interest or importance to the child, what is to be done about them is more limited. The first three functions to be expressed are almost always *Call* (to obtain somebody's attention, using rising intonation), *Ostension* (to direct attention to an object or event, usually with falling intonation), and *Want* (to obtain some object or service, with rising intonation). In this extract, Mark clearly distinguishes between calling his mother (line 1) and identifying her reflection as the object of his attention (lines 10 and 11) by using a fall-rise intonation for the Call function and a falling intonation for Ostension. (However, since the function of lines 6 and 8 is also clearly that of Ostension, it seems likely that the rising intonation in these lines also conveys a request that his mother confirm the accuracy of his observation.) In line 25, the Want function is also expressed by an operator – the idiosyncratic 'Er' pronounced in a very nasal way with rising intonation over the utterance as a whole.[4]

By the end of this stage, two further functions are typically added. In line 20, 'Jubs bread', we can see an example of a rudimentary *Statement*, though with the action linking the actor and the acted upon not yet expressed. The other Stage 2 function, *Request*, is clearly seen in 'Er fwa', and later in the same recording, Mark said, 'Up' (meaning 'Lift me up'). At the same time, we also find the meaning content of utterances beginning to develop beyond the simple naming of the object referred to. Typically, the first types of relationship to appear are those concerned with *location*. One of these, static object-location, is illustrated in the statement 'Mark there' (line 15).

At this stage, Mark still has very limited grammatical resources. As can be seen, his utterances consist either of a single word – the operator alone (line 3) or a word that in adult speech would be classed as a noun (line 18) – or of the two-word Operator + Object structure already discussed above. (Some of these utterances probably included gestures but, because this was not a video recording, no information is available about accompanying gestures. But see Chapter 11 for more discussion of the importance of gestures.) However, as can be seen from the above extract, when he is talking with someone who knows him well and who is able to interpret his intention from the combination of his utterance and its context, he is successful in 'meaning more than he can say'.

Stage 3

Mark is in the living room with his Mother. He is standing by a hot radiator.

1	**Mark:**	'Ot, Mummy?
2	**Mother:**	Hot? . yes, that's the radiator
3	**Mark:**	Been- burn?
4	**Mother:**	Burn?
5	**Mark:**	Yeh

6	**Mother:**	Yes, you know it'll burn, don't you?
7	**Mark:**	*[putting hand on radiator]* Oh! Ooh!
8	**Mother:**	Take your hand off of it
9	**Mark:**	Uh?
10	**Mother:**	What about the other shoe? (asking if he needs his other shoelace tied)
11	**Mark:**	It all done, Mummy
12	**Mother:**	Mm?
13	**Mark:**	It done, Mummy
14	**Mother:**	It's done, is it?
15	**Mark:**	Yeh
16	**Mother:**	Oh

[Mark tries to get up onto the windowsill to see out of the window]

17	**Mother:**	No, leave the curtain
18	**Mark:**	Oh, up please
19	**Mother:**	Leave the curtain, please
20	**Mark:**	No
21	**Mother:**	Leave the curtain, Mark
22	**Mark:**	No

[Looking out of window, Mark sees a man digging in his garden]

23	**Mark:**	A man- a man er- dig- down there
24	**Mother:**	A man walked down there?
25	**Mark:**	Yeh
26	**Mother:**	Oh yes
27	**Mark:**	Oh yes

[6-second pause]

28	**Mark:**	A man's fire, Mummy
29	**Mother:**	Mm?
30	**Mark:**	A man's fire
31	**Mother:**	Mummy's flower? (checking)
32	**Mark:**	No
33	**Mother:**	What?
34	**Mark:**	*[emphasizing each word]* Mummy, the man . fire
35	**Mother:**	Man's fire? (checking)
36	**Mark:**	Yeh
37	**Mother:**	Oh yes, the bonfire
38	**Mark:**	(imitating) Bonfire
39	**Mother:**	Mm
40	**Mark:**	Bonfire . oh, bonfire . bonfire . bon- a fire . bo-bonfire
41		Oh, hot, Mummy . oh, hot . it hot . it hot

42	**Mother:**	Mm . it will burn, won't it?
43	**Mark:**	Yeh . burn . it burn

From a functional point of view, Stage 3 sees the appearance of *Questions*. To begin with, they are usually limited to 'Where' and 'What' questions, in which the interrogative pronoun is followed immediately by the entity questioned (e.g. 'Where ball?' or the naming question, 'Wassat?'). When the question seeks the answer 'yes' or 'no', it is signalled by rising intonation only, instead of by the presence of an auxiliary verb (e.g. 'do' or 'is') at the beginning. Mark's only question in this extract is of the latter type: 'Ot, Mummy?' (line 1). The question 'Wassat?' and its answer also illustrate one of the major characteristics of semantic development at this stage: an insatiable interest in naming and classification. The exchange at lines 37–38 concerning the bonfire is an example. Other meanings that appear at this stage have to do with changing location – people 'coming' and 'going' or getting 'down' or 'up' (line 18) – and with simple attributes such as 'hot' (line 1), 'big' or 'nice'.

At Stage 3 we also see the clear emergence of grammatical structure, both in the combination of two constituents within the clause – Subject + Verb (line 43, 'It bum'), Verb + Object, or Subject + Object/Complement (line 41, 'It hot') – and in the various two-word combinations in the noun phrase, such as Article + Noun (line 23, 'A man'), Preposition + Noun/Adverb (line 23, 'down there'), and the possessive construction (line 28, 'man's fire'). In fact, line 28 combines two of these types of noun phrase structure in 'A man's fire', and line 23 combines two of the clause combinations to give the three-constituent structure, 'A man dig down there', with the subject and adverbial phrases having their own internal structure. Typically, such a grammatically complex utterance would not appear until Stage 4.

Stage 4

Mark is in the kitchen with his mother. He is waiting for her to finish washing the dishes so that she can play with him.

1	**Mark:**	Play, Mummy
2		Shish wash up, Mummy? (have you finished washing the dishes?)
3	**Mother:**	Pardon?
4	**Mark:**	Shish wash up?
5	**Mother:**	Yes
6	**Mark:**	Oh

7   **Mother:**   Let me just dry my hands
8   **Mark:**   Alright . in there (wants to put towel in laundry basket)
9   **Mother:**   Here
10 **Mark:**   Eyar (here you are) *[Mark gives towel to Mother]*
11 **Mother:**   Just a minute *[she dries her hands]*
12   Will you put the top back on the washing basket, please
13 **Mark:**   Uh? . uh?
14 **Mother:**   Put the top back on the washing basket
15 **Mark:**   On there, Mummy? .. on there?
16 **Mother:**   Yes
                 [Mark makes to put the towel in the basket]
17 **Mother:**   No not the towel in there
18   The top of the basket on it
19 **Mark:**   Alright
20   On there? . uh? uh? (he checks to see that he has under-
                 stood correctly – but he has not)
21 **Mother:**   Put the lid . on top of the basket
22 **Mark:**   Oh er- on there?
23 **Mother:**   Yes please
24 **Mark:**   Alright
25   You dry hands
26 **Mother:**   I've dried my hands now
27 **Mark:**   Put towel in there (he wants her to put the towel in the
                 basket)
28 **Mother:**   No, it's not dirty
29 **Mark:**   It is
30 **Mother:**   No it isn't
31 **Mark:**   'Tis
32   Mummy, play
33 **Mother:**   Well, I will play if you put the top on the basket
34 **Mark:**   All right . there . there. *[he finally puts the lid on the basket.]*
35   Play, Mummy . play . play . play, Mummy
36   Mummy, come on
37 **Mother:**   All right
38 **Mark:**   Helen play, please? (he wants his sister to play with him
                 too)
39   Helen still in bed, Mummy?
40 **Mother:**   *[from the next room]* Mm?
41 **Mark:**   Helen still- Helen still gone sleep, Mummy?
42 **Mother:**   No . she's up there talking, isn't she?
43 **Mark:**   Yes . Helen come down? (request)

44   **Mother:**   No . let her rest
45   **Mark:**   All right . all right, Mummy
     [Mother finally comes to play with him]

A few minutes later, Mark is playing with a collection of toy cars, running them down a ramp from the roof of his garage.
46   **Mark:**   Top of the coach (bus) broken (referring to one of his toys)
47   **Mother:**   Who broke the coach?
48   **Mark:**   Mark did
49   **Mother:**   How?
50   **Mark:**   Out
51   **Mother:**   How did you break it?
52   **Mark:**   Dunno (I don't know)
                   [4-second pause]
53   Mend it, Mummy
54   **Mother:**   I can't, darling
55   **Mark:**   All right
56   **Mother:**   Look, the wheels have gone as well
57   **Mark:**   Oh! I want Daddy take it to work ^ mend it
58   **Mother:**   Daddy did? (checking)
59   **Mark:**   Daddy take it away- take it to work ^ mend it
60   **Mother:**   You'll have to ask him, won't you?
61   **Mark:**   Yeh . you do it (ask him)

By Stage 4, questions are well established: Mark asks a whole spate (lines 35, 36 and 38), but they are still signalled only by rising intonation. We also see the more complex expression of wants which, as in line 57, find expression in the first type of grammatically complex sentence: the object of wanting ('Daddy take it to work') is itself a complete embedded clause. This utterance (line 57) is particularly interesting as it also illustrates a strategy that Mark employed on a number of occasions when he wasn't yet quite able to cope with the necessary grammatical structure. Between 'work' and 'mend' he left a very short gap (indicated by ^) but continued the intonation unbroken, as if to indicate that he knew a connecting word was needed at that point even though he wasn't able to produce it. 'Mend' also illustrates a development in the kind of meanings that are expressed: an action somebody carries out that causes a change in the state of the object acted upon. 'You dry hands' (line 22) is another example. At this stage, though it is not illustrated in this extract, we also typically find verbs like 'listen' and 'know' beginning to appear – verbs that refer to people's mental states. By Stage 4 there are also references to events in the past and, less frequently, to the future. The only example in this extract is line 45, 'Mark did', in answer to the question 'Who broke it?' However, we do see an example of another aspect of the temporal organization of events. 'Shish wash up?'(lines 2 and 4) asks about the *aspectual* state of the action – is it completed or not? The ongoing status of events is also regularly marked by this stage through the use of the '-ing' form of the verb. There are no examples in this extract, but in the same recording we find 'Mark doing it'; 'Helen still in bed' (line 36) expresses very much the same notion of a continuing state.

Grammatically, development at this stage is seen in three-constituent structures: Subject + Verb + Object/Adjunct (already seen in 'A man dig down there' in the previous extract), and Subject + Auxiliary Verb + Verb (e.g. 'I am going'). In the noun phrase we might similarly expect to find three-word structures, such as Preposition + Article + Noun (e.g., 'in the basket'). In line 61 we also see the first use of a 'pro-word', 'do' to stand for 'ask' in this context. Mark's longest utterance in this extract, 'I want Daddy take it to work ^ mend it' (line 57), is, as already noted, even more complex and is more typical of Stage 5 or 6.

Stage 5/6

Mark was developing rapidly at this point and I failed to make a recording that is clearly at Stage 5; several utterances in the following extract are much more typical of Stage 6 than Stage 5.

Mark is having lunch with his mother and sister. Mark has just taken a piece of cheese from the refrigerator so that he can have some.

1	**Mark:**	Oh, I wan- I want do this (cut the cheese)
2		Oh, cheese (laughs with excitement)
3	**Mother:**	That's right . sit up, then!
4	**Mark:**	Look, I'm doing it (cutting the cheese)
5		Can I do it? can I do it?
6	**Mother:**	Be careful, the knife is sharp!
7		No (that's not right) . cut it straight, not at an angle
8		All right? (can you manage?)
9		There you are (you have succeeded)

[Sister shouts in background. Mark gives the knife to Mother]

10	**Mother:**	Thank you
11	**Mark:**	Shall I cut another one?
12		I want some meat
13	**Mother:**	All right . eat your cheese first
14	**Mark:**	Can I have other piece of meat, Mummy?
15	**Mother:**	Yes

*A little while later, Mark is looking out of the window. He can see traffic going
up the hill in the distance. Mother is in another room and cannot see.*

16	**Mark:**	Why going r-round that bend, Mummy?
17	**Mother:**	Pardon?
18	**Mark:**	Why going round that bend?
19	**Mother:**	Round what bend?
20	**Mark:**	That bend
21	**Mother:**	What's going round the bend?
22	**Mark:**	Bus
23	**Mother:**	Oh, you can see a bus down on the hill?
24	**Mark:**	Yes . you go down left- you turn left and go that r- that road and go see traffic lights, see?
25	**Mother:**	Oh, it goes to the traffic lights, does it?
26	**Mark:**	Yes, it goes down there
27	**Mother:**	Oh
28	**Mark:**	By traffic lights
29		See . down there . there's a ambulance
30		Mummy! Mummy! *[demanding a response]*
31	**Mother:**	Yes
32	**Mark:**	Yes
33	**Mother:**	Does it?
34	**Mark:**	Yes

[A few minutes later, Mark wants a pen to draw with].

35	**Mark:**	Where's the pen what Pappa um gave me? Mummy?
36	**Mother:**	Pardon?
37	**Mark:**	Where's Pappa's pen ^ draw on there? (Where's Pappa's pen that I want to use to draw on there?)
38	**Mother:**	You left it at Clifton, didn't you?
39	**Mark:**	No . I want it *[noises to self]* I want it please, Mummy
40		Mark- Mark bring it home, think so

Perhaps the most striking development that occurs at Stage 5 is
the integration of the auxiliary verb into the structure of the clause, thus
allowing the production of both interrogative and negative (Stage 6)
utterances. Mark provides several examples of the former (lines 5, 11,
14), though none of the latter in this extract. With the availability of this
structure comes a diversification of the functions associated with the
control of activity. In line 5 we see him *requesting permission* and in line
11 taking a more *indirect* route to getting what he wants. At this stage we
also see the first appearance of explanation and *request for explanation*.
Usually it is the child who supplies an explanation in response to

somebody else's 'Why?' question; here it is Mark who asks the question (line 16).

Amongst the auxiliary verbs, 'do' is the first to appear, followed by 'can' and 'will' (or 'll'). Can has two possible meanings ('ability' and 'permission'), but in the child's world these are closely related: many of the things he or she is able to do also require permission, such as, for example, Mark's cutting the cheese for himself.

Two other types of semantic development occur at Stage 6 in association with developments in grammar. The first is the appearance of *complements to psychological verbs* such as 'know' (e.g. 'I know that you are there'), and the second is the qualification of a noun phrase by a *relative phrase or clause* (e.g. 'Where's the pen what Pappa gave me?' [line 35]). Both require one grammatical clause to function within the structure of another, thus introducing the principle of *recursion*. With this development, the child is well advanced towards mastery of the basic grammar of the sentence.

Also worth pointing out in this extract is Mark's continuing lack of awareness that, when his interlocutor is not in the same place as himself, they cannot identify the intended referents of *deictic* terms, such as 'that' or the pronoun 'it'. This is a very clear example of another aspect of learning to talk – taking account of the informational needs of one's listener. It is perhaps because of the difficulty of doing so that children first talk about events that are or have been shared with their interlocutor and only later become able to recount an event in which the interlocutor was not involved (Halliday, 1975).

Stage 7/8

Mark is playing with his train. His sister is trying to play too, but she is not really very welcome.

1	**Mark:**	I can't put my train over- over the bridge, Helen, if you put that like that
2		If you have . if you have . if you have, I pu- I can't put my train on the bridge

[Helen makes an unintelligible response]

3		Here it comes . here it comes, then . here it comes
4		It's coming, like that . it's coming, like that
5		Put the other bridge there
6		I want a X
7		You put that one there, Helen
8	**Helen:**	Yes

9　**Mark:**　　Don't do it again
10　　　　　　If you do, I'll smack your bottom for you
11　　　　　　Here it comes

[Some time later, Mark is doing a jigsaw puzzle with his mother.]
12　**Mother:**　There . now you've got two Camberwick Green pictures
13　**Mark:**　　Yeh
14　**Mother:**　One you made, mm? . and one on the box
15　**Mark:**　　Mm
16　**Mother:**　*[pointing to the jigsaw puzzle and a set of dominoes]* Look, these Camberwick Green men are the same as the dominoes in Camberwick Green
17　**Mark:**　　Mm (thoughtfully)
18　**Mother:**　Look!
19　**Mark:**　　Can I see which is like that one?
20　**Mother:**　There's the policeman
21　**Mark:**　　Yeh
22　**Mother:**　*[comparing the puzzle with the dominoes]* I don't think there is a man with a yellow hat
23　**Mark:**　　I made this puzzle, didn't I? (proudly)
24　**Mother:**　Mm
25　**Mark:**　　Shall we do this puzzle again?
26　**Mother:**　Yes . break it up, then
27　**Mark:**　　Break it up
[They break up the puzzle and start again]
28　**Mark:**　　And I got to start the words of it, haven't I?
29　**Mother:**　Go on, then
30　**Mark:**　　I got to start the word . you got to do-
31　　　　　　Now what does it say now?
32　　　　　　*[Pretending to read instructions]* Make the lorry
33　　　　　　You make the lorry, Mummy
34　**Mother:**　Mm (by now getting tired of doing the puzzle)
35　**Mark:**　　And make the cars, please
　　　　　　[Several seconds' pause]
36　**Mark:**　　Have I got to- um- do the most of it?
37　**Mother:**　Well, it would help

By now, Mark can use his linguistic resources for most of the major functions – giving information, asking and answering questions of various kinds, requesting (both directly and indirectly), suggesting, offering, stating intentions and expressing feelings and attitudes and also asking about those of others. In this extract, the new development we notice is the *conditional* or *hypothetical* statement (line 1). In line 10, the same grammatical structure has the function of a *threat* ('If you do, I'll smack your bottom for you'). Another, more indirect, controlling function is seen in line 30: 'I got to start the word. You got to do-'. These two utterances *formulate* the action that is required as an alternative way of getting the action performed. Very often, this function has a general applicability: whenever the appropriate conditions apply, you have got to do X.

Along with the appearance of hypothetical events and formulating functions, we find other ways in which utterances go beyond the here and now of present activity, in particular in a more differentiated expression of the time frame within which events occur. As well as general references to past and future, there is the beginning of reference to particular times as points of reference – 'before dinner', 'when Daddy comes home', 'until bedtime'. Further aspectual distinctions are also made – for example, habitual ('Daddy's always late for dinner'), repetitive ('He kept on banging the door') and inceptive ('The snow's beginning to melt').

Several of the functional and semantic options that become available at this stage require sentences that contain more than one clause. The first of these was seen in the previous stage, in the asking for and supplying of explanations, using sentences in which clauses were linked by because, and, to (in order to), and so on. However, by Stage 8 their variety has increased considerably, as can be seen from Mark's utterances in lines 1, 10 and 19. A further grammatical development at this stage is the final sorting out of the structure of questions that begin with words like 'What' and 'When'. This is illustrated in line 31: the auxiliary is now inverted with the subject after the question word: 'What does it say!'

Whereas almost all aspects of grammatical development up to this point have added to the length of the sentence, there now begin to appear the results of processes that make for greater economy of expression. These processes, collectively referred to as *Cohesion*, relate the present clause back to a preceding one by referring to the whole or a part of it by means of a pro-noun or pro-verb, or simply by ellipsis – taking it for granted. A clear example of this is given in lines 9–10. The words 'do it' in line 9 refer back to 'You put that one there' in line 7 – which Helen is not to do again – and the pro-verb 'do' in line 10 refers to 'do it again' in line 9. However, Mark's first recorded uses of this sort of cohesion were seen in the last utterances in each of the previous two extracts: 'do' to stand for 'ask' and 'so' to refer to the whole of the previous clause, 'Mark bring it home' (Stage 5/6, line 40). At that stage he had clearly grasped the idea of cohesion, but was not yet altogether sure about how to use that particular form.

By the end of Stage 8, then, the major linguistic systems are more or less in place and a basic vocabulary of several thousand words has been acquired.[5] There is certainly much more to learn, or course, particularly with respect to the socially appropriate uses of language.[6] But, from this point onwards, what is learned and the order in which it is learned becomes progressively more dependent on experience – on having opportunities to hear the relevant functions, meanings and structures used appropriately and to use them oneself. At one and the same time, then, this point marks both the end and the beginning: after an almost sheer climb up the face of the cliff, the rest of the mountain lies ahead, but there are many possible routes that may be taken and, in general, the going is somewhat easier.

The Overall Sequence of Development from Stage 1 to Stage 8 and Beyond

As explained earlier, the examples from Mark's language development were taken from continuous recordings lasting more than an hour. This enabled me to select extended passages of conversation with no interruptions. The recordings of the children in the main study, on the other hand, consisted of 90-second samples, recorded at intervals throughout the day. The advantage of this approach was that we could be fairly sure that we were obtaining a representative sample of each child's conversational experience; however, the less satisfactory consequence was that we often captured only parts of conversations. Nevertheless, using the method described at the beginning of this chapter, we were still able to chart the sequence in which each child was first observed to use the items in each of the linguistic systems in which we were interested.

In the main study, too, we studied children's development beyond the age at which the recordings of Mark ended. So, by pooling all the data we had collected over the age-span from 15 to 60 months, we were able to construct a more extended account of development in the pre-school years, which led to the production of the *Bristol Scale of Language Development* (Gutfreund *et al.*, 1989). On the basis of this much larger corpus of data, we found we could better represent the sequence of development by positing ten stages. We were also able to make use of information about items that were first observed in the later recordings of the older cohort of children. A condensed version of this scale is contained in Appendix 1.

The Relationship Between Age and Language Development

In Appendix 1, an indication is given of the median age at which each stage was reached. But this is an average; as can be seen, the age for a particular child might be many months earlier or later for – as parents and teachers know well – children do not all develop at the same rate. So, just as some children are early walkers, so some start to talk much earlier than others and may race through the stages while others proceed more slowly. However, other things being equal, those who get off to a slow start usually catch up with, or even surpass, the rapid developers. Here, an analogy with the hare and the tortoise is generally appropriate.

Nevertheless, precocity – or its opposite – is often seen as a predictor of ultimate achievement and, as will be explained in later chapters, in the short term, unfortunately, such predictions may become self-fulfilling. This applies particularly to late developers, who are often assumed to be also less intelligent. On the other hand, there are many recorded counter-examples of children who were late in learning to talk, including Albert Einstein, but who later became extremely successful in their chosen spheres.[7]

Notes

1. This next step is not, in fact, so simple. The languages of the world differ in many respects, for example, in whether relationships between the people, objects and places involved in an event are indicated by case suffixes, particles or word order, or in how time is expressed, to name but just two. As a result, it is not possible to make direct comparisons *between* languages in the order in which linguistic features are learned. On the other hand, it is possible to ask whether, within any language, the order of learning is the same for all children. It is also possible to combine these two kinds of investigation in order to seek for underlying commonalities. Dan Slobin at the University of California at Berkeley has been carrying out a cross-linguistic study of this kind over several decades (Slobin, 1985–1997, 2001).
2. A more detailed account of this method, together with a rationale for its use, can be found in the full account of the research project, *Language Development the Pre-School Years* (Wells, 1985).
3. Roger Brown provides a very detailed discussion of the early stages from a semantic point of view in *A First Language* (Brown, 1973) and David Crystal, Paul Fletcher and Michael Garman (1976) describe the complete age span from a grammatical perspective in *The Grammatical Analysis of Language Disability*. The early stages will be discussed from a more theoretical perspective in Chapter 11.
4. Michael Halliday (1975) observed essentially the same first functions in the speech of his own son. However, he made rather more distinctions – for

example, subdividing Want into Instrumental and Regulatory. He also drew attention to the systematic use of intonation at around 18 months, with falling intonation being used for 'telling' utterances and rising intonation for 'demands' of all kinds.

5.   Surprisingly, after the very early stages, there has been much less interest in the developing structure of the lexicon, but see John Macnamara's (1982) *Names for Things* and the chapters by Susan Carey and Eve Clark in *Language Acquisition: The State of the Art* (Wanner & Gleitman, 1982). For a more recent study in the United States, see Hart and Risley (1999) and also Chapter 11 of this volume.

6.   That not all the basic grammar has been learned by age five is clear from, for example, Carol Chomsky's (1969) detailed study of *The Acquisition of Syntax from 5 to 10* and Annette Karmiloff-Smith's (1979) *A Functional Approach to Child Language*.

7.   If, as a parent or teacher, you are concerned about the slow development of a particular child, it would be wise to consult a speech therapist or the local Speech and Language Advisory Service.

Chapter 3

Learning to Talk: The Construction of Language

The end of the previous chapter saw Mark well advanced towards mastery of the language of his community. By then, the most difficult part of the task had been achieved. However, the real puzzle is: how did he get started? How did he discover that the vocal sounds that people produce are intended to communicate specific meanings and to do so by virtue of the choice of particular sounds and their arrangement in particular temporal sequences?[1] Putting the question in that form, however, may be to over-emphasize the apparent arbitrariness of the language system at the expense of its functional significance as a resource in interpersonal communication. Language may be thought of as a code to be cracked, but before the child attempts that task he or she has already become familiar with the code in use. It has been encountered in meaningful interactions that also involve the more 'natural' channels of sight, sound, touch and smell.[2]

Getting Started

It has become clear from research over recent decades that newborn babies are not 'blank slates' waiting to have impressions written on them, nor are they as helpless as used to be supposed. Human infants are born with a drive to make sense of their experience and with certain effective strategies for doing so. For example, from very early they readily recognize regularities and are able to respond to abstract patterns in their environment. One very interesting experiment has shown that, by five months, infants are able to track a moving object behind a screen, anticipate its emergence at the other side, and show surprise if a different object appears (Bower, 1974). Their sense-making also seems from the beginning to be goal-directed. Everybody is familiar with the older infant who drops toys from his or her highchair or crib in order to get somebody to come and pick them up. But this sort of purposeful exploration and manipulation of the environment can be shown to be present very much earlier – for example, experiments have shown that babies discover that they can bring about changes (switching on lights, bringing pictures into focus) by turning their head or sucking on a dummy (pacifier).

Most important for language development, however, is the infant's inherent sociability. Babies show a clear preference for faces and face-like shapes and show that they distinguish human voices from other sounds. The result of these inborn traits is that they orient to other human beings in a way that parents and other family members find very appealing. They also seem to want to communicate. Split-screen film of mothers and infants as young as three months sitting facing each other show quite clearly that the infant's gestures (lip-pursing, frowning, etc.) alternate with the mother's similar gestures and are sometimes also accompanied by vocalization, in what looks to an observer very much like conversation without words. True, the temporal sequencing owes a great deal to the mother's sensitivity in timing her gestures to follow the infant's, but there is no doubt that the infant is interactively involved as well, as can be seen from his or her distress if the mother ceases to respond in a contingently appropriate manner.

By six months, then, a baby and his or her chief caregivers have established the basis for communication: a relationship of mutual attention. The establishment of this relationship and the wordless communication that takes place within it – protoconversation, as it has been called (Trevarthen, 1979) – occurs so early and so smoothly that it seems that the human infant must be biologically preadapted to initiate and engage in such interactions (see also Chapter 11).

While that may well be so, there is a further advantage that newborn babies have to help them towards language, and that is the attitude of their parents or other caretakers. Just as babies are strongly predisposed to make sense of their surroundings, particularly their human surroundings, so adults are predisposed to treat their behaviour as meaningful and potentially communicative (Bruner, 1983). The baby burps, and the mother asks, 'Have you got windypops?' The baby smiles, and she shows her pleasure that the baby is happy. The baby looks, and she follows his or her line of regard and tries to see what the baby is interested in. Thus, from the beginning, parents treat their babies as if they had intentions and respond to them in the light of the intentions that they believe their babies to be communicating. And so, by being treated as if they already had intentions, babies do in time come to have them, discovering in the process that their behaviour can affect the people in their environment and that they can indeed communicate (Newson, 1978).

However, the parent's interpretations of the baby's behaviour have another important function. As mature members of a human culture, parents have quite specific ideas about what sorts of behaviour have meaning and so, in interpreting the baby's gestures, noises, and so on, parents assimilate them to behaviours that they themselves find meaningful. The meanings attributed are therefore *cultural* meanings and, in their responses, parents provide culturally appropriate feedback that has the effect of shaping the infant's behaviour towards what is culturally acceptable and meaningful (Cole, 1993).

Finally, we should add that the baby's early environment is highly repetitive. The day is made up of a regular cycle of feeding, sleeping, cleaning and bathing. And many of the activities that the baby is involved in when awake themselves have a regular structure, involving interaction with the mother or some other regular caregiver. There are thus ample opportunities for the recognition of regularity and for the discovery of the connections that exist between persons, objects and events. This enables predictions to be made and provides the satisfaction that comes from the recognition of predictions fulfilled. It is from this experience that the infant is already beginning to construct his or her internal model of the world (Nelson, 1996).

By the second half of the first year, then, the infant is well advanced towards recognizably communicative behaviour. Through oft-repeated experiences of protoconversation, he or she has discovered the reciprocity of mutual attention: 'I know that you are attending to me, and you know that I am attending to you, and we both know that we both know that that is so'. This pattern of mutual attention has been given the name *intersubjectivity* (Stern, 1977; Trevarthen, 1979; Trevarthen & Hubley, 1978). It can be shown diagrammatically as follows:

$$\text{Adult} \longleftrightarrow \text{Infant}$$

Intersubjectivity is the essential foundation of any communication. Within this relationship infants discover, albeit as yet only partially, both their separateness from their communication partners and also their essential similarity to them. In this relationship they also learn to take a more active part in controlling the sequencing of turns that make up an interaction and discover the contingent nature of the relationship between turns, as they notice how their own specific behaviour regularly elicits particular types of behaviour from their partners, and they begin to produce particular types of behaviour themselves in response to specific behaviours by others.

The next step occurs when the world outside is drawn into the relationship of intersubjectivity and made the focus of joint attention. Typically, an interesting object will attract the child's attention and the mother will follow the child's line of regard, identify the object, and then either touch it, give it to the child, or in some other way indicate to him or her that she, too, is looking at the same object. Quite quickly the children learn to use looking to signal the direction of their own attention; they also learn to use the line of regard of another to locate what the other is interested in. And, with the achievement of deliberate engagement in joint attention, the basic triangle of communication is complete: 'I am looking at O (an object), and you are looking at O, and we both know that we are both looking at O'.

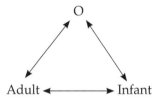

Such occasions of joint attention frequently become incorporated into playful routines, which involve handing an object back and forth, hiding it, and so forth. These routines introduce the child to two further important characteristics of linguistic communication: the basic structure of exchange – one person gives and the other receives (Halliday, 1984), with these roles being reversible – and the way in which utterances are associated with the performance of the actions that make up an exchange. In this way, the child comes to recognize and respond to certain words and phrases in familiar contexts, such as 'kyou', 'bye-bye', 'peek-a-boo' and perhaps the names of family pets or favourite objects, such as 'teddy'. Bruner describes one child's transition from action to speech as follows:

> Ann had learned between 8 and 10 months to play a well modulated exchange game involving the handing back and forth of objects. When, at 13 months, the game was well organized, Ann picked up her mother's receiving *Thank you*. She used it both when giving and receiving an object. After two weeks the expression dropped out of the giving position, nothing at first taking its place, but remained in the receiving position. Meanwhile, the demand demonstrative *Look* was appearing in Ann's lexicon, used in referential situations, as when

looking at pictures in a book. At the end of the thirteenth month, *Look* was transposed as well into the position at which AM handed her mother an object. *Look* was later replaced by *There* in the giving-taking format. (Bruner, 1975: 278)

But perhaps the most important factor urging children into speech is their desire to communicate their intentions more precisely. Almost all researchers who have studied this stage of development (which occurs around the end of the first year) have noted that the child's earliest utterances are *functional*.[3] In our own study, as noted in the previous chapter, we found that almost all the utterances in the first observations could be described as either calling for attention, expressing a want, indicating something of interest or expressing feeling (pleasure, surprise, etc.).

To begin with, these functions are often expressed by a combination of gesture and vocalization. But gradually the vocalizations take on a more regular form as distinct 'words' – though not necessarily words recognized in the adult language – and the child is able to communicate recognizable intentions, at least to those who know him or her.

One way of describing the stage that the child has now reached is to think of it as a recapitulation of the construction of the communication triangle, but at a higher level. At first, intersubjectivity was achieved entirely through gestures of various kinds; now it can be expressed through words. But, in order to complete the triangle at this second level, it is necessary for the child to be able to engage verbally in joint reference, and to do that he or she has to understand that objects have names.

The naming game is one that all parents play, and they seem to know intuitively when to start doing so. As objects are exchanged in the familiar playful routines, they begin to add the name; they look at picture books and name the pictures or name the parts of the child's body. 'What's that?' they ask and, as often as not, also supply the answer. To begin with, the child's attempts to take part involve no more than a vocalization to fill his or her turn in a familiar exchange. But associations are formed and, suddenly, the penny drops. The words the child has learned are labels. Things have names (McShane, 1980; Ninio & Bruner, 1980).

When this happens, the triangle is completed at the verbal level. The child has discovered that the words he or she utters enable him or her to communicate both *that* he or she has intentions and *what* these intentions refer to. The majority of utterances may still be restricted to single words, but the child has learned to talk.

Learning the Language of the Community

Expressing intentions and indicating what those intentions refer to are only the beginning of learning a language, of course. At this stage, children have clearly discovered the existence of the code; they have also discovered, in some sense, that it is based on an arbitrary but conventional relationship between meanings and sounds. Now they have to figure out how the code works. They have to learn the particular language that is used in their community.

To understand how they do this, it might be helpful to focus attention for a moment on the internalized representation of the world that children have been constructing from their experience of interacting with their environment. As we saw earlier, children seem to be predisposed to pay closer attention to certain aspects of their environment rather than to others. In particular, they notice people and clearly defined objects, especially if those objects can be touched and manipulated or if they move or cause other things to move. As a result, the internal model of the world that they build up is largely organized in terms of movement, appearance and disappearance and the relationships of cause and effect that bring about those perceptible changes. Summarizing his own research on what he calls the 'sensorimotor' stage of development, Piaget described the 18-month-old child as having come 'to regard himself as an object among others in a universe that is made up of permanent objects in which there is at work a causality that is both localized in space and objectified in things' (Piaget & Inhelder, 1969: 13).

Put rather differently, we could say that the basic categories in terms of which children make sense of their world are those of Agent, Object, Location, State, and so on, and the changing relationships that can hold between them. Now these are precisely the sort of categories that are encoded in language, in such utterances as the following:

- Teddy *(object)* is on the bed *(location)*
- Daddy *(agent)* is painting *(change state)* the gate *(object)*
- Mummy *(agent)* put *(change location)* the knife *(object)* in the drawer *(location)*

and it is these meaning relations that occur in a high proportion of the utterances that children hear addressed to them. Their task, then, is to match the utterances that they hear to the situation to which they apply and to work out how the former encodes the latter.

What makes this very difficult task possible is the context. A very high proportion of the utterances that people address to children are about what they can see and hear – about what is going on. Much of the time, too, these events are already familiar. So the child picks out the one or two words that he or she recognizes and uses them and an interpretation of the context to make a guess at what the speaker means.

There are usually other clues as well: gestures and exaggerated intonation. In the following example (quoted earlier, in Chapter 2) Mark wanted his mother to play with him and she agreed, but only on condition that he first replaced the lid on the laundry basket, into which he had just tried to put a towel.

[In the following extract, bold type is used to indicate heavy stress.]
Mother: Put the top back on the washing basket
Mark: On there, Mummy? on there?
Mother: Put the **lid** . on **top** of the **bas**ket

As Mark does not seem to understand the first request, his mother tries again, breaking her utterance into two parts to correspond to the two parts of the action that she wants him to perform. At the same time, by pointing to the lid by gesture and gaze and by emphasizing the word 'lid' by heavy stress and rising intonation, she uses several different cues to help him identify the object to be moved. Then, when she sees that he has understood that much, she shifts her gaze to the basket and verbally specifies the place where the lid is to be put, again using heavy stress on 'top' and 'basket' to help him to pick out the key words in her utterance. The complete utterance can be represented as follows:

Mother: Put the **lid** . on **top** of the **bas**ket

At last Mark understands and successfully carries out the action, his success being due in part to his mother's helpful guidance but also in part to his strong motivation to succeed so that she would do what he wanted, which was to play with him.

From a parent's point of view, the process of language learning must sometimes seem a painfully slow one. There is so much for children to learn: not just the words, but their pronunciation and the ways of combining them to express the relationships between the objects, attributes and actions to which they refer. They also have to learn how the more subtle distinctions of intention are expressed – indirect and direct requests, questions of various kinds, and expressions of different attitudes, such as sympathy, anger, apology and so on – through different selections and orderings of words and structures and the use of different patterns of intonation and facial and bodily gestures.

For each new linguistic distinction to be mastered, children first have to become aware that such a distinction exists in their community's way of interpreting experience; then they have to discover how it is expressed in the language spoken by that community. As has already been suggested, children usually discover the distinctions of meaning first, through nonlinguistic encounters with the environment or through observation of others' behaviour. They are then on the lookout for ways in which these meanings are expressed in the speech addressed to them. As they acquire greater command of the language, though, they are also able to learn from the conversations going on around them. Words or sentence patterns that they hear and recognize as unfamiliar alert them to possible distinctions of meaning that they have not yet discovered for themselves. A lot of children's learning, then, is dependent on making connections between what they know and what they are able to understand in the speech that they hear.

But they do not learn only by listening. Since the motivation for learning language at all is to be able to communicate, children are constantly using the resources they have already acquired to interact with other people about their needs and interests and about the activities in which they are jointly engaged. On many occasions their resources are just not sufficient to encode the meanings they want to express – distinctions they are aware of in their experience but for which they have not yet discovered the linguistic expression. On such occasions they press into service whatever means they have available, such as Mark's strategy 'I want Daddy take it to work ^ mend it'. Sometimes these strategies give rise to the sorts of 'error' that adults often find amusing – such as referring to the milkman as 'daddy' or to an elephant seen at the zoo as 'hosh' (horse) – or to neologisms, such as 'boxing' for the action of putting an object into a box, all of which are indicative of the active nature of their search for meaning and the means for expressing it (E. Clark, 1974).

Frequently, however, their attempts are not successful, and their conversational partners do not understand them. But this too can be helpful, even if only by giving children negative feedback about the adequacy of their utterances. Quite often, though, the partner will probe further, offering alternative interpretations in an attempt to discover what the child means, often in the form of expansions that, as it were, present in full what the child has been trying to say him- or herself. Such negotiations about intended meaning are likely to be particularly informative, as they provide children with evidence about the language at the very moment when they are most disposed to make use of it. Here is an example from Anthony:

Anthony: There ninny car
Mother: Mini car? yes
Anthony: Mini gone
Mother: Mini car's gone
Anthony: Daddy gone
Mother: Yes, Daddy's gone

In all these ways, then, children gradually add to and modify their representation of the language system and discover how it is used as a resource for communicating with other people. Although the process may sometimes appear slow and laborious to parents who are involved in it, when viewed from outside it appears to happen extremely rapidly, even in more slowly developing children.

Copying or Reinventing?

In the previous chapter, we traced the sequence of one child's development in some detail and briefly considered some of the evidence for believing that this sequence is followed quite closely by all children who are learning English as their first language. The question we must now consider is why there is this substantial uniformity.

In considering possible explanations, there seem to be two very different alternatives. On the one hand, the order of learning may be controlled by the model presented to children in the speech they hear – either in the form of a carefully graded programme of instruction, or simply through the effect of frequency, as they hear some words, structures, and so on, much more frequently than others. According to this explanation, children simply copy what they hear, and the sequence of learning is determined by the nature of the model, together with the effect of positive and negative reinforcement. The alternative explanation, on the other hand, attributes the order of learning to an interaction between the characteristics of the learner and the relative difficulty of what has to be learned. Provided that the speech that the child hears contains examples of what has to be learned, the precise characteristics of the input are of little importance.[4]

Clearly, these are very different explanations, with different implications for those who are concerned with helping children to learn language. We thought it important, therefore, to try to decide which (if either) seemed to square best with the evidence that we had collected. We think the results are reasonably clear.

First, there is very little evidence of deliberate instruction, graded or otherwise. Most parents do teach certain polite expressions, such as 'please' and 'thank you'. They also teach the names of familiar objects and attributes. However, in the case of the polite expressions, it is largely a matter of getting children to remember to use them, for the words themselves are very quickly learned. As for vocabulary teaching, this tends to be concentrated into quite a short period towards the end of the second year, when the principle that everything has a name is learned. Thereafter, only a minority of parents continue to teach vocabulary deliberately, and even then, this tends to be limited to common nouns and adjectives; verbs, adverbs and other parts of speech are hardly ever explicitly taught at all. As for grammar, there is barely any evidence at all of deliberate instruction. This is hardly surprising, for the vast majority of parents, although their own speech is entirely grammatical, have no conscious knowledge of the rules of grammar to which their speech conforms.

If not deliberately taught, is what children learn perhaps presented to them with differential frequency? Do they simply learn first what they hear most frequently? At first sight, this does appear quite plausible – all the more so since, in general, we found a strong correspondence between the overall frequency with which particular items (functions, meanings and structures) occurred in the speech addressed to the children and the actual sequence in which those items were learned. However, there are a number of reasons for rejecting this as a complete explanation.

First, although the correspondence was strong for the sample as a whole, it was much more variable in the case of individual children. Second, for one out of the four linguistic systems that we investigated in detail, that of the functions that utterances perform, there was not a significant correspondence at all. Children, for example, learned to answer questions before they asked them, but they heard far more questions than answers. Similarly, at a later stage, they requested permission before they granted permission to others; but in the speech addressed to them, they were granted permission far more often than they were asked for it. These results hardly seem surprising. But what they make clear is the underlying interactional basis of language learning. Children are not learning to talk in order to be able to behave like their parents for the sake of conformity, but rather to be able to communicate with them in collaborative activities in which the roles played are reciprocal rather than imitative.

However, since at one time it was thought that children did indeed learn to talk by imitating their parents, it is perhaps worth examining the role of imitation a little more closely. In one sense, of course, language *is* learned through imitation. Without examples of the different items to be learned, children would have no way of knowing how particular meanings were expressed, even though they might have made the necessary conceptual distinctions. And, in the long run, if they are to communicate successfully, they have to use the resources of the language they are learning in the same way as other members of the community. But, in the sense of immediately repeating what an adult has just said as a means of learning it, there is no evidence that this is the main way in which children learn.

Nevertheless, when children do imitate what their interlocutor has just said, the phrase or whole utterance they imitate is usually one that they have already used spontaneously on an earlier occasion. In fact, the early research that investigated infants' ability to imitate an experimenter's speech found that they were unable to imitate forms and patterns that were addressed to them unless they already had some understanding – or at least familiarity – with the items in question (Rees, 1975).

However, some researchers have reported evidence of children who develop a repertoire of whole utterance chunks they hear, which they use in constructing utterances of their own. Ruth Clark (1974), for example, reports how her son, having just heard his mother say 'Do you want to get off?' as he was riding on a roundabout (carousel), replied, 'No, I want to get on', meaning he wanted to stay on. On another occasion, he responded to his mother's statement 'We're all very mucky' with, 'I all very mucky too'. This child seemed to be reusing chunks of what he had just heard (and probably understood, at least partially, in context) without analysing them into their constituent parts. Then, when what he wanted to say taxed his productive ability too greatly, he would insert the stored chunk unmodified into an utterance, the rest of which he constructed for the occasion.

This is indeed a form of imitation. But to have stored and then recalled the chunk in order to combine it with other words on a later occasion shows that this child was doing more than simply repeating what he had heard. As William Labov once put it, the difference between a man and a parrot who both repeat the sentence 'I'll meet you downtown' is that it is only in the case of the man that one would be surprised if he didn't show up.

This is not just a quibble over the meaning of the word *imitation*. What is at issue here is how children use the information about the language they are learning that is present in the speech addressed to them. Those who argue that imitation plays an important role in language learning usually give particular emphasis to children's construction of a repertoire of ready-made phrases or routines, which are tied to and elicited by particular contextual events. Some phrases, such as 'Hello' and 'How do you do?', probably are learned in this way. But most students of child language would agree that, although this mode of learning may play a significant role in the early stages for some children, it accounts for only a small proportion of the overall process (R. Clark, 1974; Peters, 1973).

For the most part, children seem to analyse the utterances they hear into smaller units, attending to those parts they are able to understand in context and ignoring what is currently beyond their ability to comprehend. Then they store those comprehensible units, together with information about how they think they are combined, so that they can be used on future occasions to produce or comprehend new utterances. The units may be of varying size, but some are smaller than what we think of as words and some, such as 'going to' or 'got to', consist of more than one word – although it may be some time before children recognize that this is so.

At any stage, then, children have certain 'hypotheses' about the principles for combining units; and, on the whole, they seem to prefer to work with principles of maximum generalizability – principles that they construct for themselves on the basis of the regularities that they perceive in the speech of others and perhaps also in their own. However, these principles do not always correspond exactly to those that apply in adult speech – hence, such errors as 'goed', 'foots' and, later, 'How could he of done that?'

Most of the time, however, children's hypotheses correspond very closely to the regularities that characterize adult speech, so it is not possible to tell by what means they have acquired them – whether by passively absorbing the model provided or by some more autonomous process. What is important about such combinatorial 'errors', therefore, is that they provide compelling evidence that children *actively construct* their own hypotheses. Since they haven't heard these particular forms in the speech of adults, they must have put them together themselves.

Taking all the available evidence together, then, we can state the situation as follows. Children learn language because they are predisposed to do so. How they set about the task is largely determined by the way they are: seekers after meaning who try to find the underlying principles that will account for the patterns that they recognize in their experiences. At each successive stage, therefore, they are capable of dealing with new evidence of a certain degree of complexity, and they are able to incorporate it into their developing language system. But using that system as a resource for interaction with other people leads to the making of errors and to the recognition of inconsistencies. This, in turn, leads eventually to modifications of the prevailing hypotheses and to some reorganization of the language system. And this then permits evidence relating to more complex items to be considered and resolved.

In this way, children progressively construct a representation of the language of their community. And they do so on the basis of the evidence provided for them in conversation with more mature members of that community. Furthermore, because human beings are similarly endowed as language learners and grow up in environments that are similar in many important respects, the sequence in which they construct their internal representations is very similar from one learner to another, and so are the underlying principles in terms of which their representation of the language system is ultimately organized.

The Role of Adults in Language Development

From the description of children as largely autonomous constructors of their own language resources, it may appear that there is little that adults contribute to this process. But this is very far from being so. In order to proceed with the learning task, children require evidence about language in use. They also need feedback on the effectiveness of their own linguistic behaviour so that they can test the hypotheses that they are currently using in the construction of their language system. Or, to put it more simply, in order to learn to talk, they need a considerable amount of experience of conversation.

Sheer quantity is important. In the Bristol Study we found a clear relationship between the children's rate of progress in language learning and the amount of conversation that they experienced with their parents and other members of the family circle. But this can't be the whole story, for although the children who experienced the most conversation enjoyed almost 10 times as much as the children who experienced the least, even these latter children continued to make progress, though at a much slower rate. Furthermore, not all those who experienced a great amount of conversation developed rapidly.

What seems to be more important is that, to be most helpful, the child's experience of conversation should be in a one-to-one situation in which the adult is talking about matters that are of interest and concern to the child, such as what he or she is doing, has done or plans to do, or about activities in which the child and adult engage together.[5] The reason for this is the fact that, when both child and adult are engaged in a shared activity, the chances are maximized that they will be attending to the same objects and events and interpreting the situation in similar ways. This means that they will each have the best chance of correctly interpreting what the other says and so of being able collaboratively to build up a shared structure of meaning about the topic that is the focus of their intersubjective attention.

Even between mature speakers of the same language, however, there is no guarantee that they will achieve mutual comprehension; hence the frequency of requests for repetition and clarification in most conversations. When the conversation is between two participants who are as unequally matched as adult and child, the chances of misunderstanding are even greater. This therefore places a very great responsibility on the adult to compensate for the child's limitations and to behave in ways that make it as easy as possible for the child to play his or her part effectively.

This means that, as speaker, an adult must take into account the limited capabilities of the child – both the 'model of the world' and the linguistic resources that she or he has so far constructed – and select their meanings and adjust the utterances in which they are encoded so that the child is able to make sense of them. In fact adults, particularly parents, seem to be intuitively aware of the need to behave in this way; in the Bristol Study, little difference was found between the children in the extent to which they received speech that was adjusted to their capabilities as listeners – at least as far as the average length and complexity of the adult utterances was concerned (Barnes *et al.*, 1983; Ellis & Wells, 1980).

Similar findings have emerged from several other studies, carried out for the most part on European languages. From them, it seems that, compared with their behaviour when speaking to adults or other children, parents modify their speech when talking to young children in a number of ways: keeping their utterances short and grammatically simple, using exaggerated intonation to hold the child's attention and to emphasize the key words, limiting the topics talked about to what is familiar to the child, and frequently repeating and paraphrasing what they say (Cross, 1977; Snow, 1977).

In modlfying their speech in these ways, adults not only increase the chances of their children understanding what they say, but they also provide evidence that is particularly clear and easy for their children to use in their task of language construction. The episode, quoted earlier, in which Mark's mother tried to get him to put the lid on the laundry basket is a good example.

Equally important, though, are the special efforts that adults must also make as listeners. With their limited resources as speakers, children's utterances are often difficult to interpret. The adult therefore needs to make considerable use of contextual clues and knowledge about the individual child's likes and interests in order to make a good guess as to what he or she intends. Amongst researchers, this is known as 'making a rich interpretation'. And, again, we found that most parents did just that.

However, what was less common was adults' checking to ensure that they had correctly understood the child before making their next move in the conversation. Many early utterances are ambiguous and, unless the adult is alert to this possibility, what he or she says next may not be an appropriate response. In many cases this will simply lead to an abandonment of the topic; however, if the conversation continues, the child will be provided with evidence that is positively unhelpful in the task of matching what is said to the meaning he or she believes is intended.

A good example of an adult who systematically checks her interpretations is Mark's mother, in the extract quoted in Chapter 2 to illustrate Stage II of language learning. The extract begins with a successful sequence of exchanges:

Mark: 'Ot, Mummy?
Mother: Hot? *[checking]* . yes, that's the radiator
Mark: Been-burn?
Mother: Burn? *[checking]*
Mark: Yeh
Mother: Yes, you know it'll burn, don't you?

As well as illustrating the strategy of checking, this short extract also shows very clearly how, with the adult's assistance, a proposition can be jointly constructed that is far more complex than the child is able to express alone. Mark offers the first element: 'hot'. Mother confirms the appropriateness of his observation (and, of course, of the way in which he expressed it) and adds the second element: 'the radiator'. Mark then adds the third element, 'burn', to complete the complex proposition, 'hot radiator burn', which his mother confirms in the final turn.

Sometimes such checking utterances lead to the recognition that the adult's interpretation is not correct, and a sequence of negotiation over the intended meaning is begun, as in the later episode in the same extract concerning 'the man's fire'. In addition to making it more likely that the conversational participants will achieve mutual comprehension, such exchanges provide children with valuable feedback on the success with which their utterances have communicated their intentions. Such exchanges may also lead to the presentation of relevant new evidence about how to communicate a given intention more effectively, as when Mark's mother gives him the word for the particular kind of fire he is looking at – a bonfire. Note how, because that is the focus of his interest at that moment, Mark is quick to assimilate the new piece of information and relate it to other relevant knowledge that he already possesses. Interestingly, this is a clear case of imitating – with variation!

Mark: A man's fire, Mummy
Mother: *[requesting a repetition]* Mm?
Mark: A man's fire
Mother: *[checking]* Mummy's flower?
Mark: No
Mother: What?
Mark: Mummy . the man . fire
Mother: *[checking]* Man's fire?
Mark: Yeh
Mother: Oh, yes, the bonfire
Mark: *[imitating]* Bonfire
Mother: Mm.
Mark: Bonfire . oh, bonfire . bonfire . bon- a fire . bo . bonfire Oh, hot, Mummy . oh, hot . it hot . it hot
Mother: Mm, it will burn, won't it?
Mark: Yeh . burn . it burn

By chance, no doubt, but nevertheless very relevantly, the conversation comes full circle to the ideas with which the extract started. What a rich opportunity for learning – both about language and about the world to which the language refers!

As both these examples show very clearly, a really satisfying conversation needs to go beyond a single exchange. And it is in enabling this to happen that an adult can make perhaps the most important contribution to the child's development. As already emphasized, conversation involves the collaborative and cumulative construction of meaning, in which the linguistic links between utterances are like the mortar that holds together the bricks in a wall. For the child to be able to understand the nature of the meaning connections and to discover how the links are made linguistically, it is important that he or she should be able to form expectations about how the building process might proceed. For this to happen, the adult needs to try to adopt the child's perspective and, in his or her next contribution to the conversation, to incorporate some aspect of what the child has just said and to extend it or invite the child to do so him- or herself.

In the first extract from the recordings of Mark, we see very clear examples of these strategies for sustaining and extending Mark's meanings

Mark: *[looking out of the window at the birds in the garden]* Look-at-that . birds, Mummy
Mother: Mm

Mark: Jubs [birds]
Mother: *[inviting Mark to extend his own meaning]* What are they doing?
Mark: Jubs bread [birds eating bread]
Mother: *[extending Mark's meaning]* Oh, look! they're eating the berries, aren't they?
Mark: Yeh
Mother: *[extending and paraphrasing]* That's their food . they have berries for dinner
Mark: Oh

This short sequence of conversation seems an almost ideal example of the way in which parents can most helpfully contribute to their children's language development. In it we see how the mother adjusts her speech to take account of the child's capabilities and helps him to build a conversation with her about a topic that is clearly of interest to him, as it is one that he initiated. In her turns she encourages Mark to extend his initial topic and then takes what he contributes and extends it still further in a number of simple, related sentences that provide evidence for him as to how to express more fully what it is he has invited her to look at with him. Notice, too, how she is also providing him with information about the topic to which they are jointly attending (the O in the triangle of communication), thus simultaneously enabling him to extend his model of the world to which the language refers.

There is one final point to note about this example of collaborative meaning making. Although in the latter part of the sequence it is the mother who is contributing all the new material, the conversation does not become a monologue. Even though Mark may not have fully understood all that his mother is saying, he keeps up his end of the conversation, providing acknowledgments where they are required. He, too, is playing his part in the collaborative enterprise. This is important for, without these minimal but appropriate responses from Mark, his mother would not have felt able to continue to play her part.

Mark's responses have another important function. Together with his nonverbal behaviour – gestures, facial expressions, and so on – they provide his mother with feedback on the success of her contributions. And, in the light of this, she is able to 'tune' her speech fairly closely to his current ability to comprehend. As that ability increases, she increases the complexity of what she says and of the ideas that she tries to communicate. Adults do not need to know about the relative complexity of linguistic items, therefore, in order to provide appropriate evidence for children to learn from. All that is required is that they be responsive to the cues that children provide as to what they are able to understand. Rather than it being simply a matter of adults teaching children, therefore, children also teach adults how to talk in such a way as to make it easy for them to learn.

That only happens, of course, to the extent that the adult is sensitive and alert to the cues that the child offers. Some well-meaning parents, believing that instruction and correction are necessary for language learning, are so concerned with bringing their child's language system and internal model of the world into conformity with their own that they fail to pick up and respond to cues from the child and, as a result, they actually make it more difficult for the child to learn. The next example illustrates how this may happen.[6]

Thomas (age 25 months) has seen a plate of biscuits (cookies) on the table. His first utterance consists of three words, but only the third is intelligible.

Thomas: * * biscuits
Mother: Those were got specially 'cos we had visitors at the weekend Who came to see Tommy? Who came in a car?
Thomas: See Grannie Irene uh car
Mother: Grannie Irene's coming next weekend . but who came last weekend?
Thomas: Auntie Gail in a train
Mother: Auntie Gail's coming . they're coming on the train, yes
Thomas: Colin uh Anne a train
Mother: Colin- Colin and Anne came in the car, didn't they?
Thomas: Colin uh Anne . Colin uh Anne
Mother: Yes
Thomas: Colin uh Anne . Colin uh Anne
Mother: Colin and Anne came in the train
Thomas: In uh train . auntie train
Mother: No, not Auntie train, darling . Auntie Gail and Grannie Irene are coming on the train on Friday
Thomas: Auntie Gail in uh train
Mother: That's right

What was Thomas's original intention? Was he merely expressing an interest in the presence of the biscuits (as his mother decides to assume), or did he perhaps want to eat one of them? We shall never know. For, instead of negotiating to find out what his intended meaning was, his mother launches into what turns out to be a quiz on the topic of which relatives came by which mode of transport on which weekend – a topic that is considerably beyond the level of complexity that a two-year-old can cope with.

Far from being collaborative, this episode is dominated by the mother, who manages the content of the conversation by means of questions and evaluations. It is almost as if she has to assess each of Thomas's utterances to make sure that it is factually accurate and grammatically well-formed before she will allow it into the conversation. The result is that she is so concerned to ensure that Thomas should see the world from her own adult perspective that she fails to pick up his cues, and they are ignored. And, when he does volunteer an idea of his own, using the limited resources at his disposal – 'Aunty train' ('Aunty came in the train') – far from being accepted as the basis for collaboration in the construction of a more extended understanding, his utterance is rejected and his mother's 'correct' version is substituted.

There are two reasons why conversations of this kind are not helpful to the language learner. First, they fail to recognize the active and autonomous nature of the child's construction of his or her linguistic repertoire. Instead of being cued by Thomas's communicative behaviour, his mother tries to impose her own fully developed adult system and, as a result, provides evidence that is far from optimally adjusted to Thomas's current needs.

Second, such conversations are, in themselves, unrewarding: there is none of the satisfaction that comes from achieving a shared understanding of the topic. There is no real meeting of minds. What is more, if this experience is repeated too often, the child may well lose interest in conversing with adults and, as a result, also lose the opportunities for learning that such conversations can provide.

Talking with young children is thus very much like playing ball with them. What the adult has to do for this game to be successful is, first, to ensure that the child is ready, with arms cupped, to catch the ball. Then the ball must be thrown gently and accurately so that it lands squarely in the child's arms. When it is the child's turn to throw, the adult must be prepared to run wherever it goes and bring it back to where the child really intended it to go. Such is the collaboration required in conversation, the adult doing a great deal of supportive work to enable the ball to be kept in play.

Probably all parents want to help their children learn to talk, and some actively seek advice and guidance. I have one very general suggestion to make to any adult involved in caring for children: encourage them to initiate conversation, and make it easy and enjoyable for them to sustain it. The following more specific suggestions should help in achieving that result:

- When the child appears to be trying to communicate, assume he or she has something important to say and treat the attempt accordingly.
- Because the child's utterances are often unclear or ambiguous, be sure you have understood the intended meaning before responding.
- When you reply, take the child's meaning as the basis of what you say next – confirming the intention and extending the topic or inviting the child to do so him- or herself.
- Select and phrase your contributions so that they are at or just beyond the child's ability to comprehend.

In response to a similar parental request for guidance, Roger Brown had this to say:

> Believe that your child can understand more than he or she can say, and seek, above all, to communicate. To understand and be understood. To keep your minds fixed on the same target. There is no set of rules of how to talk to a child that can even approach what you unconsciously know. If you concentrate on communicating, everything else will follow. (Brown, 1977: 26)

It could hardly be put better. Children have to work out the way in which language is organized for themselves and, fortunately, they are well equipped to do so. But they can't do it all on their own. They need the collaborative help of interested conversational partners who, in aiming to achieve a shared understanding of the topics that are raised and of the activities that they are engaged in together, provide clear and relevant evidence of how the language works and feedback that enables children to evaluate the appropriateness of their current hypotheses. Above all, children need to feel that conversation is enjoyable and worthwhile and that it enables them to be effective in controlling and understanding their surroundings. This is what provides the motivation to continue to learn.

Learning to talk should thus be thought of as the result of a partnership: a partnership in which parents and other members of the community provide the evidence and then encourage children to work it out for themselves. Andrew Lock (1980: 278) sums it all up in a single phrase when he describes the process as 'the guided reinvention of language'.

Notes

1. Chomsky sees the problem to be that of discovering the relationship between sounds and meanings. But that ignores a logically prior discovery, namely, that there is a relationship to be discovered.
2. This alternative view has been advanced by a number of philosophers and psychologists (e.g. Bennett, 1976; Deacon, 1997; Donald, 1991).
3. In addition to Halliday's work, which was mentioned in Chapter 2, there are interesting studies by Elizabeth Bates and her colleagues (Bates *et al.*, 1975) and by Ann Carter (1979) on the development from gestures to words, and by John Dore (1975) on the earliest speech acts, all of which assume a functional continuity from preverbal to verbal communication.
4. These two explanations are often described as *behaviourist* and *nativist*, respectively. The former, or something rather similar, was proposed by B.F. Skinner (1957). The latter, or various versions of it, has been proposed by Noam Chomsky (1965, 1972) and by Steven Pinker (1994).
5. This is certainly true for children in Western cultures. However, some caution is needed in interpreting this finding more generally. In cultures where children and caregivers rarely take part in such activities together, children still successfully learn to talk (Gaskins, 1999; Ochs, 1988; Schieffelin & Ochs, 1986). However, at the present time, there is no evidence to show whether they develop at the same rate or not.
6. I am grateful to Margaret MacLure for this example.

Chapter 4
Talking to Learn

Conversation is rarely an end in itself, particularly where young children are concerned. They talk in order to achieve other ends: to share their interest in the world around them, to obtain the things they want, to get others to help them, to participate in the activities of the grown-up world, to learn how to do things or why things are as they are, or just to remain in contact. And similar purposes underlie their parents' reasons for talking with them. For most of the time, therefore, conversation is purposeful and goal-directed – aimed at enabling the participants to integrate their behaviour in order to achieve the purposes of one or other or both of them. In the process, a great deal of information is exchanged, either as a necessary adjunct to the performance of activities or because it is judged to be of interest in itself. In this chapter, we shall consider some examples of spontaneously occurring conversations in which children are not only learning to talk but also, through talk, learning about a great many other things.

Learning from Joint Activities

Children love to help with jobs that their parents are engaged in. When they are allowed to join in, these shared activities can provide particularly rich opportunities to learn – about the activities themselves and about the words by which to refer to them, and also about the way in which language functions to guide action. Consider the following example.

Simon, age 4 years 9 months, is helping his mother to make a cake.
Simon: *[wanting to grate a lemon]* Can I do that?
Mother: Well, you can try . but it's not very easy . you can tear your finger if you're not careful
Simon: What do you mean 'tear'?

Mother:	Well, if your finger gets too close to the grater, and you're going too fast, you can catch it on the sharp part and scrape the skin off
Simon:	I'll be very careful
Mother:	Hold it like that *[she puts the grater in Simon's hand and then gives him the lemon]*

Five seconds of concentrated effort follow, at which point the lemon slips out of Simon's hand into the bowl.

Simon:	Oh dear!
Mother:	[mock anger] Oh deary me! . whatever shall we do?

Mother hands back the lemon; Simon continues to grate.

Simon:	Look, it's coming off
Mother:	Yes, you have to turn it [the lemon] round . because when you've got it [the rind] all off one part, you have to turn it round to get the rest off . . let me show you
Simon:	No . I can do it *[he tries to turn the grater around]*
Mother:	No . you turn the lemon round, not the grater . you see, you've got it off there, so you've got to take it off another part now *[Ten seconds of grating]*
Simon:	You do it now
Mother:	Thank you . that was a help

Here Simon is not only learning to cook and testing the limits of his own competence, he is also learning how to talk about some of the activities involved.

In the next example, Jacqueline thinks she is helping but her mother takes a different view.

Jackie is playing with the clothes that her mother has tipped out on the floor from the laundry bag in preparation for the weekly wash.

Jackie:	*[putting the clothes back in the laundry bag]* I'm putting them in
Mother:	*[sharply]* No, no, no . leave Mummy's washing alone. Mummy's got to wash all that
Jackie:	I want to put those things in
Mother:	Yes, when they're washed you can . not before

Although Jackie's desire to help is unwelcome to her mother on this occasion, notice how her mother deals with the situation: as well as firmly telling Jackie to desist, she explains her prohibition in a way that recognizes her daughter's interest and desire to help and then presents a sequence of later events in which Jackie's intended activity will indeed be helpful. But from this conversation Jackie is not only learning about the sequence of stages in doing the laundry – she is also learning that, even though there may sometimes be a conflict of purposes, language provides a means for negotiating a solution that is mutually acceptable.

Later, within the same short sample, there is another episode in which Jackie and her mother have to reconcile a difference, but this time it arises from Jackie's difficulty in expressing her intended meaning in a form that her mother can understand. (Because intonation plays an important role in the negotiation of the meaning that was finally agreed, both the main, stressed, syllables and the direction of pitch movement have been marked.)

		↘ → →
1	Jackie:	**Linda** bought you **socks, Mum**

		↘ ↘
2	Mother:	**Yes**, Linda bought you **socks**

		↘ ↘
3		They're **dirty** . they've got to be **washed**
4	Jackie:	*[trying to check her understanding of Mother's words]* Did Linda bought you- me got . washed? [Have the socks that Linda bought me got to be washed? intonation unclear]

		∨↗
5	Mother:	**Par**don?

		↘ ↗↘
6	Jackie:	**Linda** wa – **wash** them

		↘ ↘
7	Mother:	**No** . **Mummy**'s going to wash them

		↘
8	Jackie:	**Linda** wash them

		↘ ↘
9	Mother:	**No** . Linda's **not** going to wash them

		↘ →
10	Jackie:	**Linda**'s not going to **wash** them

		↘ ↘
11	Mother:	**No** . **Mummy** wash them.

Jackie has seen a pair of her socks waiting to be washed, which she recalls were given to her by her Aunty Linda. She tries to share all this information with her mother, but has difficulty in organizing the form of her utterance to encode her intended meaning with the right information focus – that is to say, with the emphasis on the right words (line 4). Following a request for repetition, Jackie attempts to express her meaning in a simpler form but, as the hiatus suggests, she still has difficulty (line 6). The arrangement of the components 'Linda', 'wash' and 'them' (socks) suggests that Linda is the agent of the action of washing. But this does not correspond with the situation nor, as far as one can judge, with Jackie's intention. The problem seems to result from a conflict between two intentions: to ask for confirmation of the proposition that the socks are to be washed and to focus attention on the fact that it was Aunty Linda who gave her this particular pair of socks. In line 7, Mother rejects Jackie's utterance as inaccurate and, using marked tonic stress placement on 'Mummy', offers a contrasting true statement, which matches the surface form of Jackie's utterance. Jackie seems unable to accept this way of stating things, however, and in line 8 reaffirms her original assertion, placing contrastive stress on 'Linda'. Mother again rejects Jackie's statement, this time explicitly contradicting it: 'Linda's *not* going to wash them'. In line 10, Jackie repeats her mother's utterance but places marked tonic stress on 'Linda' to indicate her understanding that it is not Linda who is going to wash the socks and signals her wish for confirmation of this interpretation. Finally, in line 11, her mother confirms the correctness of Jackie's negative statement and, picking up the contrastive implication of the stress on 'Linda', restates the relationship positively with 'Mummy' as agent. Jackie's silence can be taken as agreement with this final version.

I have analysed this short extract in such detail because it is a very clear example of how a misunderstanding with respect to intended meaning can be quite literally *negotiated* until a collaborative resolution is achieved. At the same time, one can almost see Jackie working on the evidence supplied by the discrepancies between her own utterances, her mother's utterances, and the situation, in order to find the appropriate linguistic devices to express her original meaning. Given her inability, at this stage, to make use of a relative clause, she works on her growing control of intonation to help her resolve the problem.

Jackie was only two years three months old at the time of the previous extract. By three-and-a-half, Jonathan has much more fully developed linguistic resources and, as is seen in the next example, some skill in arguing his point of view.

Jonathan is helping his mother with the housework by polishing his wardrobe.

Jonathan: Do you think this is lovely?
Mother: I think it's a bit smeary
Jonathan: Why do you think it's a bit smeary?
Mother: Because you put far too much polish on it
Right . now you can put the things back on there
[on the dresser] and I'll put the carpet sweeper over
the room
Jonathan: Well, why can't I put the carpet sweeper over the room?
Mother: Because that's my job
Jonathan: What is my job?
Mother: You've done your job . you've polished the furniture
[A few minutes later.]
Jonathan: It doesn't matter if that polish goes in your eyes, does it?
Mother: Oh it does, yes . it makes them sting
Jonathan: [unintelligible]
Mother: It makes them sting very badly
Jonathan: Well, just now some of that polish waved in my eye
Mother: Did it?
Jonathan: Yes
Mother: Do they [your eyes] sting? or did it miss?
Don't rub them with the duster, darling . the duster's
all dirty
Jonathan: [referring to polish] Well, how can that get out, Mummy?
Mother: Why don't you go and wipe it with the flannel [facecloth]
in the Bathroom?
Jonathan: *[goes to bathroom]* No, I think I'll get it out with the
towel . Mummy, I just have to see if I can get it out
with this towel
Mother: All right

Questions and Answers

In all the preceding examples, the children were learning about how language is used for various interpersonal purposes. But, because the conversations arose from activities that had their own internal organization, through talking in order to participate in them, they were also learning about the activities themselves and their sequential structure. This sort of learning about the world through talk is perhaps even more evident in the following examples, in which the events themselves become the focus of the child's attention.

Abigail, age three, is helping her mother change the bed linen.

Mother: [referring to Abigail's nightdress] Why not take that and put
                it under your pillow? I'll just put new pillows on our bed
Abigail: Mummy, why you putting the new pillow in those? .
                because the other one's broken?
Mother: No . going to have clean ones because I want it all to look
                pretty and in the same colour to look nice when Daddy
                comes home
                So that's done . now we must find a bottom sheet and some
                other pillowcases
Abigail: Oh, yes . [referring to her nightdress]
                Shall I put and wrap it up and put it in my pillow?
Mother: Hurry up . let's see what we can find for washing

To begin with, children's questions tend to be incidental to the activity
in which they are engaged: 'Where's my ball?', 'Which one shall I take?',
'Why can't I go out in the garden?' What is being asked for is information
that will guide or facilitate action or, as in the above example, a justification
for Mother's stated plan of action. A simple answer is all that is usually
called for, as the child's attention is focused on the action rather than on
the explanation.

As they get older, though, children's questions show a developing
interest in getting to the bottom of things. Their questions seem to arise
more frequently from a sense of puzzlement – from a desire to make sense
and to get things straight in their own minds. As before, it is frequently
the activity in which they are engaged, or one in which they observe
someone else engaged, that sparks off the question; but they are no longer satisfied with the straightforward answer. They seek explanations
rather than justifications. Here is an example from the observation of
Anthony at three-and-a-half and three examples from recordings of the
older group of children.

Anthony's mother is painting the bathroom. Anthony is standing watching.

Anthony: You're painting
Mother: Oh, yes . dreadful stuff, paint . it gets everywhere
Anthony: What it do?
Mother: Gets on everything-
Anthony: [acknowledging] Mm
Mother: - and everywhere, when it's wet
Anthony: Oh, God! does it get over me and my Daddy?
Mother: No . mind, out the way, sweetheart

Anthony:	Would Daddy get it on him?
Mother:	When he does painting, it does, yes
Anthony:	He does, doesn't he? he gets it on his hair
Mother:	Does he?
Anthony:	Yes . and he gets it on his jacket
Mother:	I don't think Daddy would paint with his jacket on, darling
Anthony:	With his coat on, he do

Mother is making a jelly (Jello, in cubes) and Deirdre, age four years six months,
is stirring the jelly cubes in boiling water

Mother:	The jelly's melting, look
Deirdre:	Why's it starting to melt?
Mother:	'Cause the water's very hot . and it makes jelly melt when it's very hot

[six-second pause]

Deirdre:	Why's it making jelly melt- when it's very hot? . why does it?
Mother:	Well, because it does, that's why . butter melts when it's very hot

[eight-second pause. Mother adds cold water to the jelly.]

Deirdre:	It's very cold now, isn't it?
Mother:	It's cooler

Elizabeth, age four, is watching her mother shovel wood ash from the grate into
a bucket.

Elizabeth:	What are you doing that for?
Mother:	I'm gathering it up and putting it outside so that Daddy can put it on the garden
Elizabeth:	Why does he have to put it on the garden?
Mother:	To make the compost right
Elizabeth:	Does that make the grass grow?
Mother:	Yes
Elizabeth:	Why does it?
Mother:	You know how I tell you that you need to eat different things like eggs and cabbage and rice pudding to make you grow into a big girl
Elizabeth:	Yes
Mother:	Well, plants need different foods, too . and ash is one of the things that's good for them

James, age five, comes into the kitchen just as his mother has taken some cakes
out of the oven. There is a loud, metallic 'crack'.

James:	Who did that?

Mother:	I expect it was that tin contracting
James:	Which tin?
Mother:	The one with your pastry in
James:	Why did it make that noise?
Mother:	Well, when it was in the oven, it got very hot and stretched a bit . I've just taken it out of the oven, and it's cooling down very quickly, you see, and that noise happens when it gets smaller again and goes back to its ordinary shape
James:	Oh! Was it a different shape in the oven?
Mother:	Not very different . just a little bigger
James:	Naughty little tin . you might get smacked – if you do it again

By four years of age, most children are great askers of questions, and parents are often hard put to find appropriate answers. There is so much the children do not yet know that it is difficult to know where to start. But when, as in these examples, children are encouraged to bring their knowledge to the shared construction of an answer, there is a good chance that they will be able to assimilate some of the information that is offered; as a result, they will be able to add to and, if necessary, modify their internal model of the world.

Parents' answers are not always as full or as helpful as those in the examples quoted above. Sometimes they simply do not know the answer, or they misunderstand the question. On other occasions they are simply too busy to stop and give the question the time and attention it deserves. Nevertheless, because they are such active seekers after meaning, children do not give up and, in the absence of the necessary information, they will find an answer of their own. It is for this reason that some of the things they say seem so amusingly bizarre to adults.

However, as Tizard and Hughes (1984) pointed out after recording and observing four-year-olds at home, children do not have a problem only with gaps in knowledge; 'it is rather that they have an imperfect grasp of a vast range of concepts which an older child or adult takes for granted'. The children they observed seemed, in their words, 'in some sense aware that their conceptual framework was not yet substantial enough to cope with their experiences, and engaged themselves actively in the process of improving their intellectual scaffolding'.[1]

Children need to be persistent questioners, therefore and, provided their parents attempt on most occasions to provide an answer, they will continue to ask – using others as a resource for making sense of their experience.

Incidental Learning: The World's an Interesting Place

Questions are not the only source of information, however. As we have seen, a simple expression of interest by the child will often prompt a parent to offer information that fills in a little more of the picture and extends the child's understanding of the topic that aroused his or her interest. Here is another example, which starts with a child's interested observation of a bird.

James, age three-and-a-half, has been playing in the garden. His mother wants to get him to take his muddy shoes and socks off but, as he comes inside, he sees a bird.

Mother: There we are .. there - one slipper on

James: I can see a bird

Mother: A what, love?

James: See a bird

Mother: *[whispering]* Is there? outside?

James: *[pointing and whispering]* Yes . see

[Both continue to whisper.]

Mother: Is he eating anything?

James: No

Mother: Where? . oh yes . he's getting- do you know what he's doing?

James: No

Mother: He's going to the-the paper sack to try and pick out some pieces- Oh, he's got some food there . and I expect he'll pick out some pieces of thread from the sack to go and make his nest up underneath the roof, James .. wait a minute and I'll-

[James now wants to go out to see more closely, but at that moment the bird flies away.]

James: That bird's gone

Mother: *[speaking at normal volume again]* Has it gone now?

James: Yeh

There are countless examples of this kind, not all so dramatic as this whispered accompaniment to their jointly focused attention, perhaps, but all in their different ways helping the child to make fuller sense of an experience. It is in this way, of course, that the child gradually comes to take on the adult way of interpreting the world – not through deliberate and systematic instruction, but through shared interest and involvement in the events that make up everyday life. In fact, probably the greater part of our general knowledge is acquired in this incidental way, as we respond to the interests expressed by others and they respond to ours. Certainly, children learn a great deal in this way before they begin to receive more systematic instruction at school. Berger and Luckman (1966) refer to this sort of learning through spontaneous interaction as *the social construction of reality*. Other situations that are particularly likely to give rise to collaborative meaning making are looking out of the window, recalling past events and planning or speculating about future ones, watching television together or reading a story. The latter is potentially of particular importance and will be discussed in more detail in Chapter 8.

Since television is often considered to have an almost entirely negative influence, it is worth quoting several examples to show that it need not always be harmful. In the first, James (at three years three months) is watching a nature programme about deer. (*Note*: underlining indicates words spoken simultaneously.)

Mother: That one's got horns in the front
James: Yes, but-
Mother: In front of its head <u>it's got two horns</u>
James: <u>Yes, but it-but it</u> looks like a deer
Mother: Mm
James: But it looks like a little deer
Mother: Look! . what a nice face it's got
James: Yes . got any eyes?
Mother: Yes they have, my love . look, there's their eyes - little black marks . there you are . that's a baby one
James climbs onto his mother's lap.
Mother: <u>There's a good boy</u>
James: <u>Lovely deer</u> they are
[*10 seconds pause, while they watch. The voice of the commentator can be heard in the background.*]
Mother: Some more
James: What are they playing <u>* *</u>?
Mother: <u>Well, they were just</u> playing- I expect what they were doing is they talk to one another . they were going like this [*Mother rubs noses with James and giggles and James chuckles*]

As in the earlier extract when they looked at the bird together, what James's mother is doing here is helping him to observe more closely as she provides a framework for interpreting what he sees. Without this help, we found, children of this age were able to get very little from watching television. Certainly, in some homes the television set was switched on for much of the day, but it was part of the background and almost totally ignored by the children until their parents sat down to watch with them.

The second example involves Rosie at the age of five. With her mother, she is watching a programme about making pots.

Rosie: *[referring to the potter's wheel]* Mum, what- what's making it go round?
Mother: Er- well, like a clock
Rosie: What clock?
[Mother does not reply. 30-second pause.]
Mother: They're digging
Rosie: Why they dig-?
Mother: That's for the boilers
Rosie: Why's the boy-?
Mother: Tipping it into a machine
Rosie: Why they tipping it into the 'chine- machine?
Mother: They'll tell you now
[Commentator explains what is happening.]
Mother: Oh, that's clay
[Picture shows moulds being made.]
Mother: There it is . look, they're saucepans- not saucepans . what do you call them? basins . and that's a cup
Rosie: Is there toilet rolls?
Mother: No
Rosie: Why they trying to do that for?
Mother: Making cups, you see . that's the mold to shape the cup . . he'll get that board and put them on there
Rosie: Why? . why's he putting them on there for?
Mother: 'Cos he's got to go somewhere else
Rosie: Might fall in the fishpond

If this does not seem as successful as the previous example, that is probably due partly to the fact that the content of the programme is much more difficult for a young child to understand. But for all its limitations, it is worth noting how the mother's attention to the programme is helping Rosie to look more closely than she would otherwise have done and encouraging her to test her interpretation against her mother's understanding. Television programmes, like stories, can also be the stimulus that leads to a consideration of personal experience. In the following extract, at three years and six months,

Jonathan and his mother were watching a programme about gardening. (*Note*: underlining indicates words spoken simultaneously.)

Jonathan: Planting cabbages here . why's his Mummy with him?
Mother: Didn't you do that with Grampy- with Gran the other day?
Jonathan: Yes
Mother: Plant cabbages?
Jonathan: Yes, I did
Mother: Yes, I thought you did
Jonathan: I helped to * *
Mother: <u>What</u> did you do? . did you make the holes? or did you put the cabbages in the holes that Gran made?
Jonathan: [*getting the words 'holes' and 'cabbages' mixed up*] Gran made the cabbages, and I helped to put the holes in
Mother: Can you remember how many you planted? . did you count them or not?
Jonathan: No, we forgot to count
Mother: Oh . perhaps when we go up next week we can count them . we'll see how many you planted, eh?
Jonathan: Mm . they're for the winter
Mother: Yes, they grow in the winter, don't they? . and then we can have nice cabbages

Exploring the World of the Imagination

Nowhere is this willingness to explore the world through words more apparent than in imaginary and fantasy play. Most children readily engage in 'pretend' games alone or with other children. They also enjoy playing in this way with adults who are able to enter into the spirit of the game. Some parents find it quite difficult to join in physically, but simply to adopt the imaginary frame of reference may be sufficient to enable the play to continue, as in the following example.

Ann, age two years six months, is playing with her teddy bear.
Ann: Don't wake Teddy up, will you, Daddy?
Father: No, I won't . what's Teddy doing?
Ann: My teddy's not very well
Father: Isn't he? . what's the matter?
Ann: Gotta- Teddy's got to have some Abidec [a vitamin preparation]

Father:	Has he?
Ann:	And some aspirin
Father:	What are you going to give the aspirins to Teddy for?
Ann:	'Cos my teddy's not very comfy

But what a vivid and exciting world is created when the adult joins in completely. As James (at three years nine months) and his mother drive off in their steam train in the following example, you can almost see the green fields, the cows, and the waving farmer.

James is playing trains with his mother on the sofa. He is sitting astride the arm, as driver.

Mother:	There we are . I'll sit at the side
	Right. Are you ready? all set? . Right . off with the brake
James:	I'll start it up
Mother:	Oh, sorry! . right
James:	Mum! you don't steer it yet
Mother:	Oh . well

[James makes a noise, pretending to start the engine]

Mother:	Oh! That was a quick-starting engine . very good!
	Got enough coal at the back? Have you shoveled enough coal on, James?
James:	Yes
Mother:	Good . away we go, then . . wave good-bye to your friends

[Engine noises accelerating. James chuckles and makes a noise for the engine whistle.]

Mother:	We're going very fast now, James . can you feel the carriages swaying?
James:	Yeh
Mother:	Can you?
James:	Yeh
Mother:	Oh, they're rolling me about . oh! all my breakfast is rumbling in my tummy . oh–oh–oh!

[Engine noises.]

Mother:	I think we'll have to slow down, don't you?
James:	Mm [agreeing]
Mother:	I think we're going a bit too fast … that's better . that's easier now, isn't it?
James:	Mm
Mother:	*[hums a bit]* Look at the cows in the field, James
James:	Mm
Mother:	And there's a farmer, look . the farmer's waving to you

From Talking to Reflective Thinking

As this variety of examples shows, almost every situation provides an opportunity for learning if children are purposefully engaged and there are adults around who encourage their attempts to do and to understand and, in collaboration with them, provide a resource of skills and information on which they can draw. In such situations, language provides a means not only for acting in the world but also for reflecting on that action in an attempt to understand it.

Initially, such reflection takes place through conversation – through dialogue with another, more knowledgeable person. But gradually, if children have many positive experiences of this kind, they begin to be able to manage both roles for themselves. They come to be able to frame questions and interrogate their own experience in the search for an answer. The dialogue begins to be carried on internally in 'inner speech' (Vygotsky, 1987). In this way, language becomes a tool for thinking.

In the following example, Simon (age four years nine months) seems already to be moving in that direction. He has just eaten an apple and is left with the pips. He is explaining to his mother what he might do with them.

Simon: A pip is a seed . so he can grow . and we might be able to grow some now . got some apple seeds - apple pip seeds - and if I put even more, Daddy and me might go out one day, which isn't a rainy day, and we might be able to plant the seeds . or I could plant them tomorrow

All the examples quoted in this chapter have been taken from recordings of naturally occurring conversations in children's homes. From them we see how parents spontaneously and intuitively provide opportunities for learning as they talk with their children about the many events that occur during the course of a normal day. These parents do not feel under any pressure to instruct, but they are sensitive to their children's desire to learn – to acquire skill, understanding and control. And so, whenever possible, they encourage their children's interests and help them to extend and develop them.

In learning through talk – as in learning to talk – children are active constructors of their own knowledge. What they need is evidence, guidance and support. Parents who treat their children as equal partners in conversation, following their lead and negotiating meanings and purposes, are not only helping their children to talk, they are also enabling them to discover how to learn through talk.

Note

1. Tizard and Hughes' study involved 30 girls, half from middle-class and half from working-class families, in a comparison of the language experienced in the two settings of home and nursery class. As this is the topic of Chapter 5, I shall refer to their study in greater detail there.

Chapter 5
From Home to School

In the preschool years, as we have seen, talking and learning go hand in hand. Children talk about the things that interest them and try to increase their understanding; and, for much of the time, their adult conversational partners sustain and support their efforts, seeking, where appropriate, 'to add a pebble to the pile' (Brown, 1980).[1] What is characteristic of such learning is that it is spontaneous and unplanned and, because it arises out of activities in which one or both of the participants are engaged, it is focused and given meaning by the context in which it occurs.

This is both a strength and a limitation. It is a strength because the child's purpose in the activity sustains his or her motivation to understand, and the context provides support for the new concepts to be grasped and the new connections to be made. But it is also a limitation because such learning is sporadic and, for the most part, unsystematic: while some areas of experience are gradually illuminated from a variety of perspectives, others are encountered only rarely, and many not at all.

One of the most important functions of schooling, therefore, is to broaden the range of children's experiences and to help them to develop the sustained and deliberate attention to a topic or activity that makes more systematic learning possible. Above all, they need to be helped to become more reflectively aware of what they already know and still need to know, so that they can gradually take over more and more responsibility for their own learning (Donaldson, 1978).[2]

It is often assumed that such aims require a sharp break with the incidental style of learning experienced at home. But this is neither desirable nor necessary. The strategies that children have developed for actively making sense of their experience have served them well up to this point; they should now be extended and developed, not suppressed by the imposition of routine learning tasks for which they can see neither a purpose nor a connection with what they already know and can do. Similarly, the adult strategies that supported their talking and learning do not lose their effectiveness just because the children are now in a classroom rather than at home. Adult guidance is certainly necessary, and skill in providing it should be expected of every teacher; but knowledge still has to be 'reconstructed' by each individual child, building on what he or she brings from previous experience.

Continuity between home and school is important for social and emotional reasons, too. If children are to make the transition confidently and easily, it is important that they experience the new environment of school as an exciting and challenging one, in which the majority of their endeavours are successful and where they are given individual recognition for who they are and what they can do. First impressions – on both sides – can distort subsequent experiences. Children who feel, or who are made to feel, unaccepted and incompetent may be slow to recover their self-confidence and, as a result, their ability to benefit from the enlarged opportunities for learning that school provides may be diminished or even, in extreme cases, irrevocably damaged.

Fortunately, as we have seen, by the time children come to school, they have already acquired a considerable degree of competence as purposeful actors and as effective communicators. There is therefore a solid foundation on which to build. Certainly they differ considerably in the range and level of skills and knowledge that they have mastered, but there are very few children indeed who, in the familiar surroundings of their own homes, cannot successfully plan and carry out quite complex activities and communicate with others to seek or offer assistance, exchange information, and express feelings and respond to those of others. Each child, too, through his or her interactions with other people, has internalized a model of the world of considerable power and complexity that enables him or her to act effectively in the social and physical environment of home and its immediate surroundings.

As far as learning is concerned, therefore, entry into school should not be thought of as a beginning, but as a transition to a more broadly based community and to a wider range of opportunities for meaning-making and mastery. Every child has competencies, and these provide a positive base from which to start. The teacher's responsibility is to discover what they are and to help each child to extend and develop them.

A Typical Morning at Home and at School

How is the transition from home to school actually experienced by the majority of children? And how well do the tasks that they are given at school enable them to capitalize on the competencies they have already developed?

One difficulty that is often mentioned by teachers, particularly in schools serving areas of predominantly public housing, is the high proportion of children who are perceived to suffer from what, in Britain, is referred to as 'linguistic disadvantage'. What is meant by this term varies. In some cases, the children are perceived to be essentially without language; in other cases, the problem is thought of as a lack of the specific linguistic resources necessary to succeed in school. But are there many such children? If so, what is the nature of their disadvantage, and how far does it impede these children from adjusting easily to school?

The continuation of our longitudinal study gave us an opportunity to investigate these questions by looking more closely at the transition from home to school as it was experienced by the 32 children that we studied most intensively. For all these children, we had recordings from 15 months to 42 months. In the weeks before they started school we made another recording of each child at home and then repeated the procedure in their classrooms after they had been in school for about six weeks.

In both settings, nine five-minute samples were recorded at approximately 20-minute intervals between 9:00 am and 12:00 noon. The recording in the home was made in exactly the same way as on the earlier occasions: no observer was present, and the family was unaware of the times at which the tape recorder would be switched on. The same principle applied in the classroom, except that it was necessary to have an observer, as no class teacher could be expected to remember what a particular child had been doing at every moment throughout a morning. Having once decided that it would be necessary to have an observer, there seemed no reason not to have a mechanical observer as well, in the form of a video camera. This was mounted on a trolley and remained in a fixed position throughout the observation.

At the beginning of each session in school, the video equipment was demonstrated to the children, and each child in the class saw him- or herself on the screen in close-up and – perhaps more important – was seen by his or her friends. The children were then asked to forget about the equipment and, as our video recordings show, this is exactly what happened. As for the teachers, they no doubt continued to be intermittently aware of the camera and perhaps, therefore, not entirely relaxed. But, if this was so, any bias that was introduced was presumably in the direction of what they considered to be good teaching – though perhaps the presence of the camera inhibited them somewhat and kept them from being as adventurous as they might otherwise have been. With these small reservations, however, it can be said with considerable confidence that both home and school observations contain representative samples of naturally occurring behaviour.

Before making a detailed comparison of the language used in the two settings, however, it may be helpful to describe the activities in which the children were engaged: what they were doing and who they were doing it with.

As might be expected, there was much greater similarity between children's experiences at school than there was at home. Almost all of them spent some part of the morning on activities associated with reading and writing, and a considerable number of them spent time on activities involving numbers and counting. In most classrooms there were periods when all the children were expected to be involved together in the same activity: a story, 'news-time' ('show and tell'), a TV broadcast, a discussion. In many classrooms, too, the morning began with all the children assembled around the teacher while she called the register, collected the dinner money, and dealt with other administrative matters. Typically, though, such activities occupied only a relatively small part of the morning. For the most part, the children worked, either individually or in small groups, on tasks assigned by the teacher or engaged in self-chosen activities with the teacher's approval.

As for the teachers, the greater part of their time was spent in discussing the work of individual pupils while simultaneously monitoring the whole classroom to try to ensure that every child was profitably engaged, to forestall possible problems, and to check any unacceptable behaviour. There were, of course, quite substantial differences between the teachers in their emphases, in the proportion of time they involved the whole class in the same activity, and in their personal styles of classroom management. But there was also a very considerable degree of similarity between them in the way in which they organized the day and in what they considered it important for children to do.

To attempt a similar characterization of the children's experiences at home would be quite impossible, as they were much more varied. One important influence was the time of year at which the recordings were made. In summer, the children tended to spend a great deal of time out of doors, playing in the garden. In winter, they were confined to the house and so were more likely to play with small toys – cars, dolls, and so on. However, probably the most important factor in deciding how the children spent their time was whether or not there was a sibling or friend present in the home. As most of the recordings were made on the morning of a school day when older brothers and sisters were at school, it was only those with younger siblings who had another child to play with throughout the day. The majority of the children, therefore, spent a considerable part of the day with a parent as their only companion.

In most homes, a parent (usually the mother) engaged for a part of the morning in some shared activity with the child – reading to him or her, playing a game, cooking or performing some other household task. But for the most part the children occupied themselves, with a parent becoming involved only intermittently, either when called upon or when, between one job and another, he or she paused to talk with the child. However, the range of such impromptu conversations could be very broad, as will be seen in the examples below.

The children's activities at home, then, were much more varied than at school. But quite a number of the children voluntarily engaged in activities that were not unlike those that they would soon be doing at school – drawing, colouring, cutting out, building with bricks and construction toys, making models, listening to a story. For these children it would seem that, in this respect at least, the transition from home to school should not have been experienced as too great a discontinuity. However, for other children, there was much less similarity between the activities they performed in the two settings.

To illustrate the range of activities and the language associated with them, let us look at two of the children who were introduced in Chapter 1 to see what they were doing in each of the comparable five-minute periods at home and at school.

Like all the children, Gary was almost five years old when we recorded him on 5 January 1977. As it was during Christmas vacation, his older sister Tracey was also at home. In the first sample, made at around 10:00 a.m. on this occasion, Gary was playing alone with his toy bricks, making a squirrel. While he was doing this, his mother came into the room.[3]

Mother:	What are you making, Gary?
Gary:	Er- I'm making a- I'm making a squirrel
Mother:	A squirrel, are you?
Gary:	I can make squirrels
Mother:	Can you?
Gary:	'Cos they got- he's going to have- he's going to have a head **
Mother:	Is it?
Gary:	This one-

Mother:	You're going to make a squirrel?
Gary:	It's- it's going to go-
Mother:	Know what a squirrel is?
Gary:	Yes . I makes them in school [Gary attends the nursery school]
Mother:	What do they do?
Gary:	They climb up trees and gets nuts and acorns
Mother:	That's right! *[surprised he knows so much]*
Gary:	And they get other different things . cos I- they live in trees in a hole
Mother:	That's right
Gary:	'Cos I knows
Mother:	And they collect them up for the winter
Gary:	Yeh
Mother:	'Cos they hibernate in the winter
Gary:	Yeh, cos I knows
Mother:	Mm *[agreeing]* . who told you that?
Gary:	No one . er- I knows how to make a-
Mother:	Yeh, but who told you about the squirrels? . your teacher?
Gary:	No
Mother:	Who did?
Gary:	We knows how to paint the squirrel . sometimes we paint squirrels in school- in nursery
Mother:	Do you?
Gary:	Yeh, in holes . and I- and I can do it . cos I don't need this one [referring to bricks] I got this body . break this one
Mother:	Jolly good!

The most striking quality about this episode is Gary's confidence – both that he can make the model squirrel and that he knows about the animal itself. His mother's initial reaction is one of mild interest in what he is doing (signalled by a number of tag-question acknowledgments), but she becomes really involved and invites him to tell her more. With some surprise at the extent of his knowledge, she confirms his account ('That's right!') and then adds further information to the description that they jointly construct. Her final comment ('Jolly good!') once again reaffirms her positive evaluation of Gary's competence.

In the next sample, Gary brings some dirty ashtrays to his mother, who is washing the dishes. He then briefly watches Tracey, who is combing her doll's hair. Finally, he joins with both mother and sister in singing a Christmas rhyme.

Mother:	What has Santa in his sack
	That he carries on his back?
Tracey:	He has presents bright and gay
	All to give on Christmas Day
Gary:	Here's a lovely bouncy ball
	To play with by the garden wall
	Here a- What has Santa in his sack
	That he carries on his back?

At 10:40 am, Mother is making a cake and Gary and Tracey both want to lick the beaters from the cake mixer. They talk about the cheese and potato pie Mother is making for the midday meal (Note: underlining indicates words spoken simultaneously).

Gary:	What's that?
Tracey:	Have you done cheese and potato together?
Mother:	Cheese and potato pie
Gary:	Cheese and potato pie
Mother:	That's right
Tracey:	Is it lovely?
Mother:	Yes, I'll cook it in the oven, then I'll take it out . sprinkle some cheese on top and put it under the grill
Tracey:	Sprinkle some peas?
Mother:	Cheese
Tracey:	We've had it at home before, haven't we?
Mother:	Yes
Gary:	We had it in school and I ate the lot . <u>that's yummy</u>
Tracey:	<u>Mummy</u>
Mother:	What?
Tracey:	Remember when we used to have those potatoes still with skins on? they were lovely
Mother:	Yes. I'll do some of them
Tracey:	When?
Mother:	Well, not today
Tracey:	Might be next week?
Mother:	I'll do some tomorrow
Tracey:	Ooh! they're lovely, aren't they?

There is nothing remarkable about this extract, except perhaps the ease with which the three of them manage to integrate their various perspectives. Gary has less to say than his sister, but he's clearly involved and probably incidentally learning about making cheese and potato pie.

In the next sample, Gary tells about another child in his nursery class who is 'scared to ask for her milk'. Mother is just taking the cake out of the oven, and Gary touches it.

Gary: Touch that . it's nice and warm . not hot . Tracey, come and touch this

Tracey: Yes, I touched it . it's lovely and warm . it's not too hot

The ideal opportunity, one might say, for learning – or testing – the distinction between *hot* and *warm*.

At 11:40 Gary is playing alone, pretending that the radio-microphone (now worn on a belt around his waist) makes him the 'electric man'. Mother and Tracey are watching a television programme together, but Gary is more interested in his own game. At 12:00 noon, they sit down to dinner. During the meal, Mother explains to Gary why he must not waste his food.

Mother: They [starving children] don't even know what fish fingers taste like because they've never had 'em

Tracey: Why?

Gary: Well, it's because-

Mother: No [emphasizing what she has just said]

Gary: Do you know-

Mother: - or corned beef or anything like that

Tracey: - or boiled eggs

Mother: All they have is rice . and sometimes they don't even have that

Tracey: Sometimes they don't have nothing?

Mother: They don't have nothing

Gary: Mum, you could go up the shop . you went there, you could have gone up shop to buy them, couldn't you?

Mother: That's no good . I can't buy it and send it to them . that's why it's wasteful when you don't eat your food [This is aimed particularly at Gary, who is fussy about his food.] You think of the little children who are starving who would love to eat that

Tracey: I've got to eat it, so it's not wasted

Gary: Do you- don't they- do they have this?

Mother: No

Gary: - what I'm eating?

Mother: No, nor bread and butter

Gary: Nor butter?

Mother: No

Tracey:	Stale bread with no butter on it
Mother:	No cakes or sponges or sausage rolls or cheese flans
Tracey:	They don't ever have a party, do they?
Mother:	- or crisps [chips] . it's a luxury to them
Gary:	Yeh . we can help
Mother:	They haven't got the money
Gary:	It's not their mummy and father
Mother:	It's just a poor country, and that's it
Gary:	Mm
Tracey:	Just a poor family .. we're not a poor family . we're a very lucky family
Gary:	Yes, 'cos we- we got enough food . we know what it tastes like, don't we?
Mother:	Yeh . well, eat it, then, don't waste it

This is a difficult idea for a five-year-old to grasp, but Gary's questions and suggestions indicate that, although he doesn't fully understand, he is entering into the starving children's predicament and is trying to think of ways to help them. Tracey is quicker to see the implication for herself: 'I've got to eat it, so it's not wasted'.

In the next sample, there is not much talk. Gary is eating sweets after dinner, and his speech is not very distinct. In the final sample, he is playing with the dog, putting tissues on its head.

Gary:	Tracey, look!
Tracey:	That's funny
Gary:	He can't see that
Tracey:	If Daddy was here, he wouldn't do that
Mother:	I'll get that stick in a minute

Gary persists, however, and Mother gets really cross with him.

Mother:	You stop bloody tormenting that dog! you horrible thing, you are
Gary:	[crying] Oh, Mummy
Mother:	You'll get something you don't want in a minute
Gary:	[cries]
Mother:	Come here [holding him] how would you like me to do that to you? You wouldn't like it, would you? [Gary does not answer] would you? well, neither does the dog

These are only short samples taken at intervals from a complete morning, but there is good reason to believe that they are representative of Gary's experience of language at home. In six out of the eight samples, he engages in talk with his mother or sister about some matter that is of significance to him and, in two of the eight, the topic is treated at some depth. The last sample ends in a scolding, but here, too, the mother tries to get Gary to understand why his behaviour is unacceptable. At home, then, Gary is appreciated for what he knows and can do, and he is helped to think about the implications of his behaviour.

Let us look next at Penny. The recording cited below was made a month earlier than Gary's – in early December – and her elder brothers were at school. As in Penny's earlier recordings, several adult visitors called during the course of the morning.

At 9:10 am, her parents are talking to a friend, and Penny is playing with the dog and singing. At the end of the sample, she remembers she has to feed the fish.

At 9:36 she is writing and talking to herself as she writes:

Penny:	*[to self]* Monday, Tuesday, Wednesday, * *[singing to self]* when you've got a freezer- Jane said she'd be up with the writing pad *[to Mother]* Mum, Jane said she'd be up with the writing pad
Mother:	That'll be dinnertime she'll come
Penny:	Oh
Mother:	Where's all your writing pads?
Penny:	I haven't got none
Mother:	In Paul's room . here, you can put those in here for now
Penny:	It's going to be like keeper . all right? 'finders keepers'
Father:	'Finders keepers, losers weepers' . that doesn't always go, my girl

Penny continues to write and sing. A few minutes later:

Penny:	*[writing]* I wants to do A first . what's that for? A .. for .. apple .. a round and a little B for . balloon
Mother:	For ball

At that moment, the tape recorder switched off.

At 10:02, Penny is watching her mother do the washing. The (top-loading) washing machine is operating.

Penny:	It ain't hot- look . the froth ain't
Mother:	*[referring to the water in the machine]* It is hot
Penny:	The froth ain't
Mother:	No, not the froth
Penny:	It's not froth, it's suds
Mother:	It's suds, it is

Penny:	*[sings]* Roundy roundy roundy roundy . still it goes . *[she puts her hand in the machine]* Ma, it ain't hurting me . look
Mother:	No, it's not going, that's why
Penny:	*[thinking Mother is going to start the machine]* Ah, you dare!

[Half a minute later]

Mother:	Will you do me a favour?
Penny:	Yes
Mother:	Go upstairs and take the sheets off Paul's bed
Penny:	All right . . . *[she goes upstairs]* and bring them down?

Clearly, Penny still likes to help, and her competence is appreciated.

During the next four samples, from 10.28 until nearly noon, Penny is engaged in making Christmas cards. At various points, both her mother and her father join in. The following extract is taken from the third of these samples.

Penny:	*[to self, quietly]* I must stick that . **** . there's a little bit
Mother:	No more . you don't have no glue left
Penny:	I'm just pressing it down . that's baby Lord Jesus . Ma, shall I make a photo? . baby Lord Jesus
Mother:	Don't know *[she is engaged in making her own card and not giving her full attention]*
Penny:	I knows how to make 'em . just cut 'em out in a square *[to self, as she cuts]* come on and be straight .. *[singing]* Baby Lord Jesus looked down where she lay . la la la la Baby Lord Jesus, Baby Lord Jesus .. *[to Mother]* shall I have glue on there?
Mother:	On the other side *[telling her where to put the glue]*
Penny:	What is it?
Mother:	*[reading]* Best wishes for Christmas and the New Year
Penny:	Can I do that?
Mother:	Put that one on its top first
Penny:	Oh! I drawed it . whoops!
Mother:	Don't squeeze it no more
Penny:	Whoops! . right
Mother:	No, no, no, no!
Penny:	I know how it goes now
Mother:	Look, you've got a load on there
Penny:	Enough like that?
Mother:	Yes, you're just spreading it over, not, er . squeezing the jar
Penny:	It's not a jar!

Mother:	Well, the bottle
Penny:	Bottle
Mother:	That's it . bottle
Penny:	It's not plastic
Mother:	It is a plastic one
Penny:	Hang on a minute
Mother:	Yeh
Penny:	No, on there
Mother:	No . you've only got to have it thin, Penny
Penny:	Mum, there's a photo
Mother:	It's upside down
Penny:	It's not
Mother:	Look, some stars
Penny:	Can I have four?
Mother:	Flatten it down
Penny:	I've done Happy Christmas there . in here, look
Mother:	Let's see . oh, yes
Penny:	I've got to stick the stars .. where's the stars?
Mother:	In the- in the window in er- your room, I think
Penny:	In my room or in Vince's?
Mother:	Yours or Vince's
Penny:	Try Paul's first . *[whispers to self]* it must be our Paul's room *[she goes upstairs]*

The above represents over an hour of sustained effort, and it was obviously productive. If some of the talk is difficult to follow, this is because it is fully embedded in the context of the joint activity. When both speaker and hearer are working together on the same task, there is no need to be more explicit.

In the final sample, Penny has been locked in the house by a visiting family friend. All treat it as a great joke and there is much shouting and joking. 'Oi! I want a word with you!' she shouts, laughing, at the culprit.

Penny's morning was a happy and interesting one, during which she spent almost half the time single-mindedly on one activity. Like Gary, she enjoyed sustained interaction with her parents, talking about the activities in which she and they were engaged, and benefiting from her parents' support and assistance. In neither case is there the slightest sign of the 'verbal deprivation' that is so often assumed to be characteristic of lower-SES homes.

Some weeks later, we recorded both of them in their classrooms. Both had settled in without difficulty and were actively participating in the activities that their teachers provided for them. Let us look first at Gary who, as we saw, had already been attending a nursery school.

At 9:15, having finished marking the register, Gary's teacher was settling the children into groups for their first activity of the day. In his case, this was picture-matching Bingo, with cards depicting characters from a Dick Bruna story about a circus. At this point, however, Gary was more interested in a friend's model car.

Gary:	Can I have that car?
Darren:	No
Gary:	Can I have a look at it . just have a look at it?
Darren:	***
Gary:	I just want to have a look at it
Darren:	I'll show you
Gary:	All right . is it just that that opens up? *[referring to part of the car]*
Darren:	Look . see that? . that's the engine . and that is broken now
Gary:	It's only cheap are you allowed to keep it?

Darren does not reply to this disparaging comment and they go on to talk about the microphone that Gary is wearing. Meanwhile, the teacher is distributing the picture cards for the game.

Teacher:	Right, then . how many carrots have we got, Nicola? . how many?
Nicola:	Two
Teacher:	*[handing the cards to Nicola]* Have you got them? . ah! here's a little girl with a pretty ribbon in her hair .. anyone got this one?
Gary:	No
Teacher:	What colour's the ribbon in her hair?
Gary:	*[to friend]* She's not seen that one
Teacher:	And we've got a little chicken
Anne:	I've got that
Teacher:	*[giving her the card]* What colour is it, Anne? *[Anne does not reply]*
Gary:	*[pointing to another child's card]* Hey! there's a chicken . and there's the same chicken
Teacher:	Where?
Gary:	You've got a chicken like that one
Teacher:	But my chicken's coming out of an egg . that one isn't, is it? Now, who's got the little bunny rabbits?
Gary:	No, not us

Child:	Not us
Teacher:	Who's got the clown? *[Gary raises his hand to claim the card]* *[to Gary]* what's he doing?
Gary:	He's- he's lifting up his hand *[raising hands to illustrate. Teacher gives Gary the card to put on his board]*

The game continues in this way for another 15 minutes, with Gary becoming more and more eager for Darren and himself to complete their card and win the game. Two of the girls win, however, and at 9:35, the teacher tells the children to go and drink their milk. Gary and his friend have some difficulty getting their straws into the bottles and, in the process, the milk spills all over Gary.

Gary:	That's naughty
Darren:	There's a towel
Gary:	*[wiping his face on the towel]* Go wipe the floor with it
Darren:	Ugh! you've got some on your face
Gary:	Is it? *[wipes his face for half a minute]* It's off
Darren:	Anyway, I've got a packet of crisps in my drawer
Gary:	I got a packet of biscuits . me and my sister got a packet of biscuits
	[calls to observer] You've seen my sister, didn't you? . her name's Tracey
	[to Darren] You don't know which- when they phones up the police it's 999

After they have had their milk, the teacher tells them to fetch their writing books and pencils and get ready to write a story. But before they start, she reads them the story of a circus, which contains the pictures that they have just been matching. As the teacher reads, Gary keeps shouting out, 'We had that!', meaning that he and Darren had had that picture during the game. When it comes to the clown, he is so excited that he repeats, 'That was on mine', several times but, for whatever reason, the teacher ignores him and continues with the story. He obviously enjoys the story and relates it to a previous family visit to a circus, but this is not picked up by the teacher.

At 9:50, Gary is drawing pictures of circus animals but is more interested in chatting with Darren. When he has finished, his picture is discussed by the teacher in a rather perfunctory manner and he quickly completes his writing, though his copying of the teacher's caption is done very neatly with well-formed letters. When he shows his work to the teacher, she asks him to write one part again and, that completed, he is told to choose what he would like to do. For a few minutes, he plays with the stickle bricks and then wanders around the room to see what is going on in other groups. He joins in several of them briefly but does not settle on anything.

At 10:25, it was time to get his coat on to go out to play. While they waited in the line, the teacher distributed apples to those who had paid for them. Gary did not get an apple, as he had brought biscuits from home. After the play period, Gary went to the cloakroom to take his coat off. He notices his friend's clothes.

Gary:	Likes your brand new trouser suit jumper . that's nice . and the shirt . I got one of they shirts
Friend:	Can I see it?
Gary:	No, I haven't got it on . it's at home . this is my vest . I'm wearing my vest

At this point, the teacher comes to investigate.

Teacher:	*[to Gary]* Come and line up . can I have the boys in a straight line, please?

Organizing the line takes several minutes, during which Gary continues to chat with his friends. Finally, the children go into the school hall for the school assembly.

By the time of the next sample, at 11:10, the children are back in the classroom and Gary has gone to join the teaching assistant, who is supervising modelling in clay. Gary spends the next half hour working in this group. The following extract comes from the beginning of the session, after Gary and the others have put on aprons.

Assistant:	What are you going to make?
Gary:	*[referring to models that other children have made]* I can't make things on there
Assistant:	I'll help you . *[giving Gary a ball of clay]* you make that into a nice- nice, smooth ball . you feel it
Gary:	*[rolling clay on table]* Ugh! It's a bit soft
Assistant:	*[to the group]* Look *[showing models that other children have made]* Here's a hedgehog . and there's another one
Gary:	*[to Assistant]* I want a hedgehog . would you make a he- help me to make a hedgehog?
Assistant:	You make the ball and then I'll help you *[Gary does so]*
Gary:	I'm a- made it

Assistant: I- don't think you need paint brushes to do the clay, really
Gary: *[rolling ball on table]* I made it into a ball
Some minutes later, Gary is making an owl, using a pencil to draw the face.
He shows it to the Assistant
Gary: I done another owl
Assistant: Did you do that?
Gary: Yeh, on my own
Assistant: Oh, that's good
Gary: I knows how to do my name, I do *[he tries to write his name on the bottom of the owl but is not entirely satisfied]* Could you do my name?
Assistant: Well, I thought you were going to try
Gary: I nearly done it
Assistant: You nearly did it, didn't you?
Gary: Yeh
Assistant: You're clever at making owls, aren't you?
Gary: *[pleased to have his efforts recognized]* Yeh

The morning ends in a group activity with the teacher, counting various objects in sevens and eights. Gary seems able to carry out the task successfully, but his attention easily wanders to what other children are doing, so he doesn't always give the right answer.

Looking back over the morning, the observer wrote the following comments:

Gary is a very outgoing child, full of energy and enthusiasm. He talks a lot to the teacher, the teaching assistant, and to the other children, often in a competitive way. He is very aware of what *he* can do, what *he* possesses, etc. He seems to be well liked by the other children, although the head teacher, perhaps influenced by an episode in the nursery school, describes him as 'moody', but from 'a caring home, specially for that neighbourhood'. However, there was no sign of moodiness on this occasion. Instead, he was like a rather assertive ray of sunshine.

Gary quickly tires of an activity and looks for something more interesting to move on to. The teacher did not seem to make any effort to help him to persevere with a task and failed to engage with him on any of the occasions when he was enthusiastic about what he was doing. The absence of response was particularly noticeable when he took his completed writing for her to see. Of course, she had many other children to think about, but from Gary's point of view, although there were a number of activities organized for him to engage in, there was a lack of thematic unity, which meant that the activities were less meaningful than they might have been. The teaching assistant, on the other hand, was considerably more successful in helping Gary to complete the clay models to their joint satisfaction.

In sum, Gary has much enthusiasm and interest, but little perseverance. He needs to be encouraged to discipline his interest, but at present he is being given little help.

Penny seemed better able than Gary to harness her enthusiasm to the tasks that her teacher had organized. The day started with quite a long period in which the teacher dealt with administrative matters. This finished with her saying 'Good morning' to each child in turn. During this time, Penny sat quietly observing. Starting at 9:10, the full five-minute sample was occupied in this way. A total of 116 utterances were spoken, to which Penny contributed one: 'Good morning, Miss Evans'.

In the second sample, the teacher was reading – or, rather, retelling – a story to the whole class. This was followed by questions to check the children's understanding and recall of the main events. During this time, Penny spoke only twice, first to gain the teacher's attention and then to give her answer, which was accepted.

At 9:55, Penny was engaged on a number task, threading coloured beads on a string to match the number shown on a card.

Penny: Miss Evans, I'm winning
Teacher: I'll come and see if they're right
Penny: One, two, three, four, five, six, seven
Teacher: That's right . what's after seven?
Penny: Eight
Teacher: Eight *[shows her a card with numbers on it]* Can you find a number eight?
Penny: Can you see a eight?
Teacher: I can see one, two, three, four number eights
Penny picks up the card and starts to thread eight beads on a string. Fifteen minutes later, Penny is at the teacher's desk.
Teacher: You did that five nicely, didn't you? . how did you do your eight?
Penny: Er-
Teacher: Come on .. you go and get a pencil and we'll try the eight, shall we?

Teacher:	*[guiding Penny's hand]* Round that way and then back again . right . good girl .. let's do one with a nine, shall we? *[sending Penny away to write. Penny sings as she works]*

After playtime, the children listen to music on a record player and sing nursery rhymes. Then, at 10:30 they go into the school hall for a school assembly at which the Local Education Authority music advisor leads various activities with instruments, voices, and hand-clapping to help children focus on pitch and rhythm.

At 11:10, back in the classroom again, Penny is sent to join the teaching assistant, who has a collection of cardboard circles and cylinders prepared for the children to make a collage. The assistant is talking to the whole group.

Assistant:	Would you like to run your finger round [a section of toilet-paper roll]? What can you tell me about the round?
Penny:	*[feeling it]* Giddy
Assistant:	Your finger goes giddy . put your finger all round it . has it got any sharp corners like a square? .. put your finger round . no, it hasn't got corners like a square . it just goes all the way round, doesn't it? David, will you watch please? . scissors have got nothing to do with a round It goes all the way round, doesn't it? . what are those? *[pointing to sections from an egg container]*
Penny:	Egg box
Assistant:	Egg box . they're round, aren't they? *[demonstrating]* .. they're round that way and they're round that way. Do you know what these are?
Child:	Biscuits
Assistant:	Not biscuits, but cakes . they're out of a cake tin . they're all stuck together like that, and the cakes are all put in . they're all round . they're round that way and they're round that way, aren't they? they go all the way round

20 minutes later, having drawn and cut out circles of various sizes, they are grading the shapes by size.

Assistant:	What sort of a pattern do you think we could make? .. shall I get rid of those? *[removing those that are not immediately needed]* we don't want those, do we? we've got those, look . that's the biggest ones David, will you come and watch, please? *[crossly]* David! *[Starts to grade the shapes, as the children watch]* Those are tall

> ones, aren't they? . those are smaller . they're about the
> same, aren't they, so-and those are bigger round, aren't they,
> than that- bigger all the way round .. we want to make a
> nice pattern with all these different things . so roll your
> sleeves up ready to do some gluing

And so it continues, with Penny and the other children obediently glu-
ing and then placing the pieces where they are directed. By 11:50, the master plan is almost completed. David, who has once again wandered off, is
shouted at to 'come and stick some circles on'. Then the children wash
their hands in preparation for dinner.

At the end of Penny's morning, the observer noted that she appeared
to be confident and independent, liked by both adults and children and
able to talk freely with them. Reading through the transcript confirms
this impression – at least in part. Relative to her peers, she was indeed
confident and competent, joining in all the activities and receiving
positive feedback. In many respects, it was a useful and busy morning
for her.

Compared with her morning at home, though, was this an improvement? There was no doubt about the sense of purposefulness in the classroom. The activities themselves were carefully thought out and well
organized and, with a few exceptions, such as David, the children were
swept along by the brisk efficiency. But what opportunity was there for
the children to share in the planning of their activities or to reflect on what
they were doing in the sort of exploratory talk that we saw in both the
home recordings? Was there time and opportunity for Penny and the other
children to try out own ideas in words?

The Language of Home and School:
A Systematic Comparison

A comparison of just two children's experience of language use in the
two settings of home and school cannot be claimed to be representative,
although it does give a flavour of what we observed. To gain a more
systematic impression, therefore, we need to look at the results of a
quantitative analysis, based on the various assessments of the children as
well as on the transcribed recordings.

It will be recalled that one of the reasons for extending the original study
beyond the age of five was to find out just how much the language demands
of the classroom were different from those at home. For example, it has
been suggested that some children would not have been used at home to

hearing indirect forms of request, such as 'I think it would be a good idea if you didn't use that bottle as a hammer' or 'Who's not put away their crayons yet?' and would therefore have difficulty recognizing them as commands. Or, for similar reasons, they would not know how to answer a 'display' question appropriately – for example, 'Can you see what's in this picture?' or, following the reading of a story, 'What sort of elephant was Elmer?' It has also been suggested that the nonstandard dialect spoken by some children might impede successful communication at school.

The parallel recordings made it possible to attempt an answer to these questions, by comparing the forms and functions of utterances addressed to and produced by individual children in each of the two settings. Although the task of making the comparisons was itself quite time-consuming, the results can be stated quite briefly.

First, as far as dialect differences were concerned, for this sample of native speakers of English, there was no sign of teachers failing to understand children who spoke a nonstandard dialect or of the children failing to understand their teachers. Nor, when the teachers were asked to rate the children with respect to dialect, was there a relationship between their general level of attainment at the age of seven years and the extent to which their teachers had rated their dialect at age five as diverging from Standard English.

However, when their dialect use at age seven was compared with their concurrent level of attainment, a significant correlation *was* found. Interpretation of these apparently contradictory findings is not straightforward and must therefore be extremely tentative. At neither age did nonstandardness of dialect or accent cause a problem for teacher–pupil communication, so it is unlikely that it was in any direct manner a cause of the later associated lower attainment. It seems, therefore, that, rather than nonstandardness of dialect and accent being a source of difficulty that results from a child having learned in the preschool years a dialect that impedes successful communication at school, it is, instead, a mark of group identity that is adopted or exaggerated after entering school, perhaps in response to a growing perception of low attainment. Although this is different from Labov's (1970) account, it is not altogether incompatible with it.

With indirect requests, too, there did not appear to be a problem. In the first place, all the children had received commands addressed to them that were to varying degrees indirect and, indeed, they were making indirect requests themselves, both at home and in the classroom. Of the children's requests, 67.9% were indirect at home and 83.2% in the classroom. Furthermore, even if in some of their commands teachers used modes of indirectness that were not familiar, all the children were quite familiar, and had been for several years, with the general conversational principle that if an utterance refers to an action that you are or are not performing and there is reason to believe that the speaker would like you to perform or not to perform it, you should interpret the utterance as a request to do so or not to do so. If on occasion, therefore, a child did not respond to an indirect request in what the teacher considered an appropriate manner, the explanation was more likely to be that the child did not recognize the utterance as applying to him or her or did not see it as an appropriate action to perform in the context, rather than the form of the utterance itself being a problem.

The same was true of display questions: neither the form nor the function was unfamiliar to any of the children. All of them had taken part in rounds of the naming game when they were very young:

Adult: What's that?
Child: Pussy
Adult: That's right *[and so forth]*

If they had difficulty with particular display questions, therefore, the difficulty was in identifying what frame of reference to use in searching for an appropriate answer rather than in the recognition of the function of the utterance itself.

In general, therefore, it did not seem to be the case that the children differed in their ability to recognize the major categories of function or form that were regularly used in the classroom. There is no doubt that, for all children, there was a change in the relative frequency with which certain functional types of utterance were addressed to them as they went from home to school, and the change was more marked for some children than for others. However, this does not seem to be the explanation for the apparent incompetence of quite a number of children on entry to school.

This conclusion may seem to be at odds with reports of other research, particularly in the United States (Cazden, 1988; Mehan, 1979); but there have been few direct comparisons between recordings of naturally occurring interaction obtained in the two settings. Where such comparisons have been made, as, for example, in the study by Tizard and Hughes (1984), similar results have been obtained. A further possible reason for the discrepancy in results is that the American work has frequently investigated situations in which there is a major ethnic and cultural discontinuity between the school and the community that it serves (Philips, 1972).

This was not the case for any of the schools or social groups in the present study. It is not being claimed, however, that the overall pattern of language use was the same – or even similar – in the two settings, but rather that it was not a lack of the necessary linguistic resources that accounted for the ineptitude that some children displayed in the classroom. With Heath (1983) and others who have carried out ethnographic studies in the two settings, I agree that for all social groups, but for the less 'literacy-oriented' in particular, it is the role that language habitually plays in the construction of shared meanings that most differs between home and school. This is the problem, not the children's language resources as such (MacLure & French, 1981). Thus, in order to account for the oft-reported difficulties these children experience, we need to look at other aspects of the total conversational context.

With this aim, we selected seven of the nine five-minute samples from each child's recordings at home and at school and analysed all conversation in which an adult was involved. We looked at the contexts in which the utterances occurred, who spoke, and to whom the utterances were addressed. We classified them according to the functions they performed, the meanings they expressed and their grammatical structure. For utterances spoken by adults, we also noted how they were related to the utterances by the child that immediately preceded.

From all this analysis came a clear and consistent picture, which showed that children's experience of language in use in the classroom did differ significantly in emphasis from their experience at home. Table 5.1 shows some of the most important differences.

The fact that children speak to an adult more often at home than at school is not surprising. Quite simply, with a ratio of one adult to 30 children in the classroom, there is not the same opportunity for one-to-one conversation. In the light of this, it *is* surprising, therefore, that there is not a greater difference in the number of times the child is spoken to by an adult in the two settings. Part of the explanation is that the classroom total includes utterances addressed to the whole class or to a group, to which the child was expected to listen. However, this still represents a considerable imbalance: three teacher utterances on average for every one by the child. In the home, the distribution was much more nearly equal.

But not only do the children speak less with an adult at school. In those conversations they do have, they get fewer turns, express a narrower range of meanings, and, in general, use grammatically less complex utterances. They also ask fewer questions, make fewer requests, and initiate a much smaller proportion of conversations. Why should this be so? The answer is to be found by looking at the other side of the equation. Teachers initiate a much higher proportion of conversations than parents do and, of course, it is the initiator who chooses the topic. Furthermore, in their turns,

Table 5.1 Children's experience of language use at home and at school

Feature of language use	Home Average	School Absolute values
Number of child utterances to an adult	122.0*	45.0*
Number of adult utterances to the child	153.0	129.0
Number of child speaking turns per conversation	4.1*	2.5*
Number of different types of meaning expressed by child	15.5*	7.5*
Number of grammatical constituents per child utterance	3.1*	2.4*
Proportions (child)		
Initiates conversation	63.6%*	23.0%*
Questions	12.7%*	4.0%*
Requests	14.3%*	10.4%*
Elliptical utterances; fragments	29.4%*	49.4%*
References to nonpresent events	9.1%*	6.4%*
Proportions (adult)		
Questions	14.3%*	20.2%*
Display questions	2.1%*	14.2%*
Requests	22.5%*	34.1%*
Extends child's meaning	33.5%*	17.1%*
Develops adult's meaning	19.1%*	38.6%*

Note: Figures are averaged over 32 children in the study.
*Statistically significant differences.

teachers make a higher proportion of requests and ask a higher proportion of questions, particularly of display questions. The result is that, at school, children are reduced for a much greater part of the time to the more passive role of respondent, trying to answer the teacher's many questions and carrying out his or her requests. This is what accounts for the narrower range of meanings that they express and for the high proportion of utterances that are elliptical and fragmentary.

Most significant of all in explaining the generally reduced level of competence that children show at school is the much more dominating role that teachers play in conversation. Compared with parents, it is only half as often that they show 'uptake'[4] of the meanings offered in the children's utterances, either by extending those meanings or by inviting the children to extend them themselves. By contrast, teachers are twice as likely as parents to develop the meanings that they themselves have introduced into the conversation. Small wonder that some children have little to say or even appear to be lacking in conversational skills altogether. As repeatedly emphasized, conversation is a reciprocal activity: the more one participant dominates, the more the opportunities for the other participant to make his or her own personal contribution are reduced and constrained.

As with other researchers who have compared the language experiences of younger children at home and in the nursery or preschool play group, what we have found is that, compared with homes, schools are not providing an environment that fosters language development. For *no* child was the language experience of the classroom richer than that of the home – not even for those believed to be 'linguistically deprived'. The most similar research is the study by Barbara Tizard and colleagues (Tizard & Hughes, 1984), who observed 30 girls, half middle-class and half working-class, in their nursery classes in the morning and in their homes in the afternoon. Their results corroborate the Bristol findings, almost point for point, as can be seen from the following quotation:

> The most striking finding in the present analysis was that, for the majority of variables considered, home-school differences were very large and social class differences at home small or absent. That is, at home, conversations were more frequent, longer and more equally balanced between adult and child; further, children of both social classes asked questions at home much more frequently than they did at school, and answered adults more often. (Tizard *et al.*, 1980: 68)

A very similar picture emerged from another study of the language used in preschool play groups and nursery classes, carried out by David Wood and colleagues (Wood *et al.*, 1980). They also noted the generally passive interactional role assigned to children and the frequency of terse, even monosyllabic replies to adult questions. 'Indeed', they comment, 'the tendency to ignore children, talk over them, and generally dominate the proceedings, was the single most striking feature of the recordings that our 24 practitioners responded to when they read their own transcripts' (Wood *et al.*, 1980: 65).

This point can be made most forcibly by looking at some further examples. Here is Lee at school. He has found a horse chestnut and brings it to his teacher to show her.

Lee:	I want to show you! . isn't it big?
Teacher:	It is big, isn't it? . what is it?
Lee:	A conker
Teacher:	Yes
Lee:	Then that'll need opening up
Teacher:	It needs opening up . what does it need opening up for?
Lee:	'Cos the seed's inside
Teacher:	Yes, very good . what will the seed grow into?
Lee:	A conker
Teacher:	No, it won't grow into a conker . it'll grow into a sort of tree, won't it? . can you remember the-
Lee:	Horse chestnut
Teacher:	Horse chestnut . good . put your conker on the nature table, then

In many ways, the teacher's intention here is praiseworthy – to help Lee extend his interest more reflectively, to make the connection between the conker and the tree that it came from and will grow into. But what a price has to be paid. Lee's topic is hijacked by the teacher as she imposes her perspective as the basis for her questions – questions to which she, of course, already knows the answers. Under the constraints that she thus imposes, Lee's utterances decrease in length and complexity; from offering information about what he is planning to do with the conker, he is reduced to providing a simple labelling response to a question on a topic that he hadn't wanted to talk about at all.

The objection to this and to many other similar conversations that start with something in which the child is interested is not that teachers try to extend children's knowledge, but that they try so hard to do so that they never really discover what it is about the child's experience that he or she finds sufficiently interesting to want to share in the first place. Thus are children's enthusiasms dampened and their impulses to question and explore suppressed.

The problem is one that we have encountered before. Meaning making in conversation should be a collaborative activity. But where there is a considerable disparity between the participants in their mental models and their linguistic resources, the more mature participant has to make adjustments in order to make collaboration possible. Unfortunately, teachers often forget how different from the child's is their own model of the world, after nearly 20 years of education. Their goal is, rightly, that children should come to see the world from a similarly mature perspective but, in the way that they engage in conversation, they fail to recognize that their perspective cannot be transmitted directly but must be constructed by children for themselves, through a process of building on what they already know and gradually elaborating the framework within which they know it.

Nowhere was this lack of reciprocity so apparent as in some of the situations we observed in which the teacher talked with the whole class following the reading of a story or when introducing or reviewing a topic. Such 'discussions' form an integral part of almost every infant class's day, being seen as a means of fostering a sense of group identity and an opportunity to create shared experiences. In addition, many teachers see such discussions as being particularly important in extending children's thinking and in developing their ability to express their thoughts in language. However, in practice, quite other lessons may be what children actually learn.

In the following example, Stella's class of five- to seven-year-olds were engaged in a discussion about a visit they had made a few days previously to Berkeley Castle. They had seen many interesting things, including suits of armour, several pieces of antique furniture and the dungeon in which Edward II met a very unpleasant end. However, they were not invited to talk about what they had found most interesting. Instead, as the topic for discussion, the teacher had decided to focus on a four-poster bed that they had seen, and she had assembled a number of illustrated books on the subject. Her intention was to prompt the children to think about why such a bed was needed in olden-day castles. In reading the text of the discussion, it is worth thinking about what the children might have been learning, both about the need for four-poster beds and about strategies for learning.

Teacher:	*[holding up a picture of a four-poster bed]* Can anyone tell me why the bed's called a four-poster?
Child:	*[putting hand up and answering immediately]* Because it's cold
Teacher:	Put up- wait a minute . put your hand up and I'll ask you . Stephen?
Stephen:	Because it's got four posts
Teacher:	Four po- **why** has it got four posts? . can anyone- put your hand up if you want to say .. **why** has it got four posts? I want the little ones to try and think

[Several children put their hands up]

Teacher:	Why has it got four posts? . where's Sean?
Sean:	Here *[Sean has not got his hand up]*
Teacher:	Why has it got four- why has it got the four posts, do you think?
	[to Sean] can you think? .. *[to whole class]* think hard inside your heads everybody and-
Child 2:	I know . because it-
Teacher:	Wait a minute . wait a minute . wait a minute
Child 3:	I know
Teacher:	I want the little ones to try and answer . try and think hard .. Linda, can **you** think why it's got four posts? *[Linda stares, then shakes her head]* think hard inside your head . can you, Stella? *[Stella shakes her head]* think . can you, Karen? *[shows Karen the picture of the bed]*
Karen:	Um-
Child 4:	I know
Teacher:	All right . I know the **big** ones probably know . let's see if the little ones have got an answer first
Child:	Angela's got her hand up *[Angela is one of the 'little ones'.]*
Teacher:	Well, I know Angela has . but- we'll ask Angela if nobody else can say . why it had four posts
	[looking at Stephen] Have you got any ideas why it might have four posts? *[Stephen shakes his head]* Let's come back to Angela, then *[holds book up front of Angela]*
Angela:	'Cause it's got curtains *[several children laugh]*
Teacher:	Yes, it's got to hold the curtains, hasn't it? . what else has it got that needs four posts? *[some children put their hands up; she selects one]* Paula?
Paula:	To hold it *[pointing to roof of bed in picture]*
Teacher:	Yes, it's got a- a sort of roof- flat roof to it, hasn't it?
	Now, let's think why the bed-might have a roof on it . do you have a roof on your bed?
Children:	*[scornfully, with laughter]* No
Teacher:	I wonder why
Child:	I dunno
Teacher:	I wonder why some of these four-poster beds had roofs on top of them- why they would need a roof
Ian:	I got a bunk bed
Teacher:	Can the little ones think? . can you think why they might have needed a roof on their bed?
Ian:	I got a bunk bed

Teacher:	You've got a bunk- well, you have got a roof on yours then, haven't you? . are you on the top bunk or the lower bunk?
Ian:	No, I'm on the bottom
Teacher:	Well then you've got a roof, haven't you?
Children:	*[variously]* I'm on the top . I'm on the bottom
Teacher:	Neville . why- why do you think they might need a roof on top of their bed?
Neville:	Because there wasn't any fires in those days
Teacher:	In- where wasn't there any fires?
Neville:	In the country *[some children laugh]*
Teacher:	Yes, but-
Child:	There wasn't any matches
Neville:	* cold, and they need um- wood
Teacher:	Well, they might have had wood to make a fire, mightn't they?
Child:	They had no matches
Teacher:	As a matter of fact, I think they did have- um- fires in this castle- some beautiful fireplaces *[holding up a picture of one of the castle rooms and pointing]* there's one there .
Children:	*[in chorus]* Oh
Teacher:	*[pointing to another picture]* And there's one- there
Angela:	Yes, and one in the cooking room
Teacher:	Was there one in the bedroom?
Angela:	No . I don't expect there was
Teacher:	Well, there may have been . there were sometimes .. you can't see one there . but then you can't see the whole room, can you?
Angela:	No
Teacher:	But they did have fireplaces . and they did have large pieces of wood on the fire to keep them warm .. so why do you think they needed a roof on their bed? Joanna?
Joanna:	So when they went to sleep they wouldn't get cold on top of their- um-faces *[children laugh]*
Teacher:	*[rather surprised]* That's right. yes, that's quite right .. um- can you think of the castle? . close your eyes and think of what the castle was like *[short silence; some children shut their eyes]* was it the same as your house?
Children:	No
Teacher:	In what way were the rooms different from your house? David?

David:	'Cos they had no central heating
Teacher:	No . but when I was a little girl I didn't have central heating and I didn't have a roof on my bed either
Child:	I did
Children:	***
Child:	There's a nice * through there
Teacher:	Is there? . um- well . you're nearly there . you're nearly there
	What were the rooms like? . what were- what do you have on your walls?
Child:	Wallpaper
Teacher:	Wallpaper or . plaster, don't you? .. and what do they have on the castle walls?
Child 1:	Paint
Child 2:	Paint
Child 3:	I have paint on- *[children laugh]*
Neville:	I have-
Teacher:	*[looking through the pictures in the book]* They have plaster on some of the castle walls
Neville:	I have pictures on my walls
Teacher:	Yes, they did have plaster, didn't they? . um- what- how about the size? how about the size of the rooms in the castle?
Angela:	They weren't very big *[children laugh]*
Child:	*[shouting]* They **were!**
Children:	They **were!**
Teacher:	They were .. what about the height? what about the height of the rooms?
Child 1:	Oh
Child 2:	Very big
Children:	They were very big
Teacher:	Not very big, very-?
Child:	Tall
Children:	Tall
Teacher:	Well, high .. I would use the word 'high' .. they were very high and they were very wide, weren't they? . they were very large rooms . and the little tiny fireplace probably didn't give enough heat . so people had a roof to their beds and they drew their curtains round them and it was like being in a little- like a little tent, yes

I have quoted this example in full because it was one of the most successful teacher-led discussions we observed; many were much less coherent. The teacher was well prepared, she sustained the children's involvement – as group members, even if not in every case as active participants – and she kept the discussion tightly focused.

But the very qualities that made it successful from the teacher's point of view are what rendered it so counterproductive from the point of view of the individual pupils in their attempts to make sense, through collaborative, exploratory talk, of what they had seen in the castle. The 'correct' answer was present in the teacher's mind from the beginning (note her remark, 'You're nearly there'); and, although several pupils provided very acceptable answers on the way, it was only when she had formulated the answer in her own words, as she indicated by her intonation and her posture at the end, that the question was satisfactorily answered.

But if not successful as a discussion, it may be argued, surely the teacher was successful in fulfilling her intention of getting the children to think about why a four-poster bed would have been needed. However, such a conclusion is only warranted if we look at the discussion from the teacher's informed perspective. Clearly this was not shared by the majority of the children. And although several of them were able, from their own experience, to make appropriate connections, there were others whose answers showed that they were not being helped at all by the teacher's questions (e.g. Ian's 'I got a bunk bed' or Neville's 'We have pictures on our walls'). And the silence of the remainder gave no indication at all as to what sense they were able to make of the whole affair.

It would seem, therefore, that if teachers wish to help young children to extend their thinking, to develop their ability to express their ideas fluently and coherently, and to listen carefully and critically to the contributions of others, they should not attempt to do so through large-group discussion. Instead, they should try to plan one-to-one or, at most, small-group situations, in which more equal interaction is possible and in which children can try out their ideas in a tentative manner, free from the constraints felt by both children and teacher in the large-group situation.[5]

But, some may argue, this emphasis on one-to-one interaction is unrealistic when there are 30 or more children in the class, all needing individual attention. In any case, they may add, although an individualized, child-focused style of teaching may, ideally, be desirable, it is not really necessary, as the majority of children make satisfactory progress without it. Although understandable, these arguments are, I believe, mistaken.

In the first place, although it is undoubtedly true that some children appear to prosper under the more traditional, whole-class instructional regime, their success is only relative, being judged by comparison with those who are less successful. What progress might they have made under more supportive conditions?

The infant school, with its carefully planned resources and curricular objectives, is a place where children are encouraged, many for the first time, to reflect on what they know and how they learn. It is here that they establish strategies and expectations for learning that will influence the rest of their careers at school, and even beyond. It is worth stopping to consider, therefore, what they may be learning about learning from the sort of teacher-dominated experiences that we have been considering. What are the messages that they receive from the conversations and discussion that they have with their teachers? Are these messages those that their teachers believe they are teaching, or are children more likely to internalize the following:

- that the only valid learning is that which takes place when children are engaged in teacher-prescribed tasks;
- that personal experience, particularly that gained outside the classroom, is unlikely to be relevant for learning at school;
- that taking the initiative is unwise, as thinking things out for oneself frequently leads to unacceptable answers; it is better to play safe – to follow only the steps laid down by the teacher.

Following such precepts may be successful in the short term, leading to satisfactory scores on tests and to the ability to reproduce pre-packaged answers to preformulated problems. But they do not lead to the ultimate goals that define a worthwhile education. Both from the individual's and from society's point of view, *our aim should rather be to help children to become creative thinkers, confident in their ability to recognize problems and find ways of solving them, either alone or in collaboration with other people.*

Rosie: A Learning-Disabled Child?

If the more confident children are restricted by the style of teacher–pupil interaction that was so typical of the classrooms we observed, what must be the effect on the less confident and less able? What sense do they manage to make of this sort of classroom talk? The second argument against accepting the continuation of this style of interaction, therefore, is the positive harm that it can do to a minority of children. To gain more insight into their plight, let us look at the experience of Rosie as she made the transition from home to school.

Rosie, whom we first met in Chapter 1, is in many ways representative of a substantial minority in our schools – children from poor inner-city areas whose lives are impoverished, both materially and intellectually. Rosie is the last child in a family of five. Her father has been unemployed since she was born, and her mother has not worked since the birth of her eldest child. The terraced house they lived in (they have since been rehoused in one of the city's large housing developments) was dilapidated in the extreme; plaster was falling off the walls and the house was inade-quately furnished and overcrowded, with seven people in three small bedrooms. All this does not mean that Rosie was not loved, of course. On the contrary, her mother, a large ebullient woman, gave Rosie plenty of physical affection, and she got on well with her elder brother and sisters. Indeed, she was particularly close to her one-year-older sister, Donna; at school they were practically inseparable.

By comparison with the other children we studied, however, Rosie was a slow developer, both socially and linguistically. She was, in fact, the lowest-scoring child on almost all the developmental measures we used. Nevertheless, at the point of entry to school (at age five), she was very far from being nonverbal, as the following extract demonstrates.

Mother is doing the housework, and Rosie is eager to help

Mother: I've got to do the front room now, Rosie
Rosie: Can I do the front room? can I? [*she goes off into the front room with the carpet sweeper, whispering to herself*] I taking this in here to surprise Daddy . surprise Daddy

After about a minute she returns.

Rosie: Mum . Mum, I've picked it all up there
Mother: Have you?
Rosie: Yes
Mother: There's a good girl
Rosie: All- there ain't no bits in there
Mother: We got to make the beds later on
Rosie: Uh?
Mother: Make the beds
Rosie: Come on, then
Mother: Not yet
Rosie: What, in a minute?

Mother:	Yeh, in a minute
Rosie:	What- what time clock have we got to do it?
Mother:	I don't know- I'll see how- we got to wash up first What's the time by the clock?
Rosie:	Uh?
Mother:	What's the time? *[points to position of hands on clock]* yeh, what number's that?
Rosie:	Number two
Mother:	No it's not . what is it? .. it's a one and a nought
Rosie:	Nought . one and a nought
Mother:	Yeh . what's one and a nought? what is it?
Rosie:	There's one
Mother:	Yeh, what is it?
Rosie:	One- one and a nought
Mother:	What's one and a nought?
Rosie:	Um- that
Mother:	A ten
Rosie:	Ten
Mother:	Ten to ten
Rosie:	Ten to ten .. well, shall we wash them because they're not clean enough? *[referring to the face and hands of the clock]*

[Mother shakes her head in disagreement]

Rosie:	They're not . inside he ain't
Mother:	Well, you can't wash them inside, he'd break
Rosie:	Would he?
Mother:	Mm
Rosie:	And if- if we wash in- inside, would- would- wouldn't- would- would that thing won't go round? . on the numbers?

This is certainly not what we would consider to be an ideal conversational experience, but it demonstrates that Rosie is a reasonably competent user of English. She may not be able to tell the time, and her mother's method of teaching her may not be very effective, but there is no doubt that Rosie understands the function of her mother's display question and that she can negotiate quite complex ideas through equally complex language: 'Shall we wash them because they're not clean enough?' 'If we wash inside, ... wouldn't that thing go round?' This latter idea, in particular, with its negative consequences of a possible but not-to-be-performed action, is at least as complex as anything that a child said in the recordings that we made at school.

A few weeks after this recording, Rosie started school. Although she had been attending a nursery class, this was her first experience of formal schooling. She was placed in the same vertically grouped class as her sister and some 40 other children housed in a purpose-built cooperative unit (a unit containing one large classroom with a number of smaller adjoining workrooms) in the charge of two teachers. The following extract is taken from our observation of her when she was working in the largest of the adjoining rooms, making a calendar from one of the previous year's Christmas cards. The picture on the card showed Father Christmas skiing down a snowy mountainside. While Rosie worked, one of the teachers (Teacher A) tried to engage her in talk about this picture, although, initially, her attention was somewhat distracted by another child, who had already finished her calendar.

Child: Miss, I done it
Teacher: *[to Rosie]* Will you put it at the top?
Child: Miss, I done it, look
[Several seconds pause]
Teacher: *[to Rosie, pointing with finger at card]* What are those things?
Child: Miss, I done it . Miss, I done it
[Rosie drops something, then picks it up]
Teacher: *[to Rosie]* What are those things?
Child: Miss, I done it
Teacher: *[referring to skis in picture]* D'you know what they're called?
Rosie: *[shakes her head without speaking]*
Teacher: What d'you think he uses them for?
Rosie: *[looks at the card but does not answer]*
Teacher: *[turning to the other child]* It's very nice . after play, we'll put some ribbons at the top
Child: What?
Teacher: Ribbon at the top to hang them up by .. would you put all the cards together now? . put the cards together
Child: Oh
Teacher: *[to Rosie, pointing at the skis on the card]* What's- what are those?
Rosie: *[looks blank and does not answer]*
Teacher: What d'you think he uses them for?
Rosie: *[rubbing one eye with the back of her hand]* Go down
Teacher: Go down- ? yes, you're right . go on

[Rosie rubs both of her eyes with the backs of her hands]

Teacher: What's the rest of it? .. *[puts down card]* you have a little
                 think and I'll get- er- get the little calendar for you . I think
                 you're sitting on-

Teacher: Right *[points to the calendar she has picked up]* Could you put
                 some glue on the back there? *[Rosie takes the calendar from the
                 teacher]* He uses those to go down-
                 [5-second pause]
                 Is it a hill or a mountain?

Rosie: A hill

Teacher: A hill, yes . and what's on the hill?

Rosie: Ice

Teacher: Yes, ice .. they're called skis

Child: Miss-

*The teacher leaves to deal with the other children. When she returns, Rosie has
finished her calendar*

Teacher: That's lovely, and afterwards we'll put some ribbon- . what
                 d'you think the ribbon's for? *[points to calendar with her
                 pencil and looks at Rosie]*

[Six-second pause]

Rosie: For Father Christmas

Teacher: *[bending closer to Rosie, looking into her face]* Sorry?

Rosie: *[looking away from teacher]* For Father Christmas

Teacher: For Father Christmas? *[straightens slightly from bending
                 position and looks at the card, pointing at it again with her hand]*
                 if you want to put it up on the wall, you have a little piece
                 of ribbon long enough to hang it up by

The whole episode, excluding the interruption, lasted more than four
minutes. In that time, Rosie appeared to understand rather little of what the
teacher said and only produced five utterances herself, the last following a
request for clarification. None of them consisted of more than a simple phase.
With this evidence to go on, the teacher could perhaps be forgiven for thinking that Rosie was one of those 'linguistically deprived' children that were
believed to be so common in the sort of area that the school served.

When she had finally finished making her calendar and been out to
play, Rosie went to the other teacher (Teacher B) to do her reading. The
book she was reading was one of a series designed for beginning readers,
in which the sentence frame remained the same from page to page, with
only a single word changing, with the new word cued by the accompanying illustration. This book was called *I Am Tall.* As she read, the teacher

pointed to the words with a pencil. Rosie had reached the page showing a picture of a chimney.

Rosie:	I am tall said the . tower
Teacher:	Chimney *[correcting her]*
Rosie:	Chimbley
Teacher:	It's a big factory chimney, isn't it? *[pointing at picture]*
Rosie:	I don't like-
Teacher:	*[pointing at illustration with pencil]* There's a lot of smoke coming out of the top
Rosie:	I don't like that one *[pointing at picture of chimney]*
Teacher:	You don't like it? *[Rosie shakes her head]* why not?
Rosie:	I only likes little ones
Teacher:	Have you got a chimney in your house?
Rosie:	*[nods emphatically]*
Child:	And me
Teacher:	*[to Rosie]* D'you have smoke coming out of the top?
Rosie:	*[nods emphatically]*
Teacher:	Mm?

[Rosie nods her head again. The teacher turns the page, then closes the book.]

Teacher:	What's underneath the chimney, then, that makes the smoke come out?
Child:	I know, fire
Teacher:	*[to Rosie]* Mm?
Rosie:	Fire
Teacher:	Is it? Have you got a fire then?
Child:	Miss, can I have this one?
Teacher:	*[to Rosie]* Which room's the fire in? *[shifts gaze to other child]* Yes *[turns back to Rosie]*
Rosie:	In the front one
Teacher:	Is it? . so it keeps you warm? . lovely
Rosie:	And I got a bed
Teacher:	Where's your bed?
Rosie:	E's upstairs
Teacher:	Anybody else got a bed in your room?
Rosie:	*[very softly]* Carol got a bed .. and Kelvin . and Carol
Teacher:	Uh-huh . what about Donna?
Rosie:	Donna- we're sharing it
Teacher:	You're sharing with Donna, are you?
Rosie:	*[nods her head emphatically]*
Teacher:	D'you have a cuddle at night?

Rosie:	Yeh . I- when I gets up I creeps in Mummy's bed
Teacher:	For another cuddle? *[Rosie nods]* Oh that's nice! . it's nice in the morning when you cuddle

Here Rosie's use of language is strikingly different. In fact, if we had not been there to see, we might have thought it was a different child we were listening to. She was alert and vivacious, responding to the teacher's questions and volunteering information unasked. On the basis of this evidence, there was no reason to think of her as nonverbal. Yet it was the same child as the one who had, only a little earlier, appeared to be quite unable to converse.

However, since it *was* the same child in the same classroom on the same morning, the difference that we observed could not be attributed to Rosie herself. It could only be due to the different settings in which she found herself – to the different communication triangles in which the two teachers attempted to engage her.

On the face of it, one might have expected Rosie to cope more easily with the first situation. She was actively involved in the calendar-making task, and the topic in which the teacher tried to engage her was the subject of a picture she had chosen herself. In the second situation, by contrast, she was engaged in the much more abstract task of getting meaning from print – an activity that was still very new to her. But to look at the two episodes in these terms alone is to ignore the totality of the situation and, in particular, the ways in which the two teachers engaged with Rosie in relation to the different topics.

Teacher A was intent on getting Rosie to talk, and she used the picture as a prop. To her, the picture was quite straightforward, and her questions were asked to get Rosie to display her ability to describe the simple scene. To Rosie, on the other hand, the questions were not straightforward. Had it not been for the episode involving telling the time at home, we might have thought that she did not understand the function of the questions. But that seems most unlikely. More probably she did not fully understand the significance of the picture. After all, her limited experience had never involved skiing; perhaps she had not even seen skis before. In any event, she was unable to answer. The teacher, however, repeated her question, then tried an alternative, apparently oblivious to Rosie's obvious discomfort as she rubbed first one eye with the back of her hand and then both of them, backing away from the teacher. What was intended to be a friendly conversation had become an interrogation.

Teacher B's objective was initially rather different – to listen to Rosie read and to give feedback on the accuracy of her attempt to get meaning from the text and pictures. In this case, however, Rosie made a meaningful connection with her own experience and offered an affective response: 'I don't like that one'. Although this may have seemed somewhat irrelevant to the reading task, the teacher invited Rosie to tell her more and, from that point onwards, Rosie took over the leading role in the conversation, providing information about her own home – a topic on which she was undoubtedly the expert. When provided with the support of a listener who was interested in what she had to say, Rosie was no longer incompetent.[6]

The similarity of this comparison to the one made between the two mothers in Chapter 3 will probably have already been noticed. Here the difference between the strategies adopted by the two adults is even more striking, as was the effect on the child with whom they were talking. When adults are determined at all costs to develop the meaning that *they* see in the situation, there is little chance of achieving that collaboration in meaning making which is so essential for successful conversation. Also, there is little chance for the child to learn through talking. As we saw earlier, young children need to be helped to participate in conversation, and this means listening in order to discover what meaning they can contribute to the topic and then helping them to sustain and develop it. Teacher B intuitively recognized the value of the lead that Rosie gave her. Perhaps Teacher A would have been more successful if she had started by inviting Rosie to tell her why she liked the picture enough to choose it for her calendar!

To some, these arguments may seem to be urging an easygoing permissiveness – a failure to present an adequate challenge to children. How can it be justifiable to follow the leads that children offer when they are so often irrelevant? But the vital question, I would argue, is: irrelevant to whom? An instructional programme or scheme of work may be coherent and meaningful to an adult, carefully structured in terms of the logic and consistency of the topic as the adult perceives it, and yet still fail to engage with the children's understanding of the world – or at least be only partly meaningful to them. In such cases, their answers to an adult's questions may appear wrong and their questions, comments and suggestions misguided or irrelevant. Yet, unless they are deliberately trying to be awkward (and that in itself implies other unresolved problems), their contributions spring from their attempts to understand and are an indication of the way they are making connections between their existing model of the world and the information that is being presented to them (Donaldson, 1978).

From his study of young secondary school pupils, Douglas Barnes quotes the following extract from a chemistry lesson. The teacher was explaining that milk is an example of a suspension of solids in a liquid.

Teacher: You get the white what we call casein that's er protein which is good for you . it'll help to build bones and the white is mainly the casein and so it's not actually a solution. it's a suspension of very fine particles together with water and various other things which are dissolved in water

Pupil 1:   Sir, at my old school I shook my bottle of milk up and when I looked at it again all the side was covered with er. like particles and. er. could they be the white particles in the milk …?

Pupil 2:   Yes, and gradually they would sediment out, wouldn't they, to the bottom

Pupil 3:   When milk goes sour though it smells like cheese, doesn't it?

Pupil 4:   Well, it is cheese, isn't it, if you leave it long enough?

Teacher: Anyway can we get on? We'll leave a few questions for later

(Barnes, 1971: 28)

As in so many other teaching situations, the teacher was so preoccupied with the development of the topic – as he perceived it – that he failed to recognize the importance of the pupil's proffered example. It may have been wrong or irrelevant to the teacher, but the pupil believed it to be relevant, and the others were keen to take up and develop the suggestion. It was evidence of their attempt at active meaning making and, treated as such, could have formed the basis for a discussion that would not only have helped those pupils to approach the teacher's understanding of the topic, but would probably have been helpful to the other members of the class as well.

Learning: The Active Making of Meaning

Whether it be in the primary school or the secondary school, the essential principles are the same. Unless bludgeoned into an unthinking form of rote learning or forced to play the game of attempting to guess what the teacher wants to hear, children are active learners, attempting to construe what is new in terms of what they already know. In order to help them to learn, it is not sufficient – or indeed even necessarily helpful – to specify in advance the sequence their learning shall take, for that is to ignore what the learner can contribute to the task. It is to render passive what should be an active process.

However unequal the balance of knowledge between teacher and learner, there is no way in which the knowledge of the teacher can be transmitted directly to the learner. Indeed, the greater the disparity, the more inappropriate such a conception of teaching becomes. Teaching is essentially a matter of facilitating learning, and where that learning depends on communication between the teacher and the learner, the same principles apply as in any successful conversation. The aim must be the *collaborative* construction of meaning, with negotiation to ensure that meanings are mutually understood.

In early education, it is an oft-repeated slogan that one should 'start where the child is' – not where a child of a given age from a given background can be expected to be, but where each individual child – Gary, Penny, Ian, Rosie – *actually is*. And what better way of knowing where they are than by *listening* to what they have to say; by attending, in the tasks that they engage in, to the meanings that they make.

Of course, this is not the end of effective teaching; but it is an essential beginning – and not only at the beginning of the year, but in each new interaction. Only on this basis is it possible to negotiate challenges that will extend children's control and understanding on terms that are *mutually* relevant.

Notes

1. Describing the adult's contribution to such conversations, Roger Brown sees two major functions: 'It serves as a running check on the child's progress in building an apperceptive mass shared with his family-his psycholinguistic socialization as it were. At the same time, the adult tries to add a pebble to the pile.' [see 'The maintenance of conversation', in D. Olson (ed.), 1980.]
2. Donaldson (1978) refers to this more reflective thinking and use of language as 'disembedded' and links it very closely with the acquisition of literacy. Vygotsky (1987) sees the prime purpose of schooling as enabling the child to appropriate 'scientific' concepts, or what Halliday (1993) calls systematic educational knowledge, as this is expressed in written language.
3. Both families speak the local dialect, as do most of the families on the housing estates where they live.
4. For a definition of 'uptake', see Nystrand (1997).

5. This is the argument made for 'Instructional Conversation' by Dalton and Tharp (2002) in their 'Standards for Effective Pedagogy'.

6. Unfortunately, Rosie's subsequent school experiences were more akin to the episode with Teacher A than that with Teacher B. When I last met Rosie at the end of her primary schooling, I learned that she was to be transferred to a special school for learning disabled children. Perhaps, at that stage, this was an appropriate educational decision. But, in my view, with better support in the early years, such a decision would not have been necessary.

Chapter 6

Helping Children to Make Knowledge Their Own

The previous chapter, with its rather disturbing results from the comparison of children's language experiences at home and at school, may have given the impression that classrooms are uniformly unsatisfactory in the opportunities they provide for language learning and learning through language. This is certainly not the case, as will be clear from the extracts to be considered below. In these classrooms, in their different ways, the teachers have found ways of enabling their children to engage in that collaborative meaning making which, as we have seen, is the basis of the most effective learning in the preschool years at home.

However, there are classrooms in which, despite the teachers' good intentions and obvious dedication, such opportunities rarely occur. In a later section, we shall attempt to find reasons for this mismatch between intentions and achievement and consider ways in which the two can be brought more into line. First, though, let us look at some examples of more successful interaction.

The first comes from an observation of Jacqueline, one of the children in the pilot study, during her first term in school. The teacher was preparing the children to listen to a poem about Jack Frost and wanted them to think about their experiences of frost.

Teacher: When I woke up this morning- I don't know- who looked out of the window when they woke up this morning?
[Some children raise their hands]
Teacher: Only- only one, two, three- oh, four of you . now who can put their hand up and tell me what they **saw** out of the window this morning? Jackie?
Jackie: Ice

Teacher: Ice . ice . whereabouts was the ice?
[Another child answers but cannot be heard clearly]
Child: On the grass
Jackie: On the grass and- and on our car
Teacher: That's right . it's not- it's ice . but what do we call
                it? . <u>It's little</u> tiny bits of ice
Child 1:   <u>I call it</u>- I call it Jack Frost
Teacher: Frost really, isn't it? . frost *[waving her hands expressively]*
                What does it make the grass look like?
Jackie: White
Teacher: White . all white .. or was there some green as well?
Child 1:   <u>Some green</u>
Jackie: <u>White and green</u>
Teacher: White and green
Child 2:   Mine- mine was <u>all over the-</u>
Teacher: <u>The leaves were</u> white . *[to Child 2]* Yours was all over the
                grass, was it?
Child 3:   So was mine
Teacher: So was yours?
Ian: I had- I had a taste of grass
Teacher: And- *[about to continue but then deciding to extend Ian's
                contribution]* Did you? [she holds up her finger to indicate
                that the children should concentrate on Ian's contribution.]* Ian
                said he had a little taste of it *[to Ian]* Did it taste of anything?
[Ian does not answer]
Jackie: Yeh
Teacher: What did it taste of?
Jackie: Tastes cold
Teacher: Tastes cold .. who knows what ice is? *[pressing fingers of both
                hands together]* It's something that's frozen . ice is made up of
                something that's <u>frozen</u>
Child 2:   <u>Well</u>, I have that in my drink at <u>home</u>
Jackie: <u>Cold</u>
Teacher: That's right . you have it in your drink at home .. and how
                does Mummy make it?
Children: By water
Teacher: That's right! *[pressing fingers together]* ice is **water** that's frozen
                hard . that's why it wouldn't really taste of anything .. you're
                right, Jackie, it would taste-?
                [Jackie does not answer] - cold, wouldn't it? *[touching her lip]*
                cold . and you said you had it on your window, is that right?

Child:	<u>And me</u>
Teacher:	<u>What does it</u> do on the windows of the car?
Jackie:	Didn't do nothing
Teacher:	It didn't do anything
Child 4:	You couldn't see out the back window
Jackie:	No
Teacher:	You couldn't see out of the window, no
Jackie:	It's very dangerous . out of the back window you couldn't . 'cos there is a wire at the back window
Teacher:	Oh, and it makes- it heats up the back window so the frost disappears?
Jackie:	Yeh
Teacher:	Well, then . *[picking up the book]* this is a little poem about a man called Mister Jack Frost

As with the discussion of the four-poster bed in the previous chapter, the teacher here has a clear aim: to elicit the children's observations and experiences on the subject of frost and ice in preparation for the reading of the poem. But her initial question is much more open in the invitation it offers and, once Jackie's initial response has been refined in order to establish the general topic for discussion, the teacher follows up the children's suggestions in ways that recognize their validity and, at the same time, uses them to build up a clearer understanding of the relationship between water, freezing and ice. Although her repetition of the children's contributions to confirm their acceptability simultaneously emphasizes her control over the discussion and so, to some extent, belies the apparent openness of the initial question, her attitude throughout makes it clear that their out-of-school experience is relevant to the business of the classroom, and her ready acceptance gives them confidence to volunteer further suggestions.

The second example is taken from Connie and Harold Rosen's (1973) book, *The Language of Primary School Children*. The conversation took place in a class of six- and seven-year-olds in a dockland area of London. By chance a bird had built its nest under the school roof and, day by day, everyone had watched the building of the nest and the hatching of the chicks.

The discussion lasts for a considerable period of time and so cannot be quoted in full. At the point where we pick it up (p. 43), the class has already talked about the number of birds in the nest, their appearance and their feeding habits. Now the teacher attempts to direct their attention to a new matter: the siting of the nest and its relative immunity from certain kinds of danger.

Teacher:	I am going to ask you a question. Here's something for you to think about. Do you think the bird was clever to choose that place to build a nest?
Children:	*[several answering]* Yes. It was a good place, etc., etc.
Teacher:	Why is it?
Child:	Because the cats can't get at it. Because it is too edgery to go along … It's too narrow to go across, and because they've got small feet … Well, they wouldn't be able to get on … and they would just fall off
Teacher:	You don't think the cat could balance along there? And somebody said it's out of the rain, yes? What's another good reason why the bird would build a nest there?
Child:	Not a very good reason … Because Mark- He was trying to get- He had a big- He had a big cage and he was climbing up to get the bird down
Teacher:	Well, I'm afraid we've got one or two boys who've done unkind things like that, but most children have been very nice. John?
John:	Sometimes they build their nests under shelter to keep out the snow
Teacher:	They do. If they were going to build their nests in the winter time they would, wouldn't they? We haven't had any snow since that nest was built, have we? … Who else can think of a good thing about that nest? Why do you think the bird made the nest in that place? Tony?
Tony:	*In* my garden … when I came home from school … when I looked out of the window … when I looked on the ground … there was a broken egg … and when I looked up in the gutter, the mother bird was up there … and the babies was sitting up in turn … em … One of the babies was chewing a worm
Teacher:	Well. Our nest is safe from cats and safe from rain and safe from …?
Children:	*[together]* Snow
Teacher:	Snow … and safe from …?
Child:	The sun
Teacher:	The sun, yes … and …?
Child:	When I was going swimming Terry Booker was playing out in the street … and he looked in the gutter and he saw this little baby sparrow … It wasn't one of them like in the nest … It was just growing its feathers … It'd fell out of the

	nest ... and it had all green on his wing. He took it in and gave it some crumbs
Teacher:	To look after it
Child:	Mmmm
Teacher:	That was good ... Michael?
Michael:	You know, I saw the bird ... flying out of its nest.
Teacher:	You saw the bird, did you ... falling out of its nest?
Michael:	Flying!
Teacher:	Oh, good! You mean our bird downstairs?
Michael:	Mmmm
Teacher:	Yes ... Well, I expect that was the mother bird going to fetch ... Terry?
Terry:	I had this bird ... In the roof was this nest and this baby bird, he fell out of it ... And he was on this window sill ... So my daddy put it back up ... and it fell down ... And the cat had it
Teacher:	Oh ... what a shame. Another thing about this nest downstairs ... it's also safe from ...?
Children:	[*variously*] Wind. Dust. Children
Teacher:	People – children and people
Gary:	I got that
Teacher:	You did Gary ... That was very sensible because nobody can climb up there, can they?
Child:	No

Here, more than in the previous extract, the children are contributing freely from their own experience. And as they narrate those experiences to others they are, perhaps for the first time, discovering their significance for themselves. These are the conditions that foster language development: when one has something important to say, and other people are interested in hearing it. It is then that language and thinking most fully interpenetrate in the struggle to make meanings that capture what one has observed and understood and that communicate that understanding to others.

The success of the discussion above owes much to the teacher's support and guidance. Her questions help to maintain the focus of attention, but without imposing too tight a control over the direction it takes. She recognizes the relevance of the stories that the children tell for a consideration of the advantages of the site chosen for the nest and, sensitive to the affective and moral charge that their stories carry, she endorses their implicit evaluations of the events that they recount. As the Rosens comment: 'The conversation is particularly revealing in showing what happens when teacher and children have shared an experience of this kind. The teacher is not merely instructor and one who knows all the answers before they begin the conversation, but has found something new not only in what occurred but also in the children's comments on it' (Rosen & Rosen, 1973: 51).

A discussion with the whole class almost inevitably involves the majority of the children as listeners only. In the Jack Frost extract, for example, there were more than 20 children who remained silent throughout – though this does not mean, of course, that they were not participating actively as listeners. But if, as was suggested above, it is the formulation of one's thoughts and feelings in order to communicate them to others that is the strongest spur to actively seeking to understand them, then opportunities need to be found for one-to-one or at least for small-group interaction.

The third example is of just such a situation, which arose in the course of the morning's activities in a class of seven-year-olds in another London school. The class was being filmed over a number of weeks in order to provide material for a series of educational videotapes, and Colin had become so interested in the cameras that he had decided to make a model of one, which he had fashioned out of some pieces of balsa wood. He has just started to plan the construction of his tripod, and he has come to the teacher to discuss it.[1]

Teacher:	Colin, are you having a problem?
Colin:	Just trying to think .. out ... something .. just trying to think out how high I want the pole
Teacher:	*[to two girls with whom she had been talking]* Could you work there a while? I'll just help Colin *[to Colin]* How high do you need it?
Colin:	*[using a metre rule and a smaller ruler, trying to read off the height of the tripod he is planning to make]* One metre and-
Teacher:	Can you imagine for a minute that you're taking a photograph? . how- how high would be comfortable?
Colin:	Er, this- this is what I done-trying to find that out . I put this [the model camera] like that and held it and just pretend that I was looking through, and I thought I'd have it about that high 'cos that includes the camera on top and that's how-how far I want it- one metre and .. *[counting on small ruler while teacher talks to another child]* thirteen- one metre and thirteen centimetres

Teacher: Is that going to be the hei<u>ght of</u> your tripod?
Colin: <u>Yes</u> . of the pole
Teacher: Is each- is each pole going to be that height?
Colin: I'm go- I'm only going to have three . um- yes . I mean . the other two are going to be a bit longer
Teacher: Can you show me how you're going to do your plan? *[they go to Colin's table]*
Colin: I've got-
Teacher: Sit yourself down . you sit down
Colin: I've got a lump of wood-
Teacher: Pardon?
Colin: I've got some wood . and *[indicating plan]* that's what it's going to look like .. it's going to have those bits of, er- so I can put, something around it to hold the camera on, and- I'm going to try and get something that can- a round shape that could slide around inside the hole, that could hold on to . um . legs . which is going to be rather hard
Teacher: Have you looked in the camera book to see if it shows a diagram that would help you?
Colin: Er- I have looked in one <u>***</u>
Teacher: <u>Did you no</u>tice that there was another one there today?
Colin: No . . yes, there is
Teacher: Perhaps in a moment you'd like to look at that . that might be helpful
Colin: Yes
Teacher: What else will you need?
Colin: Um . yes . a sharp tool that I can make the ends of them rather sharp so they can dig in the ground- or I could have blunt ones that just stand out to keep it steady
Teacher: And how will you set your tripod up?
Colin: *[laughing]* It's going to always be set up .. just all I'm going to have to do is just take it outside or something . like that
Teacher: How do you think that's going to improve your photography?
Colin: It's going to keep it much stiller and the pictures- the pictures will be much better 'cos they won't go blurry through movement

With the teacher as listener and occasional prompter, Colin is helped here to think through the requirements of the task he has set himself, using language to consider alternative courses of action and to evaluate their consequences before he actually undertakes the activity. This example also shows how, in order to carry out his task more effectively, he is led quite naturally to consult reference books and to represent his proposed solution in another symbolic form – that of the plan he is drawing.

At this point it is interesting to recall the four principles that were suggested in Chapter 3 for helping children to learn through participation in conversation. Colin's teacher illustrates how each one of them applies equally validly to conversation in a deliberately educational context:

- She takes Colin's perceived problem seriously.
- She listens carefully to make sure that she understands his intentions.
- Her questions and suggestions are based on *his* intentions and are designed to help him to extend his thinking about them.
- Although they are quite challenging, these questions and suggestions are couched in terms that Colin is able to understand – as he shows by his full and informative responses.

Having helped Colin to resolve his problem and suggested that he might look at the other reference book (a suggestion that he takes up), the teacher leaves him to work with his friend, Alan, while she attends to the needs of other children.

Later in the day, she returns to see how they have been getting on.

Teacher: All right . how've you got on since I was here?
Colin: We wrote about it . I'm doing stages and we've done two stages
Alan: We've got to use another page
Teacher: What do you mean, 'stages'?
Colin: We've got to do one bit and then another bit . like a two-stage rocket-like a rocket . it's got stages . it doesn't just have one great big lump . when it-say- when it's used one bit it lets it go-
Teacher: *[pointing to diagram]* What kind of stages are they, though?
Colin: Stages of, oh- things you've got to do
Teacher: I see . and you're going to do your stages, are you?
Colin: Yeh
Teacher: Would you like to tell me how it [the tripod] is going to work with your camera?
[Turning to Alan] Have you seen his model? *[Alan nods]*
[to Colin] You show us
Alan: It turns round- that thing
Colin: It goes- I'm going to lay this on the top of my tripod-
Teacher: Yes

Colin:	- which will keep it steady . near the edge so I can go like that *[demonstrating]* . and then that'll practically be it
Alan:	He should draw a sort of square on there, so that- you know- they'll think it's-
Colin:	I'm going to cut that out
Teacher:	What would that be for then, Alan?
Alan:	The- the thing to look through
Colin:	Viewfinder
Teacher:	*[to Alan]* Did you do that on your clay one? . would you like to show me?
Alan:	I didn't cut it out . I only done the lines
Teacher:	*[to Colin]* Look at that . it's nice, isn't it? have you seen his model?
Colin:	Yeh
Alan:	*[pointing to his model]* The clicker's coming off
Colin:	He could always make another one- out of plasticene [a modeling material] or something . can I make another model of mine, a camera model out of plasticene, maybe?
Teacher:	That would be nice .. would you like first of all to show me the front of yours? . explain to me what you've been doing
Colin:	Here I've got the dials . the other picture dials are coming off . I've got to try and get those
Teacher:	They're not very clear, are they?
Colin:	No
Teacher:	Can you explain to me what they are?
Alan:	They're the weather things and the numbers on the thing-
Colin:	I've forgotten now, but I'm going to do much better, after-
Alan:	Yes . he can draw a picture of- round-
Teacher:	Do you remember in your seed diagram you drew little sketches?
Colin:	Umm
Teacher:	Could that be helpful when you're drawing on your dial?
Colin:	I could always take this off and turn it inside out . look, I didn't glue it on or anything . but it can come off
Teacher:	I should think you'll think of a way of doing that clearer, won't you?
Colin:	Yes
Teacher:	Well, if you look at the real camera and look at the sorts of pictures they've got on that-
Colin:	That's- I copied from it

Teacher:	Did you?
Colin:	Yeh
Alan:	Yeh, they've got clouds, dark clouds and light-
Colin:	It's got hazy, thunder and seaside . guess what the difference between seaside and just a normal bright sun is .. because seaside you get the water reflecting up light so it's got its own dial, and you put it on seaside whenever you're taking a picture near water
Teacher:	Do you think there's anywhere near here that we might need to put it on the seaside dial?
Colin:	*[pointing]* The pond up there
Teacher:	Do you think there would be enough light reflected off it to have that effect?
Colin:	I think there might
Alan:	Yeah, if he was in the shade
Colin:	And if you want sun and half misty sun, you put it in between the dials . and that gets it
Teacher:	You do?
Colin:	Yeh

Here the emphasis is on what has been done: reporting, explaining and evaluating. As before, language provides the means for reflecting on action – not only actions that have been performed, but also those that might be performed, such as taking a photograph by the nearby pond. In this way, Colin is helped to establish connections between different aspects of his experience, using the power of language as a system of symbols to represent objects and events that are absent or no more than hypothetical possibilities.

Language always has this potential, of course, but most of the time we don't exploit it. As Edward Sapir, the American linguist and anthropologist, put it when making exactly this point, 'It is somewhat as though a dynamo capable of generating enough power to run an elevator were operated almost exclusively to operate an electric door-bell' (Sapir, 1921). One way of helping children to harness the dynamo of language to power their own thinking is through such exploratory talk. Lev Vygotsky (1978) refers to this sort of collaborative exploration at the limits of the child's ability as working in 'the zone of proximal development', suggesting that this is one of the most important contributions that a teacher can make to a child's development. What the child is able to do today in conversation with a supportive adult, he or she will tomorrow be able to manage alone in that interior dialogue that he called 'inner speech' (Vygotsky, 1987).

Some might argue that such positive conversations are only possible in classrooms with the most able children. And there is little doubt that Colin is an able child; he is certainly very fluent for his age. Indeed, if one were to make any criticism of the teacher's contributions to their talk it would be that they weren't challenging enough. Given his interest in photography and his obvious understanding of some of the principles involved, the teacher might well have suggested that he try to make a real camera, of the simple pinhole variety. This could have led to some very interesting practical observations of the images produced and to attempts, both through experiment and discussion, to explain them.

But less able children also benefit from the opportunity to try out their ideas in conversation that is purposeful, yet collaborative and nonthreatening. In the previous extract, Alan was clearly gaining both in confidence and in fluency from working with Colin and from being included by the teacher in the discussion of their model cameras. The same is happening for Matthew in the following extract, recorded earlier the same morning, when the teacher included Amanda and Maxine as she discussed the clay model of a diver that Matthew was making.

Amanda:	Mrs M., if he put this bit in the belt and this bit in the back with the oxygen, it might look like a real diver
Matthew:	That's what I'm going to do
Teacher:	Do you think it looks like a real diver at the moment?
Matthew:	No
Amanda:	No
Matthew:	Not much . it hasn't got the equipment on it
Amanda:	Yes, but if you put the feet too small, it could easily fall down
Teacher:	How do you know about a real diver, Matthew?
Matthew:	I read a lot about it
Maxine:	[joining the group] Why? . have you got a book about divers?
Matthew:	Two . two great big annuals of divers at home and I read 'em every night 'fore bed but I'm in- . I'm in the middle book one and in book two it tells you about deep- sea divers .. in book one it tells you about frogmen
Maxine:	How to make it?
Matthew:	Not how to make 'em
Teacher:	What's the difference between frogmen and deep-sea divers?
Matthew:	'Cos deep-sea divers aren't like frogmen . deep-sea divers haven't got flippers and-

Teacher:	*[turns to answer a child in another part of the room, then turns back to Matthew]* Sorry!
Matthew:	- and they have different kinds of- frogmen don't have helmets, but deep-sea divers do .. *[pause, while teacher answers another child]* so frogmen are quite different, 'cos they haven't got helmets

Perhaps what is most striking about this teacher is the quality of her listening. It is noticeable that, even when she has to break off for a moment to respond to another child, she keeps her arm around Matthew, thereby signalling to him that it is only a temporary interruption; and, on both occasions, when she turns back, Matthew continues where he had left off.

By listening attentively in this way, giving the children her full attention, she indicates that what they have to say is important – that they have expertise that is of value. When she asks questions, it is in order to be further informed, not to check that the child's answer is in conformity with her knowledge about the topic. And by inviting other children to listen and ask questions in the same way, she builds up in each child a feeling of self-respect and confidence in what he or she knows and can do and, at the same time, a feeling of respect for others as well.

Most of this teacher's time is spent with individual children or with very small groups, helping them to plan their activities and to evaluate the outcomes in the sort of interactions illustrated above. From time to time, however, she brings a group together in order to introduce a new topic, such as the following example. Here, her purpose is to teach the children how to use reference books – consulting tables of contents, using indexes, and so forth. To this end, she has assembled on the table a variety of twigs gathered from trees on the neighbouring common and has prepared some reference books, including one entitled *Trees and Leaves*. The children begin by examining the twigs. Yelshea is fascinated by the buds on a horse chestnut twig.

Yelshea:	Miss, why has- why has it gone all furry? most plants that I see- wild plants- are not furry . but is there anything that's meant to- why it's meant to be furry?
Teacher:	What do you other children- *[to Richard]* what do you think?
Richard:	'Cos, er- it- er- protects it
Colin:	It's a warm coat that keeps it warm if it opens up too early.
Yelshea:	It could be, because I can see the green- little bit of green inside and . I see green there . sort <u>of protecting it</u>
Donna:	<u>Like my plant</u>-

Teacher:	I beg your pardon?
Donna:	It's like my plant . mine's all furry
Teacher:	Which plant is this?
Donna:	I don't know which- which one I've planted, though . might be the oak one
Teacher:	Why do you think that needs protecting?
Colin:	Protecting from the cold so's it doesn't die
Yelshea:	No, or protecting from the sticky bud . it might get up and stick all around it
Teacher:	Do you know how we- how we could find out about why it needs protecting?
Yelshea:	I know . just watch it
Richard	From a book
Colin:	Just study and <u>find out</u>
Teacher:	<u>Which book</u> would you look in, Richard?
Richard:	*[turning to get one from the shelf]* I'd look in . um . this book
Teacher:	Yes. It's not over there . I know which one you mean
Richard:	That big book *[Trees and Leaves]*
Teacher:	This one?
Richard:	Yes
Teacher:	You have a little look through that while Nicola says what she was going to say
Nicola:	Miss, you know this bit here? . It looks like- you know them sweet lollies and things? . well it looks like that . and this bit here, it's different from the other bit .. or is it another plant? *[she fingers the leaf of the horse chestnut]* because look-
Teacher:	Bring it closer <u>to yourself</u>
Colin:	<u>I think it's</u> the same- it's the same plant, except the sticky bud is still underneath it . if you can see it . all round this side . you can see it, can't you?

[The teacher speaks to another child who has just entered the room]

Richard:	*[indicating a picture in the book]* Is this the sticky bud? is this the one . this one here?
Teacher:	Hang on *[taking Richard's book]* can I show you this book, which Richard's seen before?
Colin:	*[reading] Trees and Leaves*
Yelshea:	*Trees and Leaves*
Richard:	Miss, was that it- what I just showed you . sticky bud?
Teacher:	Yes. I know that you've looked in this book . I saw you looking the other day
Donna:	****

Colin:	Is it- is it wild? . is it a wild book or just a plain book that you usually see?
Teacher:	What do you mean?
Yelshea:	Sort of . like wild plants <u>and stuff like in the common</u>
Colin:	<u>Does it have just normal</u> everyday trees, or does it have great big wild trees?
Teacher:	*[handing book to Colin]* Well, would you like to see?
Yelshea:	Um, would it, um, be like the things in the common there? If they found out about that and wild things and all things that grow in different places
Nicola:	Miss, those look like-
Teacher:	Do you know where you'd look in the book to find out whether it tells you about trees that you'd find on the common? where- where would you look in the book?
Donna:	On the <u>tree</u> page
Yelshea:	<u>Miss</u> the wildlife, wildlife
Teacher:	Shall I show you? . if you look in this book with Richard
Colin:	That's got the contents
Teacher:	Yes, right in the front it's got what's called the 'Contents'
Colin:	Which has got a list of everything that's in it .. it's got little pages or <u>little-or a few pages about</u> whatever it says, like-
[Several children speak at the same time]	
Donna:	The fruit ones
Colin:	*[reading]* 'What to look for on a tree' . that's one
Teacher:	If you wanted to find out about these horse chestnuts, Nicola, what would you look for in the Contents? . what would you look for? *[she passes the book to Nicola]* have a little read through it and see if you can find the part that will help you

And so the lesson continues: the children using the book to enrich their observation, and their observation to elucidate the text of the book. As the children themselves observed earlier, in answer to the teacher's question 'Do you know how we can find out about ..?' direct observation and consultation of reference material are complementary ways of obtaining information, each illuminating the other. However, what is understood in either case depends on what the observer/reader brings to the situation. Prior knowledge is often insufficient or inappropriate, as was the case with Colin's somewhat idiosyncratic classification of trees into the two categories 'wild' and 'everyday' (or the other boy's suggestion of sour milk as an example of the suspension of solids in a liquid, in the previous chapter). When the teacher is supportive and the topic is treated in an exploratory fashion, as in the example above, children are willing to volunteer their suggestions or ask questions and so reveal to the teacher the framework they are using to interpret the new information. The teacher can then take this into account by building on it or clarifying it, as appropriate. A teacher's manner of interacting with the children is thus at the heart of his or her style of teaching, for it is the collaborative approach – a willingness to negotiate meanings – that encourages children to explore their understanding of a topic and gives them the confidence to try out their ideas without the fear of being wrong. Risk-taking is necessary in any enterprise that aims to move beyond the status quo, and this is particularly true of learning in school, where errors as well as successes can be productive.

Central to this style of teaching is the recognition that knowledge cannot be transmitted to students in a prepackaged form in the hope that it will be assimilated in the form in which it is transmitted. Knowledge has to be constructed afresh by each individual knower, through an interaction between the evidence (which is obtained through observation, listening, reading and the use of reference materials of all kinds) and what the learner can bring to bear on it. The teacher arranges the situations – or encourages those that the children themselves have set up – and so has considerable control over the evidence that the learners encounter. But teachers cannot control the interpretations the children will make. On the other hand, teachers can provide guidance by drawing attention to additional evidence, clarifying misunderstandings and asking questions that point the learner in directions for further exploration. They can also encourage children to share their ideas with each other, facilitating the discussion where necessary by making sure that all have opportunities to contribute and that each contribution is treated with respect. In other words, to be most beneficial, the teacher needs to practice and foster a style of interaction that, like the one used for helping children to learn to talk, is supportive and collaborative.

When presented with these arguments, most teachers express their agreement with them, for they are confirmed by their own experience. Nevertheless, in many cases – as our observations showed – their practice is not guided by the principles that they claim to espouse. In the remainder of this chapter, we shall explore some of the reasons for this mismatch between theory and practice and, in later chapters, consider some practical suggestions for bringing the two more closely into line.

Schools as Environments for Learning

The first and most obvious cause of the impoverished interaction that so often occurs between teachers and pupils is the number of children involved – 30 or more in the average class, with only a single adult. All of these children have to be kept profitably occupied on tasks that stimulate their interest and promote their learning. The demands on teachers in terms of management, safety and control are therefore enormous, so it is not surprising to find that there is little sustained interaction. Added to this, at the outset, is the inexperience of children entering school for the first time. They have to learn to behave according to the norms of the classroom, wait while others take their conversational turns, and discuss the shared topic rather than changing the subject at will. The classroom thus suffers from organizational problems that can militate against children's spontaneity and restrict the opportunities for sustained adult–child interaction of the kind experienced in many homes. As a result, the more intellectually stimulating uses of language get submerged under the demands of the sheer number of children to be attended to and of the management of the tasks that have to be carried out in each day.

With respect to the latter, a further exacerbating factor seems, more and more, to be the curriculum itself – or, rather, the increasing emphasis on standardization in the interests of accountability with respect to the mastery of the 'basic skills'. Clearly, it is highly desirable that every pupil should become both literate and numerate and be conversant with certain facts about his or her social and physical environment. But these skills are only of value when they are integrated with the purposes and interests that the pupil brings from outside the classroom. As Barnes (1976) put it, to be useful, school knowledge must be converted into 'action knowledge'. Too often, though, the concern with the curriculum takes little account of what individual pupils bring to the tasks that they are required to engage in. Instead, curriculum planners concentrate on breaking down what has to be learned into smaller and smaller, relatively self-contained steps, so that they can be arranged into linear sequences for the purposes of instruction. This has led to an exaggerated belief in the efficacy of finely graded, structured programmes of work.[2]

The problem with this approach, however, is that, while certain types of learning can be promoted in this way, it is certainly not the case that children only learn – or even learn most effectively – when all the tasks in which they engage are imposed on them by others in the interests of ensuring a uniform progression through a predetermined sequence. Furthermore, it takes little account of the fact that learning is an active process that is undertaken by individual children, each of whom has different interests and abilities and that, further, in any class, children proceed at different rates, learning quickly and effectively when they are personally motivated and emotionally stable but more slowly and with greater difficulty when the task seems irrelevant or their personal motivation is low. This is not in any way to suggest that children should not be encouraged to engage in tasks that stretch them, that demand effort and concentration. But it is to suggest that the commitment that such tasks demand is only likely to be forthcoming if children perceive these tasks to be meaningful and relevant to them. As Vygotsky insisted with respect to learning to read and write, 'Teaching should be organized in such a way that reading and writing are necessary for something ... Writing should be meaningful for children ... Writing should be incorporated into a task that is necessary and relevant for life' (Vygotsky, 1978: 117–118).

A further disadvantage of centrally controlled curriculum planning is that the curriculum becomes fragmented into isolated bodies of subject matter, and children are discouraged from making connections between the various topics and types of learning in which they are engaged. In addition, under the pressures that are induced by the perceived need to 'cover the curriculum' that is imposed from above, teachers are likely to adopt a didactic style of teaching in which the roles of teacher and pupil are sharply differentiated, with the result that opportunities are seriously reduced for the sort of open-ended, exploratory interaction that encourages children to take some share in the responsibility for planning and pursuing their own learning.

But perhaps the most serious impediment to a more collaborative relationship between teacher and pupil is the mechanistic model of education that is implicit in so much of the discussion about accountability. To talk of the curriculum, or of individual units of work, in terms of 'input' and 'output' is not only inappropriate in its implicit assimilation of education to the organizational principles and ethics of industrial mass production, but it is also misguided in its simple assumption that well-prepared 'input' is all that is needed to guarantee effective learning.

It is not simply that, as has already been stressed, children bring different aptitudes and experiences to each learning task – important though it is to recognize this diversity – but that the learning itself involves an active reconstruction of the knowledge or skill that is presented, on the basis of the learner's existing internal model of the world. The process is therefore essentially interactional in nature, both within the learner and between the learner and the teacher, and calls for the negotiation of meaning, not its unidirectional transmission.

To recognize this essential characteristic of learning is to see in a new light the significance of that well-known precept 'Start where the child is'. All too often this is interpreted in practice to mean 'Administer a test or some other form of assessment in order to decide which ability group to place the child in or which reading primer or worksheet to give him or her'. But this is not discovering where the child is – what his or her mental model of the world is like or what his or her current needs and interests are. Instead, it is discovering into which of the places that are prepared in advance the child can most easily be slotted. Really to discover where a child is and, hence, how we can most helpfully contribute to his or her further learning, it is necessary to watch him or her at work and listen to what he or she has to say – to try to understand the world as he or she sees it. Only then can the teacher's contribution have that quality of contingent responsiveness that we have seen from the pre-school years to be essential in helping the child to develop his or her understanding.

The pressure of numbers, the constraints of accountability and the prevailing mechanistic model of education, then, all tend to reduce the opportunities for a collaborative style of teaching. But perhaps the most insidious influence of all is our own previous experience. Most of us have had many years of being talked *at*, first as pupils and students and, later, during our professional education, both pre-service and in-service. As a result, we have probably unconsciously absorbed the belief that a teacher is only doing his or her job properly when he or she is talking – telling, commanding, questioning or evaluating. And, in many cases, that is what we see when we look to our colleagues for a model of successful teaching. Despite the lip service that is paid to the 'student-centred' conception of education, actual practice tends on the whole to be 'teacher-centred', based on a predetermined curriculum at every level from kindergarten to university. It is not surprising, therefore, if, under pressure, teachers tend to fall back on the traditional transmission model of education without realizing how poorly it enables them to fulfill their best intentions.

How, then, can this situation be changed? How can teachers bring their practice more closely into line with the theories to which they probably already subscribe?

There is no simple panacea, of course. But there are a number of changes – some of which every teacher is in a position to make – that are likely to lead towards the style of teaching that has here been described as collaborative.

Towards a Collaborative Style of Learning and Teaching

For many teachers, the first question is, quite naturally: 'Will it work?' Of course, the only convincing answer is that of experience – and personal experience, at that. However, there is already the testimony of individual teachers, teaching in many different school systems in countries all over the world. They all say that, having taken the plunge and tried the collaborative style, they would never want to return to their old ways of doing things.

But for those who are still undecided, hesitating because of the risks that they perceive to be involved, there is a simple step that will probably be sufficient to convince them that some sort of change is necessary: they could record themselves at work. Before making the recording, they should set down in writing what they hope will be achieved, in particular what types of learning the children will engage in, and how their own behaviour will contribute. Then, afterwards, they should listen to the tape, noting how far these aims were achieved and, where they were not, asking what were the probable reasons. More specific questions that one might ask are: What are the most frequently occurring patterns of teacher–pupil exchange? Who initiates the interaction, and in which contexts? What sorts of questions are asked, by whom, and for what purpose? Most teachers who undertake this form of self-assessment find that they talk too much, repeat themselves unnecessarily, and give children too little time to respond. They also ask too many questions that restrict children's participation to that of providing minimal answers requiring only the lowest level of intellectual activity.

If, after making and listening critically to such a recording, it seems desirable to attempt to change, then there are a number of aspects of the total classroom situation that are worth thinking about. First, there is the interactive style itself. Most teachers find that they vary their strategies from one context to another, so it is worth trying to identify those contexts that allow them most readily to engage in genuine collaborative interaction. These can then be developed and the same strategies extended to other contexts. A general principle that almost all teachers find to be rewarding – although initially extremely difficult – is to talk less and to listen more, in particular allowing pupils a longer time to think out what they want to say and giving them the time to say it without interruption. It may also be worth thinking about the sorts of questions the teacher asks and about ways of encouraging pupils to ask more questions themselves.

But to focus on language alone may be self-defeating, in the same way that a millipede would probably not be helped by being advised to think about how it was moving one of its legs. More important is for teachers to think about where they are going and which route is likely to be most satisfactory. That means reconsidering what it means to be a teacher in the light of what is known about how children learn and about how others, both adults and other children, can facilitate that learning.

From observations outside school, we know that children are innately predisposed to make sense of their experience, to pose problems for themselves, and actively to search for and achieve solutions. There is every reason to believe, therefore, that, given the opportunity, they will continue to bring these characteristics to bear inside the school as well, provided that the tasks that they engage in are ones that they have been able to make their own.[3] All of us – adults and children alike – function most effectively when we are working on a task or problem to which we have a personal commitment, either because the goal is one that we are determined to achieve (balancing the family budget, repairing a machine) or because the activity is one that we find intrinsically satisfying (writing a poem, building a model), or both. In these circumstances, as the extracts concerning Colin and his model camera show, discussion with someone more skilled or knowledgeable takes on real purpose and significance, as progress to date is reviewed and alternative plans for further work are considered in terms of their feasibility and appropriateness. This is perhaps the teacher's most vital contribution: as a master providing guidance to an apprentice, who utilizes that guidance in the pursuit of his or her chosen goal, the value of which is appreciated by both of them.

For children to achieve this active involvement in their own learning, it is important to find ways of enabling them to share in the responsibility for deciding what tasks to undertake and how to set about them. This does not mean that the teacher should abnegate responsibility or tolerate a free-for-all in which children do exactly as they choose, when they choose. Few children can work productively without the support of an understood framework and clear ideas about what is expected of them, and most teachers would not feel that they were adequately fulfilling their responsibilities if they did not provide both guidelines and a clear sense of direction. What is required, therefore, is some form of negotiation in which both pupils' and teachers' suggestions are given serious consideration.

Colin's teacher had devised what were called 'choice books', in which the agenda of tasks to be completed was negotiated between the teacher and each individual pupil once each week. At the beginning of the school year, when the children were new to the class, the agenda consisted largely of activities suggested by the teacher. But, as the year progressed, the children began to add their own suggestions and, perhaps more important, to note when they had not yet completed a task satisfactorily or where they needed to make another attempt or gain further information or skill. Figure 6.1 shows a page from such a choice book.

However, not all teachers will feel comfortable with so much of the curriculum open for negotiation – at least, not initially. It is important to

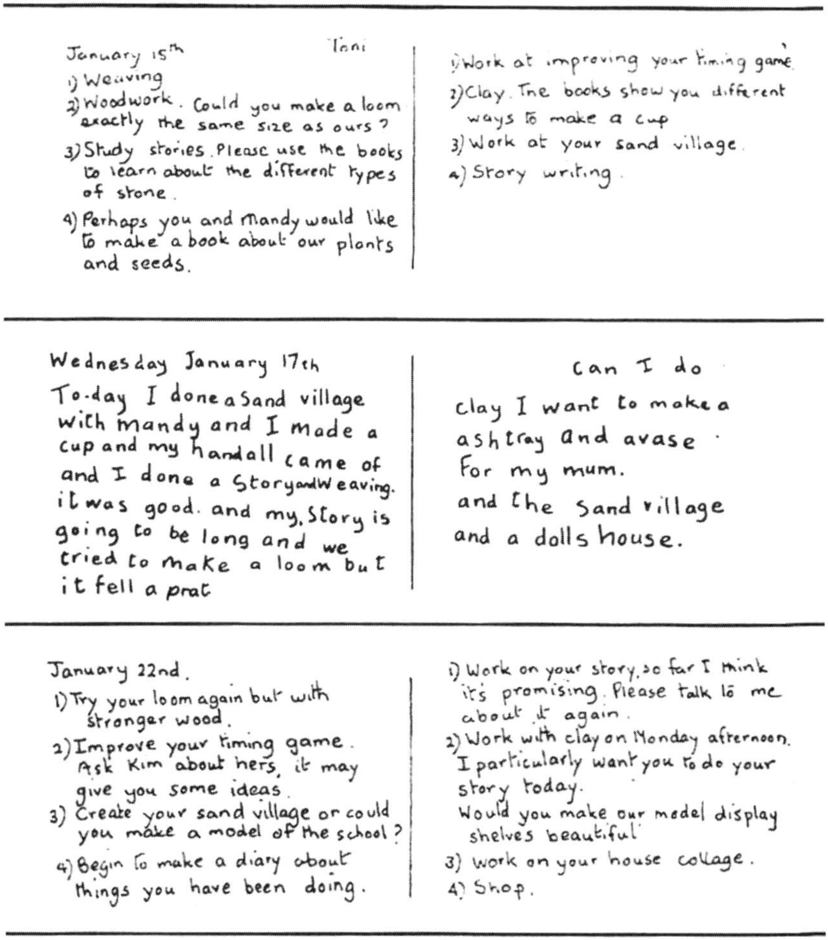

Toni

January 15th
1) Weaving
2) Woodwork. Could you make a loom exactly the same size as ours?
3) Study stories. Please use the books to learn about the different types of stone.
4) Perhaps you and Mandy would like to make a book about our plants and seeds.

1) Work at improving your timing game.
2) Clay. The books show you different ways to make a cup
3) Work at your sand village.
4) Story writing.

Wednesday January 17th
To-day I done a Sand village with mandy and I made a cup and my hand all came of and I done a Story and Weaving. it was good. and my, Story is going to be long and we tried to make a loom but it fell a prat

Can I do
Clay I want to make a ashtray and a vase for my mum. and the Sand village and a dolls house.

January 22nd.
1) Try your loom again but with stronger wood.
2) Improve your timing game. Ask Kim about hers, it may give you some ideas.
3) Create your sand village or could you make a model of the school?
4) Begin to make a diary about things you have been doing.

1) Work on your story, so far I think it's promising. Please talk to me about it again.
2) Work with clay on Monday afternoon. I particularly want you to do your story today. Would you make our model display shelves beautiful
3) Work on your house collage.
4) Shop.

Figure 6.1 A page from a child's choice book
Source: Reproduced from *Extending Literacy*. (London: Centre for Primary Education, Inner London Education Authority, p. 25.)

emphasize, therefore, that there is no one correct way to proceed. Indeed, different methods will probably work best for different teachers or for the same teachers with different classes of children. What is important is that, for at least a substantial part of the curriculum, there be genuine negotiation that enables pupils to feel that they have initiated some of their activities and have taken on others and made them their own. 'Ownership' is the word that Donald Graves (1983) uses to make the same point about children's writing, and it applies equally to other activities, right across the curriculum.

When children have a feeling of ownership and share the responsibility for the tasks that they engage in, teachers find that their relationships with the children change. Given responsibility, children behave responsibly and no longer have to be closely supervised every moment of the day. With an agreed agenda, they know what has to be achieved and spend their time productively, using resources appropriately, asking for the teacher's assistance only when other sources have proved inadequate, and moving on to a new task when the present one is completed. As a result, freed from the demands of managing resources, answering trivial questions about procedure, and continually monitoring classroom behaviour, teachers are able to spend considerable periods of time with individual children, giving assistance when it is really needed and helping them to reflect on what they are doing and to see how to extend it in various directions.

This, then, is the goal, and these are some of the benefits that are likely to result. But how can it be achieved? Here again, there is no one formula for success, but classroom management – how time, space and other resources are allocated – is one important ingredient. Having the classroom divided into different areas appropriately organized for different activities is an essential preliminary, as is arranging resources – paper, glue, scissors, apparatus, reference books, and so on – so that children can gain access to them without disturbing each other or the teacher. Arranging tables and chairs in such a way that no child has his or her back to the teacher when the teacher is addressing the whole class has been found to make a difference, as is having the children sitting in a circle for a whole-class discussion. In this way, every child can see the face of every other and can better judge how to fit their contributions into the flow of discussion.

Equally important is the organization of time. Children should have long periods of time to work on the same task, with as few interruptions as possible; and, as has already been implied, they should not all be expected to engage in the same activity at the same time. With individual agendas, there is little danger of this happening, but it will be necessary to ensure an equitable rotation of access to popular work areas and to scarce resources.

These are some of the organizational prerequisites. But perhaps the most difficult question is how to get started. From talking to others who have successfully changed their method of working, it is clear that there are many different starting points, ranging from encouraging individual children to pursue a topic that has particularly interested them to proposing a very general theme that individual children are invited to explore in a variety of different ways. Some teachers have made such a theme the centre of all curricular activity over a period of one or two weeks; others have developed a theme in the area of social or environmental studies while maintaining their normal pattern of work in the rest of the curriculum. Some teachers have used a work of literature – a story, song or poem – as the starting point for a wide range of individual activities; one first-grade teacher used the book *Watership Down* in this way, and a teacher of 10-year-olds started with the Prologue to Chaucer's *Canterbury Tales.*

The advantage of a broad theme within which all – or a majority – of the children choose topics to pursue is that there is an overall coherence to the variety of their activities. This is reassuring to the teacher, as it reduces the feeling of being pulled in too many different directions at once. It also has advantages for the children, in that they can more readily work together in groups, collaborating with each other and learning from each other's efforts. Whole-class activities, too, such as visits, reading stories related to the theme, and – most important of all – sharing what each individual or group has created or discovered, have more significance when the theme is one in which all are equally involved.

An even more ambitious – but ultimately rewarding – plan might be to choose a theme of a more abstract kind to run over the whole year. One such theme is 'transformation', which is relevant in literature, music and dance, but also in history (the transformation over generations of the town or region where the school is situated), science (water changing state, solar energy being transformed into electricity; caterpillars metamorphosing into butterflies), mathematics (fractions transformed into decimals), and so on. A further step might be to consider which transformations are reversible and which are not. The advantage of such themes is that they show the essential relatedness of the different school subjects, which are typically taught separately; they also show how abstract ideas can function as metaphors for thinking about new areas of exploration and knowledge building.

To teach in this way – collaborating in the pupils' learning and negotiating the curriculum with them – is not easy, of course. It requires a considerable degree of flexibility and an ability and readiness to meet the demands for resources of information and materials that are called for by the interests that the children wish to pursue. It also demands a constant state of open receptiveness to children's ideas and a willingness to take them seriously, even when, from an adult point of view, they seem naive or immature. At the same time, it requires clear thinking and planning in relation to broad, long-term goals and imagination in finding specific themes, activities, and materials that will spark fresh interests and make connections between those that have already been developed.

Some teachers may feel that they are simply unable to meet such demands: that the breadth of their general knowledge is insufficient or that they lack some of the necessary skills. Such doubts are understandable and very real, but they are probably unnecessary. To teach collaboratively, it is not necessary to know all the answers to pupils' questions or to be already competent in all the skills that an open curriculum may call for. Indeed, a teacher who is universally knowledgeable and competent may actually make it more difficult for pupils to gain confidence in their ability to learn on their own.[4] Learning is first and foremost a process – a continuous making and remaking of meanings in the lifelong enterprise of constructing a progressively more and more effective mental model of the world in which one lives. Learning is never complete. Furthermore, since this process is essentially interactive, it is more helpful for the apprentice learner to work with teachers who are themselves still actively engaged in learning and willing to engage with their pupils in doing so than it is to be instructed and evaluated by those who apparently no longer have the need to engage in such processes themselves. (These ideas will be taken up again in Chapter 12.)

It is important to emphasize, therefore, that there is no one correct way to proceed. The only really satisfactory solution is the one that each teacher works out for him- or herself, taking into account the particular children concerned, their parents, the school, and its resources and environment.

Notes

1. This material was recorded under the direction of Moira McKenzie, Warden of the Centre for Language in Primary Education in the Inner London Education Authority, for use in a series of video programmes entitled *Extending Literacy*. I am grateful for her permission to reproduce this and the other examples from these programmes, which are quoted here and in subsequent chapters.
2. This concern with standardization has reached such a pitch that, at the time of writing, many teachers in California, where I now live, are required to follow a scripted curriculum, in which every step of the lesson is prescribed by a 'pacing guide' from which they are not allowed to depart.
3. Piaget was convinced that if children are asked a genuine question, they will give the best answer they can, given their current understanding. Such an answer cannot be *wrong*, but it does give the teacher a basis from which to help the child reach a fuller understanding.
4. A teacher who took this view seriously describes its importance for the children's learning in 'Risking saying "I don't know"', (Rogoff *et al.*, 2001).

Chapter 7

Differences Between Children in Language and Learning

Up to this point, little has been said about the ways in which children differ from each other. Instead, the emphasis has been on the very great similarities between them in development and experience. But, as the comparisons between particular children have shown, there are also substantial individual differences, and in this chapter we shall try to understand their significance – their nature, causes and consequences.

No two children – and no two adults, for that matter – are identical. Each is unique, as a result of his or her particular combination of genetic inheritance and individual experience. The recognition of this unique quality of every individual is essential, of course, as a basis for our personal dealings with them, but it does not help us very much in our attempts to understand the major factors that contribute to this variety, nor does it help policy makers to take appropriate action to alleviate disadvantageous circumstances. For both these purposes, it is necessary to look for common patterns – for characteristics that are related to each other in predictable ways as, for example, height and weight (other things being equal, taller people tend to weigh more than shorter people). In relation to language and learning, these sorts of studies are still very much in their infancy, so conclusions can only be drawn very tentatively. However, since important decisions are being made on the basis of the conclusions that have been reached, it is worth considering the evidence that is currently available.

The Limitations of Tests and Assessments

On one matter there is unanimous agreement: as children grow older, their language ability generally increases and so does their ability to use their linguistic resources as a means of learning, problem solving, and the like. This is the assumption on which tests of almost every kind are based and, within certain limits, it is a reasonable assumption to make. If a child takes the same test under identical conditions at the beginning and end of the year, he or she will almost certainly obtain a higher score on the second occasion, unless something disastrous has happened in the interval.

But even that straightforward statement needs to be qualified. First, can one be certain that the conditions on the two occasions are identical? Not only may the person administering the test be different, with the consequent possibility of a change in the interpersonal relationship between child and tester, but the child's understanding of the test itself and what is expected of him or her may have changed as a result of intervening experiences. And if these possibilities make it difficult to interpret the significance of the change in an individual child's performance from one occasion to the next, they make it even more difficult to compare large groups of children, either on the same occasion or between successive occasions.

This qualification does not only apply to formal tests, however, but to all kinds of assessment and, indeed, to the evaluation of any form of interaction. As we saw in the comparison between the two teachers who talked with Rosie (Chapter 5), the child's 'performance' does not depend on ability alone, but on the complex interrelationship between the participants, the task and the context in which it is embedded. It is a difficult and risky business, therefore, to draw conclusions about an individual's ability from his or her behaviour in any particular situation. So, to be comprehensive as well as valid, an assessment must be based on a number of observations made in a variety of situations (Drummond, 1997; Peters, 1973). However, there has been very little research that has systematically investigated the important influence of situational factors on performance.

A second, related qualification has to do with the fact that, in almost any form of interaction, all levels of linguistic ability are drawn upon simultaneously; yet the majority of tests and even of less formal methods of assessment tend to have a very narrow focus, concentrating exclusively on just one aspect of ability – range of vocabulary comprehended, control of syntax in production, functional uses made of language, and so on. However, if the assessment is to be truly adequate, all of these aspects of ability need to be included in some form of composite profile. Children do not necessarily develop evenly across the levels: to assess just one aspect is to risk forming a biased estimate of ability.

A still further qualification arises from this last point: that ability can never be observed or measured directly, it can only be estimated from a sample of actual performance or from a number of samples. For example, if two children differ in the frequency with which they are observed to use complex sentences, one using a wide variety of sentence types in several different contexts and the other using only a small number in the same range of contexts, is this the result of a real difference in ability or is it simply a difference in the sentence types that each chooses to use? Amongst educated adults, we would assume it was the latter. One might prefer William Faulkner to Ernest Hemingway, for example, but there would be little temptation to argue that Faulkner had greater linguistic ability simply on the grounds that his sentences were typically longer and more complex.

With young children, however, this is the assumption that is frequently made. Indeed, some writers have made the further assumption that more frequent use of complex structures of various kinds is evidence of a more advanced level of intellectual functioning. As yet, however, this claim has not been systematically investigated and, until a causal connection has been clearly demonstrated, it would be wise to be more cautious. The ability to express complex relationships fully and precisely in language is certainly an aid to effective communication; it may also facilitate thinking. However, the fact that a child does occasionally produce utterances of this kind is evidence that he or she can do so when he or she judges the situation to warrant it. How the frequency with which a child uses this linguistic ability relates to his or her habitual level of thinking is a question that is much less easily resolved.

A final qualification must be made about the significance of rate of development. The fact that some children develop earlier and faster than others has been clearly demonstrated. But, apart from those children whose retardation is the result of some physiological handicap, there is little firm evidence that slow developers cannot, under appropriately supportive conditions, eventually reach the same level as – or even overtake – their more rapidly developing peers. Indeed, as is well known, many people who have become successful in adult life did not begin to show their exceptional skills until many years after they left school. There is clearly more to achievement, therefore, than simply being an early or fast developer.

This point needs to be emphasized because, in the competitive ethos that pervades our educational systems and our culture in general, we tend to attach an exaggerated importance to being faster or slower than average, particularly in the early stages. At school, considerable merit is attributed to the child who is at the top of the class and lack of it to the child who is at the bottom, despite the fact that, in Britain, the United States, and many other countries, children are allocated to grades almost entirely according to age. When comparing different varieties of plant, on the other hand, we tend to adopt very different criteria. The fact that variety A happened to flower and ripen earlier than variety B would not be considered important if variety B ultimately produced an equal yield of equally good tomatoes.

One of the dangers, therefore, of comparing children in terms of their rate of development is that it may lead us to make inappropriate inferences, which may still further exacerbate the problems of those who develop more slowly. Already at a disadvantage in being unable to do the same things as their more rapidly developing peers, they are further handicapped by being adversely labelled and by having attributed to them personal inadequacies for which there is often no justification. If such children do, in fact, in the long run fail to reach the same level of achievement as their age peers, the reason may have as much to do with the handicaps imposed on them by the reduced expectations and inappropriate treatment of those who assess them as with any intrinsic limitation in their potential ability.

For all these reasons, then, it is difficult to know just how important the differences are that have been found to exist between children in their language development. Progress is being made in describing their nature and origin; but it would be unwise, on the basis of present knowledge, to draw conclusions about their long-term consequences. This is particularly so when it comes to making predictions about the ultimate level of achievement that can be obtained by individual children.

In the Bristol Study we tried as far as possible to guard against the dangers just described by obtaining samples of naturally occurring conversation and by constructing a profile score from a wide variety of measures. This still does not completely avoid the risk of wrongly estimating the ability of an individual child; but, fortunately, we were never called upon to make an assessment in a context that might have had consequences for his or her later development. About the group as a whole, however, we did feel more confident in making general statements although, for all the reasons discussed above, even these must be treated with considerable caution.

Individual Differences

Before going on to discuss the differences we observed in greater detail, however, I want to emphasize the very great achievement of all the children we studied. Indeed, in the population as a whole, all but a tiny minority of seriously handicapped children do succeed in acquiring functional competence in their native language. In the Bristol sample of 128 children, there was not a single child who had not mastered what might be called 'basic English' by the age of five. Rosie was the least advanced child in the follow-up study and, as we have already seen, when she was talking with her mother and with Teacher B, she showed herself to be quite a competent communicator, drawing upon a variety of complex sentence types to achieve a range of conversational purposes. Furthermore, as was emphasized in Chapter 3, all children, to a very large extent, follow the same sequence of development. Considered against this background of similarity in achievement, therefore, the differences that are observed between individuals in their rate of development are relatively small and may not be of any significance in terms of their ultimate achievement.

As with such physical milestones as beginning to walk, children vary quite considerably in the age at which they begin to use speech sounds with a recognizable intention to communicate. They also differ in the age at which they show that they have discovered the grammatical organization of the language of their community by producing their first two- and three-word combinations (Bates *et al.*, 1995). In the Bristol Study, we found that a very small number of children had reached this latter stage by 15 months, while others were nearly 30 months old by the time they did so. At three-and-a-half years, the difference between the most and least advanced was equivalent to almost three years. Generally speaking, children who started early tended to stay ahead, but late starters did not necessarily continue to lag behind. Even when they did, however, they continued to make progress, although at a slower rate.

The reasons for these differences are of two basic kinds: differences in the children themselves, and differences in their environments – in the opportunities that are provided for learning. In the first category, we can include such factors as personality, learning style and general learning ability. Little is known in any detail about the contribution of these factors, but they are probably quite important. Just as people differ in their general ability to master new skills or ideas, so it seems likely that there are differences between children in their general ability to learn language, or at least in the speed at which they are able to do so. Such differences probably account for a considerable part of the variation observed in the children's rate of learning. But as constructing the language system and discovering how to use it appropriately involve different types of learning, it is possible that there are differences between children here as well. Some may be particularly quick and successful in mastering the sound system, others at forming and testing the hypotheses necessary for constructing grammar, and still others at acquiring control of the functional uses of language. In recent years a number of research studies have shown that young children may have different strategies for making sense of language or different preferences in what they attend to (Nelson, 1981;

Peters, 1973). Some of these strategies or preferences may provide an easier entry than others or lead to more rapid mastery. However, the number of children investigated from this point of view is still too small for any firm conclusions to be drawn.

Personality differences also seem likely to be of considerable importance. Children certainly differ with respect to such traits as perseverance (sticking at a problem until it is solved as opposed to giving up rather quickly when difficulties are encountered) and risk-taking (being satisfied with an approximation if it serves the immediate purpose as opposed to needing to get things absolutely right if they are to make the attempt at all), and such traits clearly influence the amount of helpful feedback they get from other speakers. Children also differ in such traits as sociability, curiosity, argumentativeness, and so on, all of which also affect the ways in which other people interact with them and, hence, the amount and kind of evidence about language that they obtain through conversation.

It is through a consideration of conversational experience that we can also best understand the influence on development of the factors that were referred to above as environmental. Parents too, like children, differ in personality; they also differ in their beliefs about how to bring up children and in the importance they attach to their own contribution to their children's development, as is clear when comparisons are made across cultures (Gaskins, 1999; Heath, 1983; Ochs, 1988). As a result, they differ quite considerably in how often they engage in conversation with their children, in what contexts, and for what purposes. They therefore provide different models for their children concerning which they treat as the most important functions of language. Clearly, a child whose experience of conversation was largely limited to obtaining satisfaction of basic needs and being required to conform to an adult's definition of 'good behaviour' would be learning a rather different and more restricted potential for meaning than would a child whose experience also included discussion of things seen and events encountered outside as well as inside the home.

In this respect, we have found that one of the more important differences between children is in the amount of conversation they have while engaged in shared activities with an adult – helping with the housework, cooking, playing together, watching television, looking at books, and so on. In such contexts, adults not only provide evidence of language in use, which is readily interpretable from the context, but they also tend to 'scaffold' the activity to make it easy for the child to play his or her role within it (Bruner, 1983; Cazden, 1983).

In the end, however, what is probably most important about the differences between parents and other adults in personality, beliefs and attitudes is the effect these have on the characteristic style they adopt when interacting with the child. Do they, for most of the time, treat the child as an equal partner, sustaining and facilitating his or her attempts to communicate, or do they impose their own views and standards? Do they, for the most part, respond fully to the child's initiations, or do they generally limit conversation to the bare minimum? There is little doubt that it is experience of the first kind in each case that provides the most effective support for language learning.

If the parents' behaviour influences the range and quality of the child's opportunities for learning, as it certainly does, it is also true that the child's behaviour influences the parents'. Parents and other adults, when talking with young children, adjust not only to the age and developmental stage, but also to the particular characteristics of the individual child. Indeed this is particularly true of the most supportive parents. For all children, language learning involves an interaction between the child and his or her environment, but where parents are really responsive to the particular characteristics of individual children, it is hardly an exaggeration to say that it is the children who are teaching their parents how to interact with them in ways that provide them with opportunities to learn.

Not all children have such a facilitative experience, however. Some children, because of their own individual characteristics, do not provide such clear cues or such rewarding experiences for their parents, so they, in turn, experience conversation that is less well adjusted to help them to learn. This tends to be particularly the case for handicapped children, for example those who are deaf or whose speech development is markedly abnormal. But, while differences in the quality of environmental support owe something to the differences between children in the communicative behaviour they elicit, the main responsibility for the variation must lie with the adults who interact with the children, since it is they who have the greater measure of control over when, why and how to engage in conversation.

Social Differences in Language Development

Because language is a social activity and is learned through interaction with other people, it is reasonable to expect that differences between children may be related to their membership in different social groups. At the level of individual families this is undoubtedly the case, though even here it is remarkable how different can be the developmental history of siblings growing up in the same home. Parents in our study often remarked on this when comparing the child we were studying with an older or younger brother or sister. What was surprising, however, was the fact that the same sorts of explanation were given for accelerated or delayed development, whether the child being described was the older or younger sibling. However, this bears out what was said earlier about the interactive nature of language learning: it may be either the younger or the older child who is the one who leads or follows, is outgoing or shy. A further factor that complicates the effect of the child's position in the family is the age gap between siblings and the child's preference for interacting with an older or a younger sibling. Overall, though, there was a slight tendency for only children or those without a sibling close in age to develop more rapidly, due most probably to the more frequent opportunities these children had for interaction with their parents on a one-to-one basis.

Possible differences due to the sex of the child have recently also come to be considered in terms of social rather than physiological causes. In fact, in the Bristol Study, no such differences were observed during the pre-school years. There were no measures on which girls as a group were consistently ahead of boys, nor vice versa. Although this is consistent with the results of other recent studies, it is in marked contrast with the picture that emerged from earlier work, in which girls were found to develop more rapidly on a number of linguistic dimensions (Cherry & Lewis, 1978). In retrospect, it seems likely that these results were due in part to the somewhat artificial conditions under which the assessments were made but even more to the rather different expectations that parents had concerning what was appropriate behaviour for boys and girls. Boys were expected to be active and boisterous, little interested in quiet and reflective activities, whereas girls were expected to be quieter and more docile, interested in helping their mothers and playing with dolls. This is no doubt something of a caricature but, despite the much greater equality with which the two sexes are now treated, there is still some evidence from the Bristol Study that parents behave differently to their children, depending on whether they are boys or girls.

This came out clearly in the sorts of toys the parents bought for the children and their reasons for buying them; but it also emerged from an analysis of the situations in which they were more likely to engage in conversation with them. With boys, a greater proportion of speech occurred while they were playing with toys; with girls while they were helping with household tasks. However, over the preschool period as a whole, these differences were not very large and, as already stated, they did not lead to consistent differences between the sexes in their rate of development nor in their use of language.

Of all the dimensions of social difference that have been investigated, however, there is no doubt that it is family background that has received the greatest attention.[1] As a result of a number of well-known studies, a rather simple account has been very widely accepted to the effect that middle-class children in general tend at any given age to be linguistically more advanced than their lower-class peers (Hess & Shipman, 1965; Tough, 1977). In many of the early studies, children's class membership was based on the father's occupation alone; in more recent studies, level of education has been included as well, and the scores used for assigning children to one social class rather than another have taken information from the mother into account as well. But, despite these refinements, the message has remained the same: compared with middle-class children, children from a lower-class background develop more slowly and, in some formulations, tend towards the expression of a more restricted range of meanings and to the use of language for a narrower and less complex range of functions.

Before reporting the results from the Bristol Study, several reservations need to be expressed concerning the way in which most previous studies obtained their evidence. First, social class was, for the most part, treated as a dichotomy: a family belongs either to the middle class or to the lower class. Further distinctions might be made within these two classes – 'lower' working class and 'professional' middle class, for example – but the major split remained the same. In practice, however, the population is not really divided in this way, even in Britain. Quite apart from the considerable amount of movement that there has been in the past, as people have 'worked themselves up' or 'fallen in the world', there has, for a considerable time, been a gradual shift in the distribution of employment from heavy manual work to secondary industry and to service occupations generally. With this has also come a trend towards more extended education. Furthermore, at the level of individual families, there is a small but significant proportion in which the parents come from different sides of the notional divide (e.g. Mr and Mrs Morel in D.H. Lawrence's *Sons and Lovers*). For all these reasons, it is clearly inappropriate to characterize individual families in terms of two crude stereotypes; class must be thought of as at least a continuum, and individual families recognized as being likely to change their position on the continuum over a limited time span.

A second problem with much of the research on language and class is that it has frequently been less interested in exploring the range of language use to be found in the population as a whole than concerned with demonstrating the existence of clear class differences. To this end, comparisons have been made between two groups, selected from near the extremes of the continuum, rather than in a manner that represents the actual class make-up of the population as a whole.

In the light of these comments, it might be predicted that if one were to study a properly representative sample of children, a quite different – or at least a less stark – picture might emerge. And this is what the Bristol Study has shown. In selecting the 128 children, information about the education and occupation of both parents was taken into account, allowing each child to be given a score on a 12-point scale. This scale was then divided into four intervals, and an approximately equal number of children was chosen to represent each interval group. When the four groups were compared on a variety of language measures, the differences between them were not statistically significant. The reason for this is quite simple. All four family background groups contained children who were relatively advanced and others who were much less so, and these differences within the groups were much greater than the relatively small differences between the *averages* for each group. On the other hand, if we were to ask about the half dozen or so most advanced children, we should find that they did tend to come from the homes of more highly educated, professional parents. It was also true that the half dozen or so least advanced children came from homes where the parents were minimally educated and worked, or had worked, in unskilled or semi-skilled occupations. But for the vast majority of the sample – representing about 90% of the population – there was no clear relationship, between family background and level of language development attained (see Wells, 1985 for details). There is therefore little justification for continuing to appeal to simple class stereotypes when thinking about the oral language abilities of children at the point of entry to school.

In summary, all the dimensions of social difference that we investigated led to the same conclusion: stereotypes are not appropriate. Whatever the mode of grouping, whether it be position in the family, family status, sex or social class, differences *between* groups in the conditions and experiences that have an influence on language development pale by comparison with the variety of individual circumstances found *within* each of the same groups.

Differences in Educational Achievement

One of the purposes of our study was to find out how far the differences we had observed in the preschool years would affect the children's success at school. Would differences in oral language ability at age five be as important as was often suggested in accounting for achievement at later ages?

To investigate this question we asked the teachers to make a comprehensive assessment of the children when they entered school, again at the end of the sixth term (at approximately age seven), and, finally, towards the end of their primary schooling, when they had reached the age of 10 years three months. At each of these points we also administered a number of tests, including: various aspects of readiness for school at age five; reading and number work at age seven; and mathematics and spoken and written language at age 10.

As might be anticipated from what has already been said, the range in achievement at each age was wide. This emerged clearly both from the tests and from the teachers' assessments. What is more, there was relatively little change in the rank order of achievement over the whole of the period studied. Children who were ahead on entry to school tended to be the high achievers five years later, and those who were behind at age five were likely to be at the lower end of the rank order at age 10. Jonathan, for example, who was amongst the two or three highest scorers at age five, was clearly the most advanced at the time of the last observation; and Rosie, who was the least advanced at age five, maintained this unenviable position at each observation.

There is nothing very surprising about this outcome, and in itself it tells us little about the effectiveness of schooling. If the aim is equally well met in all schools of enabling children to profit to the best of their ability from the opportunities that are offered, it must be expected that those who are most able – or those who are best prepared – will make the greatest progress. Indeed, there would be justifiable cause for alarm if the outcome were very different. However, what if there is an inbuilt bias in the educational system that makes it more difficult for some children than for others to progress at the rate that would be predicted by their early ability! Such is the claim that has been made about the experience of many lower-class children; and, certainly, the evidence suggests that, as a group, they do less well at school than it would be reasonable to expect, on the assumption that ability is fairly evenly distributed over the population as a whole.[2]

One way to investigate this question is to follow the progress of a representative sample of children from as early an age as possible to see whether there is a clear relationship between achievement and family background and, if there is, what bearing this has on schooling. In the Bristol Study, this was attempted for the 32 children who were observed over the full nine-year period. However, because of the original aims of

Table 7.1 Correlation between achievement and family background at successive ages

Age in years	*Correlation*
2	0.24
3.5	0.29
5	0.66*
7	0.58*
10.25	0.59*

*Significant at the 0.01% level.

the investigation, it was only linguistic achievement that was measured in the preschool years.

At first sight, the results of analysing the data in this way are rather disconcerting. At the two points in the preschool years at which correlations were calculated between oral language performance and family background (at ages two and three-and-a-half years), only a weak relationship between achievement and family background was found, which was not statistically significant. However, as soon as the children were assessed at school, the strength of the relationship increased considerably and remained at approximately the same, statistically significant, level at all three ages of assessment (see Table 7.1).

What this seems to suggest is that, while there was little difference in language performance between children from different points on the continuum of family background during the preschool years (when the assessment was based on their spontaneous conversation in their own homes), there was something about the conditions under which they were assessed at school that put the children from the lower end of the family background continuum at a relative disadvantage. Before we can explore this possibility further, however, we need to look more closely at what it was that was assessed on each occasion.

At ages two and three-and-a-half, as already explained, the assessment was concerned exclusively with oral language. The majority of the measures used were derived from analyses of the recordings of conversation and concerned the range of meanings expressed, the grammatical forms used to express them, and the functions for which speech was used. To these measures were added scores from two tests of comprehension, one of whole sentences and the other of isolated words [the English Picture

Vocabulary Test, or EPVT (Brimer & Dunn, 1963)]. This latter test was only given at age three years three months.

At age five, the tests included the EPVT again, an oral comprehension test involving the acting out of a story, a test of hand–eye coordination, and a test of knowledge of literacy, 'Concepts about Print and Letter Identification' (Clay, 1972). Neither at age five nor at age seven was there any test of oral language production. At age seven, the EPVT was repeated and two other tests were given, the Neale Analysis of Reading (Neale, 1969) and a test of number concepts and operations of our own devising. At age 10, the Neale Analysis was repeated and two further tests were added: a test of reading comprehension and one of mathematics, both provided by the National Foundation for Educational Research. At this age, the assessment also included a number of writing tasks, and five tasks involving oral language: two of comprehension and three of production. At each age, the results of all measures and/or tests were combined to give an overall achievement score.

At each age, though, there were some measures that seemed to be particularly effective in predicting overall achievement at the next assessment. At age two, it was the range of functions for which the child was able to use his or her linguistic resources; at age three-and-a-half it was the range of different sentence types that he or she was able to use appropriately. From age five onwards, however, the measures based on oral language ability ceased to be so important as predictors. Instead, what became important were measures associated with control of written language: the Knowledge of Literacy Test at age five, and Reading Comprehension at age seven. At the last assessment, at 10 years three months, performance on the reading tests still contributed substantially to overall achievement. Surprisingly, by contrast, oral language ability did not appear to make a significant contribution. However, this does not mean that the ability to speak effectively and listen with comprehension was not important for success at school, but rather that the majority of the children were able to cope with the oral language demands of the classroom, and that the differences between them in this respect did not contribute significantly to overall achievement.

These were the results that emerged from the analysis of the children's performances on the various tests. But perhaps tests do not accurately capture the differences that matter in the day-to-day work of the classroom. To discover whether this was so, we asked each child's teacher to complete detailed assessments at the same ages as those at which the tests were administered. Questions were asked about the development of social and physical skills as well as about linguistic and general intellectual achievements. In each of these areas, questions were followed by between three and five descriptions of behavior spanning the range of maturity that one might expect to find amongst children of the relevant age. By scoring the descriptions selected by the teachers for each of the children, it was possible to arrive at overall scores for the same areas of the curriculum as were assessed by the tests. The results were very similar. In the teachers' eyes, too, it was skill in reading and writing (particularly reading) and in mathematics that defined school achievement. Once again, differences between the children in oral language ability were not strongly related to the differences in the more highly valued areas.

It is not difficult to see why differences in the ability to read and write should figure so large in the overall assessment of achievement by means of tests, since successful performance on many of the tests actually requires the use of these skills. Perhaps, too, the need to be able to read and write effectively in many of the subject areas explains why the teachers evidently also rated these skills so highly. In addition, of course, throughout the elementary school years a great deal of time and effort is devoted to helping children acquire these skills and, as will be suggested in the following chapter, the acquisition of literacy and numeracy is associated with the development of more general intellectual skills that it is a central aim of schooling to foster.

However, this does not explain the much smaller importance attached to ability in using oral language. That result was quite unexpected. Even in the upper levels of the elementary school, a great deal of the content of the curriculum is still presented orally, and it might be expected that teachers would be particularly aware of their pupils' abilities, in discussion and in one-to-one dialogue, to understand and make use of the material they are being asked to learn.

Since there undoubtedly were differences between the children in their ability to express themselves coherently and fluently in speech in the oral tasks that they were asked to perform and also, to a lesser extent, in the teachers' assessments of various aspects of oral language ability, it can only be assumed that activities in which these skills are called upon do not contribute to what are seen as the more central areas of the curriculum. Or perhaps, as was suggested in Chapter 5, exploratory and collaborative talk is not thought of as playing a significant part in learning. Whatever the explanation, it seems that a valuable resource is being insufficiently utilized, particularly as there are a number of children in almost every classroom who are able to work on new ideas more effectively in speech than in writing (Barnes, 1976). If we are to match learning opportunities to individuals who differ in aptitude and learning style, this seems to be an issue that needs to be given a great deal more attention.[3]

There is a further point that needs to be emphasized in all such discussions, and that is that achievement is not the same as progress. Measurements of achievement are almost always made with respect to a group of children of approximately the same age. They are therefore biased against slow developers who, by definition, achieve low scores relative to their age peers. However, it does not follow at all that because a child remains at the bottom of the class throughout a year or even several years that he or she has made less *progress* than the child who was consistently at the top of the same class. Progress is measured relative to an initial state and is concerned with the amount of knowledge or skill gained. Low achievers in a class may thus be making just as much progress as high achievers. In a highly competitive society, however, this is often treated as less important than the fact that they are slow developers. Always coming off worse in age-related comparisons of achievement, they may easily come to be seen and to see themselves as intrinsically less well able to learn and, as a result, cease to make the progress of which they are capable.

As with the other stereotypes, therefore, we must be on our guard against treating low achievers in any age group as necessarily less capable of ultimately reaching a satisfactory level of achievement than those who are currently high achievers.[4] The important point to bear in mind is that achievement is the outcome of an interaction between potential ability and experience. Slow developers are often not less able but simply lacking in the relevant experience. When an effort is made to match the curriculum to the needs of individual children and these gaps in experience are filled, progress may be remarkable.

Theories of Linguistic Disadvantage

The issue of the place of oral language ability in the classroom is particularly relevant when we come to consider the much-debated question as to whether children from the lower end of the continuum of family background are at a disadvantage, linguistically speaking, when they come to school. Many people have argued that they are and that this is a major cause of their low educational achievement. But there has been considerable disagreement as to the precise nature of the disadvantage.

Initially, the explanation was couched in terms of deficit: lower-class children simply had fewer linguistic resources than their middle-class peers and, for that reason, were less well able to participate in the largely linguistic activities of the classroom. In the view of the proponents of this theory, the obvious remedy was to provide a highly structured compensatory educational programme that would equip these children with the skills that it was assumed they lacked and that were also assumed to be necessary for academic success. Although this view emerged most strongly in the United States at the time of Operation Head Start in the mid-1960s, it was also quite widely accepted in Britain and in other countries in which unskilled or semiskilled manual workers formed a substantial proportion of the population.

However, in reaction to this denigrating assessment of lower class children's language, an alternative explanation was proposed by Labov (1970), which was also widely accepted, particularly in the United States. During his research on the different social dialects found in all urban centres, Labov noticed how often lower-class children, particularly black children, appeared linguistically incompetent in classroom interactions with teachers and other adults. However, out in the playground with their peers or even in informal conversation with an adult, these children showed perfectly normal linguistic ability and often considerable expertise in the verbal activities valued by their friends. On the other hand, the dialect in which these verbal skills were displayed, like the dialect they spoke at home, was not Standard English, but a nonstandard dialect, black vernacular English (BVE), which differs systematically from standard English in a number of important ways. These children did not lack language, Labov argued; rather, their apparent incompetence was due to their lack of facility in situations in which they were required, or at least expected, to use Standard English. Their disadvantage, therefore, was that their dialect did not match the dialect used and valued by their teachers.

An altogether different explanation of linguistic disadvantage was proposed in Britain by Basil Bernstein. According to his account, the educationally significant difference between children from middle- and lower-class homes was not to be found in their underlying linguistic abilities, but in the uses to which they habitually put them, and these they learned from their day-by-day experience of conversation in their homes. Because of their different relationships to the means of production in their roles at work – as labourers as compared with managers or creators of information – Bernstein (1975, 1982) argued, members of the two classes were likely to emphasize different types of relationships within the family and to enact these relationships through different selections from the linguistic resources that are in principle available to all of them as members of the larger language community. Lower-class families, he suggested, emphasized 'positional' relationships and enacted them through a 'restricted' linguistic code, in which much of the speaker's meaning was implicit – assumed to be already known and shared, or tied to the immediate context of activity. Middle-class families, by contrast, were said to emphasize 'personal' relationships and, while meanings might on appropriate occasions be equally implicit, speakers would, where necessary, make their own personal point of view explicit and set it in a more universal context. This latter use of language was described as an 'elaborated' code.

The significance of these two codes for children's achievement in school, he argued, was that the habitual experience of one or other of them was said to orient children to different orders of meaning: the restricted code to context-bound, particularistic meanings and the elaborated code to more context-independent and universalistic meanings. And because education is concerned with the latter order of meanings, middle-class children, who were said to be already more familiar with the use of an elaborated code, adjusted relatively easily to the language demands of the classroom. The restricted code experience of lower-class children, by contrast, did not provide such a good preparation. Their disadvantage, therefore, was that their habitual experience of linguistic interaction at home did not match well with the expectations of the school.

For a considerable time, Bernstein's ideas remained purely theoretical and were often attacked as supporting explanations of differential school achievement in terms of working class children's linguistic deficit. However, in the 1980s, Ruqaiya Hasan, who had previously worked with Bernstein, carried out a study in which she compared the ways in which Australian middle and working class mothers talked with their preschool aged children in the course of their everyday activities (Hasan, 1986). As Bernstein had predicted, she found systematic differences which, she suggested, would be consequential in the context of the children's subsequent formal education, for the different ways in which mothers talked with their children expressed different orientations to meaning and so had the effect of encouraging different 'mental dispositions'. Summing up her argument with its supporting evidence of social class differences, Hasan concluded as follows:

> [C]hildren have a massive experience of certain specific ways of saying and meaning, which are characterised by a particular semantic direction. Participation in this discourse shapes the children's consciousness, orients them to taking certain ways of being, doing and saying as legitimate and reasonable; in short, it defines the contours of reality and provides a map for navigating that reality.
>
> There is consistent and strong evidence that, at this early stage of three and half to four years, the children belonging to these two groups have established different ways of learning, different ways of solving

problems, different forms of consciousness, or mental disposition ... Through this mediation, the mother's culture becomes the growing child's map of reality, thus ensuring its own continuance. (Hasan, 2002: 120)

It must be emphasized, however, that Hasan did not suggest that these dispositions were fixed and immutable. As children later participate in contexts beyond the home – in school or in out-of-school activities – they may encounter different ways of saying and meaning, from which they may appropriate different orientations to meaning. Thus, there is nothing deterministic about early language socialization, as is demonstrated by the significant number of young adults of working class origin who master the 'elaborated code', becoming, in the process, bidialectal.[5]

As can be seen, these theoretical explanations of the linguistic disadvantage experienced by many lower-class pupils are very different in the value that they place upon the linguistic resources that these pupils have acquired at home and in what they consider should be the appropriate response of the school. At one extreme, the proponents of the deficit theory see the problem as residing almost entirely in the child and in his or her home environment. To them, the obvious remedy is to provide highly structured compensatory educational programmes that would equip these children with the skills that it is assumed that they lack and that are also assumed to be necessary for success at school: programmes that involve much group responding to teachers' display questions; emphasizing answers in the form of grammatically complete sentences; and, as the children progress, focusing on isolated sounds and letters as a preparation for the decoding of print.

At the other extreme, Labov argued that the children he studied were in no way linguistically deficient. What was necessary for their success at school was an adaptation on the part of teachers: an acceptance of the children's dialect and a proper valuing of the uses of language that they themselves valued.[6]

Bernstein's position was somewhere in the middle. The fundamental problem, as he saw it, was in society as a whole – in the class-based inequalities of power and control. Schools needed to adjust to the different orientations to meaning that could be expected of children from different class backgrounds. At the same time, a determined effort needed to be made to give restricted code users experience of, and access to, the elaborated code.

Clearly, each of these theoretical attempts to explain the causes of the disadvantages lower class children experience in schools was a very significant advance on the earlier position that lower-class children inherited lower intelligence; if it was language rather than innate intelligence that was at issue, steps could be taken to overcome the disadvantage. In fact, all three proposed explanations have been influential, both at the level of policy decisions about the best way to use available resources and also at the level of the classroom, through the initial and in-service education of teachers. All three theories have given rise to firm – albeit different – beliefs about the typical preschool conversational experience of children from different social backgrounds, from which have been derived powerful expectations about the linguistic resources these children will have when they come to school. Unfortunately, however, in many cases, those in a position to influence the school experiences of lower-class children have selected the theory with which they feel most comfortable without taking the trouble to critically examine the evidence.

As was pointed out at the beginning of this chapter, the aim of research has often been to demonstrate the existence of theoretically predicted differences, not to discover what is actually the case. In order to discover how far children's preschool linguistic experiences do in fact differ, it is necessary to select a representative sample of children and to observe the naturally occurring conversations in which they participate in a wide variety of contexts. Only when this has been done can one talk with any confidence about the linguistic resources that children have available and about the conversational experiences through which they have acquired them.

The Evidence from the Bristol Study

One of the main aims of the Bristol Study was to obtain this sort of evidence, and every effort was made to ensure that, as far as it was possible to do so, the samples of conversation that were recorded were typical of the language that was used both by and with each child. We went to considerable lengths to ensure that the parents did not know precisely when the recorder was actually operating. If they were affected by the presence of the 'bug' in their homes (although there was very little evidence that they were), the effect was presumably to bring their practice more into conformity with their beliefs which, according to the theories just discussed, would have tended to exaggerate any class-related differences. However, the parents' styles of conversation were never discussed with them during the course of the investigation; and, when we did ask, after the observations had been completed, the vast majority said they could not think of any ways in which their behaviour had been changed by participating in the study. There is a strong reason to believe, therefore, that the evidence we obtained accurately represents the preschool linguistic experience of these children and of the population from which they were selected.

The most important finding has already been mentioned: up to the age of five, there were no systematic differences between the middle- and lower-class groups of children in their rate of development, in the range of meanings expressed, or in the range of functions for which language was used – though there were differences in the topics they were most likely to talk about with other family members. And, although it is true that the extremely fast and the extremely slow developers did show a marked tendency to be found at the upper and lower ends of the continuum of family background, these two groups together accounted for no more than 10% of the sample as a whole (Wells, 1985).

Essentially the same was true when we looked at the quality of the children's conversational experience. Certainly there was wide variation in the amount of conversation that occurred (from as few as 36 utterances to as many as 360 adult utterances addressed to different children in the 18, 90-second samples that were analysed at each observation). There was also wide variation in the quality of the conversation – in the extent to which parents sustained and extended their children's conversational contributions, as described in Chapter 3. But in both quality and quantity, the differences were not significantly associated with family background. Neither were there obvious differences in style of child or adult speech that would tend to support the theory of strongly class-associated differences in code. In fact, in all homes the range and level of conversation was for the most part highly dependent on context and restricted to familiar, everyday experiences.

It is true we did not observe the families on visits outside the home – to the launderette, the doctor's consulting room, the park or the museum. Examples claiming to show the difference between the two social classes in their styles of conversation are often taken from such settings, based on conversations that have been overheard. However, such comparisons are of dubious validity as a basis for more general statements, for two reasons. First, they represent only a very small proportion of any child's conversational experience; and second, such situations may lead parents to behave in uncharacteristic ways, which differ in a class-associated manner according to the degree of self-confidence that they feel when they are publicly on view and expected to keep their children under control.

On the basis of the evidence that we collected, therefore, there is little justification for continuing to hold the stereotyped belief that there are strongly class-associated differences in the ways in which parents talk with their children. Nor is there justification for forming expectations about children's oral language abilities on entry to school based solely on their parents' membership in a certain social class. Children differ, certainly, in the fluency and explicitness with which they habitually express themselves, but these differences do not necessarily correspond to their actual abilities, nor are they, for the most part, strongly associated with family background.[7]

When children come to school, however, the picture apparently changes. There are class-related differences in their assessed ability to cope with tests and test-like situations; furthermore, the teachers of the children in our study certainly perceived their oral language abilities to differ in ways that were quite strongly related to family background. However, we should not accept these results at their face value. In the first place, the differences in test performance, although real, may reflect different degrees of familiarity with the conventions of testing rather than a real difference in ability in relation to the actual content of the tests.

Second, it is highly probable that teacher expectations had some influence on the children's performances, and hence on the teachers' assessments of their linguistic abilities. Although, as already mentioned, there was no evidence that the teacher's perception of dialect – standard or nonstandard – had a significant relationship with their differential assessments of the children's achievement, there was little doubt that other cues, such as father's occupation or the neighbourhood in which they lived, influenced the teachers' expectations. And these expectations, in turn, sometimes influenced the ways in which the teachers engaged in conversation with the children. Where there were high expectations, teachers were more likely to encourage children to express their ideas spontaneously and to do so at length; conversely, low expectations led to a more strongly eliciting style of conversation on the part of the teacher, with few opportunities for the child to initiate or sustain a topic of conversation. (The example of Teacher A's interaction with Rosie in Chapter 5 is an extreme example of this tendency.) The result is that, with different opportunities, children produce different performances, which merely serve to confirm the teachers' initial expectations. To some extent, therefore, without having any intention to do so – indeed even with clear intentions to foster a child's language development – a teacher can interact with a child in such a way that that child is caused to appear linguistically deficient or disadvantaged.

By age 10, however, the picture has changed. Differences between pupils in their performance on the specifically oral tasks were not significantly associated with family background and the relationship, as far as the teachers' assessments of oral language ability were concerned, was barely significant. Since this result confirms the picture that we had obtained during the preschool years, it does tend to suggest that the association between oral language ability and class or family background on entry to school was more the result of differences between the children in the ease with which they adjusted to the linguistic demands of the classroom than of any more fundamental class-based difference in ability.

However, we are still left with the very substantial association between family background and overall achievement to explain. To do this, we need to return to another of the tests that we gave to the children on entry to school: the test of knowledge of literacy.

This test, better than any other, predicted overall achievement at the age of seven; it was even a good predictor of achievement at age 10. Significantly, it was also the test that was most strongly associated with family background. In fact, at all ages, all the measures concerned with literacy – tests and teachers' assessments – were significantly associated with family background. In the light of these results, we decided to look more closely at the preschool observations and at the interviews with the parents when the children were aged three-and-a-half and five to see whether we could find an explanation.

From the interviews it emerged quite clearly that the children who obtained relatively higher scores on the knowledge-of-literacy test were likely to have parents who read more and owned more books; these parents were also likely to read more often to their children. This finding was confirmed by the number of times children were observed to have stories read to them during the recorded observations. This varied from a minimum of four stories a day in the case of Jonathan to no stories at all in the case of Rosie. Simple arithmetic allows one to compute the magnitude of this difference: four stories a day for each of the 365 days in the year over the period from one to five years gives a total of nearly 6000 story-reading experiences for Jonathan; for Rosie the total – which was confirmed in the interview with her mother, was zero. The children who were read to were themselves also more likely to show an interest in literacy, asking about the meanings of words and the significance of letter shapes; they were also more likely to spend considerable periods of time on activities associated with reading and writing. And, unlike the measures of oral language use by child or parent, all these literacy-related measures in the preschool years were significantly associated with family background (Wells, 1984).

If some lower-class children did suffer from linguistic disadvantage, therefore, it was not in relation to their command or experience of oral language, but in the relatively low value placed on literacy by their parents, as shown by their own very limited use of these skills, by the absence of books – either children's or parents' – in the home, and by the infrequency with which they read to their children, if they ever did so at all.

As a result, these children came to school with a very limited understanding of the purposes of literacy and little knowledge of how to set about obtaining meaning from print. Not surprisingly, therefore, they experienced considerably more difficulty in learning to read and write; and, although they might acquire the mechanical skills of decoding print to speech and of forming letters, words and sentences in writing, unless they discovered the value of these skills at school, the children rarely achieved a level of independence by the age of 10 sufficient to make reading and writing enjoyable and rewarding activities. As a result, they tended to be less successful in other areas of the curriculum as well, as was seen earlier when the components of overall achievement were discussed.

This finding in no way contradicts the results of the substantial body of research that shows that, in a literate society, all children develop progressively more adult-like hypotheses about the organization of written language from the print in their environment (Ferreiro & Teberosky, 1982; Hall, 1987). What is at issue here is what some children were discovering in addition. That is to say, it was not whether the children had acquired any knowledge about literacy that predicted their later achievement, but the differences between them in how much they had acquired, and how closely that knowledge was related to the functions of literacy that are important in education. Heath (1983) has suggested from her research that the differences are qualitative rather than quantitative: in different subcultures, literacy is used in different ways and valued for different purposes. This may have been true to some extent of the different social groups in our study, but the more obvious difference was in the frequency with which they engaged in any of the uses of literacy.

However, lest we feel tempted to lay the blame for the plight of these children on the inadequacies of their parents, we should consider for a moment the larger social context in which both parents and children find themselves caught up. Let us follow in imagination one group of school entrants at the age of five. Some of them are already familiar with the activities of reading and writing and know how and why to use books, even though they probably cannot yet read or write for themselves. However, with such a good start, they quickly learn the necessary skills and, by age seven or eight, have become independent readers and writers. They are able to cope effectively with curricular tasks that require these skills and continue to be able to do so throughout their secondary schooling. At age 18 they continue into college or university and, having acquired qualifications, go into some form of middle-class occupation, in which they continue to use the skills of literacy. When these young adults get married and have children of their own, their regular work and leisure activities provide opportunities for their children to see the value of literacy, and they probably also share their own valuation by reading and writing with them. Their children, in turn, come to school already knowing about literacy and ready to follow the successful educational careers of their parents.

By contrast, the children who come to school knowing little about literacy frequently have difficulty in learning to read and write; and, because these skills are given such importance at school, their relative failure often leads them to lose confidence in their ability to learn. On entry to the secondary school, they are placed in the lower streams, or even in the remedial department and, unless they are very fortunate, their lack of academic success – which is largely dependent on skills in literacy – leads to disenchantment with the whole business of education. As a result, they leave school at the first possible opportunity without qualifications and, when employment is available, they go into lower-class occupations that require only minimal, if any, skills in literacy. When these young adults marry and have children, they too engage in many interesting and valuable activities with their children. But, because they do not enjoy reading and writing, they do not engage in these activities themselves nor do they share them with their children. Their children then come to school as disadvantaged, in their turn, as were their parents. In this way, the cycle of educational disadvantage is repeated: socially transmitted, as Bernstein suggested, through the characteristic patterns of activity and interaction that families of different social backgrounds engage in as a result of their own experiences as children and pupils, and in their occupations as adults.

In the late 1980s, after the first edition of this book was published, I had the opportunity to talk with Ruqaiya Hasan about the findings of our respective studies. She was convinced that the differences she had found in Australia between middle and lower class mothers' conversations with their preschool children would apply equally to the Bristol sample. I had to agree that this may have been the case, since our method of data collection – recording 90 second samples at random intervals on one day every three months – meant that we rarely captured extended exploratory conversations of the kind that Hasan (1986, 2002) found more likely to occur in the middle class homes. If they did indeed occur in the Bristol homes, such opportunities for sustained meaning-making disembedded from the children's ongoing activity could well explain the greater ease and fluency with which those from the upper end of the continuum of family background were observed – when given the opportunity – to express their ideas and opinions in the schools they attended. These qualities were certainly taken into account by the teachers in their differential evaluations of the children's language abilities.

However, another way of interpreting Hasan's findings is to see them as resulting from families' different beliefs about the value of encouraging children to adopt an inquiring attitude to the world around them rather than accepting it as they find it. Families who hold the former beliefs are probably more likely to read stories to their children and to take time to talk about the characters and the motives for their actions as a way of extending their children's experience beyond the events of daily life in which they are directly involved. Whether or not these practices are primarily engaged in as preparation for school, there is strong evidence that such exploratory talk (Barnes, 1976) does indeed lead to success in the early school years, particularly in the development of literacy. Furthermore, the shared reading of stories leads to enhanced opportunities for vocabulary development, which not only facilitates independent reading but also results in higher scores on vocabulary tests, such as the English Picture Vocabulary Test, which we found to be significantly associated with both family background and subsequent educational achievement. Thus, the frequency of story reading – which we did, but Hasan did not investigate – is in many ways comparable to the occurrence of sustained exploratory talk as an index of the use of disembedded language. And here the Bristol Study did find significant differences between children that were associated with social class.

In sum, therefore, there is considerable validity, in my view, in the theory of linguistic disadvantage with respect to success in school, when this is understood as relative unfamiliarity with the significance of literacy, its forms and functions and the kinds of exploratory talk with which it is associated. But it is important to recognize that this does not imply a general rejection of the rich oral language resources that all children have by the time they come to school, whatever the class or ethnic group to which they belong. Nor does it imply that, simply by an educator knowing certain demographic information about a child's family, he or she can predict with any accuracy how much relevant preschool experience individual children will have had or how great is their potential for success in meeting the demands of the school. However, it does help to explain why, despite their evident command of spoken language, a significant proportion of children from those groups in society that do not belong to the educated, typically middle-class 'mainstream' fail to benefit as much as they might from their formal education. However, it is important to be clear that it is not class or ethnic group membership _as such_ that explains the processes whereby some children come to be linguistically disadvantaged with respect to the opportunities provided by formal education. Rather it is the actual practices that families engage in with respect to literacy events in the home and the different values that they give to them. And, as we found, these are *not* determined by social class.

Unfortunately, schools may inadvertently be helping to perpetuate this disadvantage by weighting assessment so strongly in favour of literacy at the expense of oracy. More use, I am convinced, could be made of the undoubted abilities that many lower-class pupils have to learn and to convey the fruits of their learning through spoken language. This is an area in which they are at much less of a disadvantage with respect to their middle-class peers. Yet, on the evidence of our study, they are not being given the opportunity and encouragement to make full use of these abilities. Talking to learn is just as important as reading and writing to learn, and we ought to plan so that both are given equal value as complementary modes of thinking and communicating in all areas of the curriculum.

At the same time, there can be no diminution in the efforts that we make to enable all children to become fully literate. However, this aim will not be served by delaying the start of learning to read and write in order to give such children so-called compensatory programmes in oral language. This is doubly ineffective. In the first place, the children do not need them. They are quite able to speak in complete sentences when the occasion is appropriate and they are given the opportunity to do so. But more important, what they do need, and need urgently, is experience of books and the pleasure that comes from being read to; they also need the opportunity to try to make meanings in written language for themselves. The reason that this is so important is the subject to be considered next.

Notes

1. I use this term quite deliberately to avoid the specific interpretations given to alternative terms such as 'social class' or 'socioeconomic status' in different parts of the world. However, since much of the research on this issue has been carried out in Britain and in other parts of Europe, where the terms 'middle class' and 'lower class' are fairly well understood, I shall use these terms where it would be too cumbersome to refer to the upper and lower range of the continuum (or, more precisely, cluster of associated continua) of family background.
2. There is also the possibility that a similar bias operates against the slow developer. However, for the lack of appropriate longitudinal evidence, this possibility must for the moment remain in the realm of unproven conjecture.
3. This has indeed occurred in the years following the Bullock Report (1975) in the work of the National Oracy project (Bullock, 1975; Norman, 1992).
4. I write with feeling, as I was such a student until well into adulthood.
5. Bernstein himself was a very clear example of this bidialecticism.

6. This recommendation was taken up in Oakland, California, in the late 1990s, where the decision to include 'Ebonics' as part of the curriculum led to heated debate.
7. While we were analysing the Bristol data, Bernstein modified his way of characterizing social class, making a three-way distinction between involvement in production, symbolic control and power (police, army) (Holland, 1980) Bernstein and Holland subsequently reanalysed our maternal interview data using this new formulation and found that the mother's education and the status of her occupation, as now defined, were both significant predictors of her reported ways of dealing with her child's language and behaviour (Wells, 1985).

Chapter 8
The Centrality of Literacy

Probably the most striking finding from the whole of the longitudinal study has been the very strong relationship between knowledge of literacy at age five and all later assessments of school achievement. In the previous chapter some suggestions were made as to why this test should have had such predictive power and why the differences between the children should have been associated with family background. In a sense, those suggestions already provide a denouement to the story, but they do not fully explain the underlying mechanism. Indeed, in some respects the test results, if taken at face value, might lead to some erroneous conclusions.

The Test of Knowledge of Literacy

Let us look more carefully at the knowledge of literacy test itself. *Concepts about Print* (Clay, 1972) consists of two parts. In the first, the child is presented with an illustrated storybook called *Sand*. It is about a child going to the seaside, digging in the sand, making sand castles, and so on. The items in this part of the test are designed to measure how much the child knows about how to cope with print. At the beginning of the test, the book is handed to the child upside down and back to front. The first item is scored according to whether or not he or she turns the book the right way around. The next item asks, 'Which part tells the story?' and is scored according to whether the child points to the text or to the picture. The items increase in specificity regarding the child's concepts about print until, at the end of the test, the child is asked, 'Can you show me a word?' and 'Can you show me a sentence?'

The second part of the test is even more text-specific. The child is presented with a sheet of paper on which are displayed, in random order, all the letters of the alphabet in both upper- and lowercase forms. The child is asked to name or sound as many as he or she can recognize.

Taken together, the two parts of the test provide a very reliable estimate of how much a child knows about the conventions of written language. And, as already noted, the score a child achieves is a very good indicator of how quickly and successfully he or she will acquire the skills of reading and writing and be able to use them in tackling work in other areas of the curriculum.[1]

But is the knowledge tapped by this test what is really crucial? Is it what explains the difference between those who quickly and easily learn how to read and write and those who do not? Or is it more a byproduct of acquiring a different sort of knowledge about literacy that is of much greater fundamental importance? To put it differently, if we want to help children to become literate, is it here that we should start – by teaching the names or sounds of the letters and the operational definitions of terms like 'word' and 'sentence'?

There is no doubt that most readers do come to possess this knowledge, and it can be very useful as a means to further learning through instruction. But, as teaching methods that place the emphasis on what might be called 'the mechanics of literacy' have shown, it is possible to be very successful in teaching children to operate on the surface appearance of print but to find that they still do not understand what they read and that they never voluntarily engage in this activity, either to obtain information or for the enjoyment it offers (Gallas, 2003).

The point is perhaps made more clearly if we draw the comparison with spoken language. What use would it be for a child to know all the sounds of his or her language and the rules for combining them into words and sentences, if the child had not discovered that the whole point of this knowledge was that it was a resource for the exchange of meanings in the attainment of joint purposes of various kinds? The same is true, I believe, for an understanding of the mechanics of literacy. Important though this knowledge is for reading and writing, it is of little value if the child does not understand the *purpose* of these activities – if he or she does not know that written language conveys meaning and that it does so in ways that differ from those that apply in the use of spoken language.

Learning about Literacy in the Preschool Years

How then might some of the children in our study have discovered something of the significance of written language before they came to school? To answer this question it is necessary to look more carefully at the sorts of activities that they engaged in, or observed, during the preschool years at home in order to see which of them might provide opportunities for the necessary learning. Two sources of evidence were available for this investigation: the parents' responses to questions asked during interviews with them and the transcripts of the actual recorded observations in the children's homes.

From the first source, it was obvious that the parents' own interest in literacy was important: the number of books they owned and how much they read and wrote in accomplishing their own purposes. In this, as in so many other areas, children learn from the model provided by adult behaviour. This was particularly clearly shown with respect to the development of their writing. Children who, at age nine or 10, were amongst the more accomplished writers were much more likely to have parents who themselves wrote frequently, particularly lists, memos and notes for themselves. The reasons for this seem to be twofold: First, these forms of writing are likely to be particularly visible to children, since they occur in the course of other activities in which they may be involved, rather than in a secluded study or after the children have gone to bed. Second, because such occasions of writing occur as part of other, often shared, activities, their significance is quite readily appreciated by children and, indeed, may become a matter for actual discussion (Tizard & Hughes, 1984).

From the parental interviews, too, it was clear that the child's own interest in literacy was an important factor. This was measured not only by the number of books he or she personally owned, but by the general interest displayed in written language, in the form of signs, advertisements, labels, as well as the more conventional books and magazines. Some children more than others asked about words seen – their meaning and, in some cases, how to spell them. Even more important as an indicator of their interest in literacy was how absorbed they became in activities associated with literacy – how long, according to their parents' reports, they typically chose to spend on them.[2]

This last finding was the starting point for the next stage of the investigation, which involved a careful scrutiny of all the transcripts of the actual observations. If the extent of the child's own involvement in what we had generally labelled 'literacy-related activities' was, of all the factors asked about in the interview, most strongly related to subsequent success in school, what were these activities, and were some of them more important than others?

Obviously, there are many activities that have the potential for helping the child to learn about literacy, but they are so specific and occur, relatively speaking, so rarely that we could not expect to capture them in our short and infrequent observations – such activities as spotting signs like 'EXIT' or the names or logos of well-known brand names on goods or advertisements, watching Mother write a note for the milk or bread delivery person or reading the TV guide to find out when a favourite programme is on. These are a few examples – and there are many others – where the use of reading or writing plays a small but significant part in the lives of the majority of families. In a literate society, all children begin to form hypotheses about the functions and organization of print from such experiences. What may differ, however, is the extent to which the child is involved in these activities and how far he or she is encouraged to play an active role in them to the extent of his or her abilities.

There are other activities, however, that involve literacy much more centrally. These it did seem possible to investigate more systematically. Given the content of the knowledge of literacy test, on which the children had been so differently rated, one obvious place to start was with deliberate instruction on how to use a book and on the letters of the alphabet. However, although this no doubt took place in some homes, it was not a frequent occurrence in our recorded samples. If it was observed, it was nearly always incidental to some other activity, and so, as an independent activity, it was dropped from the investigation.

In the end, it was decided to search for occurrences of four activities. These were: looking at a picture book and talking about it; listening to a story; drawing and colouring; and writing – or pretending to write. Although not all the children had books of their own, there was no home without illustrated magazines and mailorder catalogues, and nearly all the children spent some time looking at or naming the pictures. Where an adult joined in this activity, this might provide a valuable preparation for learning to read, first because it involved handling a book or booklike object and, second, because looking at pictures and talking about the objects portrayed, their attributes, and the scenes in which they were involved might provide a valuable preparation for similar discussions at school – often an important part of a child's introduction to his or her first reading book.

Listening to a story read aloud, on the other hand, provides a different sort of introduction to written language. Here what is encountered is continuous prose, in which meaning is built up cumulatively over many sentences and even chapters. Pictures occur in many storybooks, too, but in almost all cases as accompanying illustrations.

The inclusion of drawing and colouring was based on two rather different observations. In our visits to schools, we had noticed that it was a very common practice to ask each child to draw and colour a picture and then to use the picture as the basis for the creation of a short written text. The child would talk about his or her picture and, with the teacher's help, compose a caption. This would then be traced over or copied and then finally read back to the teacher. Within such an instructional framework, therefore, drawing would be seen as intimately connected with reading and writing.

But drawing is also connected with writing in a different way. Both involve the attempt to give symbolic representation to what has been understood. As teachers and parents know, young children's spontaneous drawings are very far from realistic. Instead of drawing what they see, they try to represent what is essential about the subject as they have understood it. Indeed, Vygotsky (1978) has argued that this is an important step on the way to writing: First the child discovers that his or her understanding of objects can be represented directly, and at a somewhat later stage the child discovers that the speech in which those objects are referred to can also be represented. For some children, therefore, we might expect to find occurrences of this fourth activity as, with pencil or crayon, they engage in 'writing' – that is to say, in making marks of any kind that they themselves consider to represent a linguistic message.

Once it had been decided which activities to look for, all the transcripts were searched for evidence of their occurrence. Scores were given to each child, based on the number of occasions on which he or she was observed to engage in each activity. All the children were observed to look at picture books and to talk about them, although not equally often. 'Writing', on the other hand, was observed only twice and by a different child on each occasion. In between came listening to stories and drawing and colouring, which were each observed in one or more transcripts of about half the children. The final step was to compare the frequency scores for each activity with the children's scores on the two later literacy measures: the knowledge of literacy test at age five and the test of reading comprehension administered after two years at school.

The results of this comparison were absolutely clear-cut. Of the three frequently occurring activities that had been considered as possibly helpful preparation for the acquisition of literacy, only one was significantly associated with the later test scores, and it was clearly associated with both of them. That activity was listening to stories.

What's in a Story?

Why should listening to stories be so much more beneficial as a preparation for literacy than looking at books and magazines and talking about the pictures, or attempting to represent ideas graphically through drawing and colouring – worthwhile though these activities are for their own sake? There are, I believe, a number of reasons.

First, in listening to stories read aloud at the age of two, three, or long before they can read themselves – children are already beginning to gain experience of the sustained meaning-building organization of written language and its characteristic rhythms and structures. So, when they come to read books for themselves, they will find the language familiar.

Second, through stories, children vicariously extend the range of their experience far beyond the limits of their immediate surroundings. In the process, they develop a much richer mental model of the world and a vocabulary with which to talk about it. As a result, as the content of the curriculum expands beyond what can be experienced firsthand in the classroom, children who have been read to find themselves at a considerable advantage. This is clearly apparent in the assessment made of our 10-year-olds by their teachers. Size of vocabulary was strongly related to overall educational achievement.[3]

Stories can also provide an excellent starting point for the sort of collaborative talk between children and parents that was described in Chapter 3, as the parent helps the child to explore his or her own world in the light of what happens in the story and to use the child's own experience to understand the significance of the events that are recounted. Such talk and the stories that give rise to it also provide a validation for the child's own inner storying – that internal mode of meaning making which is probably as deeply rooted in human nature as is language itself (Spencer, 1976).

All these positive features of sharing a story can be seen in the following extract from a recording of David (age three years), who has chosen to have *The Giant Jam Sandwich* (Lord & Burroway, 1975) read to him – obviously not for the first time. Notice how the mother leaves space for the child to offer comments and ask questions and how her contributions build on his, extending his understanding of both the matter of the story and the actual wording.

[David is sitting next to Mother on the sofa so that he can see the book.]

David: The Giant Sandwich
                    [four-second pause]
Mother: Who's this here on the first page?
David: The wasps
Mother: The wasps are coming *[Turns the page]*
                    Here's some more, look . Wow!
                    [Reads] One hot summer in Itching Down
                    Four million wasps flew into town
David: I don't like wasps flying into town
Mother: Why's that?
David: Because they sting me

Mother: Do they?

David: Mm . I don't like them

Mother: They'll only sting you if they get angry . if you leave them alone they won't sting you . but four million would be rather a lot, wouldn't it? . they'd get rather in the way
[Reads] They drove the picknickers away

David: Mm

Mother: *They chased the farmers from their hay*
They stung Lord Swell [chuckles] *on his fat bald-*

David: Pate

Mother: D'you know what a pate is?

David: What?

Mother: What d'you think it is?

David: Hair

Mother: Well- yes . it's where his hair should be . it's his head, look, his bald head . all his hair's gone

David: Where is it?

Mother: Well, he's old, so it's dropped out . he's gone bald

David: Where's- is that his hat?

Mother: Mm . he's running, so his hat's fallen off
[Reads] They dived . and hummed . and buzzed . and ate

David: D'they eat him?

Mother: [laughs] I expect they might have tried to . I dunno . d'you think wasps eat people?

David: No

Mother: What do they eat?

David: [with relish] They eat vegetables

Mother: [laughing] Vegetables?

David: Yes

Mother: What sort? what do they like?

David: They like *[five-second pause]* um

Mother: What kind of vegetables were you thinking of?
[Long pause]

David: *[looking at the illustration on the next page, which shows three male inhabitants of Itching Down, each attempting in his own way to get rid of the wasps]*
Is that a spray to shoo them away? is that a spray to shoo them away?

Mother: Yes, it's probably some sort of insecticide to get rid of them . And what's that net for, do you think? [a butterfly net]

David: It's for catching them with

Mother: It doesn't seem to be much good though, does it?

Figure 8.1 Illustration from *The Giant Jam Sandwich* (Lord & Burroway, 1975)
Source: Story and pictures by John Vernon Lord with verses by Janet Burroway. Copyright ©
1972 by John Vernon Lord. Reprinted by permission of Houghton Mifflin Harcourt Publishing
Company. All rights reserved.

David:	No . they come out the holes
Mother:	[laughs] The holes are too big, aren't they? . and what about this man? what's he got?
David:	He's- . what's he got?
Mother:	What's that?
David:	A note . what does the note say?
Mother:	A note on a stick, is it? . is that what you think?
David:	Actually it's a sound
Mother:	A what?
David:	A sound . what's it called on the- on the stick? What is it? . what's that man got?
Mother:	Well you know, um-
David:	Yes . sign
Mother:	You think it's a sign? . yes it looks very like a sign with writing on, doesn't it?
David:	Yes
Mother:	But it isn't . it's like Mummy's . um-fish slice [slotted spatula]
David:	What is it?
Mother:	It's a swatter . he's going to hit the wasp with it
David:	How d'you hit wasps with otters?

Mother: [checking] Swatters? . well, they're made of plastic
David: Yes
Mother: And they- you bang them down . see if you can squash the
                      wasp .. looks very angry
                      [five-second pause]
David: Is he hurt?
Mother: It looks as if he might be . he's making a funny face
David: Why he making a funny face? . is that man- is that man
                      shouting for them to go away?
Mother: Think so . he's got his mouth open, so he could be shouting
                      [five-second pause]
                      Anyway-
David: Yes
Mother: *[reads] They called a meeting in the village hall*
                      And Mayor Muddlenut asked them all,
                      'What can we do!' And they said, 'Good question',
                      But nobody had a good suggestion.

                      Then Bap the baker leaped to his feet
                      And cried, 'What do wasps like <u>best</u> . to
David: *best*
Mother: *eat?*
                      Strawberry
David: *jam*
Mother: *Now wait a minute*
                      If we made a giant sandwich
David: Yes
Mother: *We could catch them in it*

What is particularly impressive about this last section is the timing. It is
a truly shared recreation of the story, with David chiming in at exactly the
right moment to fit the rhythm of the lines. It is also worth noticing David's
interpretation of the picture of the man with the swatter: 'a note on a stick'.
What power he attributes to written language. Even wasps can be van-
quished by a sign with writing on it: 'WASPS, GO AWAY!'

To understand the full significance of having stories read aloud from an
early age, however, we need to look more closely at the relationship
between language and experience that is found in stories – and in most
extended uses of written language.

In ordinary conversation, which is every child's first and most frequent
experience of language in use, the meanings that are communicated

arise for the most part out of the context of ongoing activity or out of past or future events about which the participants have shared knowledge or expectations. To understand what is meant, therefore, they can use the context to help them interpret what is said. Indeed, as was suggested in Chapter 3, this is what makes it possible for the child to construct his or her representation of language in the first place. In conversation, too, the participants are usually face-to-face and so can provide immediate feedback on the success of the communication and engage in negotiation if problems occur. At the same time they also have to manage their interpersonal relationship satisfactorily by posture, gaze and intonation. All of which means that, in conversation, attention is only partly on what is said. In seeking to understand each other's intentions, participants make use of a variety of other cues, and the meaning that is finally constructed is the outcome of a collaborative and negotiated interaction, which owes as much to other sources of information as it does to the actual words spoken.

In written language, by contrast, the situation is usually very different. Because writer and reader are not in face-to-face contact, and indeed probably do not even know each other, there is no need for – or even possibility of – a moment-by-moment monitoring of the interpersonal relationship. For the same reason, the writer can make no more than very general assumptions about the knowledge that the reader will bring to the text; in addition, there is no context to support the writer's meaning other than that created by the text itself and the form in which it is presented. All of this leads to a much greater focus on the text alone as the carrier of meaning and to a need for greater explicitness if the intended meaning is to be unambiguously communicated.

This is not to ignore, of course, what the reader brings by way of general expectations and personal experience to the task of constructing an interpretation of the text, nor to underestimate the importance of the cues that are available to the mature reader in the genre form in which the text is presented – verse, dramatic script, newspaper editorial, and so on – or to the novice reader in the form of illustrations. However, even these cues are text-dependent, in the sense that it is only by attending to the text that their significance is recognized. Even when a story is illustrated, as for example in the case of *The Giant Jam Sandwich*, it is the text that gives a precise significance to the illustrations rather than vice versa.[4]

In sum, the most important difference between typical instances of spoken and written language can be stated as follows. In conversation, and particularly in casual conversation around the home, what is said arises out of shared activity and only takes on its full meaning when considered in relation to that nonlinguistic context. The aim in conversational speech, therefore, is to make the words fit the world (Searle, 1977). In most writing, on the other hand, there is no context in the external world to determine the interpretation of the text. The aim must therefore be to use words to create a world of meaning, which then provides the context in terms of which the text itself can be fully understood. To understand a story therefore – or any other written text – the child has to learn to give full attention to the linguistic message in order to build up a structure of meaning. For, insofar as the writer is able to provide cues for the reader's act of construction, he or she does so by means of the words and structures of the text alone.

What is so important about listening to stories, then, is that, through this experience, the child is beginning to discover the symbolic potential of language: its power to create possible or imaginary worlds through words – by representing experience in symbols that are independent of the objects, events and relationships symbolized and that can be interpreted in contexts other than those in which the experience originally occurred, if indeed it ever occurred at all.

Compared with the longer-term effects of this discovery, it is easy to see why drawing, or matching names or sounds to the letters of the alphabet, although useful, is of much less significance for later progress at school. The same is true of the learning that takes place when looking at picture books or catalogues and discussing the names and attributes of the objects depicted. No doubt this activity helps children to enlarge their vocabularies – at least for those things that can be pictured. It also gives them practice in answering display questions of a limited kind, and this may well give them an initial advantage if they find themselves – as many do – in classrooms where such skills are emphasized. But it is a short-lived advantage and one that is, in the longer term, restricting. For ultimately – and ideally sooner rather than later – children will need to be able to answer (and also to ask) questions that go beyond naming and rote recall. They will need to follow and construct narrative and expository sequences, recognizing causes, anticipating consequences and considering the motives and emotions that are inextricably bound up with all human actions and endeavours. In a word, they will need to be able to bring the full power of storying to bear on all the subject matter of the curriculum.

This interpretation of the connection between early experience of listening to stories and later educational achievement is confirmed by the final part of the investigation of children's preschool literacy-related activities. As well as comparing the frequency scores for the three activities – looking at picture books, listening to a story, and drawing and colouring – with subsequent scores on the tests of knowledge of literacy at age five and reading comprehension at age seven, we also compared them with the scores derived from the teachers' assessments of the children's oral language ability on entry to school.

Once again, the results were clear-cut. Only the frequency of listening to stories significantly predicted the teachers' assessment of oral language ability. And this was not simply the result of the children's having acquired a larger vocabulary. Children who had been read to were also better able to narrate an event, describe a scene and follow instructions. But perhaps what was most important in accounting for the teachers' higher assessment of these children's oral language abilities was the greater ease with which they appeared to be able to understand the teachers' use of language. This is not surprising when we consider how often the topics that teachers talk about – be it four-poster beds, children in other parts of the world, or sets in mathematics – are not physically present in the classroom. Even when speaking, therefore, the teacher tends to use a literate form of language and, to understand him or her, the child has to pay particular attention to the linguistic message and use that as the basis for constructing the teacher's intended meaning. That is to say, the child has to be able to exploit the symbolic potential of language.

This becomes increasingly important as the child moves up through the school and encounters more and more curriculum content that can only be brought into the classroom symbolically, through teacher talk and through books and other forms of symbolic representation. More than anything else, therefore, schools are concerned with the development of skills in symbol manipulation, first in 'natural' language through talk and then in reading and writing and, later, in the symbol systems of mathematics, music and science (and to these we must now add the languages used in programming computers). To understand the problems posed in the curricular tasks that children are given, and to succeed in finding solutions to them, children are more and more going to need to be able to 'disembed' their thinking from the context of their own particular, taken-for-granted experience and to handle ideas of a more abstract kind, for which their own personal experience may provide only minimal support.

As Margaret Donaldson puts it:

> What is going to be required for success in our educational system is that [the child] should learn to turn language and thought in upon themselves. He must become able to direct his own thought processes in a thoughtful manner. He must become able not just to talk, but to choose what he will say, not just to interpret but to weigh possible

interpretations. His conceptual system must expand in the direction of increasing ability to represent itself. He must become capable of manipulating symbols. (Donaldson, 1978: 88–89)

This is what becoming literate really involves. And listening to stories and discussing them with adults in ways that lead children to reflect upon their own experience and encourage them to explore, through their imagination, the world created through the language of the text (as the extract from the reading of *The Giant Jam Sandwich* shows) are probably the experiences that most help young children to discover and begin to gain control of what Sapir (1921) called 'the dynamo of language'.

What does this Mean for Rosie?

Rosie, it will be recalled, was the child who had the lowest score on all the tests we administered, including the test of knowledge of literacy. This can be largely attributed, I believe, to the fact that she never had stories read to her. According to both her mother's answer to the interview question and our observations, Rosie was not read to once before she started going to school. By comparison, Jonathan had something in the order of 6000 book and story experiences before starting school.

This difference in preschool experience was not limited to Rosie and Jonathan, however. There were other children in our sample whose experience differed in similar ways. And the same would be true in any large school or school system in any of the countries of the Western world. The question is: what can be done to help Rosie and children like her to catch up with their more fortunate peers?

It is sometimes argued that it is inappropriate to think in terms of compensating for experiences missed in the preschool years. Different cultures place different values on literacy, and schools should accept the fact that children will differ in the types of literacy event that they encounter in the years before they come to school and in the ways in which those events are interpreted in their communities. These differing attitudes to literacy and the differing ways in which people engage in literacy events, even in the same broad linguistic community, are clearly brought out in Heath's (1983) study of three cultural groups in a single city in the southeastern United States. In all three communities, there were certain types of literacy event that were considered important, but it was only in the 'mainstream', highly educated group that children had the sort of experience of literacy that prepared them for the approaches to reading and writing that they would be expected to adopt at school.

However, while it is important to accept children as they are, this does not mean that steps should not be taken, when they come to school, to provide them with a firm foundation on which to acquire those skills of literacy and symbol manipulation that are so important for later success in all areas of the curriculum.

In our visits to schools, we observed a number of different strategies being adopted, with varying degrees of apparent success. In some, a language experience approach was adopted, in which children handled, observed and talked about the objects and events in their environments and used this as a basis for drawing pictures and dictating captions, which were then traced or copied and later read back to the teacher. In others, a particular emphasis was given to what I have called the mechanics of literacy: time was spent on learning from flash cards the words in the first books in the reading scheme so that the children would be able to start working their way through the graded series of reading primers; considerable attention was also given to letter formation in writing, and to spelling and later to punctuating correctly. Sometimes both these approaches were used together.

Under these conditions, some children were learning quickly and most were making reasonable progress. But in almost every classroom there were some children whose progress was extremely slow; in a few the proportion of such children was disturbingly high. What was surprising, however, was that the strategies adopted seemed to bear little relation to the preschool experiences of the children, except that, in predominantly lower-class areas, more attention was given to activities intended to extend the children's oral language resources, on the assumption that this was the area in which they were most likely to be linguistically deprived. In one such school, this policy was taken to such lengths that almost no attention was paid to written language in the first few months at school, the emphasis being placed almost entirely on remedial oral language work. The children were not allowed to have a reading book nor to borrow books from the library because they could not read; and they were not learning to read because, being judged by definition not ready, they were not allowed access to books. It was hardly surprising, therefore, that at the end of the first year these children were severely retarded in reading and writing.

However, the evidence of our study suggests that, while some lower-class children, such as Rosie, would certainly benefit from increased opportunities to engage in collaborative, exploratory conversation with adults, children who have not already achieved sufficient command of their mother tongue to be introduced to books as soon as they come to school are extremely rare. If some children made little progress in learning to read and write, the problem, as we observed it, was not that they had insufficient oral language resources, but that they had not yet discovered the purpose of reading or writing or the enjoyment to be gained from these activities. (The predicament of children who are just starting to learn English as an additional language is clearly different, but even they can enjoy books of an appropriate kind, even though they may not yet be able to read them.)

What children like Rosie need, I am convinced, is a personal introduction to literacy through stories. Listening to a story read to the whole class is no solution, for they have not yet learned to attend appropriately to written language under such impersonal conditions (Gallas, 2003). For them, what is required is one-to-one interaction with an adult centred on a story. Such an experience provides not only an introduction to literacy but also an entry into a shared world that can be explored through the sort of collaborative talk that is the most effective way of facilitating children's learning and language development. This is an essential prerequisite if programmes that emphasize phonemic awareness and phonic skills as the way into reading are to be at all meaningful for children. Fortunately, many teachers are aware of this and ensure such opportunities, despite the draconian skill-based programmes they are required to use.

By the same token, picture storybooks, both those that are written for children and those that children create themselves, provide the best material for learning to read and write, once they have discovered the pleasure of sharing a story read aloud and acquired sufficient confidence to begin to join in the actual reading. There are now sufficient picture storybooks of varying levels of difficulty to enable a complete programme to be based on books that children choose because they want to read them for themselves (Moon, 2007).

Collaboration Between School and Community

Many teachers would like to spend more time reading books with individual children or with groups of two or three. The problem is to find the time. This is an almost insoluble problem if the teacher has to meet all the needs of the children in the class single-handed. However, there are various ways in which other people can provide assistance, most importantly the children's parents.

There is little doubt that the great majority of parents recognize the importance of literacy – or at least of their children's learning to read and write. Typically, however, the responsibility for seeing that children acquire the skills of literacy is assumed to rest with the school, and all too often this assumption is reinforced by the advice that is given to parents by teachers. In interviews with parents of the children in our study, we were told more than once that they had been advised not to attempt to introduce their children to reading before they came to school, as the parents' approach might lead to the children's being confused when they began to be taught at school. No mention was made of the valuable contribution parents could make by reading stories with children; no advice was given on what would be the most suitable books to read or how to obtain them from the public library or the school. Instead parents were made to feel incompetent, and the mistaken impression was given that becoming literate is chiefly a matter of learning to decode letters to sounds, a skill that could be taught only by an expert.

Such an attitude on the part of teachers is doubly unfortunate. In the first place, it implies a denial of the spontaneous nature of children's interest in written language and of their ability actively to make sense of it for themselves if given the opportunity and encouragement (Ferreiro & Teberosky, 1982; Hall, 1987; Harste, 1994). Second, it undermines the confidence of the very people who are most likely to have both the time and the inclination to provide the conditions in which children can begin to become literate, namely by sharing books and stories with them in an enjoyable and unthreatening one-to-one interaction and by encouraging them to discover the possibilities of writing through the free exploration of the forms and uses of graphic symbols.

These are ways in which parents can and do help children to construct the foundations of literacy in the years before school. However, once children start going to school, supporting the continuing development of literacy should become a collaborative enterprise, in which the assistance of parents is positively encouraged. There are many ways in which this can be achieved. The Haringey experiment (Hewison & Tizard, 1980) showed that parents regularly listening to their children read can significantly accelerate the children's progress. This has been confirmed in other schools, where a similar practice has been adopted. Along with help at home can go parental involvement in school, not only in listening to children read but also in reading to them. In one first-grade classroom in Toronto, all these ideas have been combined. Children take home not only books that they have chosen to read to their parents, but also books for their parents to read to them; in the morning, when the children are brought to school, parents who have time are invited to read to one child or to a small group of children a book that one of the children has chosen (Hart-Hewins & Wells, 1999).

Parents can help with writing, too. In some schools, parents help in the publication of the books that children have written. They also act, along with other members of the school and community, as sources of information whom the children consult on the topics about which they are preparing to write, as recipients of the children's written communications, and as readers of the children's books, once they are published (Graves, 2003).

However, parents are not the only members of the community who can help to extend young children's experience of belonging to what Smith (1987) has called 'the literacy club'. In many schools, older children regularly read to children in first- and second-year classes and listen to them read. In some schools, these older children are also encouraged to write stories for their younger 'buddies'. Senior citizens, with time on their hands after they have retired, are often delighted to spend some of it in classrooms reading to children and talking with them about their interests. Outside the school, too, there are many opportunities for other members of the community to contribute as recipients of children's written communications and as respondents to their requests for information.

Once teachers recognize the support that is available to them from the wider community in promoting the value and enjoyment of literacy and are willing to enlist this support in various types of collaboration, their task in providing the sort of experiences that Rosie and children like her need does not appear so formidable. It may be difficult – and perhaps even undesirable – to try to persuade all parents of the importance of providing the foundations of literacy by sharing stories with their children in the years before school. But this should not mean that their children are permanently deprived of this essential experience. Means must be found to ensure that all children's first experiences of reading and writing are purposeful and enjoyable. Only in this way will they be drawn into applying their meaning-making strategies to the task of making sense of written language. Only in this way will they learn to exploit the full symbolic potential of language and so become fully literate.

Notes

1. The correlation obtained between scores on the two parts of this test combined and reading attainment at seven years, as measured by the Neale Analysis of Reading was $r = 0.79$ and the correlation between the test of knowledge of literacy and reading at age 10, as measured by the NFER test, was again $r = 0.79$.

2. The correlation between this variable and the test of knowledge of literacy was $r = 0.65$. Its correlation with overall educational attainment at age 10 was $r = 0.63$.
3. On the relationship between size of vocabulary and educational achievement, see also Hayes (1982), 'On measuring the richness of children's natural language environments: conversation, books and television'; and more recently, the focus on vocabulary in a study by Hart and Risley (1999).
4. I certainly do not want to deny the importance of intertextuality – the fact that, for both writer and reader, 'a story only exists as a story by virtue of the existence of other stories' (Rosen, 1984). But for the current story to be related to other stories, the cues must be present in the text. Although emphasizing the work carried out by the reader, Eagleton (1983: 76) makes a related point when he writes that, as readers, 'we are all the time engaged in constructing hypotheses about the meaning of the text, drawing on a tacit knowledge of the world in general and of literary conventions in particular. The text itself is really no more than a series of "cues" to the reader, invitations to construct a piece of language into meaning'.

Chapter 9
The Children's Achievements at Age 10

Our study started by investigating the early stages of language learning. The questions we set out to answer were: how far do children show a common pattern of development, and in what ways is their development influenced by their environment? In the background, though, there were always further questions that we hoped to be able to answer about the educational significance of the differences between children that we had noticed from the very first observation. What effect did it have on later achievement at school whether children were early or late in learning to talk? How important were differences in oral language ability at the point of entry to school? Was there any evidence of class-related differences in language use in the home and, if so, did such differences provide an explanation for the class-related differences that had so often been reported in educational achievement?

The continuation of the study into the years of schooling gave us an opportunity to address these latter questions and, in general terms, the answers that we arrived at have already been reported in previous chapters. However, it is also interesting to look at these same questions from the perspective of case studies of individual children. In this chapter, therefore, we shall return to the six children who were introduced in Chapter 1, in order to see how they fared over the period covered by our investigation.

At the same time, since literacy emerged as the major differentiating factor at school, we shall look in more detail at the shift in emphasis from speech to writing and consider some of the factors that are involved in making this transition. This will lead us into a reconsideration of the role of spoken language in the middle-school years (approximately ages nine to 13) and, finally, to a plea for an integrated approach to language as the medium for learning across all the subjects of the curriculum.

Linguistic Influences on Educational Achievement

Rarely, if ever, has there been an opportunity to follow the same group of children from before they were able to speak until the end of the elementary stage of their education. The number of children that were involved throughout the duration of the Bristol Study may have been small but, given the uniqueness of the undertaking, the richness and variety of the information that was collected goes a long way towards compensating for the size of the sample. In particular, the comprehensive assessment of the children at the age of 10 has made it possible to look back over the preceding years in order to identify the major linguistic factors that were important in accounting for the differences in educational achievement observed at this age.

The age range studied naturally falls into two periods: before and after the beginning of schooling. In the preschool years our information is based largely on recordings of spontaneous conversation. During this period, irrespective of family background, the differences between children in their rate of development seemed to be largely due to an interaction between the intrinsic characteristics of the children themselves (their personalities and their general learning ability – though we have no direct measurements of these characteristics) and the quantity and quality of their conversational experience. To some extent, the differences in conversational experience were almost certainly the result of differences among the parents, which made some more willing and able than others to be responsive to their children's conversational initiations. Here, too, personality differences were involved and, to some extent, awareness of how best to provide a supportive and stimulating environment. In a few cases, there were external factors, such as poverty, overcrowding or unhappy personal relationships, that made the parents' lives so stressful that they were too preoccupied to enjoy interacting with their children. But what was clear from listening to the recordings was that, although the parents were in most cases the more powerful influence on the quality of conversation, the actual conversations that occurred were always the outcome of an interaction to which both parent and child contributed, each influencing and being influenced by the other.

During these years, as already noted, the children all followed essentially the same sequence of development, although some made more rapid progress than others. In general, those who were early in beginning to speak were likely to be more advanced on entry to school, but there were a number of exceptions to this tendency. Almost certainly, slow beginners who caught up with their peers had benefited from a richer-than-average conversational experience, and the converse was probably also the case. Listening to stories was also a factor that contributed to differences between children in rate of progress.

In the second period, from entry to school at age five until the time of the last assessment at age 10, there was much less change in the rank order of relative achievement. Children who entered school ahead, as estimated by the tests administered at that time and by the teachers' assessments, were very likely still to be ahead five years later, and the same was true for those lower in the rank order. As already described in Chapter 7, the single most important factor in accounting for the differences between children in their subsequent achievement was how much they understood about literacy on entry to school. Other contributory factors were the amount of help that parents gave with schoolwork and the model they provided of the value of literacy in their own lives by the frequency with which they themselves engaged in reading and writing.

The relationships between the major factors to emerge from the analysis are shown in the form of a diagram in Figure 9.1. The numerical values inserted in the lines joining the various boxes are the correlations that were obtained. The values shown in bold type are the multiple correlations between the estimate of achievement at each point of assessment and the factors significantly influencing that achievement.

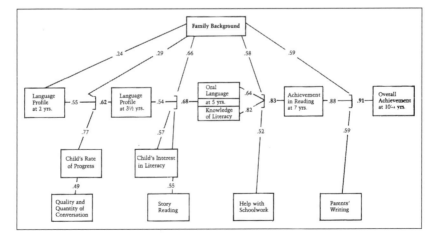

Figure 9.1 Predictors of school achievement at 10 years three months

Stories of Six Children

Figure 9.1 shows the main findings from the study in statistical terms. But what do these figures mean in terms of individual children? One way of answering this question is to present a number of case studies that illustrate the relationships identified by the statistical analysis. The children introduced in Chapter 1 – Rosie, Tony, Abigail, Gary, Penny and Jonathan – were selected because they show the main trends particularly clearly.

The six case studies that follow are based on three different sorts of evidence:

1. The scores that the children attained on the tests and other methods of assessment that were used. Rather than give the children's actual test scores, however, I have represented each score in terms of its corresponding position in the rank order of scores from all 32 children. Table 9.1 sets out the six children's ranks on some of the most significant measures discussed above.
2. Samples of their writing on two of the tasks that were set as part of the final assessment. The first of these required them to write a personal narrative with the title 'The happiest day in my life'. The second, also a narrative task, involved writing a story to fit a cartoon, in which a rather ineffectual-looking hunter was brought to bay with his dog at the edge of a cliff by a motley assortment of wild animals (see Figure 9.2). Both tasks were carried out without assistance from the teacher, and the children were given as much time as they needed to complete them.[1]
3. Answers to questions that were asked in the interviews that were conducted with all the children at the end of the study.

The interviews were conducted in a very relaxed manner by the same interviewer in every case. He was already known to the children, as he had been involved in administering the tests, some of which had involved a considerable amount of interaction. The same basic questions were asked of each child, but the order in which they were asked was varied. At some point in each interview, however, the children were asked to describe a typical day at school. They were invited to answer in as much detail as they wished, but they were told that the interviewer would not interrupt them until they had finished. This was done in order to obtain a comparable sample of continuous speech from each child as one of the ways of assessing their oral language ability. (The other oral tasks involved listening to a Russian folktale and retelling it to a friend and learning to play a new board game and then explaining how to play it to a friend.)

Table 9.1 Six children's longitudinal rank profiles

	Abigail	*Anthony*	*Gary*	*Jonathan*	*Penny*	*Rosie*
Language profile at 2	8	32	30	2	1	14
Language profile at $3\frac{1}{2}$	7.5 =	23	7.5 =	1	3	29
Story reading	5	13.5 =	13.5 =	1.5 =	26 =	32
Oral language at 5	4 =	6	20.5 =	4 =	12.5 =	29
Knowledge of literacy at 5	7.5 =	3	29	1.5 =	10	31.5 =
Child interest in literacy	4.5 =	15	27.5 =	4.5 =	12	31.5 =
Help with schoolwork	24 =	3 =	17 =	3 =	17 =	24 =
Reading at 7	8	7	24.5 =	3	10	32
Oral language at 10	2	11	6	1	8	32
Reading at 10	2	3	26	1	21.5 =	31.5 =
Writing at 10	3	4	22	1	11	32
Vocabulary at 10	2.5 =	2.5 =	22	2.5 =	5.5 =	30.5 =
Mathematics at 10	20	8.5 =	16	1	12.5 =	31.5 =
Parents' writing	5	3	9	2	26	30 =
Overall achievement at 10	2	3	22	1	13	32

Note: Equal sign indicates that several children obtained identical scores and so were placed at the same rank.

Inevitably, however, despite the efforts taken to make the interview as relaxed and informal as possible, some of the children were less at ease than others. Nevertheless, according to the answers that they gave when they were asked if they had found it difficult to talk about themselves, none of them found the experience too daunting.

Figure 9.2 The cartoon used for the story-writing task

Rosie

As may have been deduced from the discussion of Rosie's transition from home to school, she was chosen to be one of the case studies because, at least as far as educational achievement was concerned, she was the least successful child in the study. This estimate is confirmed by the information contained in Table 9.1. Nevertheless, as the interview clearly showed, she had many positive characteristics, and it was only in comparison with her age peers that she was seen to present a serious learning problem.

At age two, Rosie was very slightly above average in her level of language development (rank 14). However, by age three-and-a-half, she had dropped very nearly to the bottom, having made very slow progress in the intervening 18 months. This can be accounted for largely in terms of the amount and quality of her conversational experience. For most of the children in the study, the average number of utterances produced in the 27 minutes of recorded time analysed at each observation was around 120; about the same number of utterances was addressed to them in the same period of time. The figures for Rosie were very much lower: on average, somewhere between 30 and 40 each for Rosie and the other participants. Also, the conversation that did occur was very fragmentary; topics were rarely developed beyond two or three turns. Nevertheless, as the extract quoted in Chapter 5 demonstrated, by age five Rosie had achieved a reasonable command of language and was developing in the same way as other children, although considerably more slowly. As far as we could tell, there was no deficiency in Rosie herself; what she lacked were the experiences necessary to nourish her intellectual and linguistic development.

Perhaps the most serious deficiency in Rosie's experience, at least with respect to her subsequent progress at school, was the complete absence of stories. Compared with the other children in the study, there was very little in her home environment to stimulate an interest in literacy, and on entry to school her score on the test of knowledge of literacy was at the bottom of the rank order. Not surprisingly, therefore, she made very slow progress in learning to read (rank 32 at age seven); and, despite a certain amount of help from her parents with schoolwork, she remained at the bottom of the rank order on all the measures obtained at age 10. As her teacher put it at the end of the final assessment: 'Her present lack of reading ability is most likely to hold her back; other factors would be the home and its environment, also her lack of any real drive and initiative'. Rosie's writing was equally poorly developed. Figure 9.3 shows her account of her happiest day.

In fact, this was quite an achievement for her, given the labour that was involved in the very act of producing a written text. However, with the difficulties she still had in forming the letters, spacing words, and achieving even a phonetically consistent spelling, she could give very little of her attention to the selection and shaping of her material to produce an overall effect.

Poor Rosie! Nothing seemed to work in her favour. From a materially impoverished and intellectually unstimulating home environment, she went first to a school where her homeroom teacher (Teacher A in Chapter 5), despite her good intentions, did little to boost her confidence or to help her to become more actively interested in the new experiences of the

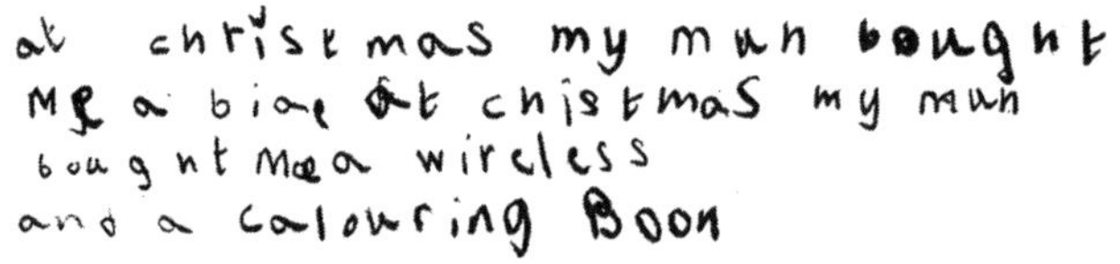
at christmas my mun bought
Me a biae at chistmas my mun
bougnt Mea wircless
and a colouring Boon

Figure 9.3 Rosie's text

classroom. No special effort was made to make up for her lack of stories at home – although it is only fair to the teacher to recognize that the majority of the children in Rosie's class were in need of the same individual story-sharing experiences. By the time Rosie and her family were rehoused and Rosie transferred to a different school, she was seen to be in need of remedial teaching. So low was her achievement, in fact, that at around the age of nine, she was assessed by an educational psychologist, who recommended that she be sent to a school for children with special learning needs. At the time of our last assessment, however, she was still attending the local school.

Something of Rosie's own feelings about school can be gleaned from the following extract from her answer to the request to describe a typical day at school.

Rosie: When I goes to school . I either gets told off . or gets smacked *[laughs]* or sometimes I gets picked on by all the rest of them . or sometimes it's either me who's getting- or it's either me laughing or it's either . Sandy, the one who sits next to me . sometimes Sandy gets it . I don't have dinners no more *[eight-second pause]* I used to get picked on in this class . when I used to go up- go somewhere for Miss, I used to go- I used to go 'Silly cow' cos I don't like our teacher. *[Laughs]* I never like that teacher

When asked whether she thought she was good at schoolwork, she first replied that she did not know; then, after a moment's reflection, she changed that to an emphatic 'No'. Despite all these negative feelings, however, she still preferred to be at school rather than at home.

Interviewer: D'you prefer being at home or at school?
Rosie: School
Interviewer: Why's that?
Rosie: 'Cos you learns there . there's nothing to do when we're at home . only just sit at the- sit down on the floor or on the sofa staring at the telly ... or help our mum wash up or ... and that's all, I think

Given Rosie's accurate assessment of her lack of success in learning at school, one can only agree with her view of her probable future:

Interviewer: What d'you think you'll do when you grow up?
Rosie: *[after long pause]* Dunno . just walk around or get a job
Interviewer: What sort of job would you get?
Rosie: Dunno

Anthony

Anthony shows almost the reverse pattern from Rosie. At age two, he was the lowest in the rank order of language development. Slow to get started, he had caught up a little by age three-and-a-half, and by age five he was ranked sixth. Part of the explanation in Anthony's case is that he was an only child who, particularly as he got older and began to talk more fluently, enjoyed a great deal of conversation with his parents. Although only average in the interest he showed in activities associated with literacy and, according to our observations, not read to more than average, he scored high on the test of knowledge of literacy (rank 3) on entry to school and achieved consistently high rankings from then onwards. At age seven, when asked 'What do you do when you read?', he replied: 'You read it in your mind . use your eyes ahead and read in your head'. At age 10 he was ranked third in overall achievement. His teacher wrote about him, 'A lively approach to life which makes the work he has to do enjoyable for him'.

From the point of entry to school – and even before – Anthony's parents were determined that he should do well at school. Reading for information as well as for pleasure was emphasized; Anthony was also encouraged to write, and his parents provided a model in the range and frequency of their own writing (rank 3). At the interview when Anthony was age seven, in which the parents were asked about ways in which they helped with schoolwork, they replied that he no longer needed help with reading or with basic number work. However, they did make a point of taking him on visits to the museum and other places of interest, and they discussed the work he was doing in class. In the week before the interview, the mother remembered, they had spent more than an hour reading about the battle of Waterloo in the *Encyclopaedia Britannica* in connection with a project that he was doing at school. From an educational point of view, Tony clearly enjoyed a very supportive home environment.

Two years before the final assessment, Tony transferred to the preparatory department of one of the prestigious local private schools. This was obviously an important event for the whole family, for it was about this that he chose to write when asked to describe the happiest day of his life.

THE HAPPIEST DAY OF MY LIFE

The happiest day of my life was a couple of years ago. It was about May and I was just collecting the post. One was for my dad and the other one was also for Mum Dad. My Mum opened a big brown one which had something for my dad's office . after reading that . she opened the other one and let out a yell and started hugging me nearly crushing me .. when I finally got her sitting down with a glass of water she told me that I had passed the test for the *** and then she started ringing up every relation saying that I had passed the exam . she said that the last few days had been hell not knowing whether I had passed because a friend had told her that they were saying who had passed and who had failed .. that was defintely my happiest day of my life.

Here is Tony's story about the hunter, showing just what he meant about imagination. It was certainly one of the most successful in its creation of a specific setting and in using that as a motive for the rest of the story. He had problems with the sequence of tenses, though, perhaps because he felt he had to explain the situation depicted in the cartoon rather than simply tell a story about it.

TRAP

It was a plesant day in North Africa. Filthy Menasty was making another trap to capture wild animals. He was doing this to make the biggest zoo in the whole world. He had lead them all this way by a dead carcus of a vison and a bowl of water. The carcus was to get the lion, snake and vulture. The water was to get the vegitirian animals. They have stopped because they are suspicious about the ground ahead which is a massive net covered with grass so they would go over it The dog is scared because Filthy treats animals awfully. Filthy also carries a gun incase they charge at him. He is whistling because he wants to get the animals to go to him and fall in the net. The cliff edge is only a few metres high and in a moment he will fall back so the animals will go and look over the edge but will fall in the net. The worm has tunneled into the net and is warning the other animals. But Filthy is at the wrong place and falls to his death. The trap had failed.

Although, like Rosie, Tony preferred to be at school, he also had an interesting life outside school, which included reading, watching home videos, and learning to play golf, as well as making a collection of lapel badges. He also talked with enthusiasm about the holidays that his parents had taken him on abroad. When asked about his future, he replied with some hesitation that, when he grew up, he thought he would be a dentist.

Gary

Gary provides a contrast of a different kind with Rosie. Initially, he was slow in starting to talk (rank 30 at age two). But over the next year and a half he made rapid progress, reaching rank 7.5 at age three-and-a-half, and this despite a slight stammer. In the interview, his parents said that they had very deliberately ignored the stammer, believing his speech would be most likely to improve if they concentrated on what he wanted to say rather than on how he said it. This policy was obviously successful, as there was no evidence of a speech problem in the final interview.

Several extracts from the recordings made when Gary was five were included in Chapter 5. From these, one gets an impression both of Gary's competence as a speaker and of the quality of his conversational experience at home. It was a surprise, therefore, to find that, on entry to school, he was judged by his teacher to be below average in oral language ability. Perhaps there were other factors that led to this low estimation, such as his nonstandard dialect or his somewhat aggressive enthusiasm. He had not shown much interest in activities associated with literacy at home, and this attitude continued at school, where he did not find it easy to settle down to tasks of an academic kind. His performance on the test of knowledge of literacy at age five was ranked almost the lowest and, despite an average amount of support at home, both in story reading in the preschool years and in help with schoolwork later, he remained in the lowest third of the rank order for reading and was ranked only slightly higher for writing. He was ranked 22 at the final assessment for overall achievement.

Here is an example of his writing: the account of his happiest day. It is full of detail, with its lists of presents and foods, and one can easily imagine his enjoyment of the Christmas holiday. But the obvious enthusiasm is also a liability, for it seems to have led Gary to neglect the need to shape his account to make a story out of what is at present only a sequence of events.

THE HAPPIEST DAY IN LIFE

dear
friend The happiest day in life was
the Christmas just gone.
        I liked it because I had the
        things I wanted, and somethings
        I dident exspect like wakietalkies,
        powertrack, torches, radiocontarlecar
        and proper scrabling cloves.
        I played with them when my mum &
        DaD went to bed. I liked the TV
        programgs like exralong cartoons,

the wondeful wizard of all
and pinochio. After watching all that.
My sister DAD ana I all
went down my nans. I had
Christmas cake, black pudding,
and welsh cakes. The day after
Christmas was boxing day. On
the night all my famiely went back down
my nans, and all the
famiely were there. We all had
a party. At fourteen oclock
We Whent home and went to
bed.

In other ways, though, Gary showed considerable talent. He was good at sports (he took part in a national archery competition just after the final assessment) and he played in the school football team. His particular passion at the time of the final assessment was motorbike scrambling (hence the reference to 'scrabling cloves' among his Christmas presents), and he talked about it with great animation.

Gary: I want to be a professional scrambler . I go scrambling every Sunday . me and my sister've got a bike- motorbike

Interviewer: A small one?

Gary: No, a big one

Interviewer: Can you ride it?

Gary: Yes, change gear on it . it's a six gear, mine is . we ride it on the common or at the airport [disused] . I goes on the grass- I used to go on the grass and now I goes on the proper bumpy track and out of our Dad's sight . . he said 'When you're ready-when you think you're ready, I'll let you go' . like wherever I want to go . like all the way round the track

He returned to the same theme later in the interview when asked what he wanted to be when he grew up:

Gary: I wanted to be a farmer . but our Dad said: 'No . you'll be an electrician and electronics . get a lot of money . it's the best job' .. if I gets a lot of money I'll buy myself a proper scrambler and just go practicing and that'll be my hobby – go weekends, go racing

At the same time he also said he was going to take his Mum and Dad on holiday and buy them a video.

Asked about other activities he enjoyed at home, Gary mentioned reading the newspaper and 'war stories' borrowed from the library. He also gave the following interesting account of a (yet to be carried out) writing project:

Gary: Me and my sister are writing- like, um . say it was a court person . like a policeman had to write a story about in court . and we writes horror stories .. me and my sister are going to discuss about writing a book and we're going to publish it and make a paperback . we're thinking of doing that

Interviewer: And what'll that be about?

Gary: Um *[long pause]* 'The Flowers in the Attic' . that might be the model . or just make up a different story- any story, what we've done

Interviewer: What? a story for children?

Gary: Yes, and adults if they want our- a paperback book

Interviewer: How are you going to publish it?

Gary: My Dad- he's got a printing machine in his work and the proper paper . he's a mechanic and he can print it there .. I don't know how I'm going to do it 'cos I'm not in charge . it's my sister, she's going to do it . it's up to her

Throughout his time at school, Gary was popular with his peers and something of a leader. To some extent this was a handicap in the classroom, as he was likely to be at the centre of any diversion, which did not endear him to his teachers – as Gary was well aware:

Interviewer: What do the teachers think about you?

Gary: [after long pause]: Dunno I reckon I'm an idiot *[A few minutes later]*

Interviewer: If you don't like them [your teachers], what are you usually upset about?

Gary: Like if you mutter to yourself you get lines . like last week . just 'cos I said, like, 'Three times three equals nine', to myself, he says, 'A thousand lines' 'cos he thinks you're talking to your partner

In fact, it is tempting to argue that the teachers generally underestimated Gary's ability. For example, at the time of the final assessment, his teacher felt unable, for lack of information, to answer the question about Gary's ability to estimate lengths. At a follow-up visit to obtain an answer to this question, Gary was sent for by the teacher, presented with a sheet of paper on which a cross was marked, and asked to estimate a distance of 20 centimetres. When he had placed a second mark, the teacher measured the distance and showed considerable surprise that the estimate was within 0.5 centimetres of the distance required.

An area in which Gary certainly showed ability well above average was in the various oral language tasks in the final assessment (rank 6). In this, he contrasted quite markedly with Tony, whose oral language rank was considerably below the ranks that he achieved in reading and writing. What is significant about this comparison, however, is that in neither case did the level of oral language ability have a noticeable effect on his rated overall achievement.

Abigail

Like Tony, Abigail was another child who improved her position in the rank order after entry to school. Although certainly never a slow developer, she was somewhat overshadowed at home by her elder sisters and did not receive a very large share of her parents' undivided attention. Although she listened to stories more frequently than most, they were not always read for her benefit alone. Nevertheless, she shared in her sisters' interest in reading and other activities associated with literacy so that, when she started school, she was very clear what books were about, even though she could not actually read.

This emerged very clearly at the first observation, when she had been at school about six weeks. Towards the end of the morning, the teacher asked her to fetch her reading book and read to her.

Abigail: *[reading]* They .. liked .. the water . Pat . likes . the water .. Pat likes-

After helping her to complete this sentence, the teacher told Abigail to put her book away and choose what she would do next. Abigail went to the book corner and, having chosen a book, she pretended to be the teacher, reading a story to two of her friends. Using the pictures as cues, she 'read' a story, which started as follows:

Abigail: When me and Tom went upstairs to the attic we- Tom pretended to be a tiger . I found a jewel and inside the jewel was- inside the jewel was a- a bit of velvet, a picture and

> a old violin . and a cupboard full of- full of buttons: silver
> buttons and gold buttons and ordinary buttons . I found an
> umbrella there, but Tom got on the pile of books and looked
> out of the attic window

The whole story was read with considerable verve and expression. It ended as follows:

Abigail: She gave her little daughter a purple fan and three beads .
then they sat downstairs and had their tea . then Grandma
said goodbye to me

Although Abigail's parents did not themselves give her much specific help with schoolwork (rank 24), the home environment they provided was both stimulating and supportive, and the example of her sisters and their occasional help were sufficient to get her 'hooked on books' and reading well by the time she was seven (rank 8). From then on she was an enthusiastic reader and writer. In fact, when asked what she thought she might be when she grew up, she replied as follows:

Abigail: I might try to be an actor but not- but I think it's much
too hard remembering all the things- the words . I don't
think I'll ever get on television .. a writer- poems and
stories, really . for young people, not for old people –
for infants really
Interviewer: D'you do writing at home?
Abigail: I write stories and I've written a lot of poems . I write
letters a lot to relatives and friends- pen-friends . I've got
two pen-friends . one lives in America and one lives in
Canada . I write to them about once every two weeks
and then if I don't get a letter back in say the next two
weeks, I'll write again

Abigail was an adventurous writer, as can be seen from her way of tackling the task relating to the cartoon. The judges were strongly divided on its merits and in the end, despite its dramatic originality and its inventive exploitation of written form, it was ranked rather low on the grounds that it did not tell a story. The following is what she wrote:

HELP!

'He,s going to fall off the edge of the cliff' murmured all the animals. 'Serves him right for almost killing us' said Leo the lion. 'I think he was quite nice' sais mussels the monkey 'you would' said Ricky the rhinoceros 'I don,t know why you are called mussels your such a softy'. 'Don,t be so mean Ricky' said Avril the elephant 'he used to be very strong'. 'You lot ssstop nattering on he,s going to fall' said silly snake. Look he,s .... 'Hellllp' 'falling' .... said Torpedo the tortoise.

Her account of her happiest moment, on the other hand, was much more conventional in form and, with its impressive control of the future-in-the-past tense and its careful shaping towards a climax, consciously literary in style. This piece was unanimously rated one of the most successful and, in its contrast with the previous piece, shows just how dangerous it is to judge a child's ability as a writer on a single text.

THE HAPPIEST MOMENT IN MY LIFE

We were going to go on a holiday round a little bit of Europe. Instead of going through France and into Spain we were going round through France into Germany then into Austria where we would stay in a small Austrian farm house for 4 days. After that we would move on to Italy there we stayed in a newly built hotel with only 10 other people staying there. Just across the road was a lake where we could swim or hire a surf sail or float or paddle in our small rubber dingy it was absolutely sensational just swimming in fresh water. But the only sad thing there was a thunder storm every evening in Italy. But then we had to turn back to go home such a sad thing when you are having fun.

Abigail regularly went on holidays abroad. Indeed, her first memory was of a camping holiday in France: 'I'm sure it's a strange thing to remember, but I remember doing the washing up in a bowl after we'd had chicken noodle soup. Just can't forget it.' Even more vivid in the impression it gives of her is her memory of another, more recent outing:

Abigail: I like visiting places- old castles and old houses. My cousins came over one day and we went to Berkeley Castle and we looked round the gravestones and there was a very old grave where a jester whose master had died . he'd carved something on the side of it – a poem or something

Abigail described herself as 'a fun person'. Her teacher wrote: 'She responds well in class to what is offered, being an industrious child with a fairly serious approach to life generally. However, she is not without a sense of humour'. Certainly both sides of her personality were revealed in the interview, which was one of the most interesting to listen to.

Like all children, Abigail enjoyed school for the opportunity it gave her to be with friends. But she also enjoyed (most of) the work that she was expected to do. In her account of a typical day at school, she referred to the project she was doing on 'British life – our homes and our country' as 'exciting' and, when asked if there was anything she did not like about school, she talked only about the things she did like, concluding 'Without school I think I'd be very bored'.

Not surprisingly, she was considered to be an excellent pupil and above average in potential. Her achievement at age 10 certainly confirmed this. She was ranked second in both oral language and in reading, and her vocabulary was judged by her teacher to be among the most extensive (four children tied for the first rank). In overall achievement, she was ranked 2.

Penny

Somewhat like Gary, Penny was a child whose achievement at school did not fulfill the expectations that one might have formed on the basis of her oral language development in the preschool years. From most advanced at age two, she dropped to rank 12.5 on entry to school and then remained at about that level. Although she apparently rarely had stories read to her, Penny engaged with interest in a variety of other literacy-related activities (as was seen in Chapter 5), entered school with a fairly good score on the knowledge of literacy test (rank 10), and was reading better than average at age seven. At age 10, however, her reading score was ranked considerably below average (21.5), well below her rank for oral language (8). On the other hand, her writing was above average (11), as was the teacher's estimate of the size and range of her vocabulary (5.5=), and this was enough for her overall achievement to be ranked 13.

A vivacious child, Penny was described by her teacher as very skilful in games and other physical activities, although physically underdeveloped for her age. She herself listed swimming and cricket among her favourite activities and also playing games with large groups of friends. When asked about the things she liked doing at home, she mentioned helping her parents with jobs around the house (already apparent in the observation at age two), but really became enthusiastic when talking about going out with her parents:

Penny: Sometimes we goes out Chew Valley Lake . my Dad and my
          Mum comes and the dog and we all runs around until it gets
          to about half past eight . then we goes home . then my mum
          says: 'Go and have a wash and get ready for bed' . and I goes
          and gets ready for bed while she makes my supper . and I goes

up to bed, she tucks me in and says good night and she turns
off the light

The same enthusiasm comes across in her account of her happiest day,
an event that she remembered in great detail. Like Abigail, Penny seems
recently to have learned how to represent direct speech with conventional punctuation. The effect here is of an event recalled with pleasure in
a good gossip.

SITUATION 1

The Happiset moment of my life was when I was sevan years old. My
uncle was getting Married and I was asked to be a bridesmaid My uncle
said to me 'Will you be a bridesmaid?' and I answered him 'What is
that?' He told me and I replied with a 'yes'. He said 'We'll have you in
a long dress and white gloves socks and sandals'. I went with his fiance
Mary. We went to a shop and chose a hairdo She said to me 'We won't-
have you dressed yet as the wedding has to be rehearsed so I left the
shop and we entered the florist and I chose a boquet. Net we went to the
dress shop and I chose an off-white creme dress. She said 'If it will go
with your shoes and socks you may have that one'. I replied 'OK'. Next
of all I went for my white shoes they were closed in and lined with a
gold strap. I put them on and I chose them. Next we went in shops for
white glove I got a pair a bit on the large side but it didn't show so I had
them and last of all I chose a hairband which was white with flowers
and it had white ribbon. Mary put all these neatly into a bag until I
wanted to see if it all went together she said you chose it nicely. When
the friday evening came I went to the hairdressers and I had my hair
curly. When Saturday came I drove to Marys and I got dressed I put on
my shoes and socks after bathing and put on my dress I then put on my
belt, and Mary put my hairband on I had my bouquet in my hand and
I turned round towards Mary She said 'You look splended' And she put
on her dress and we were off to St. Barnabas church. When I walked up
the isle I felt happier than I had ever felt before 'I said to myself Why did
I say yes?' When we got out of the church I said 'I'm glad I did' and We
had pictures taken and it started raining.

Despite her obvious enjoyment of life at home, Penny preferred to be at
school because of the opportunities it provided for sports and for social
contact with her friends. But, like Abigail, she also enjoyed the academic
work at school and liked and was liked by her teachers. In fact, to be a
teacher was her ambition for the future.

Academically, Penny was rated by her teacher to be above average in both achievement and potential. This was attributed both to her hard work and enthusiasm and to the influence of her home, which was described by her teacher as being 'sensible and supportive'. Certainly, this is the impression that emerges from her parents' answers in the interview with them and from the evidence of the preschool recordings (see Chapter 5). Penny herself mentioned reading as one of her favourite activities at home, particularly in bed at night, and she also said that she wrote stories and poems at home and kept a 'sort of diary'. It is surprising, therefore, that her reading score was so low and that, when compared with the other children in the sample, her overall achievement did not rank more highly than just above average.

Jonathan

In the whole sample, Jonathan is the child who most clearly demonstrates the connections that have been set out in the previous chapters. By age three-and-a-half he had already reached the level of oral language development typical of the average five-year-old and, as the extracts in Chapter 2 show, he was capable of conversing on a wide variety of topics. An only child, Jonathan was also outgoing and, on occasions, even argumentative. As a result, he elicited a large amount of conversation from his parents, both of whom took his comments and questions seriously and attempted to respond in ways that would extend both his thinking and his means of expression.

Jonathan's interest in stories and in written language generally was already apparent by age two and over the following three years he had a rich diet of stories and of conversation about them. By the time he entered school, he already understood the principles of reading and writing and was quick to learn to read, being ranked 3 at age seven. From then on, he was ranked first or first equal on every measure and, as will be seen below, produced at age 10 by far the most mature pieces of writing.

Reading continued to be one of Jonathan's favourite occupations. At age 10, he had this to say:

Jonathan: I do quite a lot of reading . I'm very interested in books . Mum calls me a bookworm [laughs] and I like mysteries . I like Enid Blyton, the Famous Five mysteries and the ones that she does in series, you know, with a group of people and she does, say, twelve mysteries on that .. and the ones I liked best out of those were *Famous Five* and *The Five Find Out* . I like most mysteries . I'm not all that keen on fact

> books . I like fiction most . I read one by Julie Andrews, I think it was- someone like that . it was called *The Last of the Really Great Wandoo-gles* . they've got it in the library across there . it's awfully imaginative but it's very good . I like the ones like that, you know, where . it's way out . it couldn't happen but it's lovely

Mysteries were not the only sort of books that Jonathan read, though. In describing a typical school day, he mentioned being read to by his teacher, specifically *The Lion, the Witch the Wardrobe* – a book 'which I'd read about ten times and knew nearly off by heart'. He also regularly read the newspaper.

Jonathan: I read a few articles in it. I've been reading a lot about the Falklands lately because I like to see what's happening . they don't have that on there [television], the hue and cry's died down a bit . I usually just read the headlines if they're interesting and I look at the jokes in the middle page

However, Jonathan was not only a bookworm. He talked with enthusiasm about his bikes, of which he had two, and about swimming, which he took very seriously. He would have liked to pursue this in what he called a 'sports school', but his Mum and Dad could not afford the fees. He also talked very knowledgeably about dog shows, to which he and his parents went with their own dog.

As might be expected, Jonathan enjoyed school.

Jonathan: It's a good place 'cos I got all my friends here . most of my friends I got from school . I haven't really got many other people apart from at school . if it's at home for six weeks . I do sometimes get a bit bored during the summer holidays I like nearly everything except Geography . and I do get a bit bored with decimal points 'cos Miss does have a lot of it with us . I know how to do it – a lot of people don't – so I get a bit bored with that . I like English, but not the punctuation and grammar, you know . I like the essays best of English – writing a nice long essay . Miss tries to make me do short ones, but I can't

On the writing tasks that we set, however, both Jonathan's texts were short. Perhaps the challenge of writing to a topic of someone else's choosing was valuable discipline in his case for, although short, both display a level of maturity that is considerably beyond that achieved by any of the other children. Here is his account of his happiest moment.

THE HAPPIEST MOMENT OF MY LIFE

The happiest moment of my life was as I bit into a rich, meaty cornish pasty after a day's weary travelling (at least that was what it seemed like) and a weeks holiday of golden sands, ice creams and sun stretched out before me. We were camping on a quiet grassy hill; hill especially. I felt that nothing could be better. I was right.

As I read this text, the first thing that strikes me is the writer's control of his material in the long first sentence. His happiest moment is indeed a moment – the first bite into a pasty. However, this moment is itself presented as marking a divide, a pinnacle in time, from which the writer looks back down one side into the past to the weary travelling, and forward down the other to the holiday that 'stretches out' before him. Perhaps this effect is fortuitous, however, and no more than a happy accident? I think not. For, as one reads on, one finds that the hill is a real one and the prospect from it is both literal and metaphorical. If further proof is needed of the deliberateness of the structure, one has only to note the contrast between the long first sentence and the two short final ones. In this context, the last sentence has a ring of assurance that convinces me that the writer is very conscious of the effect he is trying to achieve.

The second narrative is equally accomplished, but in a quite different way.

WHERE'S THE ARK?

Noah twisted his fingers awkwardly
behind his back as the animals stared at him.
'But how *can* you forget to build
an ark?' asked the giraffe.
'I left a lovely field of juicy
worms to come here' chirped
a bird indignantly. 'I demand
compensation!'
Meanwhile Noah was slowly walking
backwards, and eventually fell off the
cliff. Luckily he fell on a wooden raft.
'Good old Noah!' yelled the
animals, and dived on with him.

There can be no doubt about the deliberate artistry here. It is to be seen immediately in the way in which an atmosphere of tension is created in the first sentence, and in such other details as the characterization of the bird and the use of italics on 'can' to achieve the tone of incredulity in the giraffe's question. But what is most remarkable is the confidence with which he assumes his reader's knowledge of the biblical account of the building of the ark – a knowledge which is essential for an appreciation of the humour of this version. For a child of 10 to manage the allusion with such assurance is proof both of his very considerable ability as a writer and of the richness of his personal literary experience.

A year after the interview, in response to an open invitation to all the children to send further examples of their writing, Jonathan showed us what he meant by writing at length. He sent us a 37-page story – another mystery – that he had written at school. It was in eight chapters and was entitled *The Poisoned Griffin*.

It started in the local park, where two children happened one day upon a griffin, who surprised them by being able to talk. He explained that he had been poisoned by a witch and that he would die unless he found the antidote to the poison. The children agreed to help him and, towards the end of the search, they finally tracked down the old witch who, they believed, still had the antidote.

CHAPTER VII THE 'LITTLE OLD LADY'

Standing in the doorway was about the ugliest woman
imaginable. She had an egg-shaped bald head, one tooth,
bloodshot eyes and a nose that would make Pinnochio's look
like a pug's.
'Well', she hissed ungraciously, the vile stench of her
breath flooding over them, 'What is it?'
It took Anthony some time to recover from the fumes, but
when he did, he spoke up.
'We were interested in the contents of a bottle you bought
at the bric-a-brac stall', he told her.
'What's that?' she screeched.
'WE ARE INTERESTED IN THE CONTENTS OF A BOTTLE YOU
GOT AT THE JUNK STALL!!!'
'What's contents?'
'The stuff inside!!!'
'Alright, I'm not deaf, you know', she wheezed.
'So they wants the compens, does they?' she muttered. 'Yus dearies,

for ten gold peecis you can 'ave de condens
and welcome!'
'Done!'
'Oh, so dey's got the money, 'as dey? You can 'ave it for
twen'y gold pieces.'
'We've only got fifteen', lied Clare.
'Yus? Well you c'n 'ave it for dat.'

This is perhaps the most remarkable section of the story, with the invention of the special representation of the witch's speech to convey her ingratiating but untrustworthy character. But the rest of the story is equally impressive in its control of style and its management of the extremely complicated plot. Finally, after a day of nerve-racking suspense, the antidote is found and the griffin is saved. Taking to their magic carpet again, they reluctantly return to their home. The adventure is over.

Griffin gave Clare a solitary wink, shimmered and disappeared.

Jonathan was not sure what he would do when he grew up. His mother had suggested that he should be a vet, as this would be very convenient in relation to their interest in dogs. He himself had thought of being a doctor or of joining the police. But at the time of the interview he was thinking of becoming a writer! Whatever his final decision, we can predict with some confidence that he will be well prepared when he completes his schooling to embark on the training for his chosen career – whatever that may eventually be.

From Oral to Written Language

Six children cannot in themselves provide the basis for drawing conclusions that have general applicability. Those claims must be based on the results from the larger sample, which were summarized at the beginning of this chapter. However, these six children are more than isolated examples for, in many respects, they illustrate very effectively the more general trends. At the same time, comparisons between them give a sharpness to many of the issues that the study set out to investigate. One of these is the relationship between spoken and written language in the achievement profiles of the different children.

The two sets of tasks on which the assessments were based have already been described. In several important respects, they were fairly similar, despite the difference in the mode of production. Both required the children to produce extended monologues, and both included tasks with differing communication purposes. It might have been expected, therefore, that there would be a strong relationship between individual children's spoken and written performances. However, this did not prove to be the case. Certainly, there were many children, such as Jonathan and Rosie, whose ranks, either high or low, were very similar. But there was also a substantial number whose ranks on the two sets of tasks were quite widely separated. Examples would be Gary and Tony and, to a lesser extent, Penny. The questions we need to investigate, then, are why some children show such a discrepancy between their performances in speech and writing and whether this discrepancy has consequences for their more general academic achievement.

In either speech or writing, creating a text involves managing two rather different types of processes. On the one hand there are the processes of composing (forming an overall plan, selecting the appropriate content, and organizing it to fit that plan). To a considerable extent, these processes are similar whether speaking or writing is involved. The second type of processes, on the other hand, are concerned with the physical production of the text (the encoding of the content in sentences and their expression according to the conventions of pronunciation or spelling and handwriting). Because these latter processes involve a temporal sequence of skilled physical activity, they tend to lag behind the processes of composing, particularly in writing and, as a result, to constrain their operation. Whether spoken or written, texts also have to meet other constraints, arising from the purpose to be achieved, the audience to be addressed, and the genre selected. Once again, these constraints are more severe in the case of writing because written genres are more differentiated from one another than are their oral counterparts.

After many years of using oral language for a wide variety of purposes, the constraints involved in producing a spoken monologue cause children little difficulty, provided the topic is relatively familiar. The texts they produce, therefore, provide quite a reliable indication of the effectiveness of their composing processes.[2] On the other hand, for the majority of children, writing is still a relatively unfamiliar mode of linguistic communication and the constraints involved are much more daunting. As a result, the actual texts they produce may give a much less reliable indication of their composing ability.

For beginning writers, it is handwriting and spelling that provide the most serious constraints. They require so much attention that little can be spared for the task of composing or for attending to the demands of text production that are specific to writing. Typically, written texts are very short at this stage, and within this limitation, are not very different from the texts that are created in spoken monologue. Rosie is the clearest example of a child who is still at this stage.

Once some control has been gained over the means of production, however, children are freed to give more attention to the composing process and to meeting the constraints imposed by the audience and by the genre in which they are working – fictional narrative, personal narrative, argument, and so on. At this stage, their success as writers will depend to a large extent on how well they are able to manage the formal aspects of writing (choice of vocabulary and grammatical structure, control over the means for achieving explicitness and cohesion, etc.) and on their degree of familiarity with the characteristic organizing structures associated with the different genres. Jonathan is an example of a child who has acquired considerable ability to take these constraints into account in his composing: all the samples of his writing quoted above show that he can organize and encode his material in order to achieve a specific literary effect. Abigail and Tony have also both made considerable progress in the same direction.

Where children are relatively unfamiliar with these structures, however, or with the distinctive formal characteristics of written language, their tendency will be to fall back on the structures in which they might express the same content in spoken monologue. In such cases, even if the content is interesting and the conventions of grammar, spelling and handwriting are observed satisfactorily, the resulting text will still not be very effective as writing. This is the problem faced by both Penny and Gary. Penny's personal narrative of the day she was a bridesmaid, for example, contains a great deal of interesting detail, but because it is organized in essentially the form of a spoken monologue, it was not judged to be a particularly effective piece of writing.

However, such children do not necessarily lack skills in composing when these are applied to the creation of a spoken text. This is very clearly the case for Gary. His account of a typical school day was one of the most successful in terms of its overall narrative organization and the way in which interest was maintained by a combination of general statements and illustrative examples. In the following extract, he is describing what follows a physical education period on a typical afternoon.

Gary: Then we comes in gets changed . we has three minutes, or four minutes, to get changed sitting down for it . you got to change in silence 'cos if you don't you just miss another P.E. Then we-um-does English . we're doing about um- what is it? Bristol . Bristol . and when the- when the people go to camp, we're going to go to see, er- we're going to go from school to Bristol Bridge .

> then we're going to have a walk round- going to do things as if
> we people had gone to camp . then go to the Lifeboat Museum,
> and then a coach back to school . That's er- after June the
> nineteenth, I think . yeh . um- we does that till half past three .
> then it's home time

In meeting the requirements of the task and in its vigour and concern for accuracy as well as interest, this account was undoubtedly one of the most effective.

In the case of children like Gary, then, a low rank in writing does not indicate poor skills in composing or a limited command of language. The limitation is rather in *experience* of *written* language. It is perhaps significant that, whereas Abigail spoke of the poems and stories she wrote and of her correspondence with her pen-friends and Tony spoke of his enjoyment of English lessons because of the imagination he could put into writing stories, Gary described a project for writing a book that still had to be begun and, when asked about how the book might be published, he disclaimed responsibility: 'It's my sister . she's going to do it . it's up to her'.

Unlike Tony, whose strength was in writing rather than in speaking, Gary's interest was in spinning a good yarn to an interested audience. By comparison, he found writing both more difficult and less satisfying. For this situation to change, it would probably be necessary for him to become 'hooked on books', both as reader and as writer.

The Status of Oral Language in the Classroom

Such discrepancies between oral and written language ability, then, can arise from a number of causes. However, where there is strength in either mode, there is evidence both of a satisfactory command of language and an ability to use it to good effect. Now, if assessment of educational achievement took equal account of success in either mode, discrepancies such as those shown by Gary or Tony would not be a matter of great concern. Such a child could draw on his or her area of strength in tackling other curricular activities and simultaneously use it as a help in improving in the weaker language mode. However, this does not seem to be the case. From our results, it appears that it is only strength in written language that is valued; ability in oral language contributes little to the overall assessment of achievement. Despite his lower rank in relation to oral language (11), for example, Tony, with a rank of 4 on writing and 3 on reading, was still ranked 3 overall. Gary, on the other hand, with a rank of 6 on the oral tasks but 18 on writing and 26 on reading, did not achieve a better overall rank than 22.

Such unequal valuation of children's performances in speech and in writing must lead us to ask whether the spoken mode really is intrinsically less satisfactory than the written as a medium for learning. The answer may appear to have already been given in the previous chapter, where I referred to the 'centrality' of literacy. However, that is only part of the answer. Certainly, our aim should remain that of helping all children to acquire the skills of reflective thinking that are so closely associated with effective use of written language. But, as already emphasized, such skills are not developed and used only when actually reading or writing. The oral-written dimension is a continuum, and there are uses of spoken language that engage many of the same intellectual processes as are called upon in writing. For many children who lack facility with written language, therefore, oral language could perhaps provide a viable route towards the goal of effective thinking and symbol manipulation.

In other research on children of this age, it has been shown that groups of children can work successfully through discussion to solve problems (Phillips, 1985), to explore alternative possible explanations (Barnes & Todd, 1977), and to make a discriminating response to literature (Mulford, 1971). Interestingly, all these researchers noted that pupils worked much more effectively when the teacher was not present. Unless such discussions are tape-recorded, however, as was the case in each of these projects, teachers are unlikely to be aware of just how much children can achieve in speech; and, unfortunately, if their concern is largely confined to writing, they are not likely to be interested in finding out.

When we look at the skills in oral language that are typically displayed for teachers to evaluate, we begin to see why, in assessing achievement, they are accorded a so much lower status than skills in reading and writing. Consider the following extract from a lesson with children of about the same age as those under consideration; it was chosen by Sinclair and Coulthard (1975) as typical of those that their research team observed.

Teacher:	Now then, I've got some more things here that cut things that you've seen before, I think . scissors . what do I cut with scissors?
Pupil:	Paper, paper
Teacher:	Yes, paper . somebody's shouting out at the back! and I've got some more cutters here . what's that cutter called?
Pupil:	A knife
Teacher:	A knife, yes . what do I cut with a knife?
Pupil:	Food

Teacher:	I cut food . What kind of food would you cut with a knife?
Pupil:	Meat?
Teacher:	**You** tell me
Pupil:	Fish
Teacher:	Fish, yes
Pupil:	Meat
Teacher:	Meat, yes

The lesson continued in this style for more than 104 exchanges, and at no point did a pupil utter more than an elliptical sentence fragment. However, this is not surprising, since this is exactly the sort of response that the teacher's questions called for. But what is more disturbing than the constraining effect of the teacher's questions on the pupil's contributions is the fact that the pupils did not share the teacher's understanding of the purpose of the questions. Even if they had been allowed to speak without first being questioned, they would not have known the basis on which to offer relevant contributions.

In these circumstances, the teacher gets a very biased view of the pupils' oral language abilities. And yet this is the evidence on which his or her judgments are likely to be based. The pupil who appears most able will be the one who is most successful at guessing the framework within which the teacher is operating – which is indeed a skill, but not one that is particularly relevant to the task in hand. What the teacher will not be able to discover, however, from interaction of this sort is how well individual pupils are able to use their oral language resources to narrate a story, to describe a scene or situation, or to formulate, explore and attempt to resolve a problem that they have made their own, and then to communicate effectively with others in carrying out the task and reporting the outcome. Yet these are precisely the oral language abilities that can help to develop the sort of thinking skills that are most typically associated with written language. Generally speaking, these uses of spoken language do not occur because teachers are not sufficiently aware of the intellectual potential of genuinely collaborative and exploratory talk; so they make little or no provision for it to occur (Barnes, 1976).

This is particularly unfortunate for children like Gary, who, for lack of experience with written language, do not find it easy to learn through that medium. Not only are they constantly brought up against their limitations, but they are also given little opportunity to make serious use of the linguistic skills that they do possess.

To reiterate, I do not wish to suggest that mastery of written language should be accorded less importance than is presently the case – though the means used to achieve this aim may well require considerable rethinking – but rather that it should be recognized that spoken and written language provide different but complementary resources for learning. However, for children who are slower in acquiring control of the written mode, spoken language can be exploited to enable them to develop and use some of the skills in symbol manipulation that are so essential for intellectual development.

At the same time, I also want to make a plea for a greater recognition of the educational value of spoken language more generally. Although in certain respects speech clearly has limitations – its transience, for example, and the consequent difficulty of reflecting on the verbal formulations of ideas that are produced – speech also has compensating advantages. Writing and reading tend to be solitary activities and are all too often competitive. Talking and listening, on the other hand, are by definition social and, at least potentially, collaborative. They therefore provide an excellent means for fostering collaboration in learning through the pooling of ideas and the negotiation of points of view. These experiences are valuable for all pupils, of course, not simply for those whose written language skills are less well developed. But for this latter type of pupil they are likely to provide a particularly effective means of learning.

Notes

1. The children were all asked to write on the same topics in order to allow comparisons to be made between them. We were aware that this was not an ideal situation, as there is no guarantee that a topic of someone else's choosing will call forth an equal commitment from every child. We hoped, though, by asking them to write on a number of different topics, that we would obtain an overall estimate of their writing ability that would not be biased in favour of, or against, any particular individual. In retrospect, however, we are not convinced that this expectation was appropriate. It might have been better if we had been able to collect samples of the writing that they did in the course of their normal classroom activities. However, this too would have caused problems, as the frequency and type of writing that they undertook was in most cases strongly influenced by the teacher and varied considerably from one class to another. There does not seem to be any really satisfactory solution to this dilemma.

2. Other things being equal, of course. A speech impediment, for example, or a serious lack of self-confidence could cause a different sort of constraint that would effectively mask ability in composing.

Chapter 10
The Sense of Story

What has emerged in the preceding chapters as the major determinant of educational achievement is the extent of a child's mastery of literacy. As children progress through the primary years, the content of the curriculum comes increasingly to be presented symbolically through uses of language that are more characteristic of writing than of conversation. Without the ability to cope with this literate form of language, therefore – that is to say, with the linguistic representation of ideas that are disembedded from a context of specific personal experience – children become progressively less able to meet the demands of the academic curriculum and, whether justly or not, are judged to be intellectually limited.

This is not a new discovery, of course, but what has become increasingly clear from our longitudinal study is just how early these crucial differences between children begin to be established. By the time they came to school, the rank order of the children in our study was already fairly firmly established. This is not to say that school made no difference. Indeed, all the children made considerable progress during the five years of school through which we followed them. But, because the schools provided rather similar learning environments, individual children did not change their relative position in the rank order very much. Several gained or lost a few places, it is true, and there is good reason to believe that this was partly due to the quality of the teaching they received. However, there is little doubt that, in accounting for the *differences* between children, the major influence was that of the home, particularly during the preschool years and the first year or two at school.

There are many ways in which parents foster their children's development in these years, not least through the quality of their conversation with them. But what this study clearly demonstrates is that it is growing up in a literate family environment, in which reading and writing are naturally occurring, daily activities, that gives children a particular advantage when they start their formal education. And of all the activities that were characteristic of such homes, it was the sharing of stories that we found to be most important.

On the surface, this may not appear remarkable. We have always known that reading stories to children is a worthwhile activity. However, as I thought about our results, I began to wonder whether there was not more to stories than was suggested by the simple relationship between reading stories and learning to read. At the same time, I began to read some of the work that had been carried out on stories from other perspectives. Gradually, the various findings from our study began to fit together for me, forming a pattern around the concept of storying. This chapter is a first attempt to sketch out that pattern.

What I want to suggest is that stories have a role in education that goes far beyond their contribution to the acquisition of literacy. Constructing stories in the mind – or *storying*, as it has been called – is one of the most fundamental means of making meaning (Bruner, 1986); as such, it is an activity that pervades all aspects of learning. When storying becomes overt and is given expression in words, the resulting stories are one of the most effective ways of making one's own interpretation of events and ideas available to others. Through the exchange of stories, therefore, teachers and students can share their understandings of a topic and bring their mental models of the world into closer alignment. In this sense, stories and storying are relevant in all areas of the curriculum (Egan, 1988).

Making Sense Through Stories

There has probably never been a human society in which people did not tell stories. Many of them went unrecorded, of course; but, as is still the case in nonliterate societies, the most important were preserved in oral form and handed down from one generation to the next. These formed the culture's heritage of myths and legends: stories that attempted to explain and give coherence to the otherwise inexplicable. This continues to be, at least in part, the function of literature in literate societies, in which a sizeable proportion of the population have both the ability and the time to read. There are, of course, important differences between the essentially social conditions under which stories are created and recreated in an oral culture and the much more solitary conditions under which most written literature is created and interpreted. But the underlying purpose is the same: to provide a cultural interpretation of those aspects of human experience that are of fundamental and abiding concern.

Such public stories, however, are only the most highly developed and polished instances of a form of human behaviour that is both universal and ubiquitous. Whenever people come together socially, they begin to exchange stories – personal narratives, anecdotes, or just snippets of gossip. Britton (1983) refers to such stories as language used 'in the spectator role', and he contrasts this with the use that is made of language when we are involved as 'participants' in getting things done. Freed from the demands that are made on us when we are actually engaged in practical events, we are able as spectators to adopt a more reflective attitude – to look for their inner consistency and structure and to express it in the stories of everyday conversation and later, perhaps, in writing.

Such stories do not only offer a personal interpretation of experience, however. Because they occur in the context of social interaction and are produced in conversation, they, like all other conversational meanings, are jointly constructed and require collaboration and negotiation for their achievement. In this way, members of a culture create a shared interpretation of experience, each confirming, modifying and elaborating on the story of the other. Whether at home or at work, in the playground or in the club, it is very largely through such impromptu exchanging of stories that each one of us is inducted into our culture and comes to take on its beliefs and values as our own.

Even this, however, does not take us to the heart of the pervasive significance of stories. For what is done socially and verbally in conversation has its roots in the perceptual and cognitive processes through which, as individuals, we make sense of all of our experience. Each act of recognition, whether it be of objects in the external world perceived through our senses or of a conceptual relationship 'seen' through an act of the mind, involves a sort of inner storying. This is how we make sense of it.

Rarely, if ever, do we have all the necessary visual or other sensory information to decide unambiguously what it is we are seeing, hearing or touching. Instead we draw on our mental model of the world to construct a story that would be plausible in the context and use that to check the data of sense against the predictions that the story makes possible. Gregory (1974), in an article entitled 'Psychology: towards a science of fiction', refers to such stories as 'brain fictions'. He goes on to argue that essentially the same processes are involved when, in more formal contexts, we make sense of the evidence obtained through scientific observations or through other forms of research.

Waking in the middle of the night, for example, I creep downstairs without switching on the light to get a cool drink from the refrigerator. But as I pass the table in the dining room, I decide to have an apple instead and reach out my hand to the fruit bowl, which I know is in the middle of the table. To my surprise, however, the object that I touch, although spherical and apple-sized, is furry and slightly springy. It does not match my expectations at all. At this point, processes that had been going on unattended now become the focus of my attention. I search for a story that will enable me to make sense of my sensations and finally I recall an episode earlier in the afternoon when my son had found a tennis ball in the garden and asked what he should do with it. I had suggested putting it in the fruit bowl so that we would remember to give it back to our neighbours. So now, with this story, I am able to interpret my sensation: what I am grasping is not an apple but a misplaced tennis ball.

This example concerns an occasion unusual enough for the task of finding an interpretative story to require conscious attention. However, it illustrates rather clearly the processes whereby, in every act of perception, the world 'out there' is interpreted in relation to the inner mental model in terms of which that world is represented. Making sense of an experience is thus to a very great extent being able to construct a plausible story about it.

Stories in this sense surround the infant from the moment of birth. Even before they can talk, infants begin to construct a mental model of their world, based on the regularities in their experience, and in due course this model plays a major part in helping them to make sense of their linguistic experience and so to learn the language of their community. By reference to it they construct mental stories about the shared context – Mummy preparing dinner, the birds eating berries – and use them to predict the meanings of the utterances that are addressed to them. At the same time, stories provide the framework within which their own behaviours are interpreted; and, as children begin to speak and understand the speech of others, their view of the world is strongly influenced by the stories that other people offer them, as they interpret their experience for them and recount the stories of other people's experiences. In this way, stories are woven into the tapestry of a child's inner representations, producing the patterns that give it significance.

Thus, although storying may have its roots in the biologically given human predisposition to construct mental stories in order to make sense of perceptual information, it very quickly becomes the means whereby we enter into a shared social world, which is continually broadened and enriched by the exchange of stories with others. In this sense, the reality each one of us inhabits is to a very great extent a distillation of the stories that we have shared: not only the narratives that we have heard and told, read, or seen enacted in drama or news on television, but also the anecdotes, explanations and conjectures that are drawn upon in every-day conversation, in our perpetual attempts to understand the world in which we live and our experiences in it.

The Development of Narrative

What has just been suggested is that storying is one of the most funda-mental means whereby human beings gain control over the world around them. In Hardy's (1968) words, it is 'a primary act of mind'. In its begin-nings, therefore, storying is not a conscious and deliberate activity, but the way in which the mind itself works.

At a later stage, however, there does begin to be a conscious shaping. To narrate a story – to tell it in words – necessarily involves a selecting and ordering of the elements to be brought together. This is true even of two-year-olds, though to begin with they may require considerable assistance from an adult if the original impulse to link events in a narrative structure is to come to fruition. In the following example, Mark provides the embry-onic outline of a narrative structure as he makes the connection between his observation that the man has gone from view and the shop that he himself had visited in the past; his mother helps him to extend the struc-ture with her questioning prompts.

[Mark has been watching a man making a bonfire his garden]

Mark: Where man gone? where man gone?
Mother: I don't know . I expect he's gone inside because it's snowing
[A brief silence]
Mark: Where man gone?
Mother: In the house
Mark: Uh?
Mother: Into his house
Mark: No . no . gone to shop, Mummy [The local shop is close to Mark's house]
Mother: Gone where?
Mark: Gone shop
Mother: To the shop?
Mark: Yeh
Mother: What's he going to buy?
Mark: Er . biscuits
Mother: Biscuits, mm . what else?
Mark: Er . meat
Mother: Mm

Mark:	Meat and sweeties . buy a big bag of sweets
Mother:	Buy sweets?
Mark:	Yeh, m- man buy sweets
Mother:	Will he?
Mark:	Yeh, Daddy buy sweets . Daddy buy sweets
Mother:	Why?
Mark:	Oh er- uh shop . Mark do buy some sweeties . Mark buy some-um- Mark buy some- um- I did

By age four or five, children are often able to manage the narration by themselves, although the causal relationships are frequently left implicit in the ubiquitous use of 'and' or 'and then'. However, by this age we also begin to see another dimension of stories, in the form of dramatic or imaginative play. Here the function of the narrative is not reflective – to give significance to events recalled or anticipated – but rather to create a framework that will guide subsequent action and allow it to be interpreted by the other participants so that their activities may be coordinated.

[Lee (age 5) and Robert (age 6) are playing cops and robbers.]

Robert:	Right . I'm Starsky . you're Hutch
Lee:	Hello . I'm Hutch
Robert:	You don't need to go in there [imaginary building]
Lee:	I'm going in
Robert:	Come out
	[Lee makes car noises]
Robert:	I drive . Starsky drives *[pretends to drive]*
Lee:	No . I've got to take my car
Robert:	No, they have- have only got one car

One of the striking characteristics of such play is how much of the time is spent negotiating roles and appropriate actions, with the result, in some cases, that there is no time left actually to put the decisions into effect! When such play is successful, though, one clearly sees the important structuring role of the story, enabling the participants to integrate their imaginary worlds.

In the following example, Sam, John and David, all aged five, are playing with a variety of play-people and animals. David has a cardboard box: this is his base. Sam also has his own territory, a wooden boat, on which he has a family of lions. All around them is the sea – the playroom carpet. At this point in their play, John, who also has a boat and an assortment of play people, is torn between joining David on his base or Sam on his boat. The problem is that neither base nor boat has sufficient room for all John's people. As each child contributes from his own imaginary world, it is the jointly constructed narrative line that enables them to integrate those worlds in a collaborative manner and to manage the interpersonal conflicts that so often arise in the course of play. (*Note*: in the following dialogue, utterances in italics are spoken in 'play' voices appropriate to the characters concerned.)

Sam:	*[to John, to take his play-people somewhere else]* Now you have to live on your boat
David:	*[to self]* 'Tend it was put down like that *[arranging his base]*
John:	*[to Sam]:* Why? why do we?
Sam:	'Cos there was no room for you [on his boat] *[David puts people, furniture, etc. into his base]*
John:	Pretend we was sending boats back *[moves Sam's boat with the lions on]*
Sam:	*[speaking as lions] No, that's our boat . that's our boat*
John:	No, but pretend we was sav- saving them back so people could get, um- *[to David, who has got in the way]* That was your fault
Sam:	*O.K., we're living on here* [on the boat] *oh, we'll die* *[John begins to put his people on David's base.]*
David:	We- we've got all the luggage . *I'm going to sleep* *[Pretends to cry]* All our luggage is- is- one of, er- one of our boyfriends is crying in a corner *[pretends to cry]* . pretend one of the- the- their children was crying in a corner *[pretends to cry]*
Sam:	Why was that?
David:	It was because they didn't like being on the- *[pretends to cry]*
Sam:	They didn't like being on land
David:	-all squashed up, did they?
Sam:	No, they didn't like being-
David:	They went outside, didn't they?
Sam:	Yeh, and they had to go out . and it was poison on the sea and they had to die, didn't they?
John:	No, they didn't . They got on this boat [the lion's boat] . they jumped on to there . they was good jumpers

Although the reader of this extract probably has some difficulty in following the thread, the children clearly had none. Even when their suggestions were in conflict, they listened to each other's contributions to the jointly constructed story and modified their actions in ways that were mutually acceptable. One interesting feature of this particular example is the use of the past tense in those utterances which develop the narrative. It is as if they know that, to be recounted, the actions must already have happened, and it is tempting to see in this the influence of the stories they have heard, for all three boys were frequently read to. It seems likely that being read to is also the source of their much greater sophistication in making the narrative structure explicit. Certainly their experience of stories enriches the range of their imaginative play – the roles they take on and the understanding they show of their characters' thoughts and feelings in the predicaments in which they set them.

As many writers have argued, this sort of dramatic play can have particular significance in enabling children to explore and work through emotions that are too urgent to cope with in the actual world and too frightening in the world of inner reality. Play provides a relatively safe area, in many ways complementary to the imaginary worlds created by the fairy tales and other powerful stories that children hear, in which the narrative structure serves to contain and make intelligible feelings that might otherwise remain violent but inarticulate.[1]

Through Stories into Reading and Writing

In the previous section, I have traced the early development of storying and considered the interpretative power of stories in a number of interpersonal situations: narratives and anecdotes in conversation, stories told or read aloud from books or seen on television, stories explored in talk and stories created in dramatic play. In all these settings, children are able to come to a greater understanding of their own experience through relating it to the experience of others, whether real or imaginary. At the same time, through interacting with others in the creation and interpretation of stories, their own inner storying is sustained and enriched and its effectiveness as a means of making sense of experience confirmed. And since stories can only be shared with others through language, children have also been led to discover, albeit unconsciously, the enormously facilitating power that language has, as a symbolic mode of representation, in organizing and shaping the thoughts and feelings that are garnered from experience.

With this in mind, I think we can now see more clearly why the early experience of listening to stories is such a good preparation for learning to read and write. In conversation, children discover the forms of oral language that correspond to their inner storying. But in listening to stories read aloud they not only extend the range of experience they are able to understand but also begin to assimilate the more powerful and more abstract mode of representing experience that is made available by written language.

Then, having already discovered one of the chief functions of reading and writing – that of conveying stories – they are prepared for the task of mastering this new medium and the conventions and skills that this involves.

What is needed at this stage, I am convinced, is opportunities to discover how meaning and graphic representation are related, through activities involving reading and writing that have purpose and significance in their own right. As in learning to talk, children have to construct their own understanding of written language and how to use it, and the best way of helping them to do so is by enabling them to approach the tasks of reading and writing as means of communicating meaning. Guidance will certainly be necessary but, as in conversation, it will be most helpful if it is responsive to the connections that children are making between their own meaning intentions and expectations and the written language forms of the texts that they are creating or interpreting (see the discussion of *The Giant Jam Sandwich* in Chapter 8).

What this implies is that reading and writing should be treated as complementary activities, work on one informing and enhancing the other. In some schools, the practice is to concentrate first on reading and to introduce writing only when a sight vocabulary of a certain size has been acquired. Not only is this artificial – it would be odd to suggest that children should only learn to talk when they had reached a fair degree of competence in comprehending the speech of others – but it is also counterproductive. Children who already know enough about the functions of written language to be able to embark on learning to read also know enough to be able to begin to write. This has been amply demonstrated recently by a variety of experimental and observational studies of children's spontaneous learning about literacy.

What all these studies show is that, by the time they enter school, almost all children are able to write – at least in a rudimentary way – and that they gain a great deal of satisfaction from doing so and from having what they have written read by other people. In the early stages it may well be necessary to provide a transcription service – typing what the child has composed so that it can be read by other children and by the child him- or herself on a later occasion. The important thing, however, is that children make the discovery that they have experiences to share, stories to tell that others find interesting; that they belong to the fraternity of writers.

At the same time, in order to write, they must necessarily also learn to read, so that they can later interpret what they have written. For, if what a child has experienced is sufficiently significant to write about, it is likely to prove equally meaningful as material to read. An additional advantage of giving equal attention to writing in the early stages, moreover, is that writing requires a focus on the graphic display with an attention to detail of letter formation and spelling that is more concentrated than in reading. An emphasis on writing as composing can thus also be a powerful spur to the development of reading, as Clay (1983) points out. In fact, this principle is at the heart of *Reading Recovery*, the remedial literacy programme that she pioneered.[2]

The range of situations in which children may find it meaningful to read and write is extremely wide, ranging from organizing routines around the classroom (such as feeding the hamsters or recording the stages in the development of tadpoles) to corresponding with parents and other people outside the classroom. But it is likely that for the majority of children it will be stories that assume the greatest importance.

The arguments for using picture storybooks as the staple for learning to read were set out in Chapter 8. Similar arguments apply to stories as the form in which most children will find it easiest and most meaningful to learn to write. As will be clear by now, this does not only mean imaginary stories – though some children find their greatest satisfaction in creating stories about exciting worlds of princesses and dragons, monsters and space ships. Stories arise equally appropriately out of personal experience, at home or in the classroom, or from reading, watching television, or playing computer games (Dyson, 1989, 1993). One of David's earliest achievements as a writer, for example, was a book about insects, some of which he had encountered personally while others he had only met in picture reference books or through watching television. Whether based in reality or in fantasy, what is important is that what children write should be their own stories, not ones that are written to someone else's design. 'Ownership' is vital if the child is to make a real commitment of time and effort to the task of learning the craft of writing.

But perhaps the most important reason for advocating a strong emphasis on writing right from the beginning is its potential as a tool for learning. Once some proficiency in composing in this new medium has been acquired, writing provides a means of recording what has been observed or discovered through talking, listening and reading and through reflection on those observations and discoveries. And because what has been written remains, it can form the basis for further discovery when the text that has been created is reread in order to launch off anew or engage in the process of revision. If, as Donaldson (1978) suggests, one of the prime aims of schooling is to become able to direct one's thought processes in a thoughtful manner, this is most effectively learned through writing. Writing is, par excellence, the activity in which we consciously wrestle with thoughts and words in order to discover what we mean. 'The process itself unfolds the truths which the mind then learns. Writing informs the mind, it is not the other way round.'[3]

These suggestions for facilitating children's entry into literacy are based on the assumption that they have already had a wealth of experience of creating and responding to stories in a variety of interpersonal situations. Where such is the case, the transition to the more private activity of making meaning in writing, with all the new processes that this involves, is likely to be made without undue difficulty. But, as we have seen, a substantial proportion of children come to school without this advantage. It is not that they lack stories to tell or write, it is rather that they lack familiarity with the ways in which stories are constructed and given expression in writing.

For these children it is even more important that the emphasis should not be placed on the conventions and associated skills in dissociation from the purposes of reading and writing. Learning the sounds and names of the letters of the alphabet is clearly essential if they are to take possession of this new and exciting medium, but without an equal emphasis on the purpose and meaning of reading and writing *for them*, the mechanical skills may eventually be acquired, but the children will have no personal commitment to using them (Gallas, 1994, 2003). On the other hand, what better way could there be to help these children achieve this commitment than through experiences that involve the creation, interpretation, and discussion of stories, first in speech and then also in writing? As Vygotsky (1978: 117–118) emphasized, learning to read and write 'should be organized in such a way that reading and writing are necessary for something ... Writing should be incorporated into a task that is relevant and necessary for life'.

For all children, then, stories continue to provide one of the most enriching contexts for the development of language, both spoken and written. As has been emphasized, facility in using language is a means to achieving communicative purposes, not an end in itself. For the most part, it is best achieved by attending to the purposes for which language is used, rather than to the linguistic forms themselves. Stories provide a real purpose for extending control over language, all the more effective because they also tap one of the child's most powerful ways of understanding, enlarging and working on experience. In listening to, telling, reading and writing stories, children simultaneously enrich and reorganize that experience and extend their linguistic resources the better to allow them to do so.

Stories are for Understanding

Having gained this enhanced understanding of the significance of stories and storying as a fundamental way of making meaning, I began to look at their place in education more generally. What I found was that, beyond the early years, they received little official recognition, except in the literature lesson and in 'creative writing' sessions. School, it appears, is for learning about the 'real' world and, for most teachers, a concern with stories seems frivolous and pupils' personal anecdotes an annoying and irrelevant interruption of the official matter of the curriculum. Stories are all very well for preschoolers and for learning to read and write. But, once the skills of literacy have been acquired, the emphasis should shift to facts – to real-world knowledge and the subject disciplines in terms of which that knowledge is organized. However, in the light of what we now understand about the fundamental significance of storying, I believe that such a view is inappropriate and the assumptions upon which it is based are mistaken.

The first mistake is in assuming that the imaginative and affective response to experience is of less value than the practical and analytic – or, indeed, in thinking that they are in competition. The education of the whole person, which is the declared aim of probably every school system, can only be achieved if there are opportunities to explore feelings and values in specific real or imagined situations as well as lessons devoted to the consideration of general principles. Indeed, as pupils get older, it is probably more rather than less important to help them to recognize that the knowledge that they encounter in the various subjects of the curriculum is arrived at as the result of the activities of specific individuals and that it has implications for the lives and actions of other individuals in the future. Inevitably, therefore, knowledge has moral and aesthetic dimensions as well as practical and conceptual ones, and a fully mature response is one that achieves a balance between them.

Such issues are raised, for example, when studying history, by the consequences of European conquest and settlement for the indigenous populations of all the other continents; in geography, by the exploitation of the earth's resources; in biology, by the possibilities of birth control or genetic engineering. But the same need for a balanced response to knowledge applies equally in other subject areas; and, in all areas, stories have a major role to play in achieving this, in the form of biographies, historical novels, newspaper and magazine feature articles and, of course, the stories that students bring in speech or writing from their own experience.

The second mistaken assumption concerns the simple opposition that is often made between fact and fiction: facts are true while stories, if not false, are certainly less accurate or reliable. Quite apart from the difficulty involved in deciding what is a fact, such a simple dichotomy fails to do justice to the interpenetration of fact and fiction in all branches of human knowledge.

All fiction – novels, plays, even fairy tales and science fiction – is firmly based in fact, in the sense that it is about recognizable people acting in recognizable ways, but in a 'possible world' that differs in certain ways from any that has actually existed. To read or write fiction is not to abandon the search for truth, therefore, but to search for the truth within the world created by the imagination rather than the truth provided by documentary evidence, measurement, and so on.

However, if fiction is rooted in fact, so are facts embedded in something very similar to fiction. Isolated facts – items of information – only take on significance when they are related to other facts, and connections of various kinds made between them. Such coherent assemblages of related facts may then appear to correspond in a direct way to the reality that forms the background to our existence. Knowledge just is: given and unquestionable. Certainly, this is the impression that is created by many textbooks and works of reference. However, such a view is seriously misleading. As Richard Gregory showed in the article referred to above, the facts in any academic discipline are only facts within the framework of some theory, and theories share many of the imaginative 'as if' characteristics of fiction. Moreover, as theories change through radical reconceptions of the subject matter with which they deal, so do the facts they underpin.

This point is put in a somewhat more humorous vein by Harold Rosen, when he writes:

> A few days ago my son passed on to me a paper of his. It was sufficiently opaque for the title itself to be, for me, completely opaque. If I have understood the drift of one part of his argument, it is that if you aspire to becoming an invertebrate paleontologist you must be someone given to story-telling. What is geology but a vast story which geologists have been composing and revising throughout the existence of their subject? Indeed what has the recent brouhaha about evolution been but two stories competing for the right to be the authorized version, the authentic story, a macro- narrative? There are stories wherever we turn. How do we understand foetal development except as a fundamental story in which sperm and ovum triumph at the

denouement of parturition? Every chemical reaction is a story compressed into the straitjacket of an equation. Every car speeds down the road by virtue of that well-known engineer's yarn called the Otto cycle. (Rosen, 1984: 16)

If theories are 'macro-narratives', similar in many respects to the stories we class as fictions, what about the way in which theories are constructed and knowledge built up? Does that not too form a story, in the succession of contributions of different thinkers to a particular discipline (e.g. the progression in physics from Galileo to Newton to Einstein)? Equally, if we were to study the way in which intellectual and scientific advances are made by any one of these individual thinkers, would we not find that, at a rather abstract level, it involved a form of storying, as alternative hypothetical worlds were considered in order to decide which made the best sense of the available evidence?

On closer inspection, then, thinking – even advanced thinking – involves imagination as well as logical reasoning. To use Gregory's words:

By neither being tied to fact nor quite separate, fiction is a tool, necessary for thought and intelligence, and for considering and planning possibilities. Fiction is vitally important-indeed we may live more by fiction than fact. (Gregory, 1974: 439)

This is equally true for the developing thinker as well. Very young children, it is readily accepted, find it easier to assimilate new ideas when they are presented within the framework of a story. Only gradually do they learn to move from the particularized example to the general principle and from a narrative mode of expression to an expository or argumentative one. However, even older students find that illustrative anecdotes make general principles easier to grasp and, given the opportunity, will frequently look for such anecdotal examples in their own experience, as they work at new ideas in speech or writing in the attempt to assimilate the new material to what they already know. As students of all ages encounter new ideas, therefore, it is helpful to illustrate these ideas with stories – with particular contextualized examples – and to support their inner storying by encouraging them to work through the story mode themselves on the way to the expression of a more abstract formulation.

In the end, of course, it is important that students should be able to deal with abstractions and generalizations and to express them in the appropriate modes of discourse. But if, as has been suggested, storying is the most fundamental way of grappling with new experience, the best path to this achievement is likely, both developmentally and in the tackling of each new problem, to take them through the domain of stories, their own and other people's. Stories provide a major route to understanding (Bruner, 1986; Egan, 1988).

Stories Across the Curriculum

If these arguments are correct, we should expect to see stories continuing to occur in all subjects of the curriculum, in both speech and writing. Of course, the major function of stories will vary from one subject to another. In English or Language Arts, for example, there will be a concern with stories, along with plays and poems, for their own sake as works of verbal art. In science or humanities subjects, on the other hand, stories may have a much more incidental role – as a way of considering particular instances on the way to a more abstract understanding of a general principle or as illustration once that principle has been formulated. But, underpinning this diversity, we should expect to find a recognition that, in both speech and writing, a story drawn from experience can be an essential step on the route to more differentiated modes of knowing and of working on what is known.

Unfortunately, observations in classrooms suggest that this is rarely the case. In secondary schools, except in the English lesson, there is little opportunity for stories of any kind, particularly in the written mode. When a student does proffer a story from personal experience, as in the example quoted from Barnes in Chapter 5, it is often cut short as an irrelevant departure from the point of the lesson. Even in many elementary classrooms, the importance of stories is only recognized within the narrow confines of creative writing; and, if stories are read by the teacher or by individual pupils, it is often only as a way of filling odd moments when the 'serious' work has been completed.

There are classrooms, however, at both elementary and secondary levels, where the curriculum is not fragmented in this way – where activities in one area are planned to lead into activities in another and where each is enriched by connections made with the others. In such classrooms, too, pupils are encouraged to collaborate on the tasks they undertake and, as a result, they learn from each other and discover the value of their own knowledge by having it accepted and validated by their peers. Not surprisingly, perhaps, when pupils are given the freedom and the responsibility to work in this way, there is ample evidence that it is indeed their natural impulse to tell and write stories as a means of achieving understanding and of making connections between what they are learning and what they already know.

Since this more integrated approach to learning is still not particularly common, I should like to describe in some detail one particular class of 10-year-olds who were working in this way. All the activities to be described took place in the course of a single day in a longer period during which this class was being recorded.[4]

The school, which was in southwest London, was celebrating its centenary, and this occasion provided the starting point for the greater part of the curriculum for most of a term. Within the theme of 'Life a Hundred Years Ago', small groups of children, twos or threes, undertook individual projects in which they explored – through reading, writing, drama, painting, practical work and discussion – some aspect of late-19th-century life.

Not all the time was spent in these small groups, though. On the day in question, the teacher brought the whole class together to listen to the next chapter of *Journey into Yesterday* (Macnab, 1962), a sort of science fiction story in which two children were carried back into the past and met a boy who was bedridden with pneumonia. In talking with him, they found themselves having to explain such technical matters as the working of a television set, motorcars and flight in the Concorde – matters which up till then they had taken for granted. As the teacher stopped reading at the end of the chapter, discussion spontaneously broke out among the pupils as they considered how they would try to give explanations. The following extract will give a taste of this discussion. One of the boys had just described the appearance of a car.

Teacher: How does it go, though?
Pupils: The engine- by engine
Pupil 1: He might not know what an engine is
Chad: Miss, he would know what an engine was because of a- er- steam engine
Pupil 1: Oh, that's different though
Pupil 2: Yeh, that doesn't work on _steam, does it?_
Pupil 3: It's different
Pupil 4: There might be a different engine though, mightn't it?
Pupil 1: More technology
Syena: Mind you-
Teacher: Sh! Let's hear
Syena: Because it works differently . the steam engine works by fire and coal and um- the um- car-
Pupil 5: Yeh
Pupil 6: Steam
Syena: -works by petrol

After some 15 minutes, during which the teacher intervened only occasionally to assign speaking turns when several children were trying to speak at once, she posed the more general question:

Teacher: Could you actually explain something about this to somebody-

Pupils: No

Teacher: -who really didn't know anything at all about the type of things that you had?

Pupil 6: I'd ask him what their things are like

Teacher: Yes, and then?

Pupil 7: Miss, if, um- the sort of things in those days were the same like today- well- it could be, you know- he could explain a bit easier

Syena: It could be- you could compare it together in a way and see, er- say you see some things the same as ours- say it works like that but it's different

In the light of the discussion of facilitative conversation in Chapter 3, these answers seem remarkably perceptive.

Following this spontaneous discussion, the teacher called on two of the girls, Syena and Niki. They had been finding out about schools 100 years ago and had chosen to present the results of their research in the form of two related stories about a particular school. The following is a transcription of the dramatic presentation of Syena's version.

Syena: It's a story, um, about a Dame School and I'm the dame and Niki's the child . but I'm going to read **my** story
[*Reads*] The morning started when the children came in. When I thought everybody was here, I got one piece of paper- it was the only piece of paper that I had. On it was all the names in the class.
'Susan?' 'Yes, Miss Dame.'
'Abigail?' 'Yes, Miss Dame.'
'Nicolette?'
'Nicolette? Nicolette?'
Then I looked up and saw Nicolette sleeping and said, 'Susan, go and get the cane.' So Susan got the cane and brought it to me. I walked slowly to the place where Nicolette was sleeping and I tapped the back of her neck. She suddenly woke up. I said, 'Why were you sleeping in class? Stand up!' She got up- she got up and bent down. She knew what was going to

happen. I got off the shelf a metal top which fitted onto the
cane. Then I took Nicky – that is what we called her for
short – by the ear and I took the cane and hit her two times
on her bottom. In a way I felt a little sorry for her. Then
I asked her why- then I asked her why she was sleeping
in class. She said:

Niki: 'Miss Dame, I am very sorry but, er- but my mother and
father had to work in the shop and because it was very busy
I had to work too. So I went to bed very late. And
I had to get up very early and clean the shop'

Syena: In the afternoon, I did some- we did some sums and Nicky
got hers wrong. I hit her on the hand with the cane and put
a dunce cap on her. The next day we did our chanting out.
I found that Nicky could not sit down on her bottom for a
long time. She did not look at me for a long time

Teacher: Start that bit again

Syena: So I said, 'Nicky, tell me your letters, A to Z and don't get
them wrong or else!'

Niki: 'A,B,C,D,E,F,G,H,I,M,N-'

Syena: 'Stop! Stop!' I cried. 'You've done it wrong. Why don't
you learn them at home? Oh, I've forgotten, you have to
work at your mother's and father's shop. I will come to
your shop and see your mother and father and talk to them
about your sums and letters.' So after school I went with
Nicky to her house and talked to her mother and father.
In the morning, Nicky came to school on time. I asked her,
'Tell me your five times table'

Niki: One five is five. Two fives are ..

Syena: *[whispering]* Ten

Niki: Ten. Three fives are fif- er . sixteen

Syena: Sixteen is not in the five times table. I thought I told your
mother and father you had to learn your letters and sums

The other children were clearly appreciative of the story. But they also
saw it, and its authors, as a source of information. Several questions
followed about the school and its organization, with one of the other girls
showing a particular interest in the dunce cap.

The teacher indicated that these questions should be addressed to the
authors, the experts on this subject. And indeed their story does give a
very accurate picture of a dame school, with its emphasis on rote learning
and the use of corporal punishment for minor misdemeanours. It also

captures another aspect of Victorian life – the exploitation of child labour. But what is equally impressive is the quality of the writing: the dramatic conception, the characterization, and such features as the aside, 'that is what we called her for short', and the dame's moment of empathy, 'In a way I felt a little sorry for her.' Given the chance to choose a dramatic narrative form, these two girls have been able to convey what they have learned in a way that their classmates are obviously able to understand and appreciate.

However, the discussion did not stop at the historical content of the story. One of the children drew attention to the dame's apparent cruelty to Nicolette, and Syena replied at first in terms of her conception of the character of the dame. But as the discussion proceeded, the children began to explore some of the more complex issues involved, such as the difference between manner (tone of voice) and actions and the difficulty of capturing this in writing.

Syena:	I didn't like her at all . and I was very cruel anyway, and I'd hit her for anything
Eduardo:	It gives you an example of, um how it was back in the past . it was like an example
Teacher:	Good
Kurt:	But the way Syena talked, she sounded quite nice
Teacher:	Do you think she sounded nice?
Theresa:	Miss, she sounded like wicked
Teacher:	You thought she sounded wicked?
Theresa:	Yeh
Pupil:	-like she was a wicked teacher
Syena:	I think really I had to . I don't think she sounded very wicked but- 'cos in the playground we sort of play .. um .. games when *I'm* a child in a dame school and she's the teacher . and she sort of is wicked when we're in the playground
Niki:	She shouts a lot
Syena:	But it's easier to act it than to write it down, I think
William:	Miss, it's like the words are wicked but her voice- she doesn't do the right examples of being wicked . it's just the words
Teacher:	What's William trying to say? *[five-second pause]* What's he saying, Kurt?
Kurt:	He's- um . trying to say that the voice- you have to say it like the voice- like, um, you say things

William: When she was about to hit her, she should have said, 'Come
               here!' and had a kind of croaky voice, isn't it?
Patty: Miss, when we play in the playground the game of um ..
Teacher: Dame school?
Patty: Yeah, the dame school, Syena be the dame . then she has a
               sister . her sister bes kind . she bes wicked and they have a
               fight at the end . they kill each other
Kurt: Miss, Syena didn't like Nicky very much in the story . but I
               don't understand really, because she said that she felt a little
               bit sorry for her
Syena: Well, I did it because .. I like- I don't like- I didn't like her ..
               but like- er, in the playground, if I hit someone or something,
               I feel sorry inside me, and it's- I think it's the same as if
               I were a teacher

The story has obviously become more than a piece of schoolwork for
these girls; it has also been assimilated to the perennial childhood game of
'goodies and baddies'. But for Syena, in addition, it has provided an opportunity for a growth in moral understanding, as she recognizes that, although
they are in positions of power and authority, teachers, like her, may have
feelings of shame or regret when they cause suffering to others.

Later the same day, the children were at work again on their group
projects. Two were painting pictures of miners at work, others were reading and writing; a group of girls was discussing a story they had read, and
another mixed group was engaged in weaving on a hand loom. The
teacher went to join two boys, who were using a variety of books and
other source material to find out about markets. After some discussion
about what they had discovered from their reading, the teacher invited
Chad to read aloud the story he had written and beautifully illustrated,
about an escapade in a market. After he had finished, the teacher turned
to Eduardo, who had spent his early life in Portugal.

Teacher: Is that kind of market very similar to the market you would
               have in Portugal, Eduardo?
Eduardo: No
Teacher: Can you tell us something about a Portuguese market?
Eduardo: Well, it would be much busier and it have more things to
               sell . more- um . fruit and meat and . um- it did- doesn't
               have quite a lot of shops . it has more stalls . and it would
               be much busier than here because it would be more full
               of . um . fruit and meat and things . it would be much
               bigger and-

Chad:	You mean it would be more crowded than the Portobello Market on a Saturday?
Eduardo:	Yes . and it's, um- it's not very long . er . it's quite wide- wider
Chad:	You mean . it's a wide road?
Eduardo:	Yes
Chad:	It's very wide?
Eduardo:	Yes
Teacher:	Would it be a road?
Eduardo:	No
Teacher:	What would it be?
Eduardo:	Like-
Chad:	A park or something?
Eduardo:	It has a lot of pavements that are quite big
Chad:	Like a courtyard?
Eduardo:	It's like a swimming pool . um . but very big- bigger than that
Teacher:	When was the last time you saw a Portuguese market?
Eduardo:	Er-
Teacher:	Was it years ago?
Eduardo:	Yes ... it's going to have all these chickens and .. rabbits and . er-
Teacher:	Livestock?
Eduardo:	Yes, livestock
Chad:	In the country . er- in Sussex . there used to be a- by the station there used to be a kind of ... things where cows and chickens and stuff went to and there were kind of .. fair for judging- for judging the . er- best cow
Teacher:	Yes?
Eduardo:	Do they still do that?
Chad:	No, but no, no- in the country . they don't any more . they're going to turn it into a car park, I think
Teacher:	That's a shame, isn't it?

There are several characteristics of this discussion that are worth remarking on. Perhaps most important is the relaxed and easy atmosphere. Each is listening carefully in order to understand the other's intentions. This comes over very clearly in Chad's questions. As well as expressing some surprise at the claim that any market could be busier than Portobello Market on a Saturday, he is obviously trying to help Eduardo to make his meaning clear. As for Eduardo, offered the opportunity to take on the role of expert, he rises to the challenge and, although still somewhat uncertain in his command of English, he successfully manages to convey something of the appearance and atmosphere of a market in his homeland.

This sort of collaboration between pupils is, unfortunately, all too rare. However, as a result of the teacher's example, in this classroom it was the norm. And, watching the videotape, I was able to see how, on this occasion, it was achieved. Sitting between the two boys, she had been turning first to one and then to the other as the discussion prior to this extract proceeded. However, when she invited Eduardo to speak, she leaned back, so that he was speaking directly to Chad. This unobtrusive gesture, so effective in its message, makes one realize just how important teachers' non-verbal behaviour is in indicating how pupils are expected to relate to them and also to each other.

Although clearly interested in the pupils' ideas and skilled in helping them to extend those ideas, this teacher also had her own suggestions to make. Shortly after the extract quoted above, she brought the discussion back to the subject of the Portobello Market and produced some street plans of the area, which she had photocopied from the records at the public library. These had been selected from different chronological points in the development of the area and, with her help, the boys discovered how to interpret them, bringing these records of the past into relation with their firsthand knowledge of the present layout of the area. Together, they discussed some of the changes that had taken place over the previous century, as the area had become progressively urbanized. And, from this, the decision arose quite naturally that the boys should extend their project on markets to include an investigation of the way in which the Portobello Market had developed. At this point the teacher left them, having spent more than 25 minutes with them. But at the end of that time, enthusiastic about the topic, they were ready to continue on their own, collecting and sifting information in preparation for the presentation of their work, in writing, diagram, and illustration, to the rest of the class.

These few extracts from the observation made on a single day cannot do justice, of course, to the range and depth of the learning that was taking place in this classroom. But they will perhaps have served to give the feel of the place and an indication of the type of purposeful activity in which the children were engaged. They will also have conveyed an impression of the collaborative spirit in which pupils from a wide range of ethnic backgrounds were learning from each other as well as from the teacher. All the extracts show a concern for language but, both in speech and writing, the concern is with using language to learn about the topics that have been chosen and to communicate what has been learned, rather than with the development or practice of language skills for their own sake.

This classroom thus illustrates, probably as well as any could, what have been some of the main themes of this book, in particular the way in which meaning is negotiated and the collaborative quality of teacher–pupil interaction that enables pupils to make knowledge their own. In the context of this chapter, however, what is particularly striking is the central place of stories: stories read to the class by the teacher; stories read by pupils individually and in small groups; and, most obviously, stories told and written by pupils.

It also provides a fitting end to my story of the development of the making of meaning. Let me end this more personal chapter, then, with another quotation from Harold Rosen, for it is from him and from the other writers quoted in this chapter that I have learned the value of stories for my own work as a researcher and as a reporter of that research to others:

> We are in error if we believe narrative stands in complete contrast to other kinds of discourse. In fact it is an explicit resource in all intellectual activity. (Rosen, 1984: 15)

Notes

1. See, for example, James Britton (1983), 'The role of fantasy', in *Prospect and Retrospect: Selected Essays of James Britton* (Montclair, NJ: Boynton/Cook); Spencer (1976), 'Stories are for telling', in *English in Education* 10, 16–23; and Bettelheim (1976), *The Uses of Enchantment: The Meaning and Importance of Fairy Tales* (New York: Knopf). See also Meek *et al.* (1978) (eds) *The Cool Web* (New York: Atheneum) for a very comprehensive and helpful discussion of children's literature.
2. See also Graves (2003), who puts particular emphasis on individual 'conferencing' at various stages in the process of writing. As I understand this proposal, it is a particularly clear instance of the contingent responsiveness that I have suggested should characterize the guidance that the teacher gives to help children develop their mastery of this or any other craft or area of knowledge.
3. I have not been able to trace the source of this quotation, but I would not wish to claim the credit for phrasing this insight so aptly.
4. This material comes from the video program *Extending Literacy*. See Chapter 6, Note 2. For descriptions of similar secondary school classrooms, see Torbe and Medway (1981).

Chapter 11
A Functional Theory of Language Development

At the time when I was writing the first edition of this book, my concern was to present what I had learned in the Bristol Study about the relationship between learning language and using language to learn. That seemed to be a sufficient goal. But as I later reflected on the major findings, and particularly the important role of adults in the process of children's development, I felt the need to set the findings in a wider theoretical context. So I began to extend my reading on human development more generally.

Many years previously I had read and been intrigued by Vygotsky's ideas about 'inner speech' and its relationship with thinking. In 1987 a new translation of *Thinking and Speech* was published (Vygotsky, 1987) and, in reading this new edition, I was struck by the much more informative version of Vygotsky's construct of the *zone of proximal development*, and its ability to explain how adults assist children's learning. It seemed to provide a theoretical underpinning for the four guiding principles for helping children learn to talk that I had proposed in Chapter 3. So I decided to find out more about Vygotsky's overall theory.

Vygotsky's research and his writing were carried out in the period following the Russian Revolution, when there was a ferment of intellectual activity, much of it influenced by the work of Marx and Engels. But, in addition to his knowledge of Marxist theory, Vygotsky was conversant with the work of many contemporary psychologists, since he read widely in many European languages; he also conducted research on language and thinking with young children, and he was practically involved in the education of handicapped children. From these experiences arose his goal: 'to develop psychology as a science that [would be] capable of making a difference in the real world by contributing to the creation of a just and equality-based society' (Stetsenko, 2004: 503).

At the heart of this enterprise was his conviction that all human psychological processes develop out of collaborative social forms of interaction, using cultural tools, most importantly language, to transform the world rather than passively to adapt to it. However, while language played a central role in his theory, he considered it to be just one component of a unified psychological system that combined affective, practical, social, motor and symbol-based intellectual processes together in the context of larger meaningful activities that relate the individual to the world and to other people. In his theory, therefore, individual development is seen as the process of entering into an ongoing culture, gradually appropriating its tools, as well as the modes of action and thinking embodied in them, through participation in collaborative shared activities with more experienced members of the culture. As he put it, 'the whole history of the child's mental development teaches us that from the first days, his adaptation to the environment is achieved by social means through the people around him' (Vygotsky, 2004: 116).

As I read more of Vygotsky's work, I realized that here was the wider framework that I had been looking for. Furthermore, it provided the basis for a clear alternative to innatist theories of language acquisition. As I mentioned in the introduction, it was Chomsky who first engaged my interest in how children learn language. His convincing refutation of behaviourist theories of language learning and use and his proposed alternative of a language acquisition device (LAD) caused a revolution in thinking about language development and led to the first detailed investigations based on longitudinal recordings of children's early grammatical development (Brown, 1973). But it quickly became apparent that language involves more than grammar and that, although the child's speech eventually comes to conform to the grammatical 'rules' that linguists describe, to start with the assumption that this requires innate knowledge of universal grammar – as Chomsky did – might not be the best way to start.

A better alternative, Halliday (1973, 1975) proposed, was to start by asking what functions language serves for the language learner. And by recording his own son from the age of a few months, he provided convincing evidence that the child's earliest idiosyncratic utterances are produced to serve a small range of practical functions when interacting with other family members in the interests of getting things done together. Only when effective communication around a limited number of these basic functions has been established, with the use of gesture and intonation as well as a small number of 'words', does the child begin to take over the adult language of his or her community.

But for Halliday, the way in which children make their way into the particular language of their community also provided possible pointers to the way in which human language developed in the first place. And, as I shall describe below, the relationship between the beginnings of language in the distant past and the beginnings made by contemporary language learners has been profitably taken up by a number of researchers. On both 'genetic' levels, function is the key.

Adopting a 'Genetic' Approach

It was in this context that I became interested in Vygotsky's (1981) emphasis on history in studying development. In order to understand development, he argued, it is necessary to adopt a 'genetic' method of analysis, that is to say, instead of focusing on an individual's current behaviour, it is necessary to study the history of the developmental transformations that have led to the current behaviour. However, while most researchers would agree that this approach is essential in studying an individual child's development, Vygotsky argued that a true understanding can only be achieved by considering three other historical domains: phylogenesis (development in the evolution of the human species); sociocultural history (development over time in a particular culture); and microgenesis (development over the course of, and resulting from, particular activities and interactions in specific cultural and historical settings).

As I have argued elsewhere (Wells, 1999), there is considerable similarity between the perspectives offered by Halliday and Vygotsky on the subject of language development. While differing considerably in their immediate concerns – Halliday as sociolinguist and Vygotsky as psychologist – both recognized that ontogenetic development is strongly influenced by the sequence of events that make up an individual's life trajectory and that the nature of these events is both afforded and constrained by the particular historical and cultural context in which they occur, on the cultural resources available, and on what the participants bring to them as a result of their individual developmental histories and their current capabilities.

Both also subscribed to the view that language is at it is because of the functions it was originally developed to serve in the past and now serves in the present. It is this functional perspective that I wish to expand on in the remainder of this chapter. And, following Vygotsky's advice, I shall start with a brief account of current thinking about the initial emergence of language in human evolution. As I hope to show, this helps us to understand why contemporary children learn language in the way they do.

The Evolution of Culture, Mind and Language

Could language be innate?

One of the strongest objections that has been brought against Chomsky's LAD theory is that it offers no explanation for the origin of what he has more recently called the 'language organ' (Chomsky, 1972). Since he accepts a Darwinian theory of evolution, he should be able to identify the point in human evolution at which he believes this 'organ' to have emerged.

According to the most recent estimates, the evidence for the emergence of language goes back at maximum to 500,000 years ago, with some researchers arguing for no more than 50,000 years. This is far too short a time for language to have emerged through biological evolution, as Tomasello implies in the following summary of his comparative studies of young chimpanzees and human infants.

> The basic puzzle is this. The 6 million years that separate human beings from other great apes is a very short time evolutionarily, with modern humans and chimpanzees sharing something on the order of 99 percent of their genetic material – the same degree of relatedness as that of other sister genera as lions and tigers, horses and zebras, and rats and mice. Our problem is thus one of time. The fact is, there simply has not been enough time for biological evolution involving genetic variation and natural selection to have created, one by one, each of the cognitive skills necessary for modern humans to invent and maintain complex tool-use industries and technologies. (Tomasello, 1999: 2)

It is generally accepted that primitive tool manufacture preceded language by one to two million years. So, if the early development of tool manufacture cannot be ascribed to biological evolution – as most authorities argue – an evolutionary explanation for Chomsky's proposed language organ therefore seems even more implausible.

But if language did not arise through biological evolution, how did it arise? Tomasello's solution to the puzzle involves a different evolutionary explanation. Some time between six and two million years ago, he proposes, a small but highly significant development occurred. Humans – unlike other primates – began to be able 'to understand conspecifics as beings *like themselves* who have intentional and mental lives like their own. This understanding enables individuals to imagine themselves "in the mental shoes" of some other person, so that they can learn not just *from* the other but *through* the other' (Tomasello, 1999: 5–6).

What is so significant about this new form of learning 'through others' is that it makes possible, first, the transmission of knowledge and skills from one generation to the next and, second, over time, the gradual but cumulative process of *cultural evolution*, as novel practices and artifacts, created through collaboration in solving particular problems, are added to the cultural repertoire. It is this cultural form of evolution that crucially distinguishes humans from other species. However, cultural evolution started long before the emergence of language and so could not have been dependent on it. Rather, as Tomasello makes clear, language is not innate to the human species, but developed in the course of *cultural evolution* to serve the needs of inter-generational learning and teaching which, itself, was made possible by the prior biological evolution of human infants' predisposition to see other humans as intentional agents like themselves and to learn from and through them.

The sequence of phylogenetic and cultural-historical development

In *Origins of the Modern Mind*, Donald (1991) proposes four major cultural developmental stages in human development, each of which depended on a new mode of representing the experience of acting in and upon the external world. The gist of his argument is that, over the course of the human evolutionary trajectory, there have been a number of major modifications in the 'cognitive architecture', each associated with a new representational system. As he puts it, 'Humans did not simply evolve a larger brain, an expanded memory, a lexicon, or a special speech apparatus; we evolved new systems for representing reality' (Donald, 1991: 2–3).

The starting point for Donald's proposed trajectory is the culture of the australopithecines, approximately four million years ago, which can be plausibly reconstructed from the cognitive achievements of contemporary great apes. This he describes as an 'episodic' culture. Higher primates, as we know them today, are extremely adept in the realms of event perception and memory. Chimpanzees, our nearest relatives, also have social structures that depend upon remembering large numbers of individually learned dyadic relationships; they also have a nuclear family structure, with division of labour and sharing of food. The same, Donald argues, would equally have been true of the earliest hominids and, as with chimpanzees, these characteristics would have required the ability to perceive and remember complex events and to use this situationally-based knowledge to guide their actions.

However, episodic culture had serious limitations. Despite their skill in the analysis and recall of situational information, higher primates cannot deliberately construct representations in order to elicit thinking in others. They have no 'semantic' memory and, as a result, they cannot represent a situation to reflect on it, either individually or collectively. It was thus the emergence of the ability to produce conscious, self-initiated, representational acts that marked the first major transformation of mind on the trajectory from ape to modern human.

This transition occurred sometime between two and one-and-a-half million years ago with the changes that can be seen in the culture of Homo erectus. Not only did these proto-humans have a much larger brain, but they made more elaborate tools, used fire and built shelters in seasonal base camps. They were also able to pass on the required procedural forms of knowing from one generation to the next and, in this way, to transport them as, over many generations, they migrated from Africa into Eurasia. Such achievements obviously required a means of recalling and sharing information in the absence of cues from the immediate environment. From fossil evidence, however, it seems clear that Homo erectus had not yet developed language. On this basis, Donald proposes that the principal mode of communication and representation must have been 'mimetic', using a combination of gesture, mime, facial expression and modulated phonation. Mimesis would have constituted an important advance as it made possible the coordination of joint activity and the passing on of knowledge and skills to the young through demonstration and imitation.[1]

The next transition occurred as recently as half a million years ago, or less, with the advent of Homo sapiens. The biological evolution of the vocal tract and of brain size and structure, first found in Homo sapiens, made possible both rapid articulation of speech and the construction of grammatical relations between utterance segments. However, spoken language did not develop simply because of the further enlargement of the brain or the lengthening of the vocal tract. As Deacon (1997) argues, the development of language and of the brain show a pattern of co-evolution, in which the emergence of language was part of a more general pattern of adaptation that, building upon the cognitive achievements of mimetic mind, strove to integrate the unconnected bits of information in a more comprehensive and coherent account of being-in-the-world.

Clearly, the invention and gradual refinement of spoken language brought about a radical change from the cultures preceding that of Homo sapiens. Speech added a new and more powerful mode of interpersonal interaction, utilizing a representational system that made possible greater precision and comprehensiveness of reference to objects and actions and their location in space and time. Spoken language also provided means for reflectively connecting events through relationships of purpose, reason and causality and so for the development of narrative meaning making.

However, while recognizing the benefits for organizing practical action, in Donald's view the most significant achievement made possible by the use of language was 'mythic invention'. Exploiting the fundamental narrative organization of oral language (Bruner, 1986), all known cultural groups of that period began to construct overarching myths in order to explain human existence and its relation to the nonhuman world. As Donald (1991: 215) argues: 'Myth is the prototypical, fundamental, integrative mind tool. It tries to integrate a variety of events in a temporal and causal framework'.

Mythic culture emerged some 50,000 or more years ago. Underpinning it were the physical, cognitive and interpersonal skills that we still deploy in everyday life, together with the 'dynamic' everyday uses of oral language (Halliday, 1993), with their orientation towards narrative – that is to say 'storied' – construal of experience. For most people in all cultures, this way of life continued, relatively unchanged, until very recently. This may be somewhat difficult to appreciate, given the changes, particularly of a technological kind, that have taken place in the last two or three hundred years, but these only began to impinge on the lives of most of the earth's inhabitants during the course of the last century.

The emergence of writing and, with it, our contemporary theoretical culture (or 'knowledge society', as it is now called) – as with all the transitions that preceded – did not occur at all suddenly. In fact, the first recorded steps were taken some 4000 years ago, with the first use of written marks to represent articles traded and taxes due. Writing began as a system of hieroglyphics, whose function was that of giving visual representation to the meanings communicated in speech; only later, with the development of alphabetic scripts, as in written Greek, did writing represent the sounds of speech itself (Olson, 1994).

Donald characterizes the invention of writing and other visuographic systems of representation as creating 'the exact external analog of internal, or biological memory, namely, a storage and retrieval system that allows humans to accumulate experience and knowledge' (Donald, 1991: 309). However, there are important differences between the different visuographic systems in the functions that they typically serve. Drawing, together with painting and sculpture – all of which, in their first appearance, antedated writing and numerical notation by many millennia – tend to be used to create evocative, aesthetic representations, which still maintain their mythic origins; musical and choreographic notations, although functioning more like writing, also have an aesthetic purpose in allowing compositions in these media to be performed even when their composers are not present to direct them. Mathematical formulae, maps, graphs, diagrams and three-dimensional models, as well as written language, by contrast, are typically used to represent information for practical and analytic purposes. For this reason, it is these modes of representation that have played the major role in the development of theoretical understanding. This is because, as Olson (1994: 277) points out, the great major benefit of representing thinking in permanent written form is that 'it turns the thoughts themselves into worthy objects of contemplation'.

Nevertheless, these means of representation would not, in themselves, have been sufficient to give rise to theoretical culture. What was also required was a new reason for exploiting the external memory system, which was provided, in large part, by the emerging interest in scientific investigation, together with the ideological changes that accompanied it, at the time of the European Renaissance (Hacking, 1990). Donald thus argues that, although exploitation of the new modes of visuographic representation as external memory devices has clearly been instrumental in the development of our contemporary theoretical culture, equal weight in explaining the transition needs to be given to the changing cultural values and purposes that have led to the increasing importance attributed to the kind of knowledge that can be constructed by these means.

To conclude this brief summary of Donald's account of the development of the modern mind, one further important point needs to be made. Although the various transitions he describes were revolutionary in their intellectual consequences, each new means of representation did not replace the one(s) that preceded; on the contrary, the developmental process was cumulative. The result is that 'our modern minds are thus hybridizations' (Donald, 1991: 356), with a variety of modes of functioning at their disposal. Indeed, most jointly undertaken activities call for more than one mode of thinking and require the complementary and interdependent use of more than one means of representation.

Arftifacts as representations

One final contribution that I wish to include in this review of phylogenetic development is that of Marx Wartofsky, a philosopher of science. Like Donald, Wartofsky was interested in the historical development of knowing. As he put it, 'what we take knowledge to be is itself the subject of an historical evolution' (Wartofsky, 1979: xiii). For Wartofsky, knowledge is dependent on the kinds of artifact by means of which it is represented and he distinguishes three general categories of artifact that, over the course of human evolution, have come to function as representations.

First are material tools and the social practices in which they are employed; these are primary artifacts in that they are directly involved in the transformation of the material environment for the production and reproduction of the means of existence. The first such artifacts were simple tools (knives, spears and pots); today, they include aircraft, computers and automatic banking machines. Such artifacts were not created for the purpose of representing; however, they can be so used, particularly to represent the activities in which they are typically involved. The second category consists of those artifacts that are created for the purpose of preserving the tools and practices by means of which primary activities are organized and their motives, goals and knowledgeable skills passed on to new participants. These secondary artifacts are symbolic representations of primary activities and are used to plan, manage and evaluate them. Face-to-face mimetic acts would have been the earliest form of secondary artifacts; nowadays they may be in any of a variety of semiotic modes, such as speech, writing, diagrams or a combination of them. Also included among secondary artifacts are institutions and the regulations and procedures that govern their functioning. Finally, tertiary artifacts: these are the imaginative, integrative representational structures (myths, religions, works of art and literature, as well as scientific theories and conceptual models) in terms of which humans attempt to understand and explore ways of transforming the world and their existence in it.

Wartofsky's central thesis is that human cognition has developed historically as a function of the different types of artifact that have been used to represent activity and its constitutive objects and actions and, at the same time, to allow reflection on the relationships involved. As these artifacts have become capable of representing more complex relationships as well as of being given a form that remains constant over time and space, they have made possible more complex modes of perception, action and cognition and the development of more integrative modes of knowing and understanding. In sum, he argues,

> ... our own perceptual and cognitive understanding of the world is in large part shaped and changed by the representational artifacts we ourselves create. We are, in effect, the products of our own activity, in this way; we transform our own perceptual and cognitive modes, our ways of seeing and of understanding, by means of the representations we make. (Wartofsky, 1979: xx–xxiii)

Wartofsky also emphasizes the active, social nature of humans' representing – of making representational artifacts to mediate activity with other members of the cultural group to which we belong. Furthermore, as he points out, it is through these attempts to make representations to advance jointly undertaken activities that, over the course of the historical development of particular cultures, individual members develop an understanding of their situated experience of being-in-the-world in terms of the myths, value systems and theories that are made available by, and appropriated from, other members of their culture. In this, he is in agreement with Vygotsky (1981: 162) who emphasized that 'the individual develops into what he/she is through what he/she produces for others'.

In Table 11.1, I have tried to provide a succinct summary of the phylogenetic and cultural historical development of humans from the time when our species evolved the crucial predisposition that, according to Tomasello (1999), distinguishes us from other primates, up until the present, when the lives of all humans – with very few exceptions – are shaped, more or less directly, by the different modes of knowing that have developed cumulatively over the last several million years.

Two things need to be emphasized about this table. The first, which is evident from the leftmost column, is the very recent and ever increasing pace of cultural evolution. The second, which is not so evident, is the very great diversity in the trajectories that different groups of humans have taken in the last 3–5000 years. By that point in time – and probably much earlier – all groups of humans, in whatever part of the world they had settled, were using speech as well as mimetic forms of communication to organize their cultural activities and to pass on their knowledge, values and skills. No archeological evidence exists of a group that had not reached this stage in the universal developmental trajectory. However, in the last few thousand years, differences in ways of life, which probably first occurred as particular groups adopted practices appropriate to their different ecological environments, became magnified as groups that had settled in some particular geographical areas found them to be fertile and able to yield plentiful, easily exploitable resources. Over time, this led to population growth in these areas and, with it, the development of specialization of labour, more powerful production technologies, hierarchical patterns of social relations, and the creation of durable institutions, all of which have been particularly typical of prosperous and powerful civilizations.

However, in the much more recent past this cultural diversity has begun to decrease since, as a result of contact between communities – through trade, conquest or sheer proximity – many of the characteristics

Table 11.1 Modes of knowing: Phylogenetic and cultural development

Time before present	Mode of knowing	Participants	Most advanced form of representation	
			Donald (1991)	Wartofsky (1979)
6–2 million years	Actional	Solo individuals	Episodic	Primary artifacts: found objects as tools
1.5–1 million years	Procedural	Between individuals while engaged in joint action	Mimetic	Secondary artifacts: tools and practices; mimetic interaction
	Substantive	Among members of a cultural group, reflecting on action and planning further action	[Spoken Linguistic]	Secondary artifacts: representations of tools and practices; spoken interaction
50,000 years	Aesthetic	Among members of a cultural group, making sense of the human predicament	Mythic	Tertiary artifacts: artistic representations in narrative, graphic, dance and musical modes
2500 years	Theoretical	Among members of 'scientific' communities seeking to explain the natural and human world	Theoretic	Tertiary artifacts: disembedded representations, such as taxonomies, theories, models, etc.

of technologically advanced cultures have been adopted by, or imposed upon, the less technologically advanced (Diamond, 1998). Indeed, within the next few decades it seems increasingly likely that there will be much less global diversity in ways of living as compared with any previous point in recorded human history. But whereas the early similarity between hominid groups was the result of biological evolution, the currently increasing similarity is the result of cultural evolution.

Language in Ontogenetic Development

It may seem surprising that, in a book about children learning language, I should have devoted so much space to theories about the relationship between biological and cultural evolution. However, as I shall try to show, recent advances in the understanding of this relationship offer some powerful hypotheses about why ontogenetic development takes the form that it does.

Since the publication of Darwin's theory, the evidence for the stages described above in the evolution of humans over the last six million years or so have become so firmly established that there is now general agreement about the basic facts. Bipedalism preceded tool manufacture; some form of preverbal communication was required for the purposeful, collaborative use of tools; the major increase in brain size preceded the emergence of language – which itself occurred only as recently as about 50,000 to 500,000 years ago. However, what distinguishes the work of the authors discussed in the previous section is the conclusions they have drawn from this evidence about the place of language in *cultural* evolution. As each emphasizes, the emergence and refinement of language contributed enormously to the development and accumulation of the kinds of knowledge that underpin the achievements of all known civilizations, and each author, from their different disciplinary perspectives, sees language as facilitating the process of cultural evolution that was already ongoing, rather than language being a prerequisite for its commencement. In other words, once the production of speech became anatomically possible, its development was shaped by its functional potential to improve social communicative and collaborative knowledge building practices that already existed. As Donald (1991: 215) puts it, 'modern humans developed language in response to pressure to improve their conceptual apparatus, not vice versa'.

If the development of language on the phylogenetic level was driven by the functions that it was recruited to serve, might the same sort of explanation be equally appropriate for ontogenetic language development? As we have seen, this was the general orientation adopted by Halliday (1975) in his study of his son's language development. More recently it has also been explored in the field of developmental psychology.

Nelson (1996, 2007) was one of the first to treat the sequence of hominid development, described above, as an analogy for explaining ontogenetic development. Accepting with Tomasello (1999) the very considerable range of cognitive and social abilities shared between humans and other primates, she sought to understand what enabled human infants to advance intellectually beyond other primate species. Her answer to this question drew heavily upon Donald's (1991) proposed sequence of phylogenetic development, from episodic, through mimetic, to language-based modes of thinking, to suggest a similar sequence in the developmental relationship between the maturation of the brain and the unique trajectory of each child's lived experiences in a particular social and cultural environment.

Nelson was not suggesting that this parallelism constituted a recapitulation, on the ontogenetic level, of the lengthy evolutionary process that occurred on the phylogenetic level. That would be impossible, not only because the timescales are so widely different but also because the contemporary child is born into a social environment that is radically different from that of our remote ancestors, in that it is shaped by the cultural artifacts, practices and institutions that have been created and improved over many thousands of years of cultural evolution. Most importantly, the contemporary infant is born into a society that already has and uses a fully developed language. Nevertheless, as recent research – to be described below – has shown, during the early years, children go through essentially the same developmental sequence, whatever language they are learning. This sequence can be summarized as follows.

In the first few months after birth, the infant's initial encounters with the material and social world are almost entirely through the senses – as is the case with other primates; this is a period during which the infant is registering and organizing the regularities and differences in what the body senses and what it can do; by the age of six months or so, he or she has established the first level of consciousness in an awareness of the boundary between self and not-self. Then, in the second half of the first year, a new level of consciousness is achieved as the infant begins to track others' attention and intentions and to engage in reciprocal interaction about them. The development of memory also makes possible the recognition of oft-repeated events and the infant is able to participate appropriately in such activities as being fed or dressed and in playing games such as peekaboo (Bruner, 1983). This stage corresponds to what Donald called the stage of episodic representations.

During the second year, a still further expansion of consciousness becomes possible as a result of increased mobility and the beginning of linguistic communication. Critical at this stage is the emerging sense of self as an actor in the social world and the reading of the intentions of interlocutors and attempting to match the words they use with his or her interpretation of their intentions. The young child also engages in imitation and begins to draw on memory to construct intentional representations for others by means of gestures, gaze, idiosyncratic 'words' and the use of some words taken over from the adult language. This form of communication, which Halliday (1975) described as 'protolanguage', is clearly purposeful and corresponds to Donald's mimetic form of representation.

By the beginning of the third year, the child has begun to master the organization of the adult language – its vocabulary and its grammatical organization – and as this mastery increases, it gives him or her increasing access to the cultural interpretation of his or her own experience, which in turn leads to the development of reflective consciousness. Particularly important in this respect is the learning of abstract terms and the linguistic means for referring to nonpresent entities and events, causal relationships and epistemic modality (e.g. 'I think that ...', 'It might ...'). With these resources, the child is able to take part in the sharing of stories, which still further expand his or her understanding of the culture's interpretation of experience. At the same time, she or he is becoming able to manage different representations of reality – those of her or his own current and past experience, others' belief statements and narratives, both factual and imagined. Thus, during the third year and beyond, in becoming able to understand and represent meanings linguistically, the child has reached the form of representation that Donald characterized as mythic (see Table 11.2).[2]

Several further points need to be made about this trajectory. The first is that, as in phylogenetic development, early forms of representation and knowing do not atrophy or disappear as new ones are mastered. Rather, the different forms complement each other, giving rise to new levels of organization and potential in the development of the uniquely human 'hybrid mind' (Donald, 1991, 2001). Second is the key part played by collaborative interaction with others in children's construction of conceptual structures. While these inevitably remain somewhat idiosyncratic, in that they are built on personal experience, they gradually come to conform more and more with those of their immediate interlocutors and, thus, to varying degrees, with those of the culture of which they are members (e.g. separating the initial ategory of 'hosh' into 'horse', 'zebra', 'big dog'. What is particularly significant about children's learning in these early years is

Table 11.2 Developmental stages mapped onto evolutionary stages

Stage	*Age*	*Cognition*	*Language*
Infancy/*episodic*	$0–1\frac{1}{2}$	Event reps.	Sounds, first 'words'
Early childhood/ *mimetic*	$1\frac{1}{2}–4$	ERs with words Games, play, songs, social rituals	Dialogue Grammar developing, language in mimetic reps.
Middle childhood/ *narrative*	4–10	Narrative thinking, personal memory, cultural learning	Narrative Beginning reading and writing, math, categorical schemes
Adolescent/ *theoretic*	10–adult	Logical abstractions Deductive systems Extensive use of external systems Acquisition of 'scientific' social-conventional knowledge	Logical abstractions, argument and scientific reading and writing, specialization

Source: Nelson, 1996: 86. Reproduced with permission of Cambridge University Press.

that it is both predominantly conversational and that it occurs in the course of familiar activities in the local community, with a strong tendency for adult speech to be contingent upon the child's apparent understanding.

Finally, it is worth emphasizing that, while this sequence of development is universal in its broad outline, each child's trajectory is unique. Many factors influence the course it takes, such as the child's health, the characteristics of his or her physical and social environment, and the prevailing cultural beliefs about child-rearing, for on these depend the nature and sequencing of each child's personal experiences and the changing internal and external conditions that influence how he or she *interprets* them.

Functionally Oriented Studies of Children's Language Development

Nelson's (1996) approach to *Language in Cognitive Development* is predominantly that of a developmental psychologist. However, since the 1980s, many psycholinguistic students of child language have also reacted against the Chomskyan explanation of language acquisition and, like Halliday, have sought a functional explanation for the developmental path of language learning.

Among these researchers there is unanimous agreement that infants are biologically prepared to learn any human language and that they are predisposed to do so. However, the enormous diversity of organizational patterns in the 6000 or so existing languages of the world makes it highly unlikely that whatever abstract universal 'rules' might be posited could be of practical use to infants trying to learn one of those languages (Slobin, 2001). Fundamentally, the mistake is in thinking that each child has to construct language on his or her own. In reality, the child is not alone, but is born into a functioning family and community that inducts children into the particular patterns of the language of that community by enabling and encouraging them to discover and appropriate those patterns by including them in the community's life and activities.

Given this family and community support, Tomasello and Bates (2001) suggest that there are three major tasks facing any infant language learner:

- identifying the speech sounds that are critical in distinguishing words and other meaningful units and then being able to reproduce them;
- having distinguished these units, discovering what they mean;
- discovering the regular patterns in which these units are organized and constructing the wide variety of abstract relationships that these patterns convey.

Using a variety of ingenious techniques, each of these tasks has been the subject of considerable empirical research in the last quarter of a century. The questions of theoretical interest in each case are: what strategies do children use in carrying out these tasks and what can this tell us about the resources with which they are equipped that enable them to perform them? In the following sections I shall summarize the major findings of this body of research.

One technique that has been used to good effect in relation to all three tasks is to compare humans and nonhuman primates with respect to the abilities they possess that are relevant to language learning. In brief, what these studies have shown is that, to a large degree, humans and primates share the ability to distinguish the sounds of speech and, to some degree, to attach meanings to word-like units of sound; on the other hand, it is only human infants that have the ability to construct the grammatical patterns of the language in use around them (Tomasello, 1999).

Perception and production of speech

From very early, even in utero, infants begin to pay particular attention to the sounds that are characteristic of their mother's speech, and well before they show any signs of comprehension they are able to discriminate utterances in the language of their family and community from those in other languages. These sound discriminations are categorical, that is to say, in the case of a syllable that is somewhere between /ta/ and /da/, it is treated as either one or the other (Eimas, 1975). However, since primates can also perform the same tasks, it seems clear that speech perception is not specific to language as such but is part of the general vocal-auditory ability that is shared with primates and many other mammals.

On the other hand, the selective production of the speech sounds of a particular language seems to be restricted to humans, in part because it requires the particular anatomical features of the vocal apparatus that are unique to humans. Nevertheless, since these sounds must be easily discriminable by the human/mammalian auditory system, it seems that, phylogenetically, speech must have evolved to match hearing, rather than vice versa (Ramus *et al.*, 2000). In their early months the babbled sounds that infants produce occur across a wide range that is not specific to a particular language; nevertheless, by the end of their first year they have focused in on just those sounds that they hear in the speech around them. However, even before – in their second year – they begin to produce recognizable words from the community language, they utilize contrasts in intonation and stress to make known their intentions, indicating that what impels language learning is the need and desire to communicate rather than the biological maturation of a particular (language) organ, as is the case in learning to walk.

Equally important in their early communication, infants also make use of gestures. Indeed, children who are born deaf typically proceed from initial gesturing to learning a fully functional language that is realized entirely through signs. Not surprisingly, therefore, there has been considerable interest in the role of gesture in the ontogenetic development of spoken language. In addition to Donald (1991), several other scholars have argued that gesture was the precursor of language. Corballis (2002), for example, has proposed that gesture existed side by side with vocal communication from the onset of bipedalism (see also Deacon, 1997). In his view, speech did not supersede gesture, rather they co-evolved in a complex interrelationship that continues in the present in the development of both typically developing children and in children with Down and Williams syndromes.

Significantly, on the basis of their recent studies, Volterra *et al.* (2005) have found that early communication is, in fact, largely gestural, although often accompanied by vocalization. By around 14 months, words and gestures occur with equal frequency and encode similar meanings; they also begin to become disembedded, in the sense that they are used in the absence of the object or event to which they refer. However, as vocalizations become progressively more adult-like, speech begins to dominate and is further encouraged by adults. Nevertheless, Volterra and colleagues found that 'the use of gestures did not stop with the emergence of words but, rather, increased and played an important role in the transition from the one-word to the two-word stage' (Volterra *et al.*, 2005: 33). On these grounds, they were convinced that gesture is a 'robust developmental phenomenon' that is found in similar forms across languages and in atypically as well as typically developing children. Making a connection with McNeill's work on adult use of gesture, they conclude that:

> there is a remarkable continuity between prelinguistic and linguistic development ... symbolic skills that are most evident in vocal linguistic productions are inextricably linked to, and co-evolve with more general cognitive and representational abilities, as is most apparent in the tight relationship between gestures and words, which continues through adulthood. (Volterra *et al.*, 2005: 35)

Further support for this conclusion has come from ongoing investigation of 'mirror neurons' (Rizzolatti & Arbib, 1998). Believed to exist in a similar form in both monkeys and humans, the function of these neurons, which connect areas of the brain involved in vision and movement, was first considered to be that of enabling the viewer to interpret the purpose of another's action. However, further functions in which the mirror neuron system has been found to be involved include immediate repetition of actions done by others and learning by imitation. If, as discussed above, gesture was the basis of the first form of human communication, it seems likely that, as Rizzolatti and Arbib (1998) suggest, mirror neurons played an important role in ensuring the comprehensibility of gestures and so may also be involved in the perception and understanding of speech.

Word learning and the development of vocabulary

The ability to name objects and events is one of the great benefits of language and, in the later part of their second year, infants seem to recognize this, for there is typically a considerable increase in word learning at this time. While first words tend to be very specific in their reference, being tied to ongoing actions and persons, by the end of the second year children are learning words that name categories; these words function as symbols to direct the attention of other people to matters of interest or concern, both absent as well as present. By this point, too, young children are aware that their communicative signals have an impact on the mental state of their listeners and so an important part of word learning involves calibrating the categories they are constructing with those that the words denote in adult speech (Shwe & Markman, 2001). As Tomasello (1999) points out, this requires 'reading the minds' of their interlocutors and depends on cognitive development in a variety of domains.

These various findings suggest that, once the ability to identify word-like units in the stream of speech has been achieved, word learning does not differ in kind from learning other pieces of information about the world. Some of the cues involved in learning the meaning of new words are internal to language, such as the grammatical contexts in which they occur and their co-occurrence with already familiar words (Gleitman, 1990), but many are provided by the events in which child and speaker are co-involved. Two features have been shown to be particularly important: first, many of the events in which new words are heard are routine and familiar and so the child can assume the new word refers to something novel about this particular event; and second, they act on the assumption that the new word is in some way relevant to the ongoing social interaction. Having used these cues to comprehend new words, children can further assume that adult listeners will use the same cues to understand their intentions when they produce the same words in context. In sum, children learn new words as an integral part of their social interaction with others as they attempt to understand what their interlocutors are trying to get them to do or understand and as they similarly attempt to influence their interlocutors. Language learning, including word learning, can thus be seen as a bidirectional, intersubjectively facilitated entry into the symbolically represented world (Tomasello & Bates, 2001).

Most longitudinal studies of children's language development have not included systematic study of vocabulary because of the unreliability of estimates based simply on periodic sampling of naturally occurring interaction. In order to overcome this and related problems, Elizabeth Bates took the initiative in developing the MacArthur Communicative Development Inventories (Fenson *et al.*, 2003) which, using parental reports to investigate the development of children's comprehension and production of communicative forms, enable data to be collected from much larger samples of children. The CDIs consist of two scales, the Words and Gestures Scale, which is used from eight to 16 months, and the Words and Phrases Scale, which is used from 16 to 30 months. As the titles of the two parts suggest, the total inventory spans the range from the preverbal stage to the stage when children have mastered a considerable part of the grammar of whatever language they are learning.[3]

Both scales have now been used with children learning a variety of languages and the results are very similar across languages. Reporting a comparison between children learning English or Italian between the ages of eight and 30 months, Bates and her colleagues (Caselli *et al.*, 2001) found that, in both languages, a substantial proportion of children showed a rapid increase in the number of words added to their comprehension vocabulary in the second half of the second year, though this was not necessarily accompanied by a similar proportional increase in the number of different words that they produced. There were also substantial individual differences in the size of children's receptive and productive vocabularies: at 24 months, for example, in both languages the average number of words produced was around 300 words but individual children varied from as few as 50 to as many as 600.

Two of the aims of this study were to test the hypotheses, first, that early vocabulary learning would include more nouns than verbs and, second, that it would include very few (grammatical) function words. With respect to the first hypothesis, nouns predominated in both languages even though Italian is a language in which verbs are more prominent than in English. The second hypothesis was also confirmed in both languages, with the proportion of function words being closely tied to absolute vocabulary size. Very few function words occurred in the speech of children with a productive vocabulary of less than 200 words; however, while Italian speakers showed a slow but steady increase, for English speakers there was a sharp proportional increase once they reached a productive vocabulary of about 400 words. Despite these latter differences across the two languages – which can probably be attributed in part to the different grammatical structuring of the two languages – these and comparable studies of other languages suggest that vocabulary learning is not arbitrary but is strongly influenced by social, cognitive and perceptual factors. But, as with other aspects of early learning, the nature of children's vocabulary development is also closely related to their individual experiential trajectories.

Recognizing patterns, constructing grammar

However, it is over the child's construction of the grammar of his or her first language that there is the greatest disagreement between theorists. Those who subscribe to the theory of the language organ, with its innately given universal grammar, consider that children operate from the beginning with universal, abstract grammatical rules to which they assimilate the particular patterns that they hear in the language around them (e.g. Pinker, 1994). Functionalists, on the other hand, reject the notion of abstract rules, arguing that the so-called rules are constructed gradually by a process of recognizing specific, limited patterns and then generalizing from them to more abstract patterns on the basis of their linguistic experience. In recent years, the latter theoretical perspective has accumulated a considerable amount of supportive empirical evidence.

First, there is the large body of recorded child speech,[4] which clearly shows the restricted range of topics and functions that children hear talked about and initially talk about themselves: location, possession, people manipulating and moving objects, appearance and disappearance of people and objects. As a consequence, the range of semantic relationships and their syntactic realizations that young language learners need to master is also quite highly restricted whatever the language they are learning (Slobin, 1985–1997). In other words, no appeal to abstract rules is necessary to account for the generalization to new combinations from such simple patterns as 'Mummy there', 'bird gone' or 'Daddy car'.

There is also evidence of a different kind against children's use of abstract rules. Presented in a novel action context with an invented verb such as 'meek' in an intransitive utterance (e.g. 'Look, the ball is meeking') the children were found not to produce contextually appropriate utterances such as 'He's meeking the ball' or 'It got meeked', until they were three years old, in responding to questions about similar actions, which strongly suggests that they were not functioning with abstract rules that apply to the class of related familiar verbs, such as 'move', 'roll' or 'turn' (Tomasello & Brooks, 1998).

One aspect of grammar that has long been used by innatists to demonstrate the applicability of rules is that of morphology, particularly inflexions for case (e.g. accusative, dative), plural and tense. Many languages have regular inflexions that hold for most words but to which some words are exceptions. According to the innatists, regular forms are learned by reference to universal grammar but the exceptions have to be learned individually by rote and therefore behave more like lexical items. However, a number of researchers have used both experimental studies of how invented words are treated by adults and children as well as naturally occurring samples of children's speech to investigate this issue further (e.g. Köpcke, 2001). What has been found is that, rather than operating with a rule with exceptions, children form more limited schemata around words that behave similarly (e.g. the past forms of 'bring' and 'think', or 'sing' and 'drink', in English) and assimilate other words to these schemata on the basis of a variety of cues of varying strength. On this basis, it has been argued that morphology learning does not operate on the rule plus exceptions model but rather on the basis of more local pattern-seeking and schema-forming appropriate to the data of each particular language.

Slobin's cross-linguistic studies provide further support for a more empirical approach to grammar construction by language learners. Starting with a search for the particular semantic notions that are universally encoded in the morphology and syntax of the world's languages, he was finally led to the conclusion that there is too much cross-linguistic variability for human infants to make use of preconceived ideas about what kinds of notions will and will not be indicated by grammatical rather than by lexical items (Slobin, 2001). Children search for patterns based on their experience, both cognitive and linguistic, of the speech of the particular linguistic community in which they are growing up, where the distinction between what is lexical and what is grammaticized continues to change over generations. Slobin therefore concludes that, although the patterns vary across languages, the process is the same: 'in the course of development the child comes to attend to particular types of meanings and to expect them to be expressed by particular types of forms' (Slobin, 2001: 285).

Taken together, these various forms of evidence suggest that, rather than operating with abstract rules derived from universal grammar, children form and modify hypotheses about regular linguistic patterns, based on their increasing experience of language in use. Further, paralleling the fact that languages vary in their mapping from semantic categories and relationships to the manner in which they are realized across the lexical-grammatical divide, they do not act on the assumption that any particular set of semantic relations will be realized grammatically.

Bates and colleagues have addressed this relationship between lexis and grammar using a different methodological approach. Drawing on data collected by means of the MacArthur-Bates Communication Development Inventories, which were described above, they have found strong but nonlinear relationships between vocabulary size and grammatical complexity. For example, grammatical complexity at 28 months, as measured by mean length of utterance (MLU), was found to be best predicted by vocabulary size at 20 months ($r = 0.83$, $p < 0.01$) and, more specifically, the ways in which past tense in English irregular verbs was realized morphologically was found to be dependent on the size of verb vocabulary (Bates & Goodman, 1997). Comparable findings also emerged from studies of atypically developing individuals.

These and similar findings across a wide range of populations have led Bates and her colleagues to challenge the conventional categorical distinction between lexis and grammar. As she concludes, 'the most parsimonious explanation for these [findings] would be a mental/neural architecture in which grammar and the lexicon are represented together and handled by the same mechanisms for learning and processing – in short, a lexicalist view of the sort that has gained considerable acceptance in modern linguistics'[5] (Bates & Goodman, 2001: 158).

Concluding Thoughts

In summarizing recent research on language development from a functional perspective, I have tried to bring out two major lines of argument:

- The capacity for language learning does not require the positing of a language acquisition device or an innate endowment of knowledge of universal grammar. On the contrary, this capacity is part of young humans' general biological inheritance and it is brought to bear on the particular language that is spoken in the child's community, using strategies that have much wider applicability in making sense of their physical and social environment. Equally important is the assistance given by the child's caregivers through their management of the contexts of interaction and their selection of the content and form of their utterances to the child as well as their responses to those that she or he contributes.
- Just as the languages spoken today have changed over the history of their use, so has the nature of language itself developed since its first emergence. At each point in that long trajectory, and in every contemporary linguistic community, the young have constructed their version of the language in use around them in the same basic ways that enabled prelinguistic humans to learn whatever means of communication were then in use.

Without doubt, there has been development here too, but also continuity. Bates cogently sums up the argument as follows:

> [T]he human capacity for language could be both innate and species specific, and yet involve no mechanisms that evolved specifically and uniquely for language itself. Language could be viewed as a new machine constructed entirely out of old parts. (Bates & MacWhinney, 1989: 10)[6]

What I find so interesting about these findings is that they provide empirical confirmation for the ideas that Vygotsky (2004) put forward more than 75 years ago in *Tool and Sign in the Development of the Child* and in other works. At that time, the technological aids used in the research summarized above were not yet invented, as was equally the case with respect to the methods used in more recent archeological and paleonto-logical research. Vygotsky's thinking was inevitably somewhat speculative, therefore, based as it was on the limited information then available. However, the fact that the connections he theorized between phylogenetic and ontogenetic development have now received support from the sort of empirical research he recognized to be necessary makes the overall theory more compelling.

In this chapter I have focused on the resources that human children bring to language learning and on typical patterns of development. Nevertheless, it is important to recognize that there is variation both in the rate at which learning occurs – as reported in this and earlier chapters – and, depending on the sociocultural conditions under which learning occurs, in individual trajectories. In the preschool years, these differences are not of great importance, provided that there is no evidence of abnormality and progress continues to be made. However, when children enter school, such differences may present a challenge to teachers, who are nowadays expected to ensure that all children of a given age are also at the same stage of development. In the following chapters I shall report on ways in which teachers can be helped to meet this challenge. And, as here, I shall suggest that Vygotskian theory provides a helpful overall orientation.

Notes

1. Although Donald does not refer to Tomasello, their accounts are largely compatible. Donald's description of the role played by mimesis presupposes the biological evolution of the predisposition to treat others as intentional beings like oneself, which Tomasello sees as fundamental for cultural evolution.
2. I shall return to the final stage in Donald's proposed sequence in the following chapter.
3. Initially produced for studies of children learning English and Italian, versions of the CDIs have been produced in a wide range of languages.
4. Archived material from many languages can be found at http://childes.psy. cmu.edu/.
5. For example, Fillmore, 1988; Langacker, 1990.
6. Quoted in 'Elizabeth Bates's aphorisms for the study of language, cognition, development, biology, and evolution' (Tomasello & Slobin, 2005).

Chapter 12
Toward Dialogue in the Classroom

1975, the year in which Rosie, Jonathan and the other children started school, saw the publication of *A Language for Life*, the report of the Bullock Committee on the place of language in education. Many of the ideas that underlay the report had been previously discussed at the 1966 Dartmouth Seminar, at which 50 scholars and teachers of English from the United States and Britain (including some members of the Bullock Committee) met to consider desirable changes in the teaching of English (Dixon, 1966; Squire & Britton, 1975).[1] When introducing the main conclusions of the Bullock Report, the Secretary of State for Education and Science called 'for a change of approach and redirection of effort'.

The advocated change of approach was summarized in the following paragraph (4.10).

> In the Committee's view there are certain important inferences to be drawn from a study of the relationship between language and learning:
>
> (i) all genuine learning involves discovery, and it is as ridiculous to suppose that teaching begins and ends with 'instruction' as it is to suppose that 'learning by discovery' means leaving children to their own resources;
> (ii) language has a heuristic function; that is to say a child can learn by talking and writing as certainly as he can by listening and reading;
> (iii) to exploit the process of discovery through language in all its uses is the surest means of enabling a child to master his mother tongue.

As I shall discuss later in this chapter, there has been a substantial amount of research in the English-speaking countries, much of it carried out by teachers, that has explored how these inferences can be made the basis for positive changes in classroom practice. Unfortunately, however, as I shall describe below, in all these countries there have been other influences that have worked to entrench traditional 'transmissional' teaching, with the result that it still remains the case that 'instruction' remains the dominant context for learning in the majority of classrooms.

In Britain, what ultimately gained the strongest support from the government was the second set of recommendations in the Bullock Report, introduced by the statement 'We are in no doubt of the importance of monitoring standards of achievement' (3.2). And it has been the ensuing concern with standards of achievement that has led to some of the most evident changes that have taken place in the last 30 years. However, the report also contained an important qualification concerning 'monitoring', which have received rather less attention: 'Ideally, [monitoring] should not set up "backwash" effects of any kind, and by design it should rule out the possibility of specific teaching to achieve good test results' (3.5). Nevertheless, I would argue that, to a large extent, it has been the overriding preoccupation with monitoring and accountability that has militated against the adoption of the report's strong recommendations for changes in the *manner* in which learning and teaching are actually enacted.

Standards and Accountability

As the authors of the Bullock Report rightly argued, it is important that high standards should be set for public education and, clearly, some form of monitoring is essential to ensure that the learning and teaching that is taking place in schools and school districts is enabling these standards to be achieved. All children should be given the opportunity to develop their full potential and they should also develop knowledge and skills that enable them to play a productive role in the larger society beyond the school. But this was not the major reason for the increasing concern with standards. As early as 1957, there was a call to raise educational standards in the United States when the Russians were first in the space race with the launching of Sputnik. Since then, concerned about their competitiveness in the increasingly global economy, many more of the world's technologically developed countries have concluded that their schools are not adequately preparing students to fulfill the demands of the workplace and, in response, have instituted rigorous regimes of accountability in an attempt to raise standards of achievement.

However, while governmental goals of raising standards are admirable, and the use of a system of accountability to monitor progress is appropriate, these goals cannot be achieved in an equitable manner unless equal attention is given to the means by which students are enabled to make the required progress. Unfortunately, this has not been the case. In placing the emphasis on accountability through test scores, governments have to a large extent lost sight of – or simply ignored – advances that have been made in understanding about how people learn and how they should be taught (Bransford *et al.*, 2000; Olson, 2003). It becomes important, therefore, to ask why this has happened.

According to the new institutional theory of organizations (W. Scott, 2008), this widespread governmental reaction to the 'crisis in education' has occurred because, in order to gain or maintain political legitimacy, governments attempt to demonstrate their efficiency by being seen to tackle the crisis instead of actually addressing the causes, which would require a much more differentiated approach both to teaching and to assessment (Ogawa *et al.*, 2008). And because the dominant model of efficiency is that of the streamlined production line in manufacturing industries, governmental agencies engage in a search for 'the one best system' (Tyack, 1974), based on what are taken to be generally accepted beliefs, such as that, in order to ensure equality of opportunity, there should be one form of education that is provided for all children, that students learn through passive reception of transmitted information, and that standardized tests are an equitable and efficient way of evaluating student achievement.

However, as teachers know from experience and as a large body of research has shown, each of these beliefs is incorrect. Individually, children differ in their aptitudes, interests and their preferred ways of learning; equally important, they also vary in the ways in which their life outside school supports their engagement in school activities (Moll, 1992). Thus, by failing to respond to the diversity of learners' characteristics, experiences, goals and needs and, instead, putting the emphasis on all students and schools being held accountable for meeting a monolithic set of standards, such governmental policies result in an increase in the number of 'failing' students and an impoverishment of the nation's preparedness to meet new and often unexpected challenges. This consequence is even more evident in the case of non-English speaking immigrants.

Attitudes to Diversity

Forty years ago, when we were constructing the cohort of children for the Bristol Study, the large random sample – over 1000 names – that we drew from the record of births in the city contained not a single child whose family did not speak English at home. However, that would certainly not be the case if we were to draw a similar sample today. As immigration to developed countries has increased, so has the ethnic and linguistic diversity of their populations. At the same time, and partly as a result, attitudes towards immigrant groups have become more polarized and the whole issue of diversity has become increasingly contentious. Symptomatically, for many citizens, the very word 'diverse' has become a label for individuals who, for reasons of ethnicity or first language, stand out as being different from these citizens' own 'mainstream', taken-for-granted norms. Viewed from this perspective, diversity is a problem, to which assimilation is the answer. It is not surprising, then, that a mono-lithic curriculum is imposed on all schools and that all students, whatever their backgrounds, are held accountable on the basis of their performance on tests that that are constructed by and for the majority group, even when some of these students are still learning the language in which the tests are given.

This situation has been further exacerbated where provision of appro-priate learning opportunities that value and build on students' home lan-guages has been denied by 'mainstream' opposition, which has demanded that English be the only language of instruction from the day of entry to school. For example, until a decade or so ago, many states in the United States had bilingual programmes that allowed English language learners to maintain their first language by using that language to learn the content of the curriculum, while at the same time gradually increasing their com-mand of English in relation to the same content. The opposition to such bilingual instruction was based on the claim that these students were not learning English quickly enough. Nevertheless, students who, since the passing of 'English only' laws, have been instructed entirely in English have not learned English more successfully, while their mastery of curric-ulum content has lagged even more seriously behind that of their mono-lingual English peers (Cummins, 2000).

However, the harmful effects of subjecting all students to a monolithic curriculum and the same standards of achievement are not limited to chil-dren of immigrant families. There is also great diversity in children's readi-ness to succeed in school as a result of the different social and economic conditions in which they are growing up. In particular, whether character-ized in terms of social class or family income, there is great disparity between homes in the range and quality of learning experiences that they can provide. Such differences call for appropriately differentiated forms of teaching that build on students' life experiences while introducing them to the expectations for successful participation in learning in the classroom.

This was apparent in the Bristol Study when the children were assessed on entry to school. A significant correlation was found between class of family background and early school achievement, which remained more or less constant over the remainder of the longitudinal study (see Chapter 9). In the United States, Hart and Risley (1999) reported similar findings, with the sheer quantity of talk in the home in the early years being the strongest predictor of size of vocabulary, which they considered, in turn, to be a strong indicator of readiness for school. By contrast, in the Bristol Study, it was the quality of adult–child conversation that was the best predictor, with talk around shared book reading being particularly important in extending children's linguistic resources.[2] However, in both studies, it was poverty and accompanying stresses in family life, rather than social class as such, that seemed to be most responsible for the difficulties in adjusting to school that were experienced by the least successful children. This is not surprising. When parents are overtired from work and debilitated by the demands of running the home with insufficient finances, and when the children lack safe and interesting places in which to extend their horizons, there is little to stimulate conversation between parents and children in the times they spend together.

It is against this background that the arguments for tailoring the curriculum to children's needs are most compelling. As the authors of the Bullock Report emphasized, genuine learning involves discovery and the consideration of alternative solutions, yet this is rendered impossible when the classroom regime is driven by scripted instruction. Consider the following description of such a classroom, which is typical of many elementary classrooms in California, particularly those that include a preponderance of children from backgrounds of poverty and homes where a language other than English is spoken.[3]

Lessons are scripted for each day of the week, detailing where in the room they should take place. Phonics and spelling lessons, for instance, are the first part of every Monday, Tuesday, and Wednesday, and occur with students sitting in the space within the 'U' of desks decoding in unison groups of words written on the board that correspond to particular letter-sounds or phonetic patterns. Subsequently, students retire to their desks for a reading from the anthology. Early in the week, the teacher will read the story aloud, and later on students will read independently or in chorus with a taped recording. Wednesday and Thursday allow for some independence as students have 'Workshop time', during which they develop the skills identified for each particular story (spelling, handwriting, parts of speech, identifying literary and writing genre, for example) individually using workbooks that accompany the curriculum. Friday, meanwhile, is used almost exclusively for testing. In preparation for the state mandated tests in April as well as to assess the week's learning, students are subjected to a written examination consisting of bubbling in correct answers and several short written responses regarding the story of the week, the particular spelling pattern learned that week, and the particular grammatical rules learned that week. The result of this interaction is that students appreciate schooling as a mechanized, uniform process for all. Each week, regardless of story and material, students follow the same routine. At no time are they given choice of assignments, pacing, or final product. Moreover, since almost all of the instruction is direct (that is, the teacher speaks to the students, whose input is only offered as response to the teacher's solicitation), a relationship forms whereby the teacher is the bearer of knowledge and the students are simply recipients.

Given the substantial body of research that shows the long-term ineffectiveness of this form of scripted instruction, it seems extraordinary that this is what is mandated by the school district as the means of enabling these students, and the district's schools, to meet the state's achievement standards. Yet this is the widespread result of the United States' 'No Child left Behind' Act, which ostensibly aims to close the achievement gap between the 'haves' and the 'have-nots' (Darling-Hammond, 2003).

On the other hand, there are also schools and classrooms in which successful efforts *are* being made to provide a better learning environment for such children. In the United States, many of these are the result of intervention projects by university faculty, who also seek to change policy through their publications (Dalton & Tharp, 2002; Darling-Hammond *et al.*, 2009). In Britain, there have been similar initiatives, some of which will be discussed below. As the proportion of the school population that needs specific help to escape from the disenfranchised status resulting from poverty and/or linguistic minority status continues to rise in many developed countries, we can hope that these efforts will bear fruit in the recognition of the need for a differentiated curriculum that equitably meets the educational needs of all children.

So far, I have focused on diversity from the perspective of the problem of meeting the needs of various minorities. Now I want to consider the positive nature of diversity, seeing it not as a problem to be overcome but rather as a potentially valuable feature of any group of people, whether in the classroom or in society at large.

Throughout the development of the human species, there has been a tension between the need for continuity, achieved through the transmission of knowledge and skills from one generation to the next, and innovation, which is only possible if there is diversity of ideas about ways to solve emergent problems and of people with diverse talents who are willing to risk trying to put the chosen ideas into effect (Tomasello, 1999). The tendency of institutions is to emphasize continuity at the expense of innovation, and this is particularly true of education (Rowan & Miskel, 1999). However, both are necessary for the vitality of a group, whether that of a classroom or of some larger community. As I show in Figure 12.1, neither is satisfactory as the sole orientation of a group; it is only when both are valued and supported that the group can continue to develop and transform itself as well as its environment.

However, diversity is all around us. Because each individual is shaped by the confluence of biological and cultural factors that come together in his or her development over time, and by his or her resulting experiences, all individuals are unique. This emerged very clearly in the Bristol Study, when parents described the children we were studying and compared them with their siblings; and it was even more striking when we compared the children whom we followed over the whole longitudinal study (see Chapter 9). In much of the developmental literature, such diversity is described in terms of 'individual differences', which are seen as minor departures from a common norm. However, from a sociocultural perspective, who we become depends very largely on the company we keep and what we do and say together. No two individuals follow the same life trajectory; diversity among participants is therefore an intrinsic aspect of any group, even when it is culturally homogeneous (Nelson, 2007). In the classroom, this diversity is an enormous asset, for it is this that powers the co-construction of knowledge.

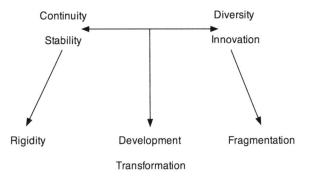

Figure 12.1 The relationship between continuity and diversity

Diversity in the Classroom

As a result of their individual life trajectories, the students who make up any classroom community come to each curriculum topic or specific activity with varying perspectives and with varying kinds of relevant experience and knowledge (Moll & Greenberg, 1990). In most classrooms this diversity is either ignored or acknowledged only indirectly in an initial 'KWL' brainstorming activity. Taken seriously, however, such differences might be expected to have several consequences. First, depending on their previous experiences, students would have different questions they wanted to ask and attempt to answer as well as different aspects of the curricular topic that they wanted to explore. Second, given the chance to express them, students would also have different opinions about many of the issues to be investigated. And, third, they could be expected to end the unit with greater personal understandings of the issues addressed but these would not be identical from one student to another.

By contrast, where the goal is to ensure that each student completes the unit having learned the same prescribed material, differences of the kind just mentioned are treated as irrelevant – or as reprehensible in the case of those who fail to provide the *correct* answers on the end-of-unit test. In such classrooms, students typically work independently on the same task, often in a regime that pits them against each other in an ethos of competition rather than one of collaboration. When there is 'discussion', it usually consists of a sequence of questions to which it is assumed that there is only one correct answer, of which the teacher is the sole judge; by contrast, student-initiated questions that seek to make connections to potentially relevant related topics are ignored or actively discouraged. As a result, the beneficial opportunities afforded by the diversity among the students are not exploited – to the detriment of all concerned.

In everyday conversation outside the classroom, on the other hand, there is typically a relative equality of participation; rarely does one participant assume a dominant role by controlling and evaluating other participants' contributions. Anyone who feels that their contributions are being ignored or suppressed is free to leave or to try to redress the balance. Equally, good conversation thrives on the expression of different points of view; without some disagreement, there would be little to keep the conversation going (Matusov, 1996).

Obviously, in the setting of the classroom, 'everyday conversation' is not appropriate for a class discussion with a curricular focus. But the two principles just mentioned – equal rights of participation and acknowledgement of different perspectives – remain important for the creation of an ambiance in which students and teacher construct knowledge together. Bereiter (1994: 9) refers to this sort of discussion as *progressive discourse* and describes it as 'progressive in the sense that understandings are being generated that are new to the local participants and that the participants recognize as superior to their previous understandings'. The question is how to create the conditions in which such progressive discourse can thrive.

The Dialogic Turn

During the second half of the twentieth century there took place what has been called the 'linguistic turn', first in philosophy and the humanities and, later, in the social sciences. Simply put, it began to be recognized, across all these disciplines, that we cannot share or discuss our understanding of the world except through language and other symbolic modalities; and, given that languages differ in the ways they categorize entities and events, as do individual users of all cultural semiotic systems, the nature of the reality we inhabit is actually constituted by the language we use to describe it and differs, at least to some degree, from one individual to another.

Vygotsky, however, offered a more radical version with his theory of semiotic mediation, in which he argued that, rather than being individually constructed, not only our linguistically-based knowledge of the world, but also the psychological processes of remembering, reasoning and evaluating, are appropriated through interaction with other members of the linguistic community of which we are members (Vygotsky, 1981, 1987). At the same time, he emphasized that these meanings and the thinking processes in which they occur are not simply copies of those people encounter in social interaction, nor are they identical from one individual to another. In the first place, signs are transformed as they become part of an individual's resources, influenced by the activity which they mediate and by the individual's past experiences. And second, the meanings of words do not remain constant for individual persons, but develop as they are encountered over time in new contexts of activity and as connections of various kinds are established with other meanings. Finally, meanings also differ between individuals because of the specific situations in which they have been encountered and of the affective loading they take on as a result.

While Vygotsky focused on semiotic mediation, it was his contemporaries, Voloshinov and Bakhtin, who emphasized the essentially dialogic nature of interaction. 'Any utterance is a link in a very complexly organized chain of other utterances', argued Bakhtin; no-one ever has the last word and equally, as he so memorably put it, nobody 'breaks the silence of the universe' (Bakhtin, 1986: 69). Thus, whenever we speak, we necessarily enter into an *ongoing* dialogue, since we are always repeating or reacting to positions that others have already expressed; our utterances are also shaped in expectation of the response of the person(s) to whom they are addressed. In Bakhtin's words,

> the speaker himself is oriented precisely toward such an actively responsive understanding. He does not expect passive understanding that, so to speak, only duplicates his own idea in someone else's mind. Rather he expects response, agreement, sympathy, objection, execution, and so forth. (Bakhtin, 1986: 69)

In dialogue, then, each utterance makes connections both to what preceded and to what is anticipated will come next, as the speaker attempts to achieve 'attunement to the attunement of the other' (Rommetveit, 1992). It is in this sense that meaning making is intrinsically dialogic, constructed over time as one voice answers another in the search for a common understanding. As Voloshinov (1973: 102) insisted, 'Any true understanding is dialogic'.

Combining Bakhtin's emphasis on dialogism with Vygotsky's emphasis on semiotic mediation leads to two further insights. First, when I contribute to joint meaning making with others, I also make meaning for myself and, in the process, extend my own understanding, both through the process of discovering what I think and want to say and through the feedback I receive in the responses of my interlocutors. And second, the dialogue I have with others can be internalized and the search for understanding continued in the dialogue of what Vygotsky (1987) called 'inner speech'. As I have explained in detail elsewhere (Wells, 1999), these insights taken together make a compelling case for reconceptualizing learning and teaching in terms of a dialogue of collaborative knowledge building. In the following section, I will discuss some important studies that suggest ways in which this goal can be achieved.

Creating Dialogue in the Classroom

Although not spelled out in detail, something like the preceding argument underpinned the first set of recommendations in the Bullock Report, which I quoted at the beginning of this chapter. The work of Vygotsky was beginning to be known in Britain in the 1970s, as is apparent in Britton's *Language and Learning* (1970) and in Barnes's *From Communication to Curriculum* (1976), both of which were extremely influential in shaping the course that research on language in the classroom would take in the succeeding decades. Particularly important was the distinction made by Britton between 'expressive' and 'transactional' uses of language and the related distinction between 'exploratory' and 'final draft' talk made by Barnes. In both cases, the first term ('expressive' and 'exploratory') can be thought of as lying at the dialogic end of a continuum that has 'monologic' discourse at the other. Lotman (1988), who developed this distinction in the Bakhtinian tradition, argued that both these forms of discourse have their place. Discourse at the monologic end is authoritative; it is unidirectional – an authority telling people what they should believe. Monologic discourse plays an important role in passing on cultural meanings, 'providing a common memory for the group' (Lotman, 1988: 35), thus preserving continuity and stability of beliefs and values within a culture. By contrast, discourse at the dialogic end serves as 'a thinking device' (Lotman, 1988: 37) because several people considering an issue or problem together are likely to generate 'new meanings'.[4] And because dialogic discourse assumes that thinking is thinking together, it is ideally suited to a commitment to taking different positions into account in the attempt to determine what is the case or what course of action should be followed.

It is this idea of dialogue as the means for thinking together that Mercer and his colleagues have taken up in their research in classrooms (Mercer, 2000; Mercer & Littleton, 2007). Coining the term, 'intermental development zone' (IDZ) as the multiperson classroom equivalent of the one-to-one interpersonal relationship that Vygotsky typically had in mind when writing about the 'zone of proximal development', Mercer (2002) argues that the IDZ is 'a mutual achievement', dependent on the interactive participation and commitment of both teacher and learner[s]'; furthermore, by engaging in 'inter-thinking' in this zone with teacher and peers, learners appropriate the 'linguistic tools' for intramental thinking on their own.

An important feature of Mercer and colleagues' work is the central role they give to thinking together in small group activities, which are designed to create opportunities for exploratory talk without the continuous involvement of the teacher. Initially they found that such groups often had difficulty in using these activities to their full advantage and so Mercer and other team members developed 'talk lessons', which help children to learn the 'ground rules' for thinking together. And, as Vygotsky would have predicted, having learned to engage in this sort of language-based thinking together, students were able to use the same strategies for problem solving on their own (Dawes *et al.*, 2004*).

Similar proposals for dialogic teaching have been made by Alexander (2006, 2008). Based on his observations in elementary/primary classrooms in five countries around the world, including Britain and the United States, he emphasizes the importance of the cultural context in which education takes place, which includes the expectations the people involved have about how they should relate to each other. These set the parameters within which pedagogical decisions are made. Nevertheless, he argues, dialogic learning-and-teaching is possible in widely different contexts if it meets five criteria: it must be collective, reciprocal, supportive, cumulative and purposeful (Alexander, 2008).

Work along similar lines has also been taking place in the United States. For example, many years ago Palincsar and Brown (1984) developed 'reciprocal teaching', an activity in which, working initially with a teacher, students learn dialogic strategies for effective comprehension of written texts, which they are then able to use in peer groups and eventually on their own. Since then, both authors have been working with teachers to develop approaches that incorporate reciprocal learning-and-teaching, more broadly across the curriculum (Brown & Campione, 1994; Brown *et al.*, 1996; Palincsar *et al.*, 1998). Other developments of a similar kind can be seen in McMahon *et al.*'s (1997) way of organizing 'book clubs' and Applebee's (1996) approach to curriculum as 'conversation'. Indeed, taking the idea of thinking together to its logical conclusion, Green and colleagues (Green & Dickson, 1993; Green *et al.*, 2008) have argued that what counts as knowledge in any classroom is not what is in the textbook but what has been constructed collaboratively by teachers and students in the course of their time together.

In addition, several important initiatives have been taken that focus on students who typically underachieve – those from ethnic and linguistic minorities and those who live in poverty, particularly in large cities. For example, Gutierrez *et al.* (1999) have developed what they call 'hybrid spaces' in classrooms in order to enable English language learners to participate fully in thinking together. Similarly, Moll and Greenberg (1990) have created what they call 'zones of possibilities', in which students are encouraged to draw on the 'funds of knowledge' in their families and communities to build bridges to the school curriculum.

Both these ideas are included in the 'Standards for Effective Pedagogy' developed at the Center for Research on Education, Diversity and Excellence (CREDE) at my own campus in Santa Cruz (Dalton & Tharp, 2002). Building explicitly on Vygotskian theory, one of the standards focuses specifically on teacher–student interaction in the context of what they call 'Instructional Conversation'. In addition to whole class instruction and discussion, CREDE gives a central place to regular meetings between the teacher and small groups in which a curricular objective is discussed in a conversational manner that allows students to offer their own experiences and opinions in relation to the topic in focus. Here is how Tharp and colleagues describe it.

> Instructional Conversation takes place in small groups. Although a teacher may have some effective dialogue with larger groups, the benefits of conversation require full inclusion of students, and that cannot be achieved in whole-group settings. Like any dialogue, IC is a 'pleasurable' event for both the students and teacher, all of whom enjoy the lively exchange of ideas and reaching shared understandings. Instruction conducted through conversation brings with it many advantages: a variety of participation formats, enhancement of students' active involvement, students' experience of Inclusion, and the teacher's opportunity to be responsive to and supportive of each student. (Tharp *et al.*, 2000: 202)

As I have seen for myself, Instructional Conversation is extremely effective in introducing young children to dialogue about curriculum content and so to a deeper understanding of it. For this reason, I decided to use the same strategy in the course I teach in our teacher credentialing programme so that my student teachers would experience its value for themselves. Interestingly, they reported that our ICs were one of the most helpful features of the course – and for just the reasons cited above. Hopefully, this experience will help them to provide similar learning experiences for their own students in the future.

In recent years, the importance of dialogue for learning has made particularly good headway in the fields of mathematics and science, which are subjects that have tended to be taught in the monologic mode. For example, in the United States both the National Council of Teachers of Mathematics' Principles and Standards and the National Science Education Standards emphasize the need for students to learn to talk the language of mathematics and science. This can only happen, they argue, if there are opportunities for students to explore the key ideas of these disciplines through dialogue in which they grapple with genuine problems. Mathematics educators talk about the importance of such discussions as an opportunity for the teacher to model and for the students to appropriate the norms of argument about mathematical issues (Cobb & McClain, 2002; Lampert *et al.*, 1996; Moschkovich, 2008; O'Connor, 2001). Lampert spells this out in more detail:

> What sort of help do children need from adults in order to do these things and to be confident of their ability to do them? I would suggest

that they need to be asked questions whose answers can be 'figured out' not by relying on memorized rules for moving numbers around but by thinking about what numbers and symbols mean. They need to be treated like sense-makers rather than rememberers and forgetters. They need to see connections between what they are supposed to be learning in school and things they care about understanding outside of school, and these connections need to be related to the substance of what they are supposed to be learning. (Lampert, 1986: 340)

Similar arguments have been put forward by science educators, particularly around the issue of 'conceptual change'. Until recently, the tendency was to talk about students' 'misconceptions' and to seek ways to correct them. However, drawing on Vygotsky's distinction between 'spontaneous' (everyday) and 'scientific' (schooled) concepts, it has been argued more recently that, rather than thinking of students as possessing concepts that need to be changed, it is more useful to think of them as learning to use the powerful scientific concepts that have been developed by others, and which form part of the cultural resources that are already available for their appropriation. In other words, rather than attempting monologically to teach scientific concepts because, unlike everyday concepts, they are considered to be 'correct', a more effective alternative is to enable students to discover their utility as they try to solve problems that arise from their own inquiries (Wells, 2009). This is the view taken by P. Scott (2008: 19), who argues that 'learning science can be seen as coming to understand and to accept the scientific view, against a "backdrop" of everyday ways of talking and thinking'. And Lemke (1990: 24) makes a similar point when he emphasizes that 'fluency in science requires practice at speaking, not just listening. It is when we have to put words together and make sense, when we have to formulate questions, argue, reason and generalize, that we learn the thematics of science'.

The Way Ahead: The Development of Shared Meanings

From the preceding account of the exciting developments that are taking place, across the curriculum, in the ways in which learning-and-teaching can be enacted, it might be thought that the centrality of dialogue would now be well understood and generally practiced in English-speaking countries. Unfortunately, that is not the case. Research carried out in the 1990s, by Galton and colleagues (Galton *et al.*, 1999) in primary schools in Britain and by Nystrand (1997) in secondary schools in the United States, showed that dialogic teaching was the exception rather than the norm; and the situation has deteriorated in subsequent years, in part as a direct result of the emphasis on testing for purposes of account-ability, and in part because most teachers have not been given guidance and encouragement about how to adopt a 'dialogic stance' (Wells & Mejía Arauz, 2006). The question, then, is how can the necessary change be brought about?

One thing is clear. The answer will not be found in government-imposed, top-down policies based on high-stakes testing and negative sanctions for districts, schools and teachers who fail to increase student scores. As those who study educational reform have made abundantly clear, in order to improve achievement, the emphasis needs to be placed squarely on the processes of learning and teaching that have been shown to lead to improvement and on local leadership that supports thoughtful change (Fullan, 2007; Hopkins, 2001). In a recent article, Hargreaves (2007) suggests that the following practices need to be given priority:

- *Putting learning first*, before achievement and testing – rather than equating achievement with tested attainment.
- *Distributing leadership widely and wisely* so improvement becomes a shared professional responsibility rather than the object of top-down government control.
- *Ensuring improvement lasts* beyond the tenure of one school leader or the government of the day's temporary election agenda.
- *Encouraging schools to work together*, helping rather than competing against each other in the quest to raise achievement standards. (Hargreaves, 2007: 17)

As Fullan and others argue, teachers are the key to improvement and teacher collaboration is the recommended means. At the heart of such efforts is the development of 'shared meanings', so it is necessary:

to make it possible both physically and attitudinally for teachers to work naturally together in joint planning; observation of one anoth-er's practices; and seeking, testing, and revising teaching strategies on a continuous basis. (Fullan, 2007: 7)

Significantly, what is being recommended is that teachers see them-selves as learners too and that, in their attempts to improve their practice, they adopt the sort of approaches to their own learning that I described in the previous section. Whether or not they explicitly label their work 'action research', those who collaborate on a shared focus across the same age-level, within subject departments, or across schools, are essentially engaged in what I have called 'dialogic inquiry', where the aim is to achieve a deeper understanding of learning and teaching and the classroom context in which it occurs so that they can improve their practice in the interests of the children for whom they are responsible.

In fact, there are many such teacher action research groups in English-speaking countries that are investigating how to create better learning opportunities for their students. Of these, one of the most important in Britain was the National Oracy Project, which drew quite heavily on the findings of the Bristol Study in making the case for the importance of dialogue in the classroom. Although the project did not continue very far beyond the initial development and dissemination phases (1987–1993), it involved teachers from many different education authorities in England and Wales, who worked in teams to investigate varied aspects of oral language use – in whole class and small group structures – and to develop strategies for using talk to its fullest advantage in children's learning across the curriculum (Norman, 1992).

The National Oracy Project was to have a significant impact on the National Curriculum in England and Wales and on the associated assessment of spoken English – but not entirely in the ways in which its initiators had hoped. As Hewitt and Inghilleri (1993) point out, the National Oracy Project's concern with spoken language as a medium for dialogue about curricular topics of importance to students was subsequently subverted by the different objectives of official government policy and, as a result, teachers often became confused by the conflicting requirements imposed on them.

Nevertheless, the teachers who participated in the project learned a great deal about what students could do when given the opportunity. As Baddely (1992) wrote about The National Oracy Project:

> The increased use of group work of various sizes and for a range of purposes provided a structure in which teachers were better able to become observers, listeners and recorders. The greater emphasis on pupils taking increased responsibility for their own learning made dialogue essential, and therefore enriched the spoken evidence available. Organising the pattern of learning so that pupils needed to use talk to plan, solve problems, make decisions, present findings and reflect on their progress, created a variety of talk and a sequence of situations from which the teacher could learn a great deal. (1992: 9)

What this quotation clearly points up is the great benefit to teachers of undertaking research in their own classrooms, school or district. This is a topic to which I shall return.

However, for teachers radically to change classroom talk to make it dialogic rather than monologic transmission with subsequent review, requires more than small strategic modifications. Certainly, allowing increased 'wait time' after asking a question – and before asking it again or providing the answer themselves – has been found to increase both student participation and the quality of their answers. Equally important is the recognition that asking questions to which there is not just one 'known answer' is more likely to elicit multiple alternative answers and perhaps to provoke discussion (Cazden, 1988). In addition, giving students time to prepare their thoughts about an issue or question – either through individual writing or in small groups – prior to a whole class discussion greatly increases the diversity of contributions (Brown *et al.*, 1993; Wells, 2002).

Nevertheless, despite the evidence of the value of these teaching strategies, few teachers are likely to persist with them if they attempt to adopt them as piecemeal changes to their normal way of conducting 'discussion'. For, as long as teachers retain a vision of teaching as ensuring that students 'learn' and remember the material predefined by the curricular guidelines, they are likely to abandon the new strategies as soon as the pressure to 'cover' the prescribed content becomes too severe. To bring about a lasting change, therefore, a different vision of teaching is required, and one that goes beyond a concern with the use of appropriate discourse moves to a recognition of the centrality of dialogue as a means of developing both group and individual understanding, coupled with the recognition that productive dialogue does not proceed independently of the activity and activity goals it mediates.

In sum, for classroom talk to become truly dialogic, two fundamental changes are necessary. First, the teacher must abandon the idea that there is one correct way of thinking about complex topics, which all students should adopt without question and, instead, he or she should encourage students to offer their own views and to treat these as the starting point for the sort of discourse that Bereiter (1994) described as 'progressive'.

This is where the diversity of students' home backgrounds and individual experiences is so important. Because of their different life trajectories they will certainly have different ways of understanding the world and different ideas to contribute to discussion. A further point is that, whatever conclusion is reached during a particular discussion, participants need to recognize that it is necessarily provisional. As new knowledge becomes available, current conclusions may need to be revised. There is no end to the possibility of deepening one's understanding.

The second major change follows from the first. If understanding can be deepened by the consideration of new information, what is required is the adoption of a *dialogic stance* toward experience and information (Wells & Mejía Arauz, 2006), that is to say, a willingness on the part of all participants – teacher as well as students – to wonder, to ask questions and to attempt to answer those questions through the collection of relevant evidence by various means, both empirical and library-based, and to present the findings to one's peers for critical review and improvement. Most importantly, the ultimate aims of a dialogic stance are to foster in each student the lifelong dispositions to be agentive in learning and to collaborate with others in seeking for understanding that enables effective and responsible action.

In the following chapter I shall describe the development of a collaborative action research project that set this as its goal.

Notes

1. Of this seminar, Marckwardt (1967: 13) wrote, 'I firmly believe that because the participation was international, the experience and indeed the quality of discussion was both broader and deeper than it would have been otherwise'.
2. It is worth noting, however, that quantity and quality of talk were significantly related.
3. This paragraph occurred in a term paper written by a graduate student in education.
4. See P. Scott (2008) for a more differentiated set of distinctions.

Chapter 13
The Interdependence of Practice and Theory

One Monday morning in February 1986, Ann Maher gathered her class round her and began to read to them.

> There are strange things done in the midnight sun
> By the men who moil for gold;
> The Arctic trails have their secret tales
> That would make your blood run cold;
> The Northern Lights have seen queer sights,
> But the queerest they ever did see
> Was that night on the marge of Lake Lebarge
>   I cremated Sam McGee.

This was her introduction to a two-week period in which her whole school explored 'The Enchantment of Winter'.

Ann Maher taught a third grade class in a school in the centre of Toronto's Chinatown. All but one of the children in her class spoke a language other than English at home, with the majority being either Portuguese or Cantonese speakers. However, since most had been attending school in Canada for several years, their English was quite proficient and they had little difficulty in participating in class activities.

I first got to know Ann at the beginning of the school year when we started observing three children in her class. I was also present at a staff meeting in the autumn when the teachers were preparing for a school-wide curriculum unit on the theme of Winter. While most were excitedly brainstorming ideas and then proceeding to plan, in detail, the activities the children would carry out, Ann remained quiet. As she later explained, she felt this theme should be approached in such a way that the children's ideas would be as important as the teacher's in making the most of the opportunity. I was delighted to hear her stance and even more delighted when she willingly agreed to allow me to videotape the whole project.

The Cremation of Sam McGee (Service & Harrison, 2006) tells the tale of Sam McGee, a miner from Tennessee, who set out to make his fortune in the Canadian gold rush. But unprepared for the harsh climate of the Yukon, he became convinced that he would die from the cold and so he asked his mate, the narrator of the ballad, to cremate him so that he would at least be warm again in death. The ballad, which is beautifully illustrated in the edition that Ann used, recounts their dog-sled journey through the snow and ice and describes how, after McGee died of cold, the narrator carried out his request by lighting the boiler of an abandoned steamer and, having placed the corpse inside, sent him up in smoke.

While they were spellbound throughout the reading, what the children enjoyed most was the ending where, opening the boiler door to check that Sam has been properly cremated, the narrator gets a surprise.

> And there sat Sam, looking cool and calm, in the heart of the furnace roar;
> And he wore a smile you could see a mile, and he said: 'Please close that door.
> It's fine in here, but I greatly fear you'll let in the cold and storm –
> Since I left Plumtree, down in Tennessee, it's the first time I've been warm.

Following this highly successful launch of the Winter unit, the children spent the rest of the day creating representations of what they had enjoyed most about the poem. One group made a model book shop from a large cardboard carton, which had windows through which 'books' could be seen and an advertisement for the Sam McGee book pinned to the door; another group, with another large carton, made a model of the boiler, with a pop-up Sam McGee.

On the third day, Ann read the ballad again and then invited the children to think of questions they would like to answer about winter and the Yukon and, when all their questions had been written on the board, she asked the children to choose a question and to work with one or more partners to try to answer it. Marilda, a Portuguese-Canadian girl, chose to work with her friend Jacinta, a Chinese-Canadian, to find out more about the weather in the Yukon and, after exploring several options, she decided to make a weather vane, based on the instructions she found in a book about the weather. Having demonstrated her creation to her friends in the playground during recess, back in the classroom again she wanted to show it to her teacher.

Marilda:	It's here, my windfinder
Teacher:	OK, so here's your windfinder . that's a good name for it, isn't it?
Marilda:	[demonstrates by blowing to make her windfinder work]
Eric:	Oh Miss-
Teacher:	Eric, have you seen this windfinder?
Eric:	Yes, last year we were studying about it
Teacher:	Mm . [to Marilda] Can you- can you explain- like . can you explain how it works?
Eric:	Yes, I know how it works
Teacher:	[to Eric] Oh excuse me, I was really speaking to Marilda [to Marilda] Can you explain it? [to Maria] Maybe you'd be interested in this . do you want to come over here? [putting her arm round her to bring her closer] [Jacinta and Maggie also join the group]
Marilda:	When you- when the wind blows . it's trying to find the wind . when the wind blows this points to which direction it's coming from [pointing to the pointer on her wind finder]
Jacinta:	Yeah like- [she takes the windfinder and demonstrates]
Marilda:	See, it's pointing round to you
Teacher:	Why's it pointing to you? [referring to Jacinta, but addressing the question to the whole group]
Eric:	Because she's the one who blew
Marilda:	And if you keep on- [takes back windfinder from Jacinta] [Maggie tries to blow]
Jacinta:	You have to blow hard [Maggie blows hard]
Marilda:	OK now blow again . [Maggie blows again] It stays in the same spot cos- cos the wind's-
Teacher:	Why?
Jacinta:	Cos it needs a big surface to blow on . to push it
Teacher:	Come on . [encouraging Marilda to continue]
Marilda:	Cos the- cos the wind's blowing that direction and it-
Jacinta:	No . why did it go?
Marilda:	- it's not coming in a different way.
Eric:	Because it doesn't have a piece of paper over here . [pointing to the end of the straw with the paperclip]
Teacher:	What would happen if you had a piece of paper over there?

Marilda:	It'd turn around?
Jacinta:	Because it needs a big surface to blow on to push it
Teacher:	So it's-
Eric:	And that's a big surface
Teacher:	So it's got something to do with the surface of the paper?
Children:	Yeah
Teacher:	And the air?
Eric:	Mm
Marilda:	And the- this thing . maybe [pointing to the bead]
Teacher:	Oh and-
Eric:	It's the needle
Jacinta:	No I think it's got to turn-
Eric:	It's the needle it's the needle that- well not the needle but the, the straw . it's the straw has the hole
Marilda:	This makes it-
Eric:	The straw has the hole and the hole like causes it to . to make a wiggly turn
Teacher:	Yes [somewhat doubtfully]
Marilda:	No, it's this that makes it-
Teacher:	Which? The bead?
Marilda:	Yeah
Teacher:	The bead . you think the bead is very important?
Marilda:	Yeah
Teacher:	Why? Why do you think that's important?
Jacinta:	Let's try it without the bead
Marilda:	Cos the-
Teacher:	[to Jacinta] That's a good idea . that- that would. be a way of finding out if it's really important . [to Marilda] First, why do you think the bead's important?
Marilda:	Well .. some machines they have a-
Eric:	It's a nuisance [referring to the bead]
Marilda:	- the little round things
Eric:	Yes, but some machines don't have them
Teacher:	Ballbearings? . you mean ballbearings
Marilda:	Yeah . so maybe like it might make it- might help by spinning it . like spinning-
Teacher:	It's got something to do with the spinning and then making it easier to spin? I like your idea, Jacinta . that's a very interesting idea,

	taking the bead out . I don't know whether Marilda
	would . <u>want to</u> do that now or not
Jacinta:	- want to-
Marilda:	[somewhat reluctantly] OK, I'll try it
	[Marilda and Jacinta go away to try the experiment]

In this particular episode, which from beginning to end lasted no more than two minutes, many different things are happening and it is quite apparent that the various participants have different reasons for becoming involved – at least to begin with. Marilda initially wants to gain the teacher's interest and approval but then, at the teacher's request, she tries to explain how the windfinder works; Eric seems to want to let the teacher know how knowledgeable he is; and Jacinta, who has been working with Marilda, joins the group out of solidarity with her friend and quickly becomes involved in the action of explaining. Toward the end, she proposes a further experiment. Also drawn in are two other children who are interested but silent onlookers.

Recognizing all these different goals, the teacher has to make a series of on-the-spot decisions. From her behaviour, it seems reasonable to attribute to her a number of simultaneous goals: first, to show her interest in Marilda's artifact and then to get Marilda to externalize her understanding of the artifact in a coherent explanation. (This goal becomes more recognizably central when one knows that Marilda has been retained in grade three because her progress in the previous year was judged to be unsatisfactory.) In gathering a group around Marilda to learn about her invention, the teacher is taking the opportunity to boost her self-confidence as a successful student. At the same time, while keeping the focus on Marilda's contribution, the teacher also wants to include the other children in the action of explaining and to help them to coordinate their contributions. Finally, she picks up Jacinta's suggestion as a means of inviting Marilda to pursue her interest in the windfinder further by testing her hypothesis about the function of the bead.[1]

This incredibly rich episode was not planned; rather, it occurred spontaneously because the teacher recognized and made the most of 'a teachable moment' when it arose. And by integrating it seamlessly into the flow of classroom activity, she demonstrated her ready appreciation of an opportunity for several children to contribute to collective meaning making about a topic of real interest to them.

Working in the Zone of Proximal Development

As I thought more about this and similar episodes that I observed in Ann's classroom over the next weeks and months, I began to see how – like some of the conversations between children and their parents at home that I quoted in earlier chapters – they exemplified what I understood Vygotsky (1987) to have had in mind when he argued that effective teaching involves 'working in the zone of proximal development (ZPD)'.

The reasoning that led Vygotsky to introduce this construct involved several steps. The first was the theoretical distinction he made between biology and culture in his attempt to understand human development. Of course he was well aware that, while theoretically useful for his purpose, the two cannot be distinguished in practice. Since the human infant is born into an ongoing culture, from the very beginning his or her biologically given functions are interpreted and responded to by his or her caregivers in accordance with the beliefs and practices of the culture of which they are members.

Biological functions, shared with other species, include active perception of the material environment, actions upon it, and memory for significant experiences that are regularly repeated. Initially, these functions do not involve conscious intentions and so cannot be deliberately controlled. Equally important, they are private in the sense that, although socially embedded, they are only meaningful to the infant in relation to his or her own experiences. However, as Tomasello (1999) later emphasized, unlike the infants of other species, the human infant is also predisposed to orient to other humans, particularly his or her principal caregiver, and to their intentional actions. And it is on this basis that, through participation in joint activities, such as feeding, dressing and playful routines, they begin to develop what Vygotsky called the 'higher mental functions' that are unique to humans.

What distinguishes humans in general from other species is that they intentionally create and use artifacts to achieve their collective purposes (see Donald & Wartofsky in Chapter 11). Some of these are material objects, such as knives, cooking utensils and cars, but others are signs and symbols, whose function is to create and communicate meaning. While both are integrally involved in all cultural activities, Vygotsky believed that it is particularly through the mastery of symbol use that children develop the *higher* mental functions. This process begins in the infant's own intentional use of signs about half way through the first year, shortly followed by his or her first communication through verbal symbols as he or she learns to talk (see the examples in Chapters 2 and 3).

The second step derived from Vygotsky's recognition that, although children are certainly active constructors of their command of language, they do not invent it by themselves. Instead, he argued, they take it over from their parents and other members of their community, who, in their conversations with their children, simultaneously provide information about the forms and organization of language and also a model of how language is used to get things done and to share intentions, thoughts and feelings about the activities in which they are jointly involved. But, as he also recognized, the opportunities for learning through conversation go still further for, as children participate in interaction with others, they also take over and make their own the cultural ways of reasoning, problem solving and valuing that are made 'visible' in the talk. In other words, the linguistic means that others use to direct children's attention and to organize and control their behaviour become resources that they themselves can eventually use to control their own actions and feelings and, still later, to solve problems and think through difficult issues on their own. In this way, speech *between* people becomes the model for *individual* thinking in the medium of 'inner speech' (Vygotsky, 1987).

For Vygotsky, then, it was clear that specifically human learning and development are essentially social in nature. This is because development involves appropriating ways of acting, thinking and feeling that are already in use between other members of the culture, and also because the means and processes of learning are also necessarily social in that they can only occur in interaction with other people. 'Human learning presupposes a specific social nature and a process by which children grow into the intellectual life of those around them' (Vygotsky, 1978: 88).

While conducting the research that underpinned his theory of children's development, Vygotsky was also the director of the Moscow Institute for what is now called special education. While there, he became concerned about the way in which slow learning or mentally retarded children were assigned to different kinds of special education simply on the basis of their scores on tests. This seemed to him to be both inappropriate and unjust and so he decided to investigate the matter further by engaging with children while they were taking one of the tests. Having waited until a child had reached the highest level of test item that she or he could answer correctly, he tried providing cues or hints as the child attempted later items, and what he found was that they could often succeed in answering several more test items correctly.

It was this that led to his idea of a zone of proximal development. He expressed it as follows: The ZPD is 'the distance between the actual developmental level as determined by independent problem solving and the level of potential development as determined through problem solving under adult guidance or in collaboration with more capable peers' – or, more simply, 'what a child can do with assistance today she will be able to do by herself tomorrow' (Vygotsky, 1978: 86–87).

The zone of proximal development thus became for Vygotsky the focus of his efforts to improve the quality of education. Effective learning-and-teaching, he believed, would be most likely to occur when teaching occurred as assistance given in response to a learner's difficulty in attempting to solve a problem just beyond what he or she could manage unaided, that is to say, in the learner's ZPD. And on this basis he argued that 'the only "good learning" is that which is in advance of development … [L]earning awakens a variety of internal developmental processes that are able to operate only when the child is interacting with people in his environment and in cooperation with his peers' (Vygotsky, 1978: 89–90).

Today the zone of proximal development is still a powerful idea for thinking about ways to make teaching effective. But it is a metaphor – a tool for thinking with – not a 'method'. In fact, Vygotsky gave very few actual examples of what the metaphor might lead to in practice. Furthermore, even if he had, such examples would not transfer easily to the very different sorts of classrooms in the schools of today. Personally, I think this is fortunate, for it means that we each have to discover how we can best use the metaphor to guide our own practice.

Collaborative Research with Teachers

The work I did with Ann Maher was my first experience of truly collaborative research and our discussions of the observations I made in her classroom led to important insights for both of us (Maher, 1994; Wells *et al.*, 1990). They also constituted my first steps in the development of an approach to enacting Vygotskyan ideas in contemporary classrooms. Other project teachers joined us and each contributed to our growing joint understanding of the value of his ideas. Most importantly, we came to see how the zone of proximal development was not only relevant in planning for and assisting children's learning; it was equally relevant for thinking about teachers' professional development.

In 1991, I was awarded a grant from the Spencer Foundation to explore these ideas further and the following year, with my colleagues, Patrick Allen and Myriam Schechter, I invited a number of teachers to join a project in which we would investigate how to create classrooms in which we enacted our understanding of Vygotsky's ideas. Three years later we were awarded a further grant, which enabled us to enlarge the group and to organize whole-day meetings at which we shared the research we were each doing, offering comments and suggestions, often based on extracts from the videorecordings we made in our classrooms. We also established an e-mail listserv that enabled us to continue our discussions between meetings and, as the project progressed, we worked together to prepare to share our research through conference presentations and articles for publication.

Early in the project, influenced by our reading of Dewey (1938, 1956) as well as of Vygotsky (1987) and Bakhtin (1986),[2] we realized that, if we wanted the sort of collaborative dialogue that Vygotsky had inspired to become the norm in our classrooms, certain conditions would need to be established. These we first formulated as follows:

- the topic must be of interest to the participants;
- individual students must have relevant ideas, opinions or experiences that they want to share;
- others must be willing to listen attentively and critically;
- the teacher must share control and the right to evaluate with students.

However, we also realized that these conditions were not enough. If the emphasis on dialogue was to be justified, it had to be relevant to the prescribed curriculum, and if we wanted it to be cumulative and sustained over time, it had to arise from a topic that posed problems or raised doubts that would motivate the student to explore further. This was where Dewey was particularly important for our thinking because, in his writing about curriculum, he placed great emphasis on inquiry, both as the motivation for engaging in, and as the organizing principle for the selection of, learning activities. These activities, he believed, should grow out of students' first-hand experiences and be relevant to their lives in the present as well as for their lives in the future – the latter being, unfortunately, the sole justification so often given for the content of the prescribed curriculum. However, while we were enthusiastic about the inquiry orientation to curriculum (Wells, 1995) and liked the idea of students having choice with respect to the topics they investigated, we also saw great value in these choices being made in relation to a single overarching theme – as in the case of Ann Maher's theme of 'Winter and the Yukon' that I described above.

As a result of our lengthy discussion of these issues, we all agreed on the importance of focusing our work on inquiry – it was, after all, what had brought us together – and on its potential for generating true dialogue, and so we made these goals explicit in the title we chose for our research: *The Developing Inquiring Communities in Education Project* (DICEP). Each of us undertook to try to create a community of inquiry in our own classroom and a similar community of colleagues in our workplace. We also saw our own group as a community of a similar kind and, to enact the values that we espoused, we decided to change our own organization in order to make it less hierarchical. Instead of the direction of the project being the sole responsibility of the university members, we made it a joint responsibility. Each member took a turn at recording the minutes of one of our meetings and acted as the chair of the next meeting, constructing the agenda and ensuring that decisions taken were put into effect. One significant outcome of this decision to share responsibility for the project, I believe, is that, eight years after I left the group on moving to California in 2000, DICEP teachers still continue to conduct collaborative research and have been successful in securing further funding to support their work (Bell-Angus *et al.*, 2009).

Between 1992 and 1998, the members of the project, who taught classes of children aged between six and 14 in Grades 1–8, planned and conducted their own inquiries with two overriding aims: to explore different approaches to creating classroom communities of inquiry; and to investigate the quality of the discourse that occurred during inquiry-oriented curricular units. The topics they chose to investigate ranged from literature to science, and from the value of class meetings to the role of writing in creating communities of inquiry.

To this end, each teacher videorecorded sequences of lessons and these recordings then served as data for their individual inquiries. In particular, by being able to review particular events undistracted by their multiple concerns as teachers while actually involved in them, they were able, as researchers, to identify aspects of their practice that they wanted to change. For example, one teacher, who regularly included the serialized reading of a novel in her grade four daily routine, took some time to view the recordings of the whole-class discussions that followed the reading of each chapter. Her intention had been that these discussions should allow the children to build on each other's ideas in order to co-construct their understanding of the story. What she discovered, however, was that, although she encouraged her students to offer their own thoughts and opinions, she always both nominated the speaker and offered some comment in response. In this way she still functioned like the hub in the wheel of discussion, with the students addressing her at the centre rather than listening to and addressing their comments to each other. As a result of this realization, she immediately introduced a new format, whereby she would nominate the first speaker and then any student who had something to add to the topic that the first speaker had initiated could do so without waiting to be nominated. The effect of this change was remarkable; the discussion progressed more coherently and led to some really thoughtful consideration of plot, character and the author's craft. Furthermore, it was conducted collaboratively by the children without need for teacher direction (Donoahue, 1998).

The video-recordings made by the participating teachers also provided evidence of changing patterns of classroom interaction over the course of the project, which resulted from the teachers' adoption of an inquiry orientation to curriculum. After six years of collecting data, with the help of a number of graduate students I carried out a systematic discourse analysis of 45 episodes of whole class discussion, from which evidence of some very significant changes emerged. What we found was that teachers asked more open-ended questions that invited a range of alternative opinions and conjectures; conversely, they asked fewer known-answer questions; they also evaluated student contributions less frequently. As a result, student contributions became more extended and elaborated. Furthermore, students much more frequently initiated sequences of discussion and teachers showed uptake of their contributions, either by building on them in their responses or by inviting further contributions on the topic raised by the student initiation. In all these ways, whole-class discussion became much more dialogic (Wells & Mejía Arauz, 2006).

During the preceding years, while most of the project meetings referred to above focused on individual members' research in progress, we also periodically spent time in trying to understand how an inquiry orientation was changing the way we thought about the relationship between learning and teaching. In particular, we wanted to understand what kinds of activities and sequences of activities were most successful in generating student engagement and in promoting the sort of dialogue that led to an enhancement of both collective and individual understanding. These discussions often occurred as we were preparing to make a conference presentation about what we were learning through our work together, but they also fed back into our practice. For me, they were particularly valuable in helping me to think through the relationship between practice and theory. And it is to this I should now like to turn.

Learning and Teaching for Understanding

Spending time in classrooms and working with teachers has convinced me that there can be no universally 'best' method of teaching. Students are too diverse in their aptitudes, interests and needs, as well as in their home cultures and life experiences – as also are teachers – for a 'one size fits all' approach to be successful in all settings. But I do think that, at a rather abstract level, there is a universal pattern in the kinds of learning that optimally lead to the increased understanding that I believe everyone would agree is one of the principal aims of education.

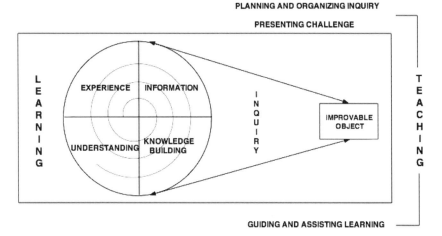

Figure 13.1 A model of the relationship between learning and teaching

Drawing on my research in homes and schools and on the writings of Vygotsky, Dewey, Bakhtin, and many others who have thought deeply about the development of understanding, I have tried to represent what I have come to believe in the diagram shown in Figure 13.1.

Over the course of our lives, we participate in many different communities – at home, at school and at work – each having its own goals, practices and values, which we have to understand in order to become a full member of the community. Learning is thus an intrinsic aspect of participation in the activities of any community (Lave & Wenger, 1991). This is represented in the left hand side of Figure 13.1 as a continuing spiral through many cycles of 'coming to understand' in order to be able to participate effectively in the activities of the community.

Not all situations demand new learning since some can be coped with in terms of our existing understanding. However, when we do encounter challenging situations that call for further learning, we first draw on our personal resource of interpreted past *experience* in an attempt to make sense of what is new. When past experience is insufficient, what is unfamiliar about the situation becomes treated as *information*, which we receive either through feedback on our actions into the world or from reading, viewing and listening to representations of the experiences, explanations and reflections of others. However, for this information to lead to an enhancement of our *understanding* – which is the goal of all useful learning – it must be actively transformed and articulated with personal experience through a process of *knowledge building*, which typically occurs in collaboration with others.

Knowledge building can take a variety of forms, but all are essentially social and interactional in nature. The aim is to create a common, or shared, understanding to which all participants contribute. Most often this takes place through face-to-face oral discourse, which often also includes use of artefacts present in the situation, such as material tools, diagrams, and written texts. In informal situations, knowledge building may occur on the fly as, for example, when two people are trying to repair a vehicle, assemble furniture or plan a holiday trip. In these situations, participants pool their expertise to understand what needs to be done. In formal situations, such as schools, on the other hand, such spontaneous knowledge building rarely occurs because of the pressure to keep moving in order to 'cover' the prescribed curriculum. For this reason it is necessary for teachers to make explicit provision for knowledge building by arranging for groups or the whole class to discuss the new information.

Very often in informal settings a key feature of knowledge building is that, as in the imagined examples above, it occurs in relation to an object that the participants are trying to improve. Having such an *improvable object* is particularly valuable in the classroom, as it provides a purpose as well as a focus for the attempt to achieve understanding. This object can take many forms, ranging from a functioning model to a work of art (e.g. a drawing, a story or poem, a musical performance) and from a scientific explanation to a geometric proof, a map or a diagram. Such an object is likely to be particularly effective if it is a representation of its creators' current understanding, for which an explanation has to be given to justify its acceptance. And since improving this object is the goal of the joint activity, recognizing weaknesses or limitations in the object is likely to motivate revision, which in turn leads to greater understanding.

Thus, instead of teaching students to accept information about 'what is known'[3] simply on the basis of authority – which is the effect of the transmission approach to teaching – a principal aim of engaging in knowledge building is to help them to recognize that all knowledge of the world in which we live is tentative and open to change – that is to say, rarely is there a single 'right answer', since there are alternative points of view that may need to be recognized as equally valid and as potential bases for improvement.

This is where *inquiry* and *diversity* come in. When students develop their own questions in relation to the theme of a curriculum unit and attempt to make their own answers to them, there is little danger of their passively accepting information provided by experts. For in this context, it is they who are providing the information, based on their own investigations; and because individual students – or groups working together – will have different information to share, there is an evident need to engage in collaborative knowledge building in order to understand how their diverse perspectives on the theme can be integrated and any discrepancies or disagreements resolved.

Finally, it is worth emphasizing that the kind of learning represented in Figure 13.1 involves the whole person. Engaging in collaborative knowledge building is not simply a matter of acquiring more knowledge. It also involves changes in attitudes and dispositions toward the topics investigated and in the knowledgeable skills that such investigations require. In other words, learning, seen as increasingly full and effective participation in inquiry about topics of interest and concern to the learner, is also a major influence on the formation of his or her identity and self-image and, by the same token, of the ways in which he or she is regarded by others.

When learning is seen, as here, to be a continuing spiral of building on past experience to convert new information into greater understanding through knowledge building (Figure 13.1), the overall responsibility of the teacher can be seen to have two major components. The first is to select a theme for inquiry appropriate for his or her particular class and to create the conditions and make available the resources necessary for students to engage with the theme according to their own interests and current expertise. Usually the theme will be related to a key curriculum topic and required outcomes, which are also likely to figure in externally imposed tests. Equally important, the theme will be such as to lead to student engagement with culturally valued knowledge and skills. On these bases, the teacher will develop a plan for the curriculum unit. The teacher will then help students to select their own specific subtopics so that they can work together with those who have similar interests but not necessarily the same expertise. He or she will also plan whole class activities in which the groups' progress and results can be the focus of collaborative knowledge building.

The teacher's second responsibility is to engage in monitoring the curriculum *as experienced* by groups and individuals, spending time with each group – or with individual students – observing and listening to how they are progressing, so that she or he is able to offer appropriate assistance, as needed, in order that the students are able to continue to improve the object on which they are working and, in the process, to develop greater understanding. In this way, the teacher uses formative assessment – which may also include students in group reflection and self-assessment – to work in the students' zones of proximal development and to provide 'just-in-time' instruction (see Figure 13.2).

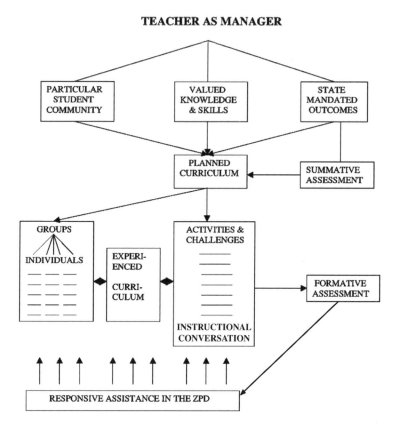

TEACHER AS FACILITATOR

Figure 13.2 A model of the teacher's roles

Clearly, this model does not prescribe how the teacher should proceed in fulfilling these responsibilities: when and how to intervene to ensure that all are making progress and that the needs of each student are being met; when to provide direct instruction; how to ensure an appropriate balance of individual, group and whole class activity; and how to evaluate the learning that is taking place. As I emphasized at the outset, these decisions are necessarily dependent on the teacher's interpretation of the total situation. However, I believe that this model is a tool that can help any teacher to think about how best to facilitate the learning of the students for whom she or he is responsible.

As I emphasized above, the models in Figures 13.1 and 13.2 grew out of the work that the DICEP group was doing. Although they have been refined in the years since I left Toronto, they are the outcome of our work together and their basic principles are those that guided our inquiries. Unfortunately, space does not allow me to do justice to the range and quality of these inquiries here, but many have been published elsewhere in book form (Wells, 2001), in *Networks, the Online Journal for Teacher Research* that we initiated in 1998,[4] and also in other journals. However, I do want to describe one inquiry in some detail because it picks up several of the issues raised in this and earlier chapters.

From Action to Writing: Learning Together in the ZPD

This inquiry, which occurred fairly early in our project, had several rather different points of departure. Mary Ann Van Tassell, a member of DICEP, and Barbara Galbraith, one of her colleagues, had for several years, arranged their timetables so that they could team-teach science with their grade two students. Together, they had developed a number of curricular units that allowed their students to explore various aspects of the natural environment through practical investigations that the students found interesting and challenging. However, as they reviewed their programme in July in preparation for the coming year, the two teachers were not entirely satisfied. In the past, when starting each new topic, they had made a point of encouraging the children to think about the questions they would like to answer; these were then written on chart paper and displayed on the classroom wall. What they now realized, however, was that that was as far as these questions went. The activities that followed were almost entirely selected by the teachers and were chosen with reference to the questions that they, the teachers, thought ought to be answered rather than to those that the children had actually asked.

In planning the first science unit for the new school year, therefore, they decided they would try to allow the unit to evolve more organically in response to the children's questions. With this intention, they invited me to join them in considering how to do so and, over the summer months, we met several times to consider how to proceed.

Meanwhile, Mary Ann had been reading Vygotsky's ideas about learning-and-teaching and was wondering whether the way she and Barbara organized their science units really provided opportunities for children to receive assistance in their zones of proximal development and, if so, what conditions made such occasions likely to occur. As we pondered this question together, we realized that, since Vygotsky had provided rather little in the way of concrete exemplification of this concept, we ourselves would have to search through the video-recordings we planned to make in order to identify incidents that met what we considered to be the defining criteria of Vygotsky's construct, as we had understood it.

I also had a question. As recounted in previous chapters, I had been intrigued by the degree of parallelism between the phylogenetic sequence in the emergence of the different modes of knowing that Donald (1991) described and the sequence in which these same modes of knowing emerged in contemporary children's development. In particular, like Donald, I was convinced that these different modes were cumulative and complementary rather than arranged in a hierarchy of value, with theoretical knowing superseding those that preceded. My question was how to ensure that children were given the opportunity to make use of, and to further develop, all the modes of knowing in their curricular activities in school.

When children come to school at five or six, they are already competent knowers in the modes of action, gesture and speech. So, by this age, most are ready to learn to read and write and, thereby, to enter gradually into the mode of theoretical knowing. But we were convinced that this did not mean that the earlier modes should be treated as inferior and unimportant – as all too often happens when, once literate, children's learning becomes almost entirely oriented to theoretical knowing through the study of textbooks and teacher lectures. Would it not be more effective, we wondered, if we were to bear in mind the primacy (genetically speaking) of knowing through action, and therefore to start each new unit with an opportunity to explore the relevant material through individual hands-on action? This could then be followed by demonstration, with opportunities for gesture and drawing. Soon this could be expected to lead to talk about what was done and observed in order to create a shared understanding, which in turn could form a basis for reading what others had come to know about the topic and for engaging in theoretical knowing through writing.

This theory-based sequence was, in fact, close to what Mary Ann and Barbara had actually been doing in previous units and so the forthcoming unit promised to provide a good opportunity for us to observe how it played out in practice.

Having discussed all these issues, the teachers decided to start the year with a unit on 'energy', to be explored through the making and testing of 'rollers' powered by elastic bands. The children brought from home a variety of cylindrical containers and, following the design found in a children's guide to technology (Richards, 1990), they each began to make their own roller and to conduct tests to see how far it would travel for a given number of turns of the elastic band. Immediately, however, there were problems. Apart from the difficulties of construction encountered by these seven-year-olds, there were unexpected variations in the manner in which the rollers functioned. In some cases, it took a very large number of turns to get the roller to move at all; others unwound very fast but hardly moved; and some veered to one side or the other. As can be imagined, these problems generated a number of very real questions as to how the problems could be 'fixed'. These were addressed through trial and error, tempered by suggestions arising from teacher-led discussion.

The problem of the rollers that did not go straight gave rise to a particularly interesting discussion. In some cases, the difficulty had occurred because a child had used a container such as a film canister that, with its lid on, had a greater diameter at one end than at the other. In other cases, the problem had been created by adding rubber bands round the circumference of the container in order to give the roller better traction on the wooden floor. Part way into the discussion, one of the teachers took one of the rollers that had an elastic band around one end (thus making it slightly conical) and asked the children to predict whether it would travel in a straight line or veer to one side. Most predicted that it would veer, but they were divided as to which way it would circle – to the right or to the left. After it had been observed to circle to the right, I wondered aloud what would happen if the elastic band was moved to the other end of the canister. When the adjustments had been made, the children were asked to predict again and then invited to explain their predictions. Most who tried were unable to be at all specific, but Alexandra made an interesting connection:

> I think it will [turn] because on a car if you turn the wheel this way (motioning to the left) the car goes this way (motioning to the left) if you turn it this way (right) it goes this way (right).

However, when the roller was released, contrary to all predictions, it travelled in an almost straight line. Finally, after the rubber band had been moved even further towards the end of the container, another trial was conducted and the roller circled – somewhat erratically – around the end with the smaller diameter.

After seeing the enthusiastic interest aroused by the behaviour of the rollers, the teachers changed the plan they had prepared and, following Alexandra's connection between the performance of the roller and the wheels of a car, they decided to continue the exploration of elastic power by making and testing similarly powered 'cars'. Again, each child brought from home a small cardboard carton and, with lengths of dowel and wooden wheels provided by the teachers, constructed vehicles that were powered by an elastic band that was attached to the front of the box and the centre of the rear axle. After a period of general experimentation (and modification of malfunctioning vehicles), it was decided in a general class discussion that the questions to which they now wished to find answers were: how far the vehicle would travel for a given number of turns, and whether the addition of rubber bands or Scotch tape as 'tyres' would affect the vehicle's performance on the wooden floor as compared with on the carpet.

Since no-one, teachers nor children, had attempted such an experiment before, it took some time to develop a satisfactory procedure. One very important invention proposed by one of the children, was to make a mark on the circumference of one of the rear wheels so that the number of turns could be counted accurately. Conventions also had to be established concerning the use of a tape measure to calculate the distance travelled. Once these procedures were in place, systematic trials were carried out by children, working in pairs, and the results were recorded in a chart, the form of which had been collaboratively constructed for the purpose.

Despite these preparations, several children had difficulty in carrying out the procedures and so they sought assistance. Whitney and her friends approached Mary Ann because the car they were testing did not seem to go further as they added more turns to the wound up elastic. Mary Ann first checked with them that they had been accurately using the mark when counting the revolutions as they pushed the car backwards to wind up the elastic. Then, when she had helped the children count four turns, she took the tape measure and placed the zero end next to the place where the back wheel made contact with the floor. Then she released the car and, with the children, identified the point on the tape measure next to where the back wheels now contacted the floor: the distance travelled was 78 cm. The teacher then asked the girls whether they were sure they had followed these steps when carrying out their trials before and suggested they should start over again, paying particular attention to the accuracy of their procedures.

A little earlier, Julia and Simon had been working side by side to test the hypothesis that increasing the wheels' grip would increase the distance travelled. Their task was to measure how far their respective cars would go for a given number of turns under three conditions: bare wheels, with elastic bands round the wheels, and with masking tape round the wheels. At the moment the camera begins to record them, Julia is preparing the table in which to record her results, following the format agreed on in the preceding class discussion. Simon seems to be uncertain what to do and he looks over to see how Julia is constructing her table. Noticing this, Julia takes Simon's book and turns to the next blank page.

Julia: There .. just ... do that .. [demonstrating to Simon how to prepare his table] and then turn it like that, draw a line and then ******

Simon: No, I'm doing it this way [turning back to the previous page in his book, which is two-thirds written on]

Julia: But you're going to have to write that stuff and that's not going to be enough room [pointing to Simon's page]
You have to write 'rubber band', 'no rubber band', 'masking tape'

Simon: [decides to follow Julia's suggestion and starts on a fresh page]

A few minutes later, they have finished preparing their tables and are ready to start their trials. Julia suggests that Simon take the first turn. When she sees that he is having difficulty, she instructs him on how to do it and, as Simon starts to push his car backwards to wind it up, Julia monitors his actions.

Julia: Did you put a mark? - how many times?

When Simon seems uncertain, Julia takes over and pushes the car back, counting the turns, while Simon watches. Together, they count three turns. Then Julia places the car with its front wheels approximately lined up with the end of a tape measure stretched out on the floor and releases it. When it stops, she marks the point the front of the car has reached along the tape measure and they both read off the distance.

Julia: Oh . thirty-two . you- . OK
Simon: Thirty-three [correcting her]
Julia: Thirty-three ... put 'thirty-three' on your chart
Simon 'No rubber bands' [writing in his science log]
Julia: Thirty-three . put- . put 'cm' [leaning over to supervise]
Simon: 'cm' [adding this to his entry]

Both Julia and Simon then proceed to carry out the next trial independently.

Later – a few minutes before the end of this session – Whitney (whose group Mary Ann helped earlier) approached me in great excitement. She was clearly in the grip of 'a wonderful idea' (Duckworth, 1987). From looking at her chart of results, she had noticed that, for each additional turn of the rear wheels when it was pushed backwards, her car travelled forwards

Table 13.1 Whitney's results

Turns	Distance (cm)
1	20
2	39
3	57
4	76
5	95
6	113

a further 19 cm – approximately. I shared her excitement and asked her if she could think about these interesting results and come up with an explanation by the following week's lesson. When the time came, Whitney did not, in fact, have an explanation (or was perhaps too shy to attempt one in public). However, the problem was taken up in a class discussion and, when Teacher 2 had written the chart of results (Table 13.1) on the blackboard,[5] a collaborative attempt was made to solve the question concerning the relationship between the number of turns and the distance travelled.

Initially, although the children were able to see the pattern, they could not make a connection between an additional turn and the additional 19 cm the car travelled. This, I surmised, was because of the difficulty of 'seeing' the relationship between the circumference of the wheel and the linear distance the wheel travelled in one revolution. So, after several minutes, in which little progress was being made, I asked one of the children to stand on one end of a tape measure. Her foot was exactly 20 cm long and, as she stepped along the tape, each additional footstep added a further 20 cm. 'So now, what connection can we make?' I asked. Immediately there was a rush of suggestions, all of them inaudible because spoken at once.

Meanwhile, Matthew, sitting unseen on the floor beside the teacher, made a circular gesture in the air with his hand. Eventually, Lindsay can be heard.

Lindsay: The first foot was on- . the first foot was twenty-one . and then her next foot was forty-one, so that's twenty in between . and that's exactly like that [Whitney's results] with nineteen in between

Teacher 2:   So how does that connect to the pattern?

Peter: How much- how long is the box [Whitney's car]?

Teacher 2: How long is this box? [checking] OK, let's measure the box and see how long the box is [taking tape measure and measuring] it's twenty-three centimeters

When it has been generally agreed that it is not the length of the box that is relevant, Teacher 1 prompts them again by asking what else on the car they could measure, but nobody has a suggestion.

At this point, I take one of the children's cars and put a drop of ink on the elastic band that had been added to the marked rear wheel as a tyre and I push the car across a large sheet of chart paper. With each turn of the wheel, it leaves an ink-spot on the paper. Several children immediately fetch tape measures and Teacher 2 measures the distance between the marks and announces the distance between them.

Teacher 2: Kind of between nineteen and twenty actually
Teacher 1: Lindsay?
Lindsay: When she <moves> her box . when she's doing that . when she moves all the centimetres, the reason why it's doing . nineteen - maybe more - is because- …
[Other children are indicating that they want to speak]
Teacher 2: Yes . the distance-
Lindsay: - the distance of her turning around her wheel
Teacher 1: - is-
Lindsay: - is . twenty
Matthew: Each time . she winds it back it's twenty centimetres [making a circular gesture]
Teacher 1: So . how can we find out . for sure?
Carrie: <Count> it?
Teacher 1: - of what? . you've just said the distance of the -
Lindsay: Measuring the distance .. back wheel
Children: - of the wheel
Teacher 1: Measure what?
Matthew: Measure um <the distance between the wheels>
Sam: Maybe . you can take a tape measure round and round it
Teacher 1: Around the wheel?

Teacher 2 then measures the circumference of the wheel and reports the results.

Teacher 2: It's kind of between nineteen and twenty
Teacher 1: Which is why you get the difference, right? [referring to Whitney's less than consistent results]
Charlie: That's why- that's why she's getting nineteen in between

Children:	Yeah
Charlie:	That's why she's -
Matthew:	That's nineteen .. adding nineteen every- every minute [? turn]
GW:	[to Whitney] You go and tell everybody because you made this discovery
Whitney:	[gives her explanation with much hand gesture to indicate the wheel's circumference, but her speech is too soft to hear]
Teacher 2:	So what would happen if everybody measured . their wheel the way I just measured this?
Child:	They would see-
Matthew:	They could see how much it would keep on going . like ***
	[Several children speak at once]
Teacher 2:	You should be able to PREDICT . how far it will go

Action, Talk and Text

There are many interesting events that are worth commenting on in these episodes. Most striking, perhaps, is the central role performed by the rollers and cars, first as the outcome of the action-based knowing involved in their construction, and subsequently as artefacts that helped the children to move towards the theoretical knowing involved in explaining the results of the trials they had carried out. These 'vehicles', constructed by the children, thus functioned both as working mechanical artefacts and as embodied, material representations of the mathematical relationship between wheel circumference and distance travelled, which latter role they performed for precisely the reason offered by Wartofsky, namely that that they 'carried' information about the mode of their own production and functioning.

Initially, the children's concern was to have their cars work properly and this involved them first in instrumental (action-based) knowing as they each attempted to construct one, and then in procedural knowing as they assisted each other with those aspects that were proving problematic. Later, this same concern led to a search for ways of getting the cars not to skid on the smooth surface of the floor, in the course of which they generated substantive knowledge about the properties of different surfaces and the function of tyres in enabling the wheels to get a better grip. (The term 'traction' was mentioned by one child in talking about this.)

However, from early on, the children were also interested in the relationship between the number of turns of the rubber band as it wound up on the rear axle and the distance the vehicle would travel. This started, as one might expect, in a context of competition, as children sought to outdo each other with respect to the prowess of their respective cars. But it did not take much persuasion on the part of the teachers to turn this into a more general problem, to be tackled experimentally through systematic trials. And it was the pattern that Whitney noticed in her results that led to the discussion quoted above which, from the point of view of the move towards theoretical knowing, must count as one of the most successful episodes in the whole unit.

Throughout the unit, then, in their dual role as artefacts and representations, the elastic-powered vehicles not only mediated different modes of knowing, but they also mediated *between* the different modes, integrating them into a larger activity structure of doing, talking and thinking theoretically.

Equally striking were the mimetic meanings expressed through facial expression, gesture and posture as the children used their whole bodies to communicate. Indeed, I would argue that it was Matthew, in his silent circular gesture as one of the other children was stepping along the tape measure, who first 'saw' the direction in which the solution might be found. Certainly his contribution at 165, 'Each time . she winds it back it's twenty centimeters', suggests that he had by then figured it out, and it is probable that it was his desire to share his growing understanding that earlier prompted him to make his unnoticed gesture. For Matthew, at least, it seems that it was easier to represent his knowing through gesture than through speech.

Taken together, then, these various sources of evidence suggest that it may indeed be more effective to embark on a new topic through practical activity that enables knowing through action and demonstration before expecting children to share their knowing through words. A major benefit of this approach is that, when patterns and relationships are expressed linguistically, children have their own direct experience to which to relate these more abstract representations.

This argument receives further support from the children's weekly writing in their science journals, where what they had done and observed provided concrete material on which to reflect and attempt to provide an explanation. Here is what Alexandra wrote as they were still perfecting their cars:

> Today our group made sure we got acurat answers on how far our cars move. First we looked at Jansens car. After 2 minutes me and katie realizised that Jansons cars wheels were rubbing against the box

thats called friction. Then the car wouldent go very far because there was to much friction.

The teachers also made a practice of recording ideas that emerged in whole class discussion on large sheets of chart paper, the exact formulation being negotiated with the children. Here, the process of collaborating in composing the written text worked in the opposite direction, helping the children to focus on what was happening, and why. The resulting text, posted on the classroom wall, also provided a collective record of the group's emerging understanding, to which individual children could refer as they made their own journal entries.

Engaging in writing as well as in doing and talking certainly helped the children to extend and consolidate their understanding of the concepts involved in this investigation of energy. They themselves were aware of its importance as an integral part of 'doing science' and approached it enthusiastically. This was apparent from their comments in the interviews that were conducted at the end of the unit, which included a question asking if writing in science had helped their learning. Alexandra replied:

> When you write stuff .. You can always remember it and then, when you share in groups you can write more stuff so . so whatever you share you learn more.

It was these seven-year-old children's understanding of the interdependence of doing, talking and writing as modes of knowing that led us to choose 'Action, talk and text' as the title for the book in which the DICEP group shared our collective findings (Wells, 2001).

Although there is not space to demonstrate it in detail, the above episodes also show the children spiraling through the four quadrants of the model of learning discussed earlier. Both their own actions in building and trialing their cars and the results thus obtained provided the critical information, while the teachers provided regular opportunities for collective knowledge building about this information. At the same time, these discussions and their journal writing gave evidence of their increasing understanding of the functioning of the elastic-powered cars and also of how they were developing this understanding.

Working in the ZPD

Looking back over the recordings, we identified numerous examples of individuals and groups receiving assistance that enabled them 'to go beyond themselves' – as Vygotsky put it when writing about the ZPD.

Mary Ann checking that Whitney and her friends had understood the importance of following the procedures for conducting trials was one very clear example of a teacher providing assistance in the students' collective zone. And the effectiveness of this assistance became apparent when Whitney subsequently noted the regularity of increasing distance in relation to the number of turns of elastic round the car's rear axle.

Equally effective was the assistance that Julia – a 'more capable peer' – offered when she saw that Simon had not fully understood the purpose of the table of results. Again the evidence of the assistance enabling progress through the zone was seen when Simon was able to manage the next trial on his own. Thus, in both examples, the 'scaffolding' provided served its over-all purpose of enabling the learner subsequently to reach the stage of carry-ing out the action without the need for assistance (Maybin *et al.*, 1992).

But the most important insight occurred as Mary Ann and Barbara reflected together on what had been achieved during the unit. On this occasion, they felt, they had succeeded in taking up the students' questions, and the reason was that they had recognized the importance of 'listening'. As Mary Ann later wrote:

> In coming to understand more fully what it means to teach and learn in the zone of proximal development, we have identified the act of being responsive and the shift in perception of our role as being neces-sary to authentically help anyone in their ZPD. These two elements have been the most significant contributing factors to our feelings of success in science instruction this year. And, as with all learning, they have carried over into all other areas of our teaching.

> The change in us, as teachers, was reflected in our interactions with the children and in the changed climate of the classroom. Students' questions and knowledge were as valued in the learning process as those of the teachers. Consequently, the students were supported in their efforts to make sense of their world and were motivated to take risks to further their own understandings. Because of this act of being responsive, both to the students and to each other, the knowledge we constructed over the course of the unit was much deeper and more meaningful than we had anticipated.

Concluding Reflections

These words of Barbara and Mary Ann speak powerfully to the value of teachers researching the learning and teaching that takes place in their classrooms. Not only do they gain insights that enable them to improve their own practice but also, by reflecting on how their own and their students' actions and utterances are mutually constitutive of what is achieved on particular occasions, they enrich and extend the more abstract theories that underpin their work. As Maria Kowal, one of the DICEP members, explained:

> At first action research was a means of taking the theory I had been reading and applying it to my practice – a means of making theory useful; but it also quickly became a means of allowing me to see how the theory needed changing in my individual context. I also think that it then gave me the confidence to refute aspects of the research I was reading about and thereby to contribute to the theory base and develop it further ... It helped me to stop looking for the 'right' way to do things and to recognize the many variables that influence the teaching/learning context. (McGlynn-Stewart, 2001: 199–200)

These benefits are further enhanced when individual teachers get together to form a community of inquiry, as was the case with the members of DICEP. Zoe Donoahue summed up her experience as follows:

> Having a group with whom to talk, share my findings, hear about other people's inquiries, has kept me going with my research. Writing and presenting together, as well as presenting my current work at meetings, gives me a reason to analyze and think about my data on a regular basis. Getting feedback from others, answering their questions and hearing how my thinking links with other members of the group helps me to develop ideas and gives me ideas for future inquiries. (McGlynn-Stewart, 2001: 195–196)

But perhaps most important is the collective message they communicate to other teachers: that it is both possible and enormously worthwhile to create classrooms that are more open and democratic – communities of inquiry – where students and teachers learn with and from each other. As Dewey (1916) pointed out, how today's students will respond, in the future, to the challenges facing the world and its diverse inhabitants depends not only on the knowledge and skills they encounter and appropriate in the classroom but also on the values and dispositions they develop in the process. For this reason, the model that we, as teachers, provide for our students is just as important as the specific content that we teach. For, as we learn from Vygotsky: 'Who we become depends on the company we keep and what we do and say together'.

Notes

1. Marilda and Jacinta did go on to test the hypothesis but the results were inconclusive: the windfinder functioned equally well both with and without the bead. However, Marilda's interest in the wind was not dampened and she went on to create another demonstration of how convection currents occur. Two weeks later, the class prepared their work for a parents' evening, where they would show and talk about what they had learned. So enthusiastic had Marilda become about her projects that, in addition to preparing her displays, including a written version of her explanation of the working of the windfinder, she also made a tape recording explaining her work so that, if she happened to be away from her display, an interested visitor could play the tape and listen to her account (Wells & Chang-Wells, 1992).

2. Most of the members of the group had read these and other authors during the classes for the Masters degree they were taking or had taken.

3. Much would be gained, I believe, if there were greater recognition of the distinction between 'knowing' and 'what is known'. In colloquial speech, 'what is known' is often referred to as 'the knowledge out there' – known by somebody but not necessarily by the person speaking. It is this impersonal knowledge that constitutes the content of the prescribed curriculum – what teachers are required to teach and students are held accountable for being able to reproduce. By contrast, 'knowing' is what individuals do as they thoughtfully carry out actions on a particular occasion and for some purpose to which they are committed. Therefore, learning-and-teaching is – or should be – not the transmission and memorization of 'what is known' for the purpose of accreditation, but an active engagement in knowing on the part of the teacher and students together through the processes of knowledge building for some purpose that is meaningful for the students.

4. Volume 6 (1) (February 2003) is devoted to articles by DICEP teachers. The journal can be found at http://journals.library.wisc.edu/index.php/networks. Accessed 6.6.09.

5. For convenience, I refer to Barbara as Teacher 1 and to Mary Ann as Teacher 2.

Epilogue: Making Meaning Together

Two main claims have been repeated at intervals throughout this book, like the refrain in a ballad or traditional story. They are that children are active meaning makers and that the best way in which adults can help them to learn is by giving them evidence, guidance and encouragement. The first claim is based on the evidence that we collected in our longitudinal study, and I have tried to give it more immediacy by quoting at length from the recordings, writings and interviews of a small number of children. The second claim is a corollary of the first, and it too has been supported by quotations from the homes and classrooms of parents and teachers who have intuitively understood its correctness and tried to find ways of relating to the children in their care in such a way as to facilitate this development. I wrote the above sentences 20 years ago and nothing has led me to change those claims. Indeed they have been strongly supported by my more recent research with teachers who adopt a dialogic stance.

The Nature of Conversation

For the most part, I have placed the emphasis on the empirical evidence for these claims. But there are also grounds for accepting them of a different kind: namely, the nature of conversation itself. In talking about conversation, we often use such phrases as 'sharing ideas' or 'exchanging opinions' as if, through what he or she says, a speaker were able to cause another person to have the very same thoughts or feelings as were in his or her own mind. We are all aware, of course, of occasions when this is patently not the case – when a misunderstanding occurs for any of a variety of reasons – but we still continue to act as if this were the exception rather than the rule, believing that, if we say things clearly enough, our listeners will 'know what we mean'. Taken literally, such phrases express an optimism which is, I believe, mistaken, as I think will be clear from a closer examination of the processes that are involved in any instance of linguistic communication.

When I communicate with other people, whether it be to inform, request, or persuade, what I have in mind is an idea – an event, action or outcome – that I intend they should understand. However, this idea arises from my personal understanding of the world, which is itself the product of my unique personal biography. Nobody else has exactly the same mental model of the world, since nobody else has had exactly the same experiences. It follows, therefore, that nobody can have exactly the same ideas as I have.

Even if my listener were able to form the same ideas as I have, however, I still am not able to transmit my ideas directly to him or her in all their simultaneity and multifaceted particularity, since language, the most effective means of communication available, requires that I select and arrange what I mean in an ordered sequence that is compatible with the temporally organized possibilities of syntax and vocabulary. Furthermore, while my ideas are personal and particular, the categories of language, in terms of which I now have to represent them, are public and general. It is simply not possible, therefore, to convey the ideas that I have in mind in a form that does full justice to their simultaneous complexity and specificity.

However, this is still not the end of the problem for, in order to reach my intended audience, my message must be further re-encoded into a stream of vocally produced sounds – or, if writing, into a sequence of marks on a page – that has only an arbitrary but conventional relationship to the meanings that I intend. All that is available to the receiver, therefore, is a patterned sequence of vocal sound, or a graphic display, which in itself is totally meaningless. This is immediately apparent if we listen to a speaker of an unknown language or attempt to interpret a text in an unknown script- as was forcibly brought home to me on a visit to Yugoslavia some years ago, when I found that the menu in the hotel where I was staying was completely impenetrable. Unable to recognize the letters of the Cyrillic alphabet, I could not even begin to decipher the words that were written there, let alone work out what they might mean.

Even to a listener/reader who knows the code, however, the task of reconstructing the intended meaning is not simply a matter of working 'from the bottom up' – of decoding the sequence of sound into a pattern of words in a syntactic structure and then reading off the corresponding meaning. In the first place, as anyone who has tried to transcribe recorded speech will know, one cannot even hear the sounds until one knows their meaning[1] and, second, even if one can decipher the words and structures, they only make sense when one can give them a specific interpretation in the light of one's own previous experience and the context in which they are encountered. Interpreting another person's message, therefore, requires that one also have expectations, based on prior knowledge or information derived from the situational context. Comprehension is the result of an act of *meaning construction* by the receiver. It occurs only when the meaning derived from a decoding of the linguistic message fits with the meaning that the receiver predicts from an interpretation of the context in the light of the relevant aspects of his or her understanding of the world.[2]

What all this leads to is a recognition that one never *knows* what other people mean by what they say or write. One can only make an informed guess, taking into account all the cues that are available: from the communication context, from one's own relevant experience, and from the actual linguistic signal. To put it differently, I cannot know what idea is in your mind as you speak or write. I can only know what ideas I would have had in mind if I had produced the same lexico-grammatical sequence as I believe you to have produced in the context that I think you think we currently share.

In normal conversation between mature adult members of the same culture, however, this does not normally cause a problem. Their past experience, both of language and of the world to which it refers, is sufficiently similar for there to be a considerable overlap between them in the ideas they might wish to communicate. Furthermore, in speech at least, there are strategies available for negotiating the intended meaning if a mismatch is suspected. Finally, where conversational meaning is jointly constructed over successive turns, there are opportunities to amplify or modify what one has said in the light of the feedback received in subsequent contributions. Although participants in a conversation never know for sure what the other meant by a particular utterance, over the conversation as a whole there are sufficient opportunities for each to calibrate his or her interpretation of what is meant against that of the other for a consensus to be reached that is usually adequate for most of the purposes for which people communicate with each other.

On the other hand, where the conversational participants come from different cultural backgrounds, or where they differ greatly in their level of cognitive and linguistic maturity – as is the case in interactions between children and their parents or teachers – the possibility of misunderstanding is both substantial and ever-present. And unless they – or at least the more mature of the participants – take the necessary steps, the meanings that they construct on the basis of their differing mental models and linguistic resources are likely to become increasingly divergent (Michaels, 1981).

What these steps are has already been dealt with at some length when considering the ways in which adults can facilitate their children's language development (Chapter 3) and they apply equally to interaction between teachers and students. The four principles that were suggested were:

- to treat what the child has to say as worthy of careful attention;
- to do one's best to understand what he or she means;
- to take the child's meaning as the basis for what one says next;
- in selecting and encoding one's message, to take account of the child's ability to understand – that is, to construct an appropriate interpretation.

However, when these principles are followed by both participants, it is possible for minds to make contact – even when they are separated by wide differences in maturity and experience. Although it may not be possible literally to share the thoughts of another person, it is possible, through the collaborative construction of conversational meaning through dialogue, to extend and modify one's own thoughts in response to the cues provided by the other and, in turn, to provide cues that enable the other to estimate how close one has come to the ideas that he or she originally had in mind.

Dialogue may not be perfect as a means of information exchange and knowledge building, therefore, but when engaged in collaboratively, it can be an effective medium for learning and teaching. In any case, since there is no better alternative, we must do the best we can.

The Guided Reinvention of Knowledge

If the argument of the previous section is correct, together with the evidence from our own study, as I have interpreted it, it follows that the conception of teaching as 'transmission' must be a mistaken one. First, it is not possible, simply by telling, to cause students to come to have the knowledge that is in the mind of the teacher. Knowledge cannot be transmitted. It has to be constructed afresh by each individual knower on the basis of what is already known and by means of strategies developed over the whole of that individual's life, both outside and inside the classroom. On both these counts there are bound to be substantial differences between the individuals in any class of students and, hence, a wide variation in the interpretations that they put upon the teacher's words. Unless students are given opportunities to formulate the sense they make of new topics in their own way, using their own words, an important means of gaining understanding is lost. In addition, the teacher loses the opportunity to discover what meanings the students bring to the topic and so is unable to make his or her contributions contingently responsive.

Second, a unilateral definition by the teacher of what is to count as worthwhile knowledge and of how it is to be constructed undervalues the contributions that students can make in terms of their own experience, interests, and methods of inquiry, thereby impoverishing the learning experience. Furthermore, to override their natural predisposition to attempt to construct their own knowledge is to force them into a relatively passive role, with a consequent reduction in their commitment to the endeavour and an increase in the likelihood that what is learned will not be integrated into their action-oriented model of the world and so will soon be forgotten.

In sum, what is wrong with the transmission model is that it places the teacher or textbook at the center of the educational enterprise and focuses almost exclusively on the input, in the mistaken belief that, to obtain the desired outcomes, what is most important is to ensure that the input is well selected, sequenced and presented in terms of the educated adult's understanding of what is to be learned.

However, once we give due recognition to the fact that knowledge can only be constructed by individual knowers and that this occurs most effectively when they have an active engagement in all the processes involved, it becomes clear that a different model of education is required – one that is based on a partnership between students and teachers, in which the responsibility for selecting and organizing the tasks to be engaged in is shared (Green & Dixon, 1993).

To urge that classrooms should be places in which the curriculum is negotiated – where students are encouraged to take the role of expert when they are able to do so, and where they have a part in determining the goals to be aimed for and the procedures to be followed – may seem to be reducing the importance of the role of the teacher. However, this is very far from being the case. What is required, though, is a different conception of the relationship between teacher and students – one in which the teacher aims to facilitate learning rather than to direct it. This is not to deny the teacher's greater expertise and experience, but to argue that it will be of much greater value to students if it is offered collaboratively and 'just in time' when it is needed rather than being imposed according to the teacher's plan.

Nor am I suggesting that the teacher should relinquish the overall responsibility for setting directions, proposing specific content or evaluating achievement (see Chapter 12). On the contrary, final decisions on these matters require informed judgment that can only be gained through professional development and experience. Nevertheless, in fulfilling these responsibilities, the teacher should explain the criteria on which decisions are based so that, within the limits of their capabilities, students can share in the day-to-day planning of learning activities to an increasing degree (Gipps, 2002). The aim, therefore, should be to foster the development of students' ability to take control of their own learning so that eventually they become self-directed learners who assume these responsibilities for themselves.

Following these principles, teaching can no longer be seen as the imparting of information to relatively passive recipients and then checking to see that they can correctly reproduce it. Instead, it is more appropriately characterized as a dialogic partnership in learning. The tasks of the partners are necessarily different as a result of their differing levels of expertise, but the goal is the same for students and teacher alike. Without too much exaggeration, it can be described as the 'guided reinvention of knowledge'. As the philosopher, Karl Popper, put it:

> We can grasp a theory only by trying to reinvent it or to reconstruct it, and by trying out, with the help of our imagination, all the consequences of the theory which seem to us to be interesting and important ... One could say that the process of understanding and the process of the actual production or discovery are very much alike. (Popper & Eccles, 1977: 461)

From Practice to Theory – And Back Again

Abstract theory is all very well, I suspect some readers are saying, but what does it amount to in practice? Or, if those readers are teachers, their question is probably more specifically, 'What should I do in my particular situation?' This is a very important question, and one that is urgently in need of an answer. However, it would be inappropriate for me to attempt to provide a detailed response because there is not one but many answers. Furthermore, the only valid answers are the ones that individual teachers construct in the light of their knowledge of themselves, their students, the curriculum and the setting – the colleagues, school system and community – in which they work.

Nevertheless, it is possible to offer a number of general suggestions, and this I have attempted to do in the preceding chapters. More important, I have described and quoted from work in classrooms in which teachers have found their own specific and practical answers, which are appropriate to their own particular circumstances.

In practical terms, what is common to them is that they have arranged the daily programme so that a variety of activities can be going on simultaneously. This has made it relatively easy for them to allow individual children to follow different patterns within the total curriculum so that, at any time, the teacher can give help where it is most needed. And from there to allowing the child to share the responsibility for designing and taking responsibility for his or her own individual curriculum is a small and relatively easy step to take. Some teachers are happy for the greater part of each child's work to be carried out individually, but others feel that there is much to be gained by encouraging collaborative group work. In my view, there should, ideally, be a balance of individual, group and whole class activity that is appropriate to the nature of each particular curriculum unit (Wells, 2002). Where this is the case, there is much to be said for starting with a broad theme, with the expectation that small groups will choose their own specific aspect to work on, as in the example reported in Chapters 10 and 13, where the broad themes of life 100 years ago and winter in the Yukon allowed for a wide range of topics to be investigated, using a variety of methods of inquiry and subsequent presentation. By guiding individual or group choices of topic, the teacher can ensure that, over a reasonable length of time, each child is tackling topics across the range of the curriculum.

For those who find this too large a change to make – at least at first – a similar strategy might be adopted for just one part of the day, for example in social studies or in science. The 'writing workshop' described by Graves (2003) is another possible starting point, but this would need to be linked to some other major area of learning if the strategies developed in the workshop were to permeate the curriculum more widely.

However, what these examples show is that the best source of suggestions is to be found in other teachers. What is needed, therefore, is more, and more frequent, opportunities for teachers to meet together to pool their ideas and experiences – putting together, for example, a list of themes that have proved successful starting points and compiling a central pool of resources of various kinds that could be drawn upon in exploring these themes. There are already schools where the staff meet together regularly in this way, and the encouragement and support that this provides for individual teachers is out of all proportion to the initial difficulty of finding a time in the lunch hour or at the end of the working day when all the staff can meet on a regular basis. In other cases, support groups have got together on a wider front, involving teachers in a group of neighbouring schools or in an area served by a teachers' center.

Clearly principals and head and advisory teachers have an important leadership role to play in facilitating the functioning of such groups (Tharp & Gallimore, 1988). But it is important that they do not take on too directive a role. If teachers are to discover effective ways of helping their students to take some of the responsibility for their own learning, they must themselves have the opportunity to learn in the same way. The same is true of more formally provided teacher education, whether at the level of initial preparation, in-service courses, or programmes leading to higher degrees. Unless teachers' experiences as adult students are of this kind, they can hardly be expected to take easily to working in this way with their own students.

Every teacher needs to become his or her own theory-builder, but a builder of theory that grows out of practice and has as its aim to improve the quality of practice. For too long, 'experts' from outside the classroom have told teachers what to think and what to do. They have even designed programmes and materials that are 'teacher-proof' in an attempt to bypass teachers' professional expertise, in the same way that so many teachers have bypassed the contributions that students can make to collaborative knowledge building. Such programmes must be rejected for exactly the same reasons as were given above for rejecting a transmission model of classroom teaching. At every level, learners must be encouraged actively to take responsibility for their own learning, and this applies as much to teachers as learners as it does to the students that they teach.

Conclusion

We are the meaning makers – every one of us: children, parents and teachers. To try to make sense, to construct stories and explanations, and to share them with others in speech and in writing is an essential part of being human. For those of us who are more knowledgeable and more mature – parents and teachers – the responsibility is clear: to interact with those in our care through 'action, talk and text' in such a way as to foster and enrich their meaning making and develop their understanding.

Notes

1. In most passages of recorded speech, I have found, there are utterances that are, initially, completely unintelligible. Even after several replayings, I am simply not able to 'hear' them. However, it has been my frequent experience that, on replaying them on a later occasion in a different context, the problem disappears. With a different set of expectations, I am able to reconstruct a meaning; and, when I have an interpretation, the speech signal itself immediately becomes clear.
2. This was demonstrated very clearly in a number of experiments reported by Bransford and McCarrell (1974). One of their examples involves the sentence 'The notes were sour because the seams had split'. This initially uninterpretable message becomes clear when one knows that the reference was to music played on the bagpipes – at least if one has any knowledge of the construction of that instrument.

Appendix 1: The Bristol Language Development Scale

Appendix 1: The Bristol Language Development Scale

Stage	Function	Meaning relations	Time modality	Noun phrase	Clause syntax	Examples	Median, range
1	Call; Want; Ostension	Operator + Referent		Gesture; "Noun"	1 constituent	"(Gesture) + bird \"; "Dink \ " "Mummy /"; "e a \ = look at that (+ Pointing Gesture)	12 9–21
2	Statement; Direct Request	Want + Entity; Agent Act; Static Location		Noun; Pronoun; Adverb		"There Mummy \"; "Want Teddy /"; "Mark do it \"; "Up please / "	21 12–24
3	Express State; Content Question	Agent Change Location; Classification		Possessor + Noun; Prep + Head; Indef Art + Noun; Interrog Pronoun	2 constituents	"That [is] doggie \"; "Man's fire \"; "In there /"; "A ball \"; "Go shop /"; Jon tired \"; "Who came /"	24 15–30
4	Intend; Yes/No Question	Want + Embed Cl; Agent Cause Cogn Exper; Change Possession; Agent Change Attribute	Past Time; Contin Aspect; Perfect Aspect; "and"	Def Art + Noun; Prep + Det + Noun; Adj + Noun; Indef Pronoun	S + cop + C; S + V (+O)	"Mummy have it \"; "I want daddy mend it \"; "The man gone \"; "Mark running \"; "Helen come down /"; "Read the book \"; "Me have chips and Daddy \"; "I do that /"	27 18–36

(Continued)

Appendix 1: Continued

Stage	Function	Meaning relations	Time modality	Noun phrase	Clause syntax	Examples	Median, range
5	Request Permission; Explain	Cogn Experience; Agent Act on Object	Future Time; Permission; Ability	Det + Mod + Head; Poss Adj + Noun; Dem Adj + Noun;	S + aux + V (+ O/A); Aux + S + V (+ O); S + V + O + A; Wh + cop + S; S + V + Non-finite Cl	"Where's my shoe?"; "I want to see that picture"; "I'll eat the big one"; "Can I cut the cheese?"; "I've picked the bricks up"	30 21–42
6	Indirect Request; Suggestion	Agent Change Existence; Cogn Exper + Embed Cl		Head + Defining Phrase	S + aux + cop + X; S + aux + neg + V (+X); Aux + S + V + O/A; A + S + aux + V + O + A	"I will be a good boy"; "I thought Daddy was making it"; "Perhaps we'll get my anorak tomorrow"; "Could you bring my blocks out now?"; "Make one with two heads"	36 24–51
7	Request; Explain; Query State/ Attitude; Formulation	Agent Cause + Embed Cl; Benefactive Relation	Possibility; Obligation; Necessity; "because"	Head + Defining Cl; Prep + Det + Mod + Head	Main Cl + Subord Cl; S + aux + aux + V + X; Passive; Main Cl + Tag; Wh + aux + S + V	"I want my tea cos I'm hungry"; "They might be eaten by the monster"; "I made this puzzle for you, didn't I?"; "The man's got to make them go away"; "Are you cross, Mummy?"; "Where did you put my book?"	42 27–57

8	Why Question; Conditional		Habitual; Extent Time; "if"; "when"	Interrog Adj + Head; Relative Pronoun	Why + aux + S + V + X; 3 clause utterance	"That's what we wear when it's raining, isn't it?"; "Which is the one that keeps going for ever?"; "Why can't I have another one?"; "I can't put my train over the bridge if you put that like that"	48 33–60+
9		Change Affective Exper; Classific + Embed Cl; Purposive	Inference	Reflexive Pronoun	S + aux + neg + aux + V + X	"What made you cross?"; "What's this for?"; "Tomorrow is when I have my birthday party"; "I can do it by myself"; "That one must be Mr Wooden then"; "You shouldn't have done that"	57 39–60+

References

Alexander, R. (2006) *Towards Dialogic Teaching: Rethinking Classroom Talk*. Thirsk, North Yorks: Dialogos.

Alexander, R. (2008) Culture, dialogue and learning: Notes on an emerging pedagogy. In N. Mercer and S. Hodgkinson (eds) *Exploring Talk in School* (pp. 91–114). London: Sage.

Applebee, A.N. (1996) *Curriculum as Conversation: Transforming Traditions of Teaching and Learning*. Chicago: University of Chicago Press.

Baddeley, G. (ed.) (1992) *Learning Together Through Talk*. London: Hodder.

Bakhtin, M.M. (1986) *Speech Genres and Other Late Essays*. Austin: University of Texas Press.

Barnes, D. (1971) *Language, the Learner and the School*. Harmondsworth, Middlesex: Penguin.

Barnes, D. (1976) *From Communication to Curriculum*. Harmondsworth, Middlesex: Penguin.

Barnes, D. and Todd, F. (1977) *Communicating and Learning in Small Groups*. London: Routledge & Kegan Paul.

Barnes, S., Gutfreund, M., Satterly, D. and Wells, G. (1983) Characteristics of adult speech which predict children's language development. *Journal of Child Language* 10, 65–84.

Bates, E., Camaioni, L. and Volterra, V. (1975) The acquisition of performatives prior to speech. *Merrill-Palmer Quarterly* 21 (3), 205–226.

Bates, E., Dale, P. and Thal, D. (1995) Individual differences and their implications for theories of language development. In P. Fletcher and B. MacWhinney (eds) *Handbook of Child Language* (pp. 96–151). Oxford: Blackwell.

Bates, E. and Goodman, J.C. (1997) On the inseparability of grammar and the lexicon: Evidence from acquisition, aphasia, and real time processing. *Language and Cognitive Processes* 12 (5/6), 507–586.

Bates, E. and Goodman, J.C. (2001) On the inseparability of grammar and the lexicon: Evidence from acquisition. In M. Tomasello and E. Bates (eds) *Language Development: The Essential Readings* (pp. 134–162). Malden, MA: Blackwell.

Bates, E. and MacWhinney, B. (eds) (1989) *The Crosslinguistic Study of Sentence Processing*. New York: Cambridge University Press.

Bell-Angus, B., Davis, G., Donoahue, Z., Kowal, M. and McGlynn-Stewart, M. (2009) DICEP: Promoting collaborative inquiry in diverse educational settings.

In A.P. Samaras, A.R. Freese, C. Kosnik and C. Beck (eds) *Learning Communities in Practice* (pp. 19–30). New York: Springer.

Bennett, J. (1976) *Linguistic Behaviour*. Cambridge: Cambridge University Press.

Bereiter, C. (1994) Implications of postmodernism for science, or, science as progressive discourse. *Educational Psychologist* 29 (1), 3–12.

Berger, P.L. and Luckman, T. (1966) *The Social Construction of Reality*. Garden City: Doubleday.

Bernstein, B. (1975) *Class, Codes and Control, Vol. 3: Towards a Theory of Educational Transmissions*. London: Routledge & Kegan Paul.

Bernstein, B. (1982) Codes, modalities and the process of cultural reproduction: A model. In M. Apple (ed.) *Cultural and Economic Reproduction in Education* (pp. 304–355). London: Routledge & Kegan Paul.

Bettelheim, B. (1976) *The Uses of Enchantment*. New York: Knopf.

Bower, T. (1974) *Development in Infancy*. San Francisco: W.H. Freeman.

Bransford, J.D., Brown, A.L. and Cocking, R. (eds) (2000) *How People Learn*. Washington, DC: National Academies Press.

Bransford, J.D. and McCarrell, S. (1974) A sketch of a cognitive approach to comprehension. In W.B. Weiner and D.S. Palermo (eds) *Cognition and the Symbolic Processes*. Hillsdale, NJ: Lawrence Erlbaum.

Brimer, A. and Dunn, L. (1963) *English Picture Vocabulary Test*. Windsor: National Foundation for Educational Research.

Britton, J. (1970) *Language and Learning*. London: Allen Lane.

Britton, J. (1983) Writing and the story world. In B.M. Kroll and G. Wells (eds) *Explorations in the Development of Writing*. Chichester: Wiley.

Brown, A.L. and Campione, J.C. (1994) Guided discovery in a community of learners. In K. McGilly (ed.) *Integrating Cognitive Theory and Classroom Practice: Classroom Lessons* (pp. 229–270). Cambridge, MA: MIT Press/Bradford Books.

Brown, A.L., Ash, D., Rutherford, M., Kakagawa, K., Gordon, A. and Campione, J.C. (1993) Distributed expertise in the classroom. In G. Salomon (ed.) *Distributed Cognitions: Psychological and Educational Considerations* (pp. 188–228). Cambridge: Cambridge University Press.

Brown, A.L., Metz, K.M. and Campione, J.C. (1996) Social interaction and individual understanding in a community of learners: The influence of Piaget and Vygotsky. In A. Tryphon and J. Vonèche (eds) *Piaget-Vygotsky: The Social Genesis of Thought* (pp. 145–170). Mahwah, NJ: Erlbaum.

Brown, R. (1973) *A First Language: The Early Stages*. London: G. Allen and Unwin.

Brown, R. (1977) Introduction. In C. Snow and C. Ferguson (eds) *Talking to Children: From Input to Acquisition* (pp. 1–27). Cambridge: Cambridge University Press.

Brown, R. (1980) The maintenance of conversation. In D. Olson (ed.) *The Social Foundations of Language and Thought*. New York: Norton.

Bruner, J.S. (1975) From communication to language – a psychological perspective. *Cognition* 3, 255–287.

Bruner, J.S. (1983) *Child's Talk*. New York: Norton.

Bruner, J.S. (1986) *Actual Minds, Possible Worlds*. Cambridge, MA: Harvard University Press.

Bullock, A. (1975) *The Bullock Report: A Language for Life*. London: Her Majesty's Stationery Office.

Carter, A. (1979) Prespeech meaning relations. In P. Fletcher and M. Garman (eds) *Language Acquisition*. Cambridge: Cambridge University Press.

Caselli, M.C., Casadio, P. and Bates, E. (2001) Lexical development in English and Italian. In M. Tomasello and E. Bates (eds) *Language Development: The Essential Readings* (pp. 76–110). Malden, MA: Blackwell.

Cazden, C.B. (1983) Adult assistance to language development: Scaffolds, models and direct instruction. In R.P. Parker and F.A. Davis (eds) *Developing Literacy: Young Children's Use of Language*. Newark, DE: International Reading Association.

Cazden, C. (1988) *Classroom Discourse: The Language of Teaching and Learning*. Portsmouth, NH: Heinemann.

Cherry, L. and Lewis, M. (1978) Differential socialization of girls and boys: Implications for sex differences in language development. In N. Waterson and C.E. Snow (eds) *The Development of Communication*. Chichester: John Wiley.

Chomsky, C. (1969) *The Acquisition of Syntax from 5 to 10*. Cambridge, MA: MIT Press.

Chomsky, N.A. (1965) *Aspects of the Theory of Syntax*. Cambridge, MA: MIT Press.

Chomsky, N.A. (1972) *Language and Mind*. New York: Harcourt Brace Jovanovich.

Clark, E. (1974) Some aspects of the conceptual basis for first language acquisition. In R. Schiefelbusch and L. Lloyd (eds) *Language Perspectives: Acquisition, Retardation and Intervention*. Baltimore: University Park Press.

Clark, R. (1974) Performing without competence. *Journal of Child Language* 1, 1–10.

Clay, M. (1972) *The Early Detection of Reading Difficulties: A Diagnostic Survey*. London: Heinemann Educational Books.

Clay, M.M. (1983) Getting a theory of writing. In B.M. Kroll and G. Wells (eds) *Explorations in the Development of Writing*. Chichester: Wiley.

Cobb, P. and McClain, K. (2002) Supporting students' learning of significant mathematical ideas. In G. Wells and G. Claxton (eds) *Learning for Life in the 21st Century: Sociocultural Perspectives on the Future of Education* (pp. 154–166). Oxford: Blackwell.

Cole, M. (1993) Remembering the future. In G. Harman (ed.) *Conceptions of the Human Mind. Essays in Honor of George A. Miller* (pp. 247–265). Hillsdale, NJ: Erlbaum.

Corballis, M.C. (2002) *From Hand to Mouth: The Origins of Language*. Princeton, NJ: Princeton University Press.

Cross, T.G. (1977) Mothers' speech adjustments: The contribution of selected child listener variables. In C.E. Snow and C. Ferguson (eds) *Talking to Children: Language Input and Acquisition*. Cambridge: Cambridge University Press.

Crystal, D., Fletcher, P. and Garman, M. (1976) *The Grammatical Analysis of Language Disability*. London: Arnold.

Cummins, J. (2000) *Language, Power, and Pedagogy: Bilingual Children in the Crossfire*. Clevedon: Multilingual Matters.

Dalton, S.S. and Tharp, R.G. (2002) Standards for pedagogy: Research, theory and practice. In G. Wells and G. Claxton (eds) *Learning for Life in the 21st Century: Sociocultural Perspectives on the Future of Education* (pp. 181–194). Oxford: Blackwell.

Darling-Hammond, L. (2003) Standards and assessments: Where we are and what we need. *Teachers College Record* (16 February 2003).

Darling-Hammond, L., Oakes, J. and Underwood, J. (2009) *From Inequality to Quality*. San Francisco: Jossey-Bass Wiley.

Dawes, L., Mercer, N. and Wegerif, R. (2004) *Thinking Together: A Programme of Activities for Developing Speaking, Listening and Thinking Skills*. Birmingham: Imaginative Minds Ltd.

Deacon, T.W. (1997) *The Symbolic Species: The Co-evolution of Language and the Brain*. New York: Norton.

Dewey, J. (1916/1966) *Democracy and Education*. New York: The Free Press.

Dewey, J. (1938) *Experience and Education*. New York: Collier Macmillan.

Dewey, J. (1956) *The School and Society & The Child and the Curriculum*. Chicago: University of Chicago Press.

Diamond, J. (1998) *Guns, Germs, and Steel: The Fates of Human Societies*. New York: Norton.

Dixon, J. (1966) *Growth through English*. Oxford: Oxford University Press.

Donald, M. (1991) *Origins of the Modern Mind: Three Stages in the Evolution of Culture and Cognition*. Cambridge, MA: Harvard University Press.

Donald, M. (2001) *A Mind so Rare: The Evolution of Human Consciousness*. New York: Norton.

Donaldson, M. (1978) *Children's Minds*. London: Fontana.

Donoahue, Z. (1998) Giving children control: Fourth graders initiate and sustain discussions after teacher read-alouds. *Networks* 1 (1). On WWW at http://journals.library.wisc.edu/index.php/networks. Accessed 4.6.09.

Dore, J. (1975) Holophrases, speech acts and language universals. *Journal of Child Language* 2, 21–40.

Drummond, M.J. (1997) *Learning to See*. Portland, ME: Stenhouse Publishers.

Duckworth, E. (1987) *'The Having of Wonderful Ideas' and Other Essays on Teaching and Learning*. New York: Teachers College Press.

Dyson, A.H. (1989) *Multiple Worlds of Child Writers: Friends Learning to Write*. New York: Teachers College Press.

Dyson, A.H. (1993) *Social Worlds of Children Learning to Write in an Urban School*. New York: Teachers College Press.

Eagleton, T. (1983) *Literary Theory: An Introduction*. Oxford: Blackwell.

Egan, K. (1988) *Teaching as Storytelling*. Chicago: University of Chicago Press.

Eimas, P.D. (1975) Auditory and phonetic coding of the cues for speech: Discrimination of the (R-L) distinction by young infants. *Perception and Psychophysics* 18 (5), 341–347.

Ellis, R. and Wells, G. (1980) Enabling factors in adult-child discourse. *First Language* 1, 46–62.

Fenson, L., Marchman, V.A., Thal, D.J., Dale, P.S., Reznick, S. and Bates, E. (2003) *MacArthur-Bates Communicative Development Inventories (CDIs)*. Baltimore, MD: Brookes.

Ferreiro, E. and Teberosky, A. (1982) *Literacy Before Schooling*. Portsmouth, NH: Heinemann Educational Books.

Fillmore, C.J. (1988) The mechanisms of 'Construction Grammar'. *Proceedings of the Berkeley Linguistics Society* 14, 35–55.

Fullan, M. (2007) *The New Meaning of Educational Change*. New York: Teachers College Press.

Gallas, K. (1994) *The Languages of Learning: How Children Talk, Write, Dance, Draw, and Sing Their Understanding of the World*. New York: Teachers College Press.

Gallas, K. (2003) *Imagination and Literacy: A Teacher's Search for the Heart of Learning*. New York: Teachers College Press.

Galton, M., Hargreaves, L., Comber, C., Pell, T. and Wall, D. (1999) *Inside the Primary Classroom: 20 Years On*. London: Routledge.

Gaskins, S. (1999) Children's daily lives in a Mayan village: A case study of culturally constructed roles and activities. In A. Göncü (ed.) *Children's Engagement in the World: Sociocultural Perspectives* (pp. 25–61). Cambridge: Cambridge University Press.

Gipps, C. (2002) Sociocultural perspectives on assessment. In G. Wells and G. Claxton (eds) *Learning for Life in the 21st Century: Sociocultural Perspectives on the Future of Education* (pp. 73–83). Oxford: Blackwell.

Gleitman, L. (1990) The structural sources of word meaning. *Language Acquisition* 1, 3–55.

Graves, D. (1983) *Writing: Teachers and Children at Work*. Exeter, NH: Heinemann Educational Books.

Graves, D. (2003) *Writing: Teachers & Children at Work (20th Anniversary Edition)*. Portsmouth, NH: Heinemann.

Green, J.L. and Dixon, C.N. (1993) Talking knowledge into being: Discursive and social practices in classrooms. *Linguistics and Education* 5 (3–4), 231–239.

Green, J., Yeager, B. and Castanheira, M.L. (2008) Talking texts into being: On the social construction of everyday life and academic knowledge in the classroom. In N. Mercer and S. Hodgkinson (eds) *Exploring Talk in School* (pp. 115–130). London: Sage.

Gregory, R. (1974) Psychology: Towards a science of fiction. *New Society* (23 May 1974).

Gutfreund, M., Harrison, M. and Wells, G. (1989) *The Bristol Language Development Scales*. Windsor: NFER-Nelson.

Gutiérrez, K., Baquedano-Lopez, P. and Tejeda, C. (1999) Rethinking diversity: Hybridity and hybrid language practices in the third space. *Mind, Culture, & Activity* 6 (4), 286–303.

Hacking, I. (1990) *The Taming of Chance*. Cambridge: Cambridge University Press.

Hall, N. (1987) *The Emergence of Literacy*. Portsmouth, NH: Heinemann Educational Books.

Halliday, M.A.K. (1973) *Explorations in the Functions of Language*. London: Arnold.

Halliday, M.A.K. (1975) *Learning How to Mean*. London: Arnold.

Halliday, M.A.K. (1984) Language as code and language as behaviour: A systemic functional interpretation of the nature and ontogenesis of language. In R. Fawcett, M.A.K. Halliday, S.M. Lamb and A. Makkai (eds) *The Semiotics of Culture and Language* (Vol. 1) (pp. 3–35). London: Frances Pinter.

Halliday, M.A.K. (1993) Towards a language-based theory of learning. *Linguistics and Education* 5, 93–116.

Hardy, B. (1968) *Novel: A Forum on Fiction*. Providence, RI: Brown University.

Hargreaves, A. (2007) The long and short of educational change. *Education Canada* 47 (3), 16–23.

Harste, J. (1994) Literacy as curricular conversations about knowledge, inquiry and morality. In M.R. Ruddell and R.B. Ruddell (eds) *Theoretical Models and Processes of Reading*. Newark, DE: International Reading Association.

Hart, B. and Risley, T.R. (1999) *The Social World of Children Learning to Talk*. Baltimore: Paul H. Brookes.

Hart-Hewins, L. and Wells, J. (1999) *Better Books! Better Readers!: How to Choose, Use, and Level Books for Children in the Primary Grades*. Portsmouth, NH: Heinemann.

Hasan, R. (1986) The ontogenesis of ideology: An interpretation of mother child talk. In T. Threadgold, E.A. Grosz, G. Kress and M.A.K. Halliday (eds) *Language, Semiotics, Ideology* (pp. 125–146). Sydney, NSW: The Sydney Association for Studies in Society and Culture.

Hasan, R. (2002) Semiotic mediation and mental development in pluralistic societies: Some implications for tomorrow's schooling. In G. Wells and G. Claxton (eds) *Learning for Life in the 21st Century: Sociocultural Perspectives on the Future of Education* (pp. 112–126). Oxford: Blackwell.

Hayes, D. (1982) *On Measuring the Richness of Children's Natural Language Environments: Conversation, Books and Television*. San Francisco: American Sociological Association.

Heath, S.B. (1983) *Ways with Words*. Cambridge: Cambridge University Press.

Hess, R. and Shipman, V. (1965) Early experience and the socialization of cognitive modes in children. *Child Development* 36, 869–886.

Hewison, J. and Tizard, J. (1980) Parental involvement and reading attainment. *British Journal of Educational Psychology* 50, 209–215.

Hewitt, R. and Inghilleri, M. (1993) Oracy in the classroom: Policy, pedagogy, and group oral work. *Anthropology & Education Quarterly* 24 (4), 308–317.

Holland, J. (1980) Social class and changes in orientations to meaning. *Sociology* 15, 1–18.

Hopkins, D. (2001) *School Improvement for Real (Education and Change Development)*. London: RoutledgeFalmer.

Karmiloff-Smith, A. (1979) *A Functional Approach to Child Language*. Cambridge: Cambridge University Press.

Köpcke, K-M. (2001) The acquisition of plural marking in English and German revisited: Schemata versus rules. In M. Tomasello and E. Bates (eds) *Language Development: The Essential Readings* (pp. 203–226). Malden, MA: Blackwell.

Labov, W. (1970) The logic of non-standard English. In F. Williams (ed.) *Language and Poverty*. Chicago: Markham Publishing.

Lampert, M. (1986) Knowing, doing, and teaching multiplication. *Cognition and Instruction* 3 (4), 305–342.

Lampert, M., Rittenhouse, P. and Crumbaugh, C. (1996) Agreeing to disagree: Developing sociable mathematical discourse. In D.R. Olson and N. Torrance (eds) *The Handbook of Education and Human Development* (pp. 731–764). Cambridge, MA: Blackwell.

Langacker, R.W. (1990) *Concept, Image, and Symbol: The Cognitive Basis of Grammar*. Berlin: Mouton de Gruyter.

Lave, J. and Wenger, E. (1991) *Situated Learning: Legitimate Peripheral Participation*. New York: Cambridge University Press.

Lemke, J.L. (1990) *Talking Science: Language, Learning, and Values*. Norwood, NJ: Ablex.

Lock, A. (ed.) (1980) *The Guided Reinvention of Language*. London: Academic Press.

Lord, J.V. and Burroway, J. (1975) *The Giant Jam Sandwich*. Boston: Houghton Mifflin.

Lotman, Y.M. (1988) Text within a text. *Soviet Psychology* 26 (3), 32–51.

McGlynn-Stewart, M. (2001) Look how we've grown! In G. Wells (ed.) *Action, Talk, and Text; Learning and Teaching through Inquiry* (pp. 195–200). New York: Teachers College Press.

McMahon, S.I., Raphael, T.E. with Goatley, V.J. and Pardo, L.S. (eds) (1997) *The Book Club Connection: Literacy Learning and Classroom Talk*. New York: Teachers College Press.

McNeill, D. (1992) *Hand and Mind: What Gestures Reveal about Thought*. Chicago: University of Chicago Press.

McShane, J. (1980) *Learning to Talk*. Cambridge: Cambridge University Press.

MacLure, M. and French, P. (1981) A comparison of talk at home and at school. In G. Wells (ed.) *Learning through Interaction*. Cambridge: Cambridge University Press.

Macnab, R. (1962) *Journey into Yesterday*. Cape Town: Timmins.

Macnamara, J. (1982) *Names for Things*. Cambridge, MA: MIT Press.

Maher, A. (1994) An inquiry into reader response. In G. Wells (ed.) *Changing Schools from Within* (pp. 81–97). Toronto: OISE Press and Portsmouth, NH: Heinemann.

Marckwardt, A.H. (1967) From the basic issues conference to the Dartmouth Seminar: Perspectives on the teaching of English. *Publications of the Modern Language Association of America* 82 (4), 8–13.

Matusov, E. (1996) Intersubjectivity without agreement. *Mind, Culture, and Activity* 3, 25–45.

Maybin, J., Mercer, N. and Stierer, B. (1992) 'Scaffolding' learning in the classroom. In K. Norman (ed.) *Thinking Voices: The Work of The National Oracy Project* (pp. 186–195). London: Hodder & Stoughton.

Mehan, H. (1979) *Learning Lessons: Social Organization in the Classroom*. Cambridge, MA: Harvard University Press.

Mercer, N. (2000) *Words and Minds: How We Use Language to Think Together*. London: Routledge.

Mercer, N. (2002) Developing dialogues. In G. Wells and G. Claxton (eds) *Learning for Life in the 21st Century: Sociocultural Perspectives on the Future of Education* (pp. 141–153). Oxford: Blackwell.

Mercer, N. and Littleton, K. (2007) *Dialogue and the Development of Children's Thinking*. London: Routledge.

Meek, M., Warlow, A. and Barton, G. (1978) *The Cool Web*. New York: Atheneum.

Michaels, S. (1981) "Sharing time": Children's narrative styles and differential access to literacy. *Language in Society* 10, 423–442.

Moll, L. (1992) Funds of knowledge for teaching: Using a qualitative approach to connect homes and classrooms. *Theory into Practice* 31 (2), 132–141.

Moll, L.C. and Greenberg J.B. (1990) Creating zones of possibilities: Combining social contexts for instruction. In L.C. Moll (ed.) *Vygotsky and Education: Instructional Implications and Applications of Sociohistorical Psychology* (pp. 319–348). Cambridge: Cambridge University Press.

Moon, C. (2007) *Individualised Reading 2007: A Teacher Guide to Readability Levels for Children Aged 3–11*. Reading: National Centre for Language and Literacy.

Moschkovich, J. (2008). "I went by twos, he went by one": Multiple interpretations of inscriptions as resources for mathematical discussions. *Journal of the Learning Sciences* 17 (4), 551–587.

Mulford, J. (1971) Reading. *English in Education* 5 (3), 3–7.

Neale, M. (1969) *Neale Analysis of Reading Ability*. Basingstoke: Macmillan Education.

Nelson, K. (1981) Individual differences in language development: Implications for development and language. *Developmental Psychology* 17, 170–187.

Nelson, K. (1996) *Language in Cognitive Development: The Emergence of the Mediated Mind*. New York: Cambridge University Press.

Nelson, K. (2007) *Young Minds in Social Worlds: Experience, Meaning and Memory.* Cambridge, MA: Harvard University Press.

Newson, J. (1978) Dialogue and development. In A. Lock (ed.) *Action, Gesture and Symbol: The Emergence of Language* (pp. 31–42). New York: Academic Press.

Ninio, A. and Bruner, J.S. (1980) The achievement and antecedents of labelling. *Journal of Child Language* 5, 5–15.

Norman, K. (ed.) (1992) *Thinking Voices: The Work of the National Oracy Project.* London: Hodder & Stoughton.

Nystrand, M. (1997) *Opening Dialogue: Understanding the Dynamics of Language and Learning in the English Classroom.* New York: Teacher College Press.

Ochs, E. (1988) *Culture and Language Development: Language Acquisition and Language Socialization in a Samoan Village.* Cambridge: Cambridge University Press.

O'Connor, M.C. (2001) "Can any fraction be turned into a decimal?" A case study of a mathematical group discussion. *Educational Studies in Mathematics* 46, 143–185.

Ogawa, R.T., Crain, R., Loomis, M. and Ball, T. (2008) CHAT-IT: Toward conceptualizing learning in the context of formal organizations. *Educational Researcher* 37 (2), 83–95.

Olson, D. (ed.) (1980) *The Social Foundations of Language and Thought.* New York: Norton.

Olson, D.R. (1994) *The World on Paper.* Cambridge: Cambridge University Press.

Olson, D.R. (2003) *Psychological Theory and Educational Reform: How School Remakes Mind and Society.* New York: Cambridge University Press.

Palincsar, A.S. and Brown, A.L. (1984) Reciprocal teaching of comprehension-fostering and monitoring activities. *Cognition and Instruction* 1, 117–175.

Palincsar, A.S., Magnusson, S.J., Collins, K.M. and Cutter, J. (1998) Designing a community of practice: Principles and practices of the GIsML Community. *Teaching and Teacher Education* 14 (1), 5–20.

Peters, A. (1973) *The Units of Language Acquisition.* Cambridge: Cambridge University Press.

Philips, S. (1972) Participant structures and communicative competence. In C.B. Cazden, V.P. John and D. Hymes (eds) *Functions of Language in the Classroom.* New York: Teachers College Press.

Phillips, T. (1985) Talk among yourselves: It's not my style. In G. Wells and J.C. Nicholls (eds) *Language and Learning: An Interactional Perspective.* Philadelphia: Taylor and Francis.

Piaget, J. and Inhelder, B. (1969) *The Psychology of the Child.* London: Routledge and Kegan Paul.

Pinker, S. (1994) *The Language Instinct: How the Mind Creates Language.* New York: HarperCollins.

Popper, K.R. and Eccles, J.C. (1977) *The Self and its Brain.* Berlin: Springer-Verlag.

Ramus, E., Hauser, M.D., Miller, C. and Morris, D. (2000) Language discrimination by human newborns and by cotton-top tamarin monkeys. *Science* 288, 349–351.

Rees, N.S. (1975) Imitation and language development: Issues and clinical implications. *Journal of Speech and Hearing Disorders* 40, 339–350.

Richards, R. (1990) *An Early Start to Technology.* London: Simon & Schuster.

Rizzolatti, G. and Arbib, M.A. (1998) Language within our grasp. *Trends in Neuroscience* 21, 188–194.

Rogoff, B., Goodman Turkanis, C. and Bartlett, L. (eds) (2001) *Learning Together: Children and Adults in a School Community.* New York: Oxford University Press.

Rommetveit, R. (1992) Outlines of a dialogically based social-cognitive approach to human cognition and communication. In A.H. Wold (ed.) *The Dialogical Alternative: Towards a Theory of Language and Mind* (pp. 19–44). Oslo: Scandinavian University Press.

Rosen, C. and Rosen, H. (1973) *The Language of Primary School Children*. Harmondsworth, Middlesex: Penguin.

Rosen, H. (1984) *Stories and Meanings*. Sheffield: National Association for the Teaching of English.

Rowan, B. and Miskel, C.G. (1999) Institutional theory and the study of educational organizations. In J. Murphy and K. Seashore-Louis (eds) *Handbook of Research in Educational Administration* (pp. 359–383). San Francisco: Jossey-Bass.

Sapir, E. (1921) *Language*. New York: Harcourt Brace.

Schieffelin, B.B. and Ochs, E. (eds) (1986) *Language Socialization Across Cultures*. Cambridge: Cambridge University Press.

Scott, P. (2008) Talking a way to understanding in science classrooms. In N. Mercer and S. Hodgkinson (eds) *Exploring Talk in School* (pp. 17–36). London: Sage.

Scott, W.R. (2008) *Institutions and Organizations*. Thousand Oaks, CA: Sage.

Searle, J. (1977) A classification of illocutionary acts. *Language in Society* 5, 1–23.

Service, R. and Harrison, T.I. (2006) *The Cremation of Sam McGee*. Tonawanda, NY: Kids Can Press.

Shwe, H.I. and Markman, E.M. (2001) Young children's appreciation of the mental impact of their communicative symbols. In M. Tomasello and E. Bates (eds) *Language Development: The Essential Readings* (pp. 62–75). Malden, MA: Blackwell.

Sinclair, J.M. and Coulthard, M. (1975) *Towards an Analysis of Discourse: The English Used by Teachers and Pupils*. London: Oxford University Press.

Skinner, B.F. (1957) *Verbal Behavior*. New York: Apple-Century-Crofts.

Slobin, D. (1985–1997) *The Crosslinguistic Study of Language Acquisition, Volumes 1–5*. Hillsdale, NJ: Lawrence Erlbaum.

Slobin, D. (2001) Form/function relations: How do children find out what they are? In M. Tomasello and E. Bates (eds) *Language Development: The Essential Readings* (pp. 267–289). Malden, MA: Blackwell.

Smith, F. (1987) *Joining the Literacy Club: Further Essays into Education*. Portsmouth, NH: Heinemann.

Snow, C.E. (1977) Mothers' speech research: From input to interaction. In C.E. Snow and C. Ferguson (eds) *Talking to Children: From Input to Acquisition*. Cambridge: Cambridge University Press.

Spencer, M. (1976). Stories are for telling. *English in Education* 10, 16–23.

Squire, J. and Britton, J. (1975) Foreword. In J. Dixon (ed.) *Growth Through English Set in the Context of the Seventies* (pp. vii–xviii). Oxford: Oxford University Press.

Stern, D. (1977) *The First Relationship: Infant and Mother*. London: Open Books.

Stetsenko, A. (2004) Introduction to Vygotsky's "Tool and sign in the development of the child". In R.W. Rieber and D.K. Robinson (eds) *The Essential Vygotsky* (pp. 501–512). New York: Kluwer Academic/Plenum.

Tharp, R.G., Estrada, P., Dalton, S.S. and Yamauchi, L.A. (2000) *Teaching Transformed: Achieving Excellence, Fairness, Inclusion and Harmony*. Boulder CO: Westview Press.

Tharp, R. and Gallimore, R. (1988) *Rousing Minds to Life*. New York: Cambridge University Press.

Tizard, B., Carmichael, H., Hughes, M. and Pinkerton, G. (1980) Four year olds talking to mothers and teachers. In L.A. Hersove (ed.) *Language and Language Disorders in Childhood.* Oxford: Pergamon.

Tizard, B. and Hughes, M. (1984) *Young Children Learning: Talking and Thinking at Home and at School.* London: Fontana.

Tomasello, M. (1999) *The Cultural Origins of Human Cognition.* Cambridge, MA: Harvard University Press.

Tomasello, M. and Bates, E. (2001) Perceiving intentions and learning words in the second year of life. In M. Tomasello and E. Bates (eds) *Language Development: The Essential Readings* (pp. 111–128). Malden, MA: Blackwell.

Tomasello, M. and Brooks, P. (1998) Young children's earliest transitive and intransitive constructions. *Cognitive Linguistics* 9, 379–395.

Tomasello, M. and Slobin, D. (eds) (2005) *Beyond Nature-Nurture. Essays in Honor of Elizabeth Bates.* Mahwah, NJ: Lawrence Erlbaum.

Torbe, M. and Medway, P. (1981) *The Climate for Learning.* London: Ward Lock Educational.

Tough, J. (1977) *The Development of Meaning.* London: Allen and Unwin.

Trevarthen, C. (1979) Communication and cooperation in early infancy: A description of primary intersubjectivity. In M. Bullowa (ed.) *Before Speech: The Beginning of Interpersonal Communication.* Cambridge: Cambridge University Press.

Trevarthen, C. and Hubley, P. (1978) Secondary intersubjectivity: Confidence, confiding and acts of meaning in the first year. In A. Lock (ed.) *Action, Gesture and Symbol: The Emergence of Language* (pp. 183–230). New York: Academic Press.

Tyack, D.B. (1974) *The One Best System: A History of American Urban Education.* Cambridge, MA: Harvard University Press.

Voloshinov, V.N. (1973) *Marxism and the Philosophy of Language.* Cambridge, MA: Harvard University Press.

Volterra, V., Caselli, M.C., Capirci, O. and Pizzulo, E. (2005) Gesture and the emergence and development of language. In M. Tomasello and D.I. Slobin (eds) *Beyond Nature-Nurture: Essays in Honor of Elizabeth Bates* (pp. 3–40). New York: Psychology Press.

Vygotsky, L.S. (1978) *Mind in Society: The Development of Higher Psychological Processes.* Cambridge, MA: Harvard University Press.

Vygotsky, L.S. (1981) The genesis of higher mental functions. In J.V. Wertsch (ed.) *The Concept of Activity in Soviet Psychology* (pp. 144–188). Armonk, NY: Sharpe.

Vygotsky, L.S. (1987) Thinking and speech. In R.W. Rieber and A.S. Carton (eds) *The Collected Works of L.S. Vygotsky, Volume 1: Problems of General Psychology* (pp. 39–285). New York: Plenum.

Vygotsky, L.S. (2004) Tool and sign in the development of the child. In R.W. Rieber and D.K. Robinson (eds) *The Essential Vygotsky* (pp. 513–569). New York: Kluwer Academic/Plenum.

Wanner, E. and Gleitman, L.R. (eds) (1982) *Language Acquisition: The State of the Art.* New York: Cambridge University Press.

Wartofsky, M. (1979) *Models, Representation and the Scientific Understanding.* Boston: Reidel.

Wells, G. (1984) Preschool literacy related activities and success in school. In D. Olson, A. Hildyard and N. Torrance (eds) *Literacy, Language, and Learning:*

The Nature and Consequences of Literacy (pp. 229–255). Cambridge: Cambridge University Press.

Wells, G. (1985) *Language Development in the Pre-school Years.* Cambridge: Cambridge University Press.

Wells, G. (1995) Language and the inquiry-oriented curriculum. *Curriculum Inquiry* 25 (3), 233–269.

Wells, G. (1999) *Dialogic Inquiry: Towards a Sociocultural Practice and Theory of Education.* Cambridge: Cambridge University Press.

Wells, G. (ed.) (2001) *Action, Talk, and Text: Learning and Teaching through Inquiry.* New York: Teachers College Press.

Wells, G. (2002) Learning and teaching for understanding: The key role of collaborative knowledge building. In J. Brophy (ed.) *Social Constructivist Teaching: Affordances and Constraints* (pp. 1–41). Oxford: Elsevier/JAI.

Wells, G. (2009) Researching together: Collaborative action research in education. In B. Somekh and S. Noffke (eds) *The Sage Handbook of Educational Action Research.* Thousand Oaks, CA: Sage.

Wells, G., Chang, G.L. and Maher, A. (1990) Creating classroom communities of literate thinkers. In S. Sharan (ed.) *Cooperative Learning: Theory and Research.* New York: Praeger.

Wells, G. and Chang-Wells, G.L. (1992) *Constructing Knowledge Together: Classrooms as Centers of Inquiry and Literacy.* Portsmouth, NH: Heinemann Educational Books.

Wells, G. and Mejía Arauz, R. (2006) Dialogue in the classroom. *Journal of the Learning Sciences* 15 (3), 379–428.

Wood, D., McMahon, L. and Cranstoun, Y. (1980) *Working with Under Fives.* London: Grant McIntyre.

Index